ESSENTIAL SKILLS IN MATHS

BOOK 3

Nelson

Graham Newman and Ron Bull

Thomas Nelson and Sons Ltd
Nelson House Mayfield Road
Walton-on-Thames Surrey
KT12 5PL UK

First published by Thomas Nelson and Sons Ltd 1996

I(T)P Thomas Nelson is an International Thomson Publishing Company.

I(T)P is used under licence.

ISBN 0-17-431442-6
NPN 9 8 7 6 5 4

Printed in China

Acknowledgements

The authors and publishers would like to thank the following for permission to use their maps:

Maps of Stony Stratford and Milton Keynes Area from *Official City Atlas, Milton Keynes*, GEOprojects UK (based on Ordnance Survey)

Map of Aldeburgh and District from *Ordnance Survey Atlas of Great Britain*, Guild Publishing/Hamlyn Publishing, London 1984

Map of Le Havre and District from *Motoring Atlas of Great Britain*, Philips 1991

Contents

NUMBER

ALGEBRA

SHAPE, SPACE AND MEASURES

HANDLING DATA

Number

1/ MULTIPLYING AND DIVIDING BY POWERS OF 10

Simple rules with whole numbers

$\times 10$	'add' a zero	$\div 10$	'remove' a zero
$\times 100$	'add' two zeros	$\div 100$	'remove' two zeros
$\times 1000$	'add' three zeros	$\div 1000$	'remove' three zeros

EXAMPLES

▶ $32 \times 10 = 32\underline{0}$ $\quad$ $8300 \div 10 = 830$

$53 \times 1000 = 53\,\underline{000}$ $\quad$ $700 \div 100 = 7$

Exercise 1A

1	76×10	**2**	217×100	**3**	$5000 \div 1000$	**4**	$20 \div 10$
5	95×100	**6**	$27\,000 \div 1000$	**7**	$400 \div 10$	**8**	81×100
9	$2000 \div 1000$	**10**	$5700 \div 100$	**11**	24×1000	**12**	$350 \div 10$
13	89×1000	**14**	219×10	**15**	$42\,000 \div 100$	**16**	$42\,000 \div 1000$
17	27×100	**18**	$4300 \div 100$	**19**	91×1000	**20**	98×10
21	25×1000	**22**	$9200 \div 10$	**23**	$8800 \div 100$	**24**	187×100
25	$7000 \div 10$	**26**	33×1000	**27**	108×10	**28**	$40\,000 \div 1000$
29	65×10	**30**	$35\,000 \div 100$				

Exercise 1B

1	$700 \div 100$	**2**	56×1000	**3**	21×10	**4**	$2400 \div 100$
5	$420 \div 10$	**6**	$33\,000 \div 100$	**7**	18×10	**8**	$73\,000 \div 1000$
9	87×1000	**10**	891×10	**11**	$5000 \div 100$	**12**	$94\,000 \div 1000$
13	918×100	**14**	$3200 \div 10$	**15**	13×1000	**16**	105×10
17	89×100	**18**	$17\,000 \div 10$	**19**	$34\,000 \div 1000$	**20**	213×100
21	$62\,000 \div 1000$	**22**	107×10	**23**	44×100	**24**	$5000 \div 10$
25	912×100	**26**	$32\,000 \div 1000$	**27**	$50\,000 \div 1000$	**28**	503×10
29	$4000 \div 1000$	**30**	420×100				

Simple rules with decimals

× 10	'move' decimal point one place to the right
× 100	'move' decimal point two places to the right
× 1000	'move' decimal point three places to the right
÷ 10	'move' decimal point one place to the left
÷ 100	'move' decimal point two places to the left
÷ 1000	'move' decimal point three places to the left

It may be necessary to add extra zeros to the number.

EXAMPLES

▶ 3.5 × 100 = 350.0 or 350 — 53.27 ÷ 100 = 0.5327

0.27 × 1000 = 270 — 10.12 ÷ 10 = 1.012

Exercise 1C

1 71.2 × 10	**2** 6.27 × 100	**3** 4.2 × 10	**4** 221 ÷ 100
5 0.79 × 100	**6** 21.3 ÷ 10	**7** 3.12 × 1000	**8** 2.9 ÷ 100
9 0.4 × 100	**10** 3.71 × 100	**11** 0.15 ÷ 100	**12** 0.007 × 100
13 0.9 ÷ 10	**14** 2.8 ÷ 1000	**15** 3.1 × 100	**16** 1.27 × 100
17 7.9 ÷ 100	**18** 417 ÷ 100	**19** 2.13 × 100	**20** 275 ÷ 10
21 0.05 × 10	**22** 4.1 ÷ 10	**23** 0.8 ÷ 1000	**24** 0.97 × 1000
25 0.03 ÷ 10	**26** 0.49 ÷ 1000	**27** 0.71 ÷ 100	**28** 0.03 × 1000
29 6.05 × 10	**30** 4.79 ÷ 100		

Exercise 1D

1 21.1 × 100	**2** 1.24 × 10	**3** 417 ÷ 10	**4** 2.76 × 100
5 1.22 ÷ 10	**6** 1.21 × 10	**7** 4.1 ÷ 1000	**8** 1.27 × 10
9 275 ÷ 1000	**10** 0.4 × 1000	**11** 0.15 ÷ 10	**12** 4.2 ÷ 100
13 49.8 × 1000	**14** 0.9 ÷ 1000	**15** 14.8 × 10	**16** 2.9 ÷ 1000
17 0.05 × 1000	**18** 0.8 ÷ 10	**19** 7.9 ÷ 10	**20** 4.21 × 1000
21 2.8 ÷ 100	**22** 0.71 ÷ 1000	**23** 0.007 × 100	**24** 2.23 ÷ 100
25 21.3 ÷ 100	**26** 3.71 × 1000	**27** 0.03 ÷ 100	**28** 3.1 × 1000
29 4.09 ÷ 1000	**30** 0.49 ÷ 100		

2/ MULTIPLICATION BY A 2-DIGIT NUMBER WITHOUT A CALCULATOR

When multiplying by a number such as 29, it is important to remember that the '2' is 2 tens or twenty. When multiplying by 20, remember to put a nought at the end and multiply by 2.

EXAMPLE

▶ 317 × 29

$$\begin{array}{cccc} & 3 & 1 & 7 \\ \times & & 2 & 9 \\ \hline 2 & 8^1 & 5^6 & 3 \\ 6 & 3^1 & 4 & 0 \\ \hline 9^1 & 1 & 9 & 3 \\ \hline \end{array}$$

Exercise 2A

1 119 × 13	**2** 403 × 14	**3** 513 × 16	**4** 210 × 21
5 470 × 27	**6** 231 × 14	**7** 315 × 16	**8** 346 × 76
9 215 × 14	**10** 473 × 15	**11** 532 × 39	**12** 204 × 21
13 845 × 67	**14** 894 × 79	**15** 163 × 23	**16** 825 × 23
17 232 × 31	**18** 172 × 35	**19** 943 × 64	**20** 354 × 29
21 634 × 23	**22** 843 × 69	**23** 925 × 21	**24** 647 × 47

25 There are 363 parts in a radio. How many parts are needed for 25 radios?

26 A woman makes 279 components every hour. How many will she make in 84 hours?

27 A ticket for a celebrity party costs £34. What is the total amount collected from the sale of 940 tickets?

28 There are 79 matches in a box. What is the total number of matches you might expect in 943 similar boxes?

29 A small vase weighs 98 g. What will be the total weight, in grams, of 397 vases?

30 There are 79 items of crockery in each set sold. What is the total number of items of crockery in 657 sets?

Exercise 2B

1 185 × 16	**2** 146 × 13	**3** 427 × 21	**4** 397 × 23
5 214 × 63	**6** 163 × 16	**7** 376 × 72	**8** 132 × 16
9 621 × 68	**10** 507 × 16	**11** 421 × 23	**12** 712 × 39
13 429 × 21	**14** 387 × 22	**15** 738 × 97	**16** 640 × 18
17 243 × 72	**18** 497 × 94	**19** 897 × 94	**20** 946 × 87
21 376 × 13	**22** 763 × 49	**23** 247 × 84	**24** 493 × 94

25 There are 64 parts in a CD player. How many parts are needed to make 878 CD players?

26 It takes a snail 19 minutes to travel 1 metre. How many minutes will it take to travel the length of a 374-metre path?

27 A designer car will travel 59 miles on one litre of petrol. How far will it travel with 768 litres of petrol?

28 There are 243 special chocolate bars each with a prize of 98p. What is the total cost of the prizes?

29 Tickets cost £31 each for a charity ball. What is the total amount raised from the sale of 573 tickets?

30 A company sends out 97 parcels in each shipment. Over a year, how many parcels have been sent in 378 shipments?

3/ DIVISION BY A 2-DIGIT NUMBER

When dividing by a number that is bigger than 10, long division can be used. This method is better for large numbers than short division but it is not essential as both methods will give the correct answer. However, if you prefer, use short division.

EXAMPLE

▶ 3536 ÷ 34

Short division:

```
       1  0  4
34 ) 3  5 ¹3 ¹³6
```

Long division:

```
       1  0  4
34 ) 3  5  3  6
   - 3  4
        1  3  6
      - 1  3  6
              0
```

Exercise 3A

1 408 ÷ 12	**2** 6230 ÷ 70	**3** 1568 ÷ 14	**4** 627 ÷ 19
5 4864 ÷ 64	**6** 6764 ÷ 76	**7** 7812 ÷ 84	**8** 2523 ÷ 29
9 3953 ÷ 59	**10** 2773 ÷ 47	**11** 3591 ÷ 57	**12** 5056 ÷ 64
13 770 ÷ 14	**14** 1134 ÷ 18	**15** 6370 ÷ 65	**16** 3136 ÷ 14
17 7990 ÷ 17	**18** 5192 ÷ 11	**19** 11 392 ÷ 16	**20** 4536 ÷ 14
21 4410 ÷ 21	**22** 6461 ÷ 13	**23** 3888 ÷ 16	**24** 4512 ÷ 12

25 A car does 23 miles per gallon. How many gallons will be used on a journey of 4899 miles?

26 There are 21 different parts that are used to make up a model kit. A total of 13 587 parts are waiting to be packaged. How many kits will this number of parts make?

27 There are 17 turnstiles at a large soccer stadium. If 5882 people are divided equally amongst the turnstiles, how many is this per turnstile?

28 A batch of 18 546 eggs is packed into containers which will each hold 22 eggs. How many containers are needed?

29 A game needs 19 counters. How many games can be made from a box of 8892 counters?

30 Prize money of £8874 is divided equally among 18 people. How much does each one receive?

Exercise 3B

1 272 ÷ 16	**2** 294 ÷ 14	**3** 544 ÷ 17	**4** 1053 ÷ 27
5 2597 ÷ 49	**6** 1872 ÷ 39	**7** 3420 ÷ 45	**8** 6460 ÷ 76
9 3724 ÷ 49	**10** 4464 ÷ 48	**11** 345 ÷ 15	**12** 2523 ÷ 29
13 608 ÷ 19	**14** 810 ÷ 18	**15** 1281 ÷ 21	**16** 6764 ÷ 76
17 5759 ÷ 13	**18** 7192 ÷ 31	**19** 8140 ÷ 22	**20** 5145 ÷ 15
21 5664 ÷ 16	**22** 2996 ÷ 14	**23** 8092 ÷ 17	**24** 6358 ÷ 11

25 A lorry has 22 tyres on its wheels. How many lorries can be fitted with new tyres from a stock of 8734 tyres?

26 If 13 041 mice have been put into cages each of which can hold a maximum of 21 mice, how many cages are there?

27 A gift set contains 23 glasses. A company has a total of 17 549 glasses in stock. How many gift sets will these make?

28 Car-parking tickets cost 25p. A total of £211.25 has been collected in an afternoon. How many tickets have been issued?

29 A lottery prize of £16 492 is to be divided equally among 31 people. How much will each receive?

30 The total cost of posting a batch of letters is £229.23. Each letter cost 27p to post. How many letters were posted?

4/ ORDERING POSITIVE AND NEGATIVE NUMBERS

EXAMPLE

▶ Rewrite the following numbers in descending order of size: 3, –8, 0, 6, –5, 1

The number 6 is the largest (6 means +6) and –8 is the smallest.
In descending order of size: 6, 3, 1, 0, –5, –8

Remember: **Ascending** order means smallest first with numbers increasing in size.
Descending order means largest first with numbers getting smaller.

Exercise 4A

Rewrite the numbers in the order stated.

1 0, –4, –9, 9, –6, 5, 7; ascending
2 –8, 5, 8, –7, 10, –4, 1; ascending
3 –5, –1, 7, 3, –8, 4, –7; descending
4 –8, –1, 4, –7, 3, 0, –6; descending
5 10, –2, –9, 6, –4, 0, 9; ascending
6 –4, 1, –2, 7, –5, 8, 3; descending
7 –4, 6, 8, –1, –9, 5, 9; ascending
8 –8, –2, 4, –4, 1, –9, 10; descending
9 6, 0, 5, –9, –6, –7, 2; descending
10 –5, 7, 10, –3, –9, 2, 4; ascending
11 –4, 0, 9, –7, 7, –3, 6; ascending
12 4, –3, 9, –5, –6, –1, 3; descending
13 1, –4, 7, 6, –9, –6, 2; descending
14 –10, 5, –4, 10, 0, –1, 8; ascending
15 –8, 2, 6, –1, –6, 5, –4; ascending
16 4, 0, –9, –5, 2, –6, 1; descending
17 4, –3, 7, –9, 3, 0, –4; ascending
18 –8, –2, 3, –1, 7, 2, –5; ascending
19 –5, 3, 4, –4, –8, 6, –1; descending
20 0, –9, –2, –6, –8, –3; descending
21 –8, 4, –9, –3, 1, 10, –7; descending
22 –6, 0, 8, –2, 5, –4, 7; ascending
23 –21, 18, –13, 25, –9, –29, 4; descending
24 –10, 33, –40, 25, 19, –27, 39; ascending
25 –50, –21, 4, –32, –42, 29, –53, 14; ascending
26 –9, 9, 30, –24, 22, –1, –18; descending
27 49, –16, 19, 54, 37, –23, –4; descending
28 24, 31, –14, 3, –28, 17; ascending
29 18, –18, –40, 49, 32, –31, 28; descending
30 –33, –21, 30, 9, –7, –27, 22; ascending

Exercise 4B

Rewrite the numbers in the order stated.

1 1, –2, –8, –3, 5, 6, 9; descending
2 –3, –8, –5, 6, 8, 5, 0; ascending
3 –3, –4, –9, –1, 3, 0; ascending
4 –5, 3, 5, 0, 1, –1, –7; ascending
5 9, 2, –5, –3, 6, 4; descending
6 8, –1, –7, –9, –3, 5, 4; descending
7 –10, 3, –4, 6, 5, 1, –5; ascending
8 9, 3, –3, 0, 7, –4, 6; descending
9 –2, –9, 2, –1, –4, 0, 1; ascending
10 –5, 2, 7, –4, –8, 1, 5; ascending
11 4, –5, –6, 0, 6, –1, 3; descending
12 –1, –10, 8, 0, 9, 7, –5; ascending
13 –9, –1, 8, –8, 4, –5; ascending
14 9, 0, –7, –1, 4, –5, 1; descending

15 8, –7, –10, –4, –1, –6, 5; descending
16 –2, 5, 0, –6, 7, –1, 1; ascending
17 –4, 0, –7, –1, 4, 3, –3; ascending
18 1, –3, –6, 2, 6, –5, 3; descending
19 0, –5, 9, –7, –3, 3, 4; descending
20 –3, –8, 4, –9, –6, 1, 2; descending
21 5, –3, –9, –2, 4, 1; descending
22 –6, –10, –3, 0, –9, 1, –7; descending
23 5, –4, –3, 7, 8, 3, –9; descending
24 –18, –24, 10, 0, 16, –21, –9; ascending
25 0, –22, 16, 20, –31, 4, –28; ascending
26 5, 13, –14, 0, –9, 21, 18; ascending
27 –4, 25, –15, –21, 29, 34, –14; descending
28 21, –21, –3, 32, 43, –19, –15; descending
29 –14, 2, –23, 19, –27, 33, 27; ascending
30 –10, –30, 15, 28, –38, 32, –23; descending

5/ NEGATIVE NUMBERS IN CONTEXT

EXAMPLE

► A temperature falls by 12 degrees from 7°C. What is the new temperature?

7 – 12 = –5
The new temperature is –5°C.

EXAMPLE

► I want to buy a new CD player for £75. I find I am £14 short. How much money do I actually have?

£75 – £14 = £61

(Note: BCE ≡ BC and CE ≡ AD.)

Exercise 5A

1 At breakfast the temperature was –3°C. By lunchtime the temperature was 4°C. By how many degrees had the temperature risen?
2 What year is 15 years before 6 CE?
3 I have £55, but need £80 for a new portable CD player. How much do I need to borrow?
4 It is –4°C outside. The temperature is forecast to rise by 9 degrees. What will the temperature be then?
5 A man was £50 in debt to a bank. He paid £125 into his bank account. How much money did he have to spend in his account?
6 How many years are there from 34 BCE to 70 CE?
7 A lift rises from the third basement (–3) to the fifth floor. How many floors has it risen? (The ground floor is Floor 0.)
8 At sunset the temperature was 3°C and at midnight it was –6°C. By how many degrees had the temperature fallen?
9 Martin owes £43. He repays £22. How much does he still owe?
10 A train on a bridge is 12 metres above the surface of a river. The river is 5 metres deep. How high is the train above the river bed?
11 Plato was born in 429 BCE. Hypatia was born in 370 CE. How many years are there between the years of their births?
12 What year is 120 years after 35 BCE?

13 After buying a new hi-fi unit for £350, I find I owe the bank £24. How much did I have in the bank before I bought the hi-fi?

14 Sharon arrives 12 minutes before her train is due to leave the station. The train is 20 minutes late leaving the station. How long does she have to wait before the train leaves?

15 How many years are there between 19 CE and 25 BCE?

16 The temperature in a room is 11°C. The temperature outside is –3°C. What is the difference in temperature?

17 Aristotle was born in 384 BCE. Euler was born in 1707 CE. How many years are there between the years of their births?

18 My watch shows five minutes to one, but my watch is eight minutes slow. What is the real time?

19 The scale of a kitchen weighing machine shows zero with a 1.3-kg pan on it. The pan is removed and a 2-kg bag of sugar is placed on the scales. What will the scales now show?

20 What is the difference in temperature between –9°C and –1°C?

Exercise 5B

1 When the temperature in London was –3°C, it was –12°C in Glasgow. What was the difference between these two temperatures?

2 I ordered a new car for £15 000, but found I was £2500 short of the money needed. How much money did I have in the bank to spend on the car?

3 One morning a thermometer read –5°C. By lunchtime it had risen by 8 degrees. What was the temperature at lunchtime?

4 A lift descends from the eighth floor to the second basement level. By how many floors has it descended? (The ground floor is called Floor 0.)

5 Pythagoras was born in 582 BCE. Ptolemy was born in 89 CE. How many years are there between the years of their births?

6 What year is 22 years after 15 BCE?

7 A diver is working 12 metres below sea level. The deck of an oil platform is 15 metres above sea level. How far is the diver below the level of the deck?

8 Barry owes £27. He repays £18. How much does he still owe?

9 How many years are there between 48 BCE and 10 CE?

10 The temperature inside a fridge is –4°C. The door is left open to defrost it, and the temperature rises by 8 degrees. What is the new temperature?

11 Ben arrived at the bus stop 8 minutes before the bus was due to arrive. The bus actually arrived 12 minutes late. How long was Ben waiting at the bus stop?

12 My watch shows 3 minutes past 3, but my watch is 8 minutes fast. What is the real time?

13 A sonar reading shows zero when the depth is 13 feet. What will the sonar reading show when the depth is 32 feet?

14 What year is 37 years before 12 BCE?

15 Euclid was born in 300 BCE. Fibonacci was born in 1170 CE. How many years are there between the years of their births?

16 My watch is 6 minutes fast. When my watch shows 12.25 p.m., what is the correct time?

17 Martin owes the bank £41. He pays £96 into the bank. How much of this money is available for him to spend?

18 The temperature falls 12 degrees from 5.5°C. What is the new temperature?

19 How many years are there between 31 CE and 14 BCE?

20 Shazia wants to buy a new washing machine priced at £350, but finds that she is £45 short. How much money does she actually have?

6/ NUMBER LINES

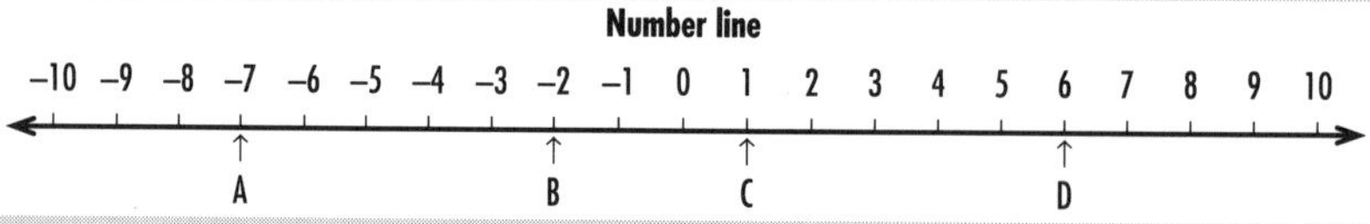

EXAMPLE

► State the values at the positions marked B and D.

B is at –2 and D is at 6.

EXAMPLE

► How far is it from A to D?

It is 13 units from A to D.

Exercise 6A

State the value at each of the points marked with a letter.

1

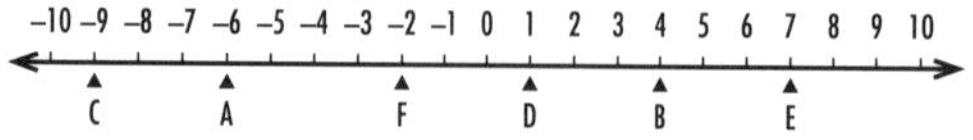

2

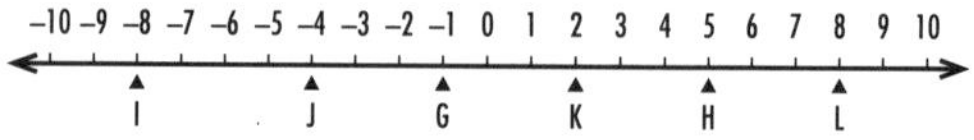

3

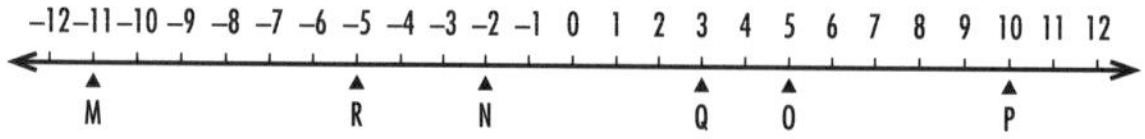

4

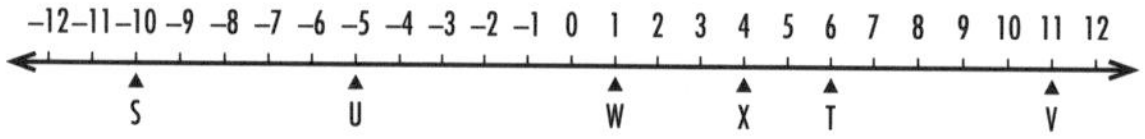

5 Using the diagrams in questions 1–4, state how far it is between the following points.

(a) A to F (b) C to B (c) A to B (d) G to H (e) J to L (f) I to G
(g) N to Q (h) M to R (i) R to P (j) U to T (k) S to X (l) U to V

Exercise 6B

State the value at each of the points marked with a letter.

1

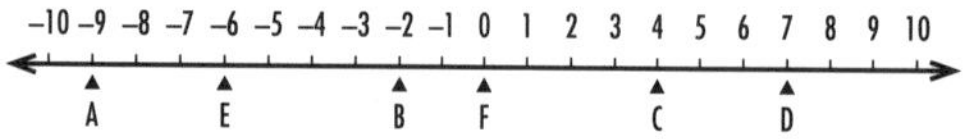

2

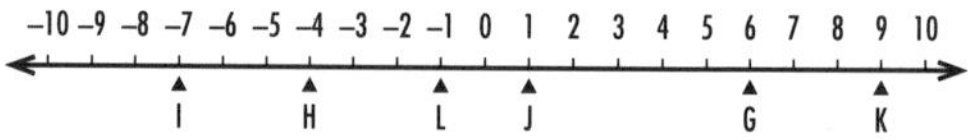

3

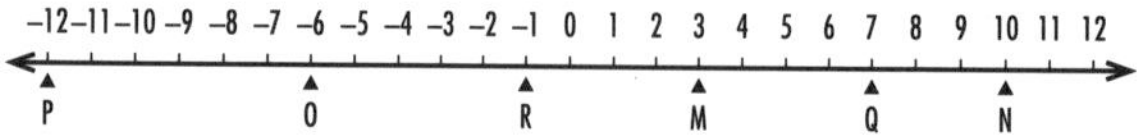

4

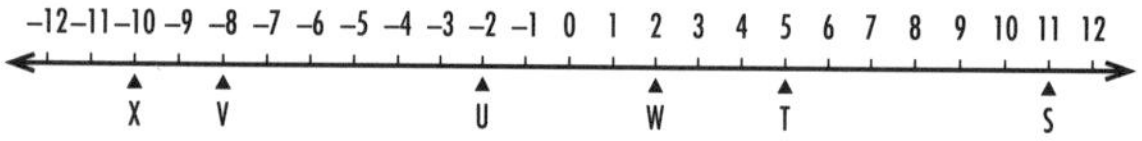

5 Using the diagrams in questions 1–4, state how far it is between the following points.

(a) B to C (b) E to F (c) A to D (d) H to G (e) J to K (f) I to G
(g) P to M (h) R to N (i) O to Q (j) U to T (k) V to T (l) X to S

7/ NEGATIVE NUMBERS: ADDITION AND SUBTRACTION

+ + and − − are replaced by +.

+ − and − + are replaced by −.

EXAMPLE

▶ Simplify (+5) – (+2).

– (+2) is replaced by –2.

The calculation is now:

+ 5 – 2 = +3

EXAMPLE

▶ Simplify (+4) – (–3).

– (–3) is replaced by +3.

The calculation is now:

+ 4 + 3 = 7

Exercise 7A

Simplify.

1 (+3) + (+1)
2 (–2) + (+2)
3 (–1) + (+1)
4 (+3) + (+2)
5 (+1) + (–2)
6 (–1) + (+3)
7 (+5) – (+7)
8 (+4) + (–1)
9 (–3) + (–4)
10 (+3) + (–1)
11 (–5) – (–7)
12 (+7) + (–3)
13 (–1) – (–4)
14 (–4) – (+8)
15 (–5) + (–4)
16 (–2) + (–7)
17 (+8) + (–7)
18 (–5) – (–3)
19 (–6) – (–7)
20 (+10) – (–5)
21 (–11) + (+7)
22 (–7) – (–8)
23 (–21) – (+14)
24 (–17) + (+10)
25 (–22) – (+20)
26 (+7) – (–14)
27 (–13) + (+10)
28 (–17) – (+17)
29 (+24) + (–19)
30 (–29) – (–14)

Exercise 7B

Simplify.

1 (+1) + (+2)
2 (–2) + (0)
3 (+4) + (–4)
4 (+3) + (–3)
5 (–3) + (–2)
6 (+1) + (–4)
7 (+2) + (–4)
8 (–4) + (–1)
9 (+5) + (–8)
10 (+9) – (+2)
11 (–2) – (–4)
12 (+4) – (–3)
13 (–2) – (–5)
14 (+3) – (–2)
15 (+4) + (–7)
16 (+12) + (–7)
17 (+4) – (–5)
18 (+2) – (–3)
19 (–11) – (–10)
20 (+4) – (–10)
21 (+12) + (–7)
22 (+20) + (–17)
23 (–8) + (–21)
24 (+10) – (+18)
25 (+13) – (–13)
26 (+20) + (–11)
27 (+11) – (+19)
28 (–15) + (+15)
29 (–23) – (+19)
30 (+24) – (–17)

8/ NEGATIVE NUMBERS: MULTIPLICATION AND DIVISION

+ and + gives + − and − gives +
+ and − gives − − and + gives −

The rule is: LIKE SIGNS give +
UNLIKE SIGNS give −

EXAMPLES

▶ $(+4) \times (-2) = -8$ ($4 \times 2 = 8$; unlike signs give a minus sign)
$(-16) \div (-8) = +2$ or just 2 ($16 \div 8 = 2$; like signs give a plus sign)

Exercise 8A

Simplify.

1 $(+5) \times (+2)$
2 $(+6) \times (-4)$
3 $(-8) \times (+3)$
4 $(+4) \times (-3)$
5 $(-8) \div (+4)$
6 $(+1) \times (-5)$
7 $(+6) \div (-3)$
8 $(-6) \div (+2)$
9 $(-1) \times (+5)$
10 $(-15) \div (-3)$
11 $(-4) \times (+6)$
12 $(-12) \div (+6)$
13 $(-8) \times (-7)$
14 $(+10) \div (-2)$
15 $(-9) \times (-3)$
16 $(+9) \times (-3)$
17 $(+16) \div (-4)$
18 $(+8) \times (-2)$
19 $(-12) \div (+3)$
20 $(+4) \times (+7)$
21 $(+30) \div (+3)$
22 $(-27) \div (-3)$
23 $(-40) \div (+5)$
24 $(-7) \times (+8)$
25 $(-36) \div (-12)$
26 $(+18) \div (-3)$
27 $(+14) \times (-11)$
28 $(+24) \div (+8)$
29 $(-36) \div (+9)$
30 $(-9) \times (-12)$

Exercise 8B

Simplify.

1 $(+7) \times (+2)$
2 $(-6) \times (+2)$
3 $(-49) \div (+7)$
4 $(-35) \div (-7)$
5 $(-6) \times (+8)$
6 $(+6) \times (-1)$
7 $(-10) \div (+5)$
8 $(-9) \times (-4)$
9 $(-7) \times (+11)$
10 $(-24) \div (-6)$
11 $(+6) \times (+7)$
12 $(-30) \div (-15)$
13 $(-12) \div (+4)$
14 $(-3) \times (-8)$
15 $(-6) \times (-6)$
16 $(-5) \times (+1)$
17 $(+9) \div (-3)$
18 $(-14) \div (+2)$
19 $(-18) \div (-9)$
20 $(-4) \times (-8)$
21 $(+20) \div (+4)$
22 $(-2) \times (+6)$
23 $(+18) \div (-6)$
24 $(-28) \div (-7)$
25 $(+8) \times (-3)$
26 $(-10) \div (+5)$
27 $(+25) \div (-5)$
28 $(+9) \times (-9)$
29 $(+8) \div (-2)$
30 $(+10) \times (-9)$

9/ NEGATIVE NUMBERS: MIXED EXAMPLES

Exercise 9A

Simplify.

1 $(-1) + (+4)$
2 $(+1) \times (-2)$
3 $(+4) - (-3)$
4 $(-6) \div (+2)$
5 $(+4) + (+2)$
6 $(+2) + (-5) - (-2)$
7 $(-6) \times (+3)$
8 $(-5) \times (-1)$
9 $(-9) + (+3) - (-4)$
10 $(-4) + (+2)$
11 $(-18) \div (-3)$
12 $(-2) \times (-3)$
13 $(+7) - (+4) + (-2)$
14 $(+21) \div (-7)$
15 $(-2) - (+1)$
16 $(-9) \div (-3)$
17 $(-3) + (+2) + (-5)$
18 $(+2) \times (-3) \times (+2)$
19 $(-3) - (+5)$
20 $(+12) \div (-3)$
21 $(-1) + (-5)$
22 $(+3) - (-9)$
23 $(+7) \times (-5)$
24 $(-8) \div (+4)$
25 $(-6) + (-2) - (-4)$
26 $(+2) - (+8) - (-4)$
27 $(+4) - (-3) + (-3)$
28 $(-2) + (-4) - (-2)$
29 $(+49) \div (+7)$
30 $(-7) \times (+5)$

Exercise 9B

Simplify.

1 (+1) − (+3)	**2** (−5) + (+2)	**3** (−2) + (−6)	**4** (+6) × (+4)
5 (−10) ÷ (−2)	**6** (+3) × (+3)	**7** (−6) + (−1)	**8** (−2) − (+7)
9 (+5) − (−6)	**10** (+3) + (+7) − (+6)	**11** (−18) ÷ (+3)	**12** (−3) × (+3)
13 (−32) ÷ (+8)	**14** (+5) + (−4) − (−3)	**15** (+4) × (+5)	**16** (−24) ÷ (−4)
17 (+2) × (−2) × (+2)	**18** (−2) + (+3) − (−3)	**19** (+5) − (−5)	**20** (+2) − (+5) − (−2)
21 (−21) ÷ (+7)	**22** (−9) + (−5) − (−3)	**23** (+3) − (+3)	**24** (−6) × (−3)
25 (+35) ÷ (−5)	**26** (−1) − (+7) + (−3)	**27** (+2) + (−1) − (+2)	**28** (+24) ÷ (−6)
29 (−6) − (+7) + (−3)	**30** (−4) × (+4) × (−2)		

10/ THE VALUE OF A DIGIT WITHIN A DECIMAL NUMBER

The value of a digit within a decimal number depends upon its position within that decimal number.

	10s	units	.	$\frac{1}{10}$s	$\frac{1}{100}$s	$\frac{1}{1000}$s	$\frac{1}{10\,000}$s
94.167	9	4	.	1	6	7	
5.0498		5	.	0	4	9	8

EXAMPLE

▶ State the value of the underlined digits in (a) decimal form (b) fraction form: $94.\underline{1}\underline{6}7$, $5.0\underline{4}9\underline{8}$.

$94.\underline{1}\underline{6}7$ 1 has the value (a) 0.1 (b) $\frac{1}{10}$

6 has the value (a) 0.06 (b) $\frac{6}{100}$

$5.0\underline{4}9\underline{8}$ 4 has the value (a) 0.04 (b) $\frac{4}{100}$

8 has the value (a) 0.0008 (b) $\frac{8}{10\,000}$

Exercise 10A

State the value of the underlined digits in (a) decimal form (b) fraction form.

1 $1.\underline{4}2\underline{7}$	**2** $0.0\underline{8}7\underline{5}$	**3** $0.\underline{4}7\underline{6}3$	**4** $0.8\underline{9}7\underline{2}$	**5** $0.06\underline{7}\underline{9}$
6 $0.0\underline{4}9\underline{1}$	**7** $0.04\underline{7}\underline{2}$	**8** $0.0\underline{8}9\underline{1}$	**9** $0.00\underline{1}\,4\underline{2}$	**10** $0.0\underline{9}\underline{4}1$
11 $0.\underline{1}9\underline{2}$	**12** $0.002\,\underline{7}\underline{6}$	**13** $0.\underline{3}7\underline{4}$	**14** $0.0\underline{7}\underline{5}5$	**15** $0.000\,\underline{1}\underline{6}$
16 $1.\underline{1}4\underline{3}$	**17** $4.7\underline{3}\underline{2}$	**18** $20.0\underline{1}\underline{4}5$	**19** $1.02\underline{7}\underline{9}$	**20** $12.00\underline{5}\,2\underline{9}$
21 $4.07\underline{6}\underline{5}$	**22** $47.000\,\underline{9}\underline{3}$	**23** $8.00\underline{1}\,8\underline{2}$	**24** $12.0\underline{2}4\underline{9}$	**25** $14.\underline{4}\underline{4}9$
26 $8.00\underline{5}\,6\underline{4}$	**27** $10.000\,7\underline{1}\underline{3}$	**28** $123.\underline{8}\underline{5}7$	**29** $4.00\underline{9}\,8\underline{7}$	**30** $53.0\underline{1}3\underline{2}$

Exercise 10B

State the value of the underlined digits in (a) decimal form (b) fraction form.

1	$2.\underline{5}9\underline{7}$	**2**	$0.02\underline{3}\underline{5}$	**3**	$0.\underline{9}84\underline{3}$	**4**	$0.2\underline{3}\underline{5}6$	**5**	$0.0\underline{7}5\underline{3}$
6	$0.0\underline{8}\underline{9}4$	**7**	$0.04\underline{7}\underline{9}$	**8**	$0.4\underline{7}5\underline{6}$	**9**	$0.00\underline{2}\,6\underline{3}$	**10**	$0.\underline{3}\underline{9}1$
11	$0.00\underline{5}\,1\underline{4}$	**12**	$0.\underline{5}6\underline{3}5$	**13**	$0.000\,\underline{7}\underline{5}2$	**14**	$0.08\underline{6}\underline{4}$	**15**	$0.00\underline{9}\,7\underline{7}$
16	$4.0\underline{1}8\underline{5}$	**17**	$9.\underline{1}6\underline{9}4$	**18**	$12.6\underline{2}9\underline{4}$	**19**	$17.003\,\underline{9}\underline{5}$	**20**	$4.0\underline{4}9\underline{3}$
21	$40.000\,\underline{4}\underline{5}$	**22**	$812.\underline{5}9\underline{6}$	**23**	$15.00\underline{6}\,8\underline{4}$	**24**	$16.0\underline{6}7\underline{5}4$	**25**	$8.00\underline{8}6\underline{7}$
26	$29.00\underline{9}\,\underline{5}6$	**27**	$105.7\underline{4}\underline{2}$	**28**	$77.0\underline{1}2\underline{6}$	**29**	$53.7\underline{2}9\underline{3}$	**30**	$4.00\underline{3}\,\underline{7}2$

11/ ROUNDING TO DECIMAL PLACES

A number can be rounded to a specified number of **decimal places** (d.p.).

```
4 3 . 0   5   7
      ↑   ↑   ↑
    1st 2nd 3rd decimal place
```

EXAMPLE

► Round the number 3.8397 to (a) 1 d.p. (b) 2 d.p. (c) 3 d.p.

(a) 3.8 (The next number is 3 so round *down.*)
(b) 3.84 (The next number is 5 or more, so round *up.*)
(c) 3.840 (The last 0 is important because it shows the 3rd decimal place.)

Exercise 11A

Round each of these decimal numbers to (a) 1 d.p. (b) 2 d.p. (c) 3 d.p.

1	4.3129	**2**	2.3615	**3**	2.3157	**4**	6.4078	**5**	8.7145
6	8.0723	**7**	4.1732	**8**	4.1931	**9**	8.3891	**10**	4.5162
11	9.5358	**12**	6.9024	**13**	10.8623	**14**	3.9596	**15**	13.5804
16	29.9561	**17**	7.2441	**18**	6.2045	**19**	10.7761	**20**	4.5132
21	3.2178	**22**	3.8435	**23**	28.9234	**24**	7.878 225	**25**	10.8721
26	8.1214	**27**	5.3889	**28**	2.3867	**29**	3.3346	**30**	5.9174

Exercise 11B

Round each of these decimal numbers to (a) 1 d.p. (b) 2 d.p. (c) 3 d.p.

1	53.9874	**2**	4.7291	**3**	7.1522	**4**	6.2792	**5**	10.2156
6	32.2564	**7**	90.8875	**8**	17.4523	**9**	25.3134	**10**	3.2254
11	3.1553	**12**	13.2794	**13**	7.3573	**14**	28.4414	**15**	36.1598
16	2.3646	**17**	4.0835	**18**	3.0181	**19**	2.3019	**20**	75.1802
21	12.7621	**22**	3.3612	**23**	2.3103	**24**	1.1824	**25**	2.5024
26	8.4144	**27**	1.0035	**28**	5.0296	**29**	7.3002	**30**	5.6891

12/ ORDERING DECIMAL NUMBERS

EXAMPLE

▶ Place these numbers in ascending order: 0.501, 1.6, 0.5, 0.4999.

First compare the whole numbers, then the 1st decimal place, 2nd decimal place, 3rd decimal place etc.:
0.4999 (smallest), 0.5, 0.501, 1.6 (largest)

Exercise 12A

Place these numbers in ascending order.

1 0.42, 0.41, 0.49
2 0.91, 0.18, 0.32
3 0.794, 0.432, 0.914, 0.222
4 0.2143, 0.9141, 0.1042, 0.8132
5 0.012, 0.039, 0.022
6 0.3, 0.8, 0.2, 0.9
7 0.132, 0.012, 0.232
8 0.1, 0.01, 0.001
9 0.4, 0.2, 0.6
10 0.101, 0.011, 0.041
11 5.109, 5.039, 5.009
12 0.0999, 0.009, 0.9
13 13.321, 13.123, 13.331
14 4.111, 4.011, 4.101
15 4.0059, 4.009, 4.0089
16 0.32, 2.3, 0.23, 3.2
17 9.909, 9.099, 9.990
18 0.2, 0.02, 2.2, 0.22
19 232.01, 231.39, 231.42
20 0.0199, 0.009 99, 0.0109
21 0.252, 0.254, 0.214, 0.241
22 4.0, 0.75, 0.04, 6.7
23 1.25, 0.125, 0.525, 0.55
24 5.306, 5.305, 5.202, 5.204
25 5.08, 8.8, 8.08, 9.8
26 1.0, 1.01, 0.110, 0.011
27 6.554, 5.623, 5.754, 6.556
28 0.03, 0.003, 3.0, 0.3
29 9.904, 9.99, 9.804, 9.9
30 1.10, 11.1, 11.3, 1.12

Exercise 12B

Place these numbers in ascending order.

1 0.7, 0.3, 0.4
2 0.234, 0.849, 0.915, 0.111
3 0.4, 0.9, 0.1, 0.7
4 0.7040, 0.8247, 0.3143, 0.2024
5 0.53, 0.52, 0.59
6 0.81, 0.19, 0.23
7 0.156, 0.024, 0.204
8 0.102, 0.022, 0.052
9 0.023, 0.048, 0.033
10 0.2, 0.0222, 0.002
11 0.4, 0.04, 0.004
12 23.331, 23.123, 23.321
13 2.007, 2.0067, 2.0037
14 3.007, 3.037, 3.107
15 0.0266, 0.0206, 0.006 66
16 0.77, 0.07, 0.7, 7.7
17 7.088, 7.888, 7.808
18 1.2, 2.1, 0.12, 0.21
19 3.330, 3.033, 3.303
20 1.08, 9.8, 10.8, 9.08
21 0.456, 0.472, 0.474, 0.465
22 0.8, 0.08, 0.008, 8.0
23 4.512, 6.443, 6.448, 4.643
24 0.03, 3.0, 0.75, 5.7
25 8.701, 8.88, 8.801, 8.8
26 4.32, 5.02, 5.52, 4.42
27 0.125, 0.66, 0.626, 1.25
28 8.80, 88.1, 88.5, 8.83
29 6.202, 6.305, 6.306, 6.204
30 0.022, 2.0, 2.02, 0.220

13/ ROUNDING TO SIGNIFICANT FIGURES

A number can also be rounded to a specified number of **significant figures** (s.f.).

4	5	.	0	1	2
↑	↑		↑	↑	↑
1st	2nd		3rd	4th	5th significant figure

To round a decimal number which is less than 1, follow the same process as for rounding to decimal places. (The zeros immediately after the decimal point are not significant figures.)

EXAMPLE

▶ Round 0.003 021 5 to (a) 3 s.f. (b) 4 s.f.

(a) 0.003 02 (Round down after the 2 as 2 is the 3rd significant figure.)

(b) 0.003 022 (Rounding up.)

To round a number that is 1 or more, the value of the significant figure within the number is important.

EXAMPLE

▶ Round 229.45 to (a) 1 s.f. (b) 2 s.f. (c) 3 s.f.

(a) 200 (The 1st significant figure is to the nearest 100.)

(b) 230 (The 2nd significant figure is to the nearest 10.)

(c) 229 (The 3rd significant figure is to the nearest unit.)

Exercise 13A

Round each of these numbers to (a) 1 s.f. (b) 2 s.f. (c) 3 s.f.

1	3.1145	**2**	0.3582	**3**	2.6452	**4**	0.7542	**5**	3.3459
6	0.3645	**7**	0.025 47	**8**	2.8481	**9**	0.036 936	**10**	2.1654
11	14.523	**12**	49.623	**13**	46.235	**14**	254.56	**15**	484.12
16	150.87	**17**	197.856	**18**	374.945	**19**	42.1963	**20**	0.045 29
21	69.954	**22**	0.5478	**23**	8.1946	**24**	0.078 899	**25**	1.5207
26	128.96	**27**	2262.5	**28**	282.23	**29**	8362.1	**30**	2694.5

Exercise 13B

Round each of these numbers to (a) 1 s.f. (b) 2 s.f. (c) 3 s.f.

1	3.4197	**2**	0.631 24	**3**	1.3270	**4**	0.9205	**5**	0.0292
6	0.3633	**7**	0.0774	**8**	0.8746	**9**	1.1106	**10**	7.1156
11	187.16	**12**	96.101	**13**	71.335	**14**	0.017 55	**15**	1.0226
16	32.7999	**17**	90.725	**18**	396.72	**19**	0.9635	**20**	0.052 41
21	213.256	**22**	114.856	**23**	12.9351	**24**	2303.52	**25**	1493.2
26	692.045	**27**	4059.2	**28**	409.46	**29**	4775.4	**30**	6422.5

14/ EVALUATING POWERS

$2^1 = 2$
$2^2 = 2 \times 2 = 4$
$2^3 = 2 \times 2 \times 2 = 8$
$2^4 = 2 \times 2 \times 2 \times 2 = 16$

EXAMPLE

▶ $5^n = 125$. Find n.

$5 \times 5 \times 5 = 125$
So: $5^3 = 125$
$n = 3$

EXAMPLE

▶ Evaluate $2^4 \times 5^3$.

$2^4 \times 5^3 = 16 \times 125$
$= 2000$

Exercise 14A

Evaluate.

1 3^2 **2** 4^3 **3** 6^2 **4** 2^7 **5** 4^5
6 3^4 **7** 7^2 **8** 10^3 **9** 3^5 **10** 11^2
11 9^2 **12** 13^2 **13** 8^4 **14** 15^3 **15** 20^2

Find the value of the number n in each of the following.

16 $5^n = 625$ **17** $2^n = 512$ **18** $4^n = 4096$
19 $6^n = 7776$ **20** $11^n = 1331$ **21** $12^n = 144$

Evaluate.

22 $3^3 \times 4^4$ **23** $7^2 + 8^4$ **24** $4^2 \times 6^2$ **25** $2^4 \times 3^3$ **26** $2^6 + 5^5$
27 $4^4 - 5^3$ **28** $8^3 + 4^6$ **29** $6^4 + 2^8$ **30** $3^6 - 5^4$

Exercise 14B

Evaluate.

1 5^2 **2** 6^3 **3** 2^5 **4** 4^2 **5** 6^4
6 10^2 **7** 7^3 **8** 8^2 **9** 9^3 **10** 10^4
11 9^4 **12** 3^7 **13** 14^2 **14** 7^4 **15** 16^2

Find the value of the number n in each of the following.

16 $2^n = 256$ **17** $3^n = 6561$ **18** $8^n = 512$
19 $5^n = 3125$ **20** $11^n = 14\,641$ **21** $13^n = 2197$

Evaluate.

22 $2^3 \times 4^5$ **23** $5^4 + 3^2$ **24** $3^6 + 6^3$ **25** $2^5 \times 4^3$ **26** $5^2 + 6^5$
27 $6^4 - 2^{10}$ **28** $7^3 \times 2^7$ **29** $7^3 - 3^4$ **30** $9^3 + 3^5$

REVISION

Exercise A

Questions 1–4 should be worked out without the use of a calculator, but you should show any working out that you find necessary.

1 (a) 52×100 (b) $35\,000 \div 100$ (c) 43×1000 (d) $1400 \div 10$
2 (a) 0.33×1000 (b) $4.5 \div 100$ (c) 1.7×100 (d) $25.14 \div 10$

3 (a) 254×14 (b) 103×28 (c) 741×35 (d) 431×56

4 (a) $3486 \div 14$ (b) $6710 \div 22$ (c) $16\,014 \div 34$ (d) $13\,581 \div 27$

5 Rewrite the numbers in ascending order.

(a) 6, –3, 1, 8, 0, –8, 5 (b) –7, 9, 3, –2, –10, 7, –1

6 Rewrite the numbers in descending order.

(a) 4, –5, 1, 6, –6, –3, 9 (b) 5, –7, –2, 10, –6, –9, 4, 0

7 Work out.

(a) $(+4) + (-7)$ (b) $(+7) - (-2)$ (c) $(-2) \times (-4)$ (d) $(+9) + (-3)$

(e) $(+3) \times (+5)$ (f) $(-12) \div (-6)$ (g) $(-3) - (-5)$ (h) $(-4) + (-5)$

(i) $(-21) \div (+7)$ (j) $(-3) \times (+4)$ (k) $(+18) \div (-3)$ (l) $(+5) - (+9)$

8 State the value of the underlined digits in (i) decimal form (ii) fraction form.

(a) $1.\underline{4}3\underline{7}9$ (b) $0.0\underline{4}0\underline{2}$ (c) $0.00\underline{7}\,61\underline{2}$ (d) $4.\underline{2}15\underline{7}$

9 Place the following decimals in ascending order.

(a) 0.22, 0.12, 0.222, 0.2 (b) 0.14, 1.104, 0.401, 0.104

(c) 3.333, 3.303, 3.330, 3.030 (d) 0.1568, 0.1685, 0.1658, 0.1856

10 Round each of these decimal numbers to (i) 1 decimal place (ii) 2 decimal places (iii) 3 decimal places.

(a) 1.3542 (b) 15.0914 (c) 6.7987

11 Round each of these numbers to (i) 1 significant figure (ii) 2 significant figures (iii) 3 significant figures.

(a) 4.5842 (b) 36.874 (c) 1837.5

12 Evaluate.

(a) 5^4 (b) 2^9 (c) 3^3 (d) 6^2

(e) $5^4 \times 9^2$ (f) $3^5 + 8^3$ (g) $7^3 - 2^8$ (h) $6^2 + 4^4$

Exercise AA

All these questions should be worked out without the use of a calculator, but you should show any working that you find necessary.

1 If 1500 counters are shared equally between 100 pupils, how many counters does each pupil receive?

2 There are 40 matches in a single matchbox. How many matches should there be in 100 matchboxes?

3 A prize of £3000 is to be shared equally among 10 people. How much should each person receive?

4 There are 12 felt-tip pens in a packet. How many pens are needed to fill 1000 packets?

5 There are 48 packets of crisps in a box. How many packets of crisps are there in 130 boxes?

6 There are 132 sweets in a bag. How many sweets are there in 14 bags?

7 A coach can carry 52 pop fans. How many fans can be taken to a series of concerts if 120 coaches have been booked?

8 A child's bucket of bricks contains 548 pieces. What is the total number of pieces required for 35 buckets of bricks?

9 Rubbers are to be packed in boxes of 48. How many boxes will be needed to pack 6000 rubbers?

10 An airmail package contains 144 silicon chips. How many packages are needed to send 3456 chips to South Africa?

11 A game uses 16 pegs in a board. How many games can be put together from 3424 pegs?

12 There are 10 251 people divided evenly among 17 sections of seats in an arena. How many people are there in each section?

13 A temperature of 3°C falls by 7 degrees. What is the new temperature?

14 How many years are there between 80 BCE and 130 CE?

15 Tim wants to buy a new pair of trainers for £48, but finds he is £9 short. How much money does he have?

16 At midnight the temperature was –5°C. At noon the temperature was 3°C. By how many degrees has the temperature risen?

15/ EQUIVALENT FRACTIONS

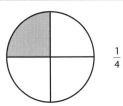

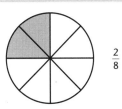

As you can see from the diagram, $\frac{1}{4}$ and $\frac{2}{8}$ cover the same area of the circle. The fractions $\frac{1}{4}$ and $\frac{2}{8}$ are **equivalent fractions**. The fraction $\frac{2}{8}$ can be cancelled down to $\frac{1}{4}$ by dividing top and bottom numbers by 2. Alternatively, $\frac{1}{4}$ becomes the equivalent fraction $\frac{2}{8}$ by multiplying top and bottom numbers by 2.

$$\frac{1}{4} = \frac{2}{8} = \frac{3}{12} = \frac{4}{16} = \frac{5}{20} = \ldots$$

EXAMPLE

▶ Complete the following by filling in the missing numbers.

$$\frac{2}{3} = \frac{4}{?} = \frac{?}{12} = \frac{12}{?}$$

$$\frac{2}{3} = \frac{4}{6} = \frac{8}{12} = \frac{12}{18}$$

(× 2) (× 4) (× 6) ← The original fraction is multiplied by these.

Exercise 15A

Complete the following.

1 $\frac{1}{2} = \frac{?}{4} = \frac{3}{?} = \frac{?}{8}$

2 $\frac{2}{5} = \frac{?}{15} = \frac{?}{25} = \frac{12}{?}$

3 $\frac{?}{6} = \frac{10}{?} = \frac{?}{24} = \frac{25}{30}$

4 $\frac{3}{4} = \frac{?}{8} = \frac{?}{12} = \frac{15}{?}$

5 $\frac{1}{5} = \frac{?}{15} = \frac{5}{?} = \frac{7}{?}$

6 $\frac{5}{9} = \frac{?}{18} = \frac{15}{?} = \frac{?}{54}$

7 $\frac{3}{8} = \frac{6}{?} = \frac{?}{24} = \frac{12}{?}$

8 $\frac{1}{7} = \frac{?}{21} = \frac{?}{35} = \frac{7}{?} = \frac{9}{?}$

9 $\frac{7}{10} = \frac{?}{30} = \frac{28}{?} = \frac{49}{?} = \frac{?}{100}$

10 $\frac{?}{8} = \frac{14}{?} = \frac{?}{24} = \frac{35}{40} = \frac{49}{?}$

11 $\frac{9}{?} = \frac{18}{40} = \frac{?}{60} = \frac{?}{104} = \frac{72}{?}$

12 $\frac{13}{24} = \frac{?}{48} = \frac{39}{?} = \frac{?}{96} = \frac{65}{?}$

Exercise 15B

Complete the following.

1 $\frac{1}{3} = \frac{?}{9} = \frac{?}{15} = \frac{6}{?}$

2 $\frac{5}{8} = \frac{?}{16} = \frac{?}{24} = \frac{20}{?}$

3 $\frac{3}{5} = \frac{6}{?} = \frac{?}{15} = \frac{?}{25}$

4 $\frac{1}{6} = \frac{2}{?} = \frac{?}{24} = \frac{5}{?}$

5 $\frac{?}{9} = \frac{21}{27} = \frac{?}{45} = \frac{49}{?}$

6 $\frac{3}{?} = \frac{9}{30} = \frac{?}{40} = \frac{18}{?}$

7 $\frac{1}{8} = \frac{?}{16} = \frac{5}{?} = \frac{6}{?} = \frac{?}{64}$

8 $\frac{5}{12} = \frac{15}{?} = \frac{25}{?} = \frac{?}{84} = \frac{?}{108}$

9 $\frac{5}{24} = \frac{?}{48} = \frac{20}{?} = \frac{?}{144} = \frac{35}{?}$

10 $\frac{5}{32} = \frac{?}{96} = \frac{?}{160} = \frac{30}{?} = \frac{?}{224}$

11 $\frac{7}{?} = \frac{28}{80} = \frac{?}{100} = \frac{56}{?} = \frac{?}{200}$

12 $\frac{4}{15} = \frac{?}{30} = \frac{20}{?} = \frac{?}{90} = \frac{?}{120}$

16/ FRACTIONS OF QUANTITIES

EXAMPLES

▶ Find $\frac{1}{5}$ of 30.

$\frac{1}{5}$ of 30 = 30 ÷ 5
= 6

Find $\frac{5}{6}$ of £4.20.

$\frac{1}{6}$ of £4.20 = £4.20 ÷ 6
= £0.70 or 70p

So, $\frac{5}{6}$ of £4.20 = £0.70 × 5 = £3.50

Exercise 16A

Find the following.

1 $\frac{1}{7}$ of 42 **2** $\frac{1}{3}$ of 72 **3** $\frac{1}{8}$ of 16 **4** $\frac{1}{9}$ of 36p

5 $\frac{1}{5}$ of 25 g **6** $\frac{1}{6}$ of £9 **7** $\frac{1}{3}$ of 72 km **8** $\frac{1}{15}$ of £60

9 $\frac{4}{5}$ of 3.5 kg **10** $\frac{5}{9}$ of £38.34 **11** $\frac{5}{7}$ of 21 metres **12** $\frac{2}{5}$ of 12.4 metres

13 $\frac{2}{3}$ of 48 g **14** $\frac{3}{7}$ of £52.22 **15** $\frac{2}{3}$ of £5.16 **16** $\frac{3}{5}$ of £100

17 $\frac{7}{9}$ of 27 litres **18** $\frac{5}{8}$ of £19.68 **19** $\frac{3}{10}$ of 800 g **20** $\frac{9}{25}$ of £9

21 $\frac{5}{12}$ of 738 kg **22** $\frac{9}{20}$ of £95.80 **23** $\frac{5}{6}$ of £27.54 **24** $\frac{13}{16}$ of £184.16

25 $\frac{3}{10}$ of 59.2 km **26** $\frac{3}{8}$ of £52.40 **27** $\frac{5}{9}$ of 270 mm **28** $\frac{5}{6}$ of £1.38

29 $\frac{3}{8}$ of £12.24 **30** $\frac{7}{8}$ of 88 ml

Exercise 16B

Find the following.

1 $\frac{1}{6}$ of 24 **2** $\frac{1}{4}$ of 48 **3** $\frac{1}{5}$ of 40 **4** $\frac{1}{2}$ of £1.12

5 $\frac{1}{7}$ of £35 **6** $\frac{1}{5}$ of 45 g **7** $\frac{1}{12}$ of £42 **8** $\frac{1}{10}$ of £3

9 $\frac{3}{4}$ of £18.68 **10** $\frac{2}{5}$ of 800 g **11** $\frac{3}{4}$ of 15.4 metres **12** $\frac{3}{10}$ of 50 kg

13 $\frac{7}{10}$ of £16.30 **14** $\frac{7}{15}$ of \$60 **15** $\frac{2}{3}$ of £21.75 **16** $\frac{3}{10}$ of 4.5 kg

17 $\frac{19}{20}$ of 91 litres **18** $\frac{2}{5}$ of £7.25 **19** $\frac{7}{16}$ of £43.84 **20** $\frac{5}{11}$ of 479.6 km

21 $\frac{5}{6}$ of 48 litres **22** $\frac{7}{12}$ of 28.2 litres **23** $\frac{3}{8}$ of £25.04 **24** $\frac{5}{6}$ of £9

25 $\frac{4}{5}$ of 5.65 kg **26** $\frac{7}{10}$ of £58.80 **27** $\frac{3}{5}$ of £17.10 **28** $\frac{3}{20}$ of £74.40

29 $\frac{7}{20}$ of 300 kg **30** $\frac{11}{12}$ of £42

17/ CANCELLING FRACTIONS

Fractions can be simplified by cancelling the top and bottom numbers. This is done by dividing both the top and bottom numbers by any common factor.

EXAMPLES

▶ Cancel these fractions to their lowest terms: $\frac{8}{10}$, $\frac{24}{30}$.

$\frac{8}{10} = \frac{4}{5}$ (÷ 2)

$\frac{24}{30} = \frac{4}{5}$ (÷ 6)

Notes: Check your cancelled fraction to make sure you cannot cancel it again.
Always try to divide by the *largest* common factor.

Exercise 17A

Cancel these fractions to their lowest terms.

1 $\frac{9}{12}$ **2** $\frac{12}{15}$ **3** $\frac{35}{42}$ **4** $\frac{6}{8}$ **5** $\frac{30}{36}$ **6** $\frac{4}{8}$

7 $\frac{24}{32}$ **8** $\frac{60}{84}$ **9** $\frac{80}{90}$ **10** $\frac{25}{55}$ **11** $\frac{56}{77}$ **12** $\frac{18}{24}$

13 $\frac{36}{64}$ **14** $\frac{54}{72}$ **15** $\frac{20}{35}$ **16** $\frac{16}{24}$ **17** $\frac{12}{18}$ **18** $\frac{45}{48}$

19 $\frac{11}{22}$ **20** $\frac{2}{14}$ **21** $\frac{72}{90}$ **22** $\frac{12}{15}$ **23** $\frac{75}{150}$ **24** $\frac{84}{112}$

25 $\frac{48}{120}$ **26** $\frac{48}{64}$ **27** $\frac{27}{108}$ **28** $\frac{12}{160}$ **29** $\frac{28}{70}$ **30** $\frac{192}{448}$

Exercise 17B

Cancel these fractions to their lowest terms.

1 $\frac{21}{27}$ **2** $\frac{3}{12}$ **3** $\frac{48}{72}$ **4** $\frac{7}{35}$ **5** $\frac{6}{9}$ **6** $\frac{16}{24}$

7 $\frac{100}{160}$ **8** $\frac{65}{85}$ **9** $\frac{12}{32}$ **10** $\frac{140}{200}$ **11** $\frac{48}{80}$ **12** $\frac{35}{75}$

13 $\frac{36}{90}$ **14** $\frac{48}{108}$ **15** $\frac{168}{480}$ **16** $\frac{8}{12}$ **17** $\frac{18}{24}$ **18** $\frac{48}{60}$

19 $\frac{12}{24}$ **20** $\frac{99}{108}$ **21** $\frac{75}{200}$ **22** $\frac{12}{18}$ **23** $\frac{45}{144}$ **24** $\frac{18}{81}$

25 $\frac{27}{39}$ **26** $\frac{56}{80}$ **27** $\frac{76}{92}$ **28** $\frac{254}{308}$ **29** $\frac{42}{105}$ **30** $\frac{105}{189}$

18/ CONVERSION TO AND FROM MIXED NUMBERS

Mixed numbers are numbers which have a 'whole number' part, and a 'fraction' part. A mixed number can be changed into an 'improper' or 'top-heavy' fraction.

EXAMPLE

▶ Change into improper fractions: (a) $7\frac{3}{4}$ (b) $4\frac{2}{5}$.

(a) $7\frac{3}{4} = 7 + \frac{3}{4} = \frac{28}{4} + \frac{3}{4} = \frac{31}{4}$

(b) $4\frac{2}{5} = 4 + \frac{2}{5} = \frac{20}{5} + \frac{2}{5} = \frac{22}{5}$

Improper fractions can be changed into mixed numbers if the top part of the fraction is larger than the bottom part. The fraction might also need cancelling.

EXAMPLE

▶ Change into mixed numbers: (a) $\frac{20}{9}$ (b) $\frac{136}{12}$.

(a) $9\overline{)\,2\ 0}$ = 2 r 2

(b) $12\overline{)\,1\ 3\ {}^{1}6}$ = 1 1 r 4

So: $\frac{20}{9} = 2\frac{2}{9}$

So: $\frac{136}{12} = 11\frac{4}{12}$

$= 11\frac{1}{3}$ (cancelling the $\frac{4}{12}$)

Exercise 18A

Change these mixed numbers into improper fractions.

1 $3\frac{2}{3}$	**2** $1\frac{1}{2}$	**3** $4\frac{2}{5}$	**4** $4\frac{1}{4}$	**5** $3\frac{1}{4}$	**6** $9\frac{1}{2}$
7 $8\frac{9}{10}$	**8** $2\frac{9}{11}$	**9** $7\frac{3}{4}$	**10** $11\frac{5}{6}$	**11** $6\frac{1}{7}$	**12** $13\frac{3}{5}$
13 $5\frac{3}{10}$	**14** $10\frac{4}{9}$	**15** $5\frac{6}{7}$	**16** $5\frac{2}{7}$	**17** $12\frac{3}{4}$	**18** $4\frac{6}{7}$
19 $3\frac{9}{10}$	**20** $5\frac{4}{5}$	**21** $9\frac{11}{18}$	**22** $9\frac{5}{7}$	**23** $8\frac{8}{9}$	**24** $13\frac{3}{8}$
25 $1\frac{5}{12}$	**26** $5\frac{4}{5}$	**27** $30\frac{1}{3}$	**28** $4\frac{5}{12}$	**29** $19\frac{5}{8}$	**30** $9\frac{7}{10}$

Exercise 18B

Change these mixed numbers into improper fractions.

1 $2\frac{2}{3}$	**2** $3\frac{1}{2}$	**3** $5\frac{3}{5}$	**4** $3\frac{3}{4}$	**5** $8\frac{11}{12}$	**6** $7\frac{1}{6}$
7 $2\frac{3}{4}$	**8** $7\frac{1}{4}$	**9** $5\frac{1}{6}$	**10** $9\frac{2}{5}$	**11** $1\frac{5}{6}$	**12** $5\frac{1}{16}$
13 $7\frac{2}{3}$	**14** $5\frac{5}{6}$	**15** $8\frac{4}{9}$	**16** $1\frac{6}{7}$	**17** $1\frac{3}{10}$	**18** $7\frac{1}{7}$
19 $10\frac{2}{7}$	**20** $4\frac{2}{5}$	**21** $9\frac{4}{9}$	**22** $12\frac{5}{12}$	**23** $9\frac{5}{6}$	**24** $8\frac{7}{8}$
25 $3\frac{11}{12}$	**26** $11\frac{3}{8}$	**27** $18\frac{4}{7}$	**28** $3\frac{5}{12}$	**29** $12\frac{7}{9}$	**30** $10\frac{3}{5}$

Exercise 18C

Change these improper fractions into mixed numbers.

1 $\frac{5}{4}$	**2** $\frac{17}{3}$	**3** $\frac{19}{4}$	**4** $\frac{9}{2}$	**5** $\frac{9}{5}$	**6** $\frac{41}{6}$
7 $\frac{38}{7}$	**8** $\frac{11}{4}$	**9** $\frac{49}{12}$	**10** $\frac{61}{8}$	**11** $\frac{73}{10}$	**12** $\frac{89}{6}$
13 $\frac{49}{8}$	**14** $\frac{82}{9}$	**15** $\frac{100}{3}$	**16** $\frac{83}{9}$	**17** $\frac{35}{6}$	**18** $\frac{31}{4}$
19 $\frac{23}{3}$	**20** $\frac{31}{9}$	**21** $\frac{41}{7}$	**22** $\frac{57}{8}$	**23** $\frac{128}{15}$	**24** $\frac{127}{6}$
25 $\frac{25}{2}$	**26** $\frac{32}{3}$	**27** $\frac{100}{9}$	**28** $\frac{109}{25}$	**29** $\frac{97}{24}$	**30** $\frac{97}{16}$

Exercise 18D

Change these improper fractions into mixed numbers.

1 $\frac{3}{2}$	**2** $\frac{5}{2}$	**3** $\frac{9}{4}$	**4** $\frac{19}{12}$	**5** $\frac{11}{5}$	**6** $\frac{25}{2}$
7 $\frac{63}{8}$	**8** $\frac{27}{4}$	**9** $\frac{57}{10}$	**10** $\frac{24}{5}$	**11** $\frac{77}{8}$	**12** $\frac{23}{12}$
13 $\frac{48}{7}$	**14** $\frac{84}{5}$	**15** $\frac{24}{10}$	**16** $\frac{51}{4}$	**17** $\frac{93}{6}$	**18** $\frac{19}{4}$
19 $\frac{14}{9}$	**20** $\frac{76}{9}$	**21** $\frac{28}{5}$	**22** $\frac{93}{7}$	**23** $\frac{56}{15}$	**24** $\frac{41}{6}$
25 $\frac{79}{5}$	**26** $\frac{93}{14}$	**27** $\frac{47}{20}$	**28** $\frac{129}{25}$	**29** $\frac{79}{12}$	**30** $\frac{19}{3}$

19/ ADDITION OF SIMPLE FRACTIONS

When fractions with the same denominators are added, do *not* add the denominators. Always cancel an answer to its simplest form.

EXAMPLES

▶ $\frac{2}{5} + \frac{1}{5} = \frac{3}{5}$

$\frac{5}{8} + \frac{7}{8} = \frac{12}{8} = 1\frac{4}{8} = 1\frac{1}{2}$

When fractions of different denominators are added, first change one of the fractions to an equivalent fraction so that the two fractions have a common denominator (that is the denominators are the same).

EXAMPLES

▶ $\frac{1}{3} + \frac{7}{12} = \frac{4}{12} + \frac{7}{12} \quad (\frac{1}{3}\frac{\times 4}{\times 4} = \frac{4}{12})$

$= \frac{11}{12}$

$\frac{3}{4} + \frac{7}{8} = \frac{6}{8} + \frac{7}{8} \quad (\frac{3}{4}\frac{\times 2}{\times 2} = \frac{6}{8})$

$= \frac{13}{8}$

$= 1\frac{5}{8}$

$1\frac{1}{2} + 2\frac{3}{4} = 3 + \frac{1}{2} + \frac{3}{4}$ (The whole numbers are dealt with separately.)

$= 3 + \frac{2}{4} + \frac{3}{4}$

$= 3 + \frac{5}{4}$

$= 3 + 1\frac{1}{4}$

$= 4\frac{1}{4}$

Exercise 19A

1	$\frac{3}{4} + \frac{1}{4}$	**2**	$\frac{5}{8} + \frac{4}{8}$	**3**	$\frac{1}{6} + \frac{5}{6}$	**4**	$\frac{5}{9} + \frac{4}{9}$	**5**	$\frac{1}{2} + \frac{1}{8}$
6	$\frac{1}{2} + \frac{1}{16}$	**7**	$\frac{1}{4} + \frac{3}{8}$	**8**	$\frac{7}{16} + \frac{3}{32}$	**9**	$\frac{3}{4} + \frac{1}{32}$	**10**	$\frac{3}{4} + \frac{1}{16}$
11	$\frac{1}{2} + \frac{15}{32}$	**12**	$\frac{3}{4} + \frac{3}{8}$	**13**	$\frac{1}{2} + \frac{3}{32}$	**14**	$\frac{3}{4} + \frac{7}{8}$	**15**	$\frac{1}{2} + \frac{3}{4}$
16	$\frac{9}{16} + \frac{5}{8}$	**17**	$\frac{1}{2} + \frac{15}{16}$	**18**	$\frac{1}{4} + \frac{13}{16}$	**19**	$\frac{7}{8} + \frac{11}{16}$	**20**	$\frac{3}{4} + \frac{1}{16}$
21	$\frac{5}{6} + \frac{1}{12}$	**22**	$\frac{2}{3} + \frac{5}{6}$	**23**	$\frac{3}{5} + \frac{7}{10}$	**24**	$\frac{4}{9} + \frac{1}{3}$	**25**	$\frac{2}{3} + \frac{7}{12}$

26 Two parcels, which have weights of $\frac{3}{4}$ kg and $\frac{5}{12}$ kg, are posted. What is the total weight?

27 If $3\frac{2}{5}$ litres and $4\frac{1}{5}$ litres of oil are poured into a tin, how much oil is in the tin?

28 A platform $9\frac{7}{8}$ ft long is extended by $\frac{9}{16}$ ft. What is the total length?

29 Two pieces of carpet, $3\frac{1}{2}$ metres and $2\frac{7}{8}$ metres wide, are joined together. What is the total width?

30 A cake that is $8\frac{3}{7}$ in deep has icing added of thickness $\frac{9}{14}$ in. What is the new depth of the cake?

Exercise 19B

1 $\frac{3}{5} + \frac{2}{5}$ **2** $\frac{4}{7} + \frac{5}{7}$ **3** $\frac{3}{7} + \frac{5}{7}$ **4** $\frac{8}{9} + \frac{4}{9}$ **5** $\frac{1}{2} + \frac{1}{4}$

6 $\frac{1}{4} + \frac{1}{16}$ **7** $\frac{1}{4} + \frac{11}{32}$ **8** $\frac{1}{8} + \frac{3}{16}$ **9** $\frac{3}{4} + \frac{7}{32}$ **10** $\frac{5}{8} + \frac{1}{32}$

11 $\frac{3}{8} + \frac{1}{4}$ **12** $\frac{3}{4} + \frac{5}{8}$ **13** $\frac{1}{2} + \frac{5}{8}$ **14** $\frac{1}{2} + \frac{15}{16}$ **15** $\frac{5}{8} + \frac{13}{16}$

16 $\frac{3}{4} + \frac{31}{32}$ **17** $\frac{9}{16} + \frac{15}{32}$ **18** $\frac{3}{4} + \frac{5}{16}$ **19** $\frac{17}{32} + \frac{5}{8}$ **20** $\frac{5}{8} + \frac{1}{16}$

21 $\frac{2}{5} + \frac{7}{30}$ **22** $\frac{3}{4} + \frac{5}{8}$ **23** $\frac{8}{9} + \frac{2}{3}$ **24** $\frac{3}{8} + \frac{1}{4}$ **25** $\frac{1}{2} + \frac{1}{12}$

26 A length of carpet that is $5\frac{3}{8}$ feet long has another piece added to it of length $2\frac{1}{4}$ feet. What is the total length of carpet?

27 One bag of shopping weighs $2\frac{2}{5}$ kg and another weighs $4\frac{3}{5}$ kg. What is the total weight of shopping?

28 A table of length $6\frac{2}{3}$ feet is extended by $2\frac{7}{9}$ feet. What is the new length of the table?

29 A plank $8\frac{4}{5}$ cm in width is laid alongside another plank $3\frac{7}{15}$ cm in width. What is the total width?

30 Mark has $8\frac{3}{4}$ hectares of land. He buys another $1\frac{7}{12}$ hectares. How much land does he now have?

20/ SUBTRACTION OF SIMPLE FRACTIONS

When a fraction is taken away from a whole number, remember that the whole one can be expressed as a fraction.

EXAMPLES

▶ $1 - \frac{2}{3} = \frac{3}{3} - \frac{2}{3} = \frac{1}{3}$

$4 - \frac{4}{5} = 3 + 1 - \frac{4}{5} = 3 + \frac{5}{5} - \frac{4}{5} = 3\frac{1}{5}$

Subtraction of fractions involves the same processes as for adding fractions.

EXAMPLES

▶ $\frac{7}{8} - \frac{1}{4} = \frac{7}{8} - \frac{2}{8} = \frac{5}{8}$

$3\frac{4}{5} - 1\frac{1}{10} = 2 + \frac{8}{10} - \frac{1}{10} = 2\frac{7}{10}$

Exercise 20A

1 $1 - \frac{3}{4}$ **2** $1 - \frac{1}{16}$ **3** $3 - \frac{5}{8}$ **4** $2 - \frac{3}{4}$ **5** $1 - \frac{5}{8}$

6 $2 - \frac{17}{32}$ **7** $5\frac{2}{3} - 3\frac{1}{3}$ **8** $8\frac{7}{9} - 2\frac{5}{9}$ **9** $\frac{1}{2} - \frac{1}{4}$ **10** $\frac{3}{4} - \frac{3}{8}$

11 $\frac{2}{3} - \frac{1}{6}$ **12** $\frac{1}{4} - \frac{1}{8}$ **13** $\frac{7}{8} - \frac{1}{2}$ **14** $\frac{13}{16} - \frac{3}{4}$ **15** $\frac{3}{4} - \frac{1}{8}$

16 $\frac{1}{2} - \frac{1}{20}$ **17** $\frac{7}{8} - \frac{13}{16}$ **18** $\frac{5}{8} - \frac{1}{16}$ **19** $\frac{15}{16} - \frac{1}{2}$ **20** $\frac{15}{32} - \frac{1}{4}$

21 $\frac{7}{12} - \frac{1}{3}$ **22** $4\frac{7}{8} - 2\frac{1}{2}$ **23** $\frac{5}{6} - \frac{7}{12}$ **24** $\frac{3}{4} - \frac{5}{28}$ **25** $4\frac{4}{5} - 2\frac{7}{20}$

26 A door $5\frac{1}{4}$ ft high has $\frac{1}{12}$ ft trimmed off it. What is its new height?

27 A pen $3\frac{1}{2}$ cm long has its end, which is $1\frac{1}{4}$ cm long, snapped off. What is its new length?

28 The distance across the outside of a pipe is $7\frac{1}{2}$ cm. The distance across the inside is $6\frac{15}{32}$ cm. What is the difference between the distances?

29 One child has a height of $3\frac{3}{8}$ ft; another has a height of $1\frac{5}{16}$ ft. How much taller is the first child?

30 A package that has a weight of $2\frac{3}{4}$ kg is posted. The packaging weighs $1\frac{9}{16}$ kg. What is the weight of the contents?

Exercise 20B

1 $1-\frac{3}{8}$	**2** $2-\frac{1}{8}$	**3** $6-\frac{15}{16}$	**4** $1-\frac{31}{32}$	**5** $3-\frac{17}{32}$
6 $6-\frac{11}{16}$	**7** $2\frac{4}{5}-1\frac{3}{5}$	**8** $6\frac{3}{5}-2\frac{1}{5}$	**9** $\frac{1}{2}-\frac{1}{12}$	**10** $\frac{3}{4}-\frac{1}{2}$
11 $\frac{7}{9}-\frac{2}{3}$	**12** $\frac{3}{4}-\frac{1}{2}$	**13** $\frac{1}{2}-\frac{1}{8}$	**14** $\frac{7}{8}-\frac{1}{4}$	**15** $\frac{13}{16}-\frac{1}{2}$
16 $\frac{5}{8}-\frac{1}{2}$	**17** $\frac{3}{4}-\frac{7}{32}$	**18** $\frac{7}{8}-\frac{3}{4}$	**19** $\frac{17}{32}-\frac{1}{2}$	**20** $\frac{3}{4}-\frac{9}{16}$
21 $3\frac{5}{8}-1\frac{1}{4}$	**22** $\frac{11}{32}-\frac{1}{4}$	**23** $\frac{14}{20}-\frac{1}{2}$	**24** $\frac{7}{8}-\frac{5}{24}$	**25** $3\frac{5}{8}-2\frac{1}{2}$

26 A tank contains $\frac{1}{2}$ litre of oil. How much needs to be added to make $6\frac{7}{8}$ litres?

27 A $4\frac{3}{4}$ kg block of cheese has $1\frac{3}{8}$ kg removed. How much is left?

28 A package weighs $4\frac{1}{4}$ kg. Its contents weigh $3\frac{3}{16}$ kg. What weight is the packaging?

29 A cupboard of height $9\frac{3}{4}$ feet has its legs removed. It now stands $8\frac{23}{32}$ feet tall. What length were the legs?

30 A piece of wood $4\frac{3}{8}$ cm long has $3\frac{3}{16}$ cm cut off. What length remains?

21/ SIMPLE MULTIPLICATION OF FRACTIONS

When multiplying fractions first multiply the top numbers, then multiply the bottom numbers. Cancelling top and bottom numbers first might make the problem easier to solve.

EXAMPLES

▶ $\frac{3}{5} \times \frac{1}{2} = \frac{1\times 3}{5\times 2} = \frac{3}{10}$

$\frac{3}{4} \times 6 = \frac{3\times 6}{4} = \frac{3\times 3}{2} = \frac{9}{2} = 4\frac{1}{2}$

$\frac{1}{4} \times \frac{8}{9} = \frac{1\times 8}{4\times 9}$ (Cancel the 8 and the 4.)

$= \frac{1\times 2}{1\times 9}$

$= \frac{2}{9}$

Exercise 21A

1 $\frac{4}{5}\times\frac{2}{3}$	**2** $\frac{1}{2}\times\frac{4}{5}$	**3** $\frac{3}{5}\times\frac{1}{4}$	**4** $\frac{2}{3}\times\frac{1}{4}$	**5** $\frac{5}{2}\times\frac{3}{10}$
6 $\frac{2}{3}\times\frac{5}{7}$	**7** $\frac{1}{3}\times\frac{2}{3}$	**8** $\frac{5}{12}\times\frac{4}{5}$	**9** $\frac{2}{3}\times\frac{3}{8}$	**10** $\frac{3}{7}\times\frac{21}{10}$

11	$\frac{4}{5} \times \frac{5}{8}$	**12**	$\frac{3}{7} \times \frac{14}{9}$	**13**	$\frac{8}{9} \times \frac{3}{4}$	**14**	$\frac{2}{3} \times 8$	**15**	$\frac{4}{5} \times \frac{15}{16}$
16	$\frac{2}{5} \times \frac{7}{8}$	**17**	$\frac{4}{5} \times \frac{15}{24}$	**18**	$\frac{3}{4} \times 2$	**19**	$\frac{8}{9} \times \frac{3}{4}$	**20**	$\frac{9}{27} \times \frac{8}{4}$
21	$\frac{2}{3} \times 12$	**22**	$\frac{3}{8} \times \frac{1}{4}$	**23**	$\frac{2}{3} \times \frac{4}{3}$	**24**	$\frac{2}{3} \times \frac{6}{5} \times \frac{1}{7}$	**25**	$\frac{7}{8} \times \frac{1}{2}$
26	$\frac{5}{19} \times 38$	**27**	$\frac{2}{7} \times 28$	**28**	$\frac{3}{4} \times \frac{3}{16}$	**29**	$15 \times \frac{4}{9}$	**30**	$\frac{1}{4} \times \frac{5}{3}$

Exercise 21B

1	$\frac{2}{3} \times \frac{2}{7}$	**2**	$\frac{6}{5} \times \frac{1}{3}$	**3**	$\frac{3}{7} \times \frac{2}{6}$	**4**	$\frac{5}{6} \times \frac{1}{3}$	**5**	$\frac{4}{7} \times \frac{2}{3}$
6	$\frac{1}{2} \times \frac{7}{8}$	**7**	$\frac{2}{3} \times \frac{3}{4}$	**8**	$\frac{3}{4} \times \frac{5}{7}$	**9**	$\frac{1}{8} \times \frac{2}{3}$	**10**	$\frac{3}{4} \times \frac{4}{9}$
11	$\frac{5}{12} \times \frac{6}{7}$	**12**	$\frac{2}{3} \times \frac{6}{7}$	**13**	$\frac{4}{5} \times \frac{10}{12}$	**14**	$\frac{7}{8} \times \frac{4}{7}$	**15**	$\frac{6}{7} \times 14$
16	$\frac{4}{9} \times \frac{7}{8}$	**17**	$\frac{6}{18} \times \frac{3}{9}$	**18**	$\frac{4}{7} \times 8$	**19**	$\frac{3}{2} \times \frac{1}{4}$	**20**	$\frac{4}{5} \times 5$
21	$\frac{2}{5} \times \frac{4}{3}$	**22**	$\frac{3}{4} \times 8$	**23**	$\frac{5}{2} \times \frac{3}{4}$	**24**	$\frac{4}{5} \times \frac{3}{7} \times \frac{1}{8}$	**25**	$\frac{1}{2} \times \frac{5}{16}$
26	$20 \times \frac{5}{8}$	**27**	$\frac{11}{32} \times \frac{1}{4}$	**28**	$\frac{3}{4} \times \frac{1}{8}$	**29**	$\frac{15}{4} \times \frac{3}{2}$	**30**	$\frac{3}{2} \times \frac{3}{2}$

22/ SIMPLE DIVISION OF FRACTIONS

When dividing fractions, an 'inverse' property can be used to change the division problem into a multiplication problem, for example:

$\frac{3}{5} \div \frac{1}{2}$ is the same as $\frac{3}{5} \times \frac{2}{1}$ (Using the inverse of division, which is multiplication, *and* the inverse second fraction.)

So: $\frac{3}{5} \div \frac{1}{2} = \frac{3}{5} \times \frac{2}{1} = \frac{6}{5} = 1\frac{1}{5}$

EXAMPLE

▶ $\frac{1}{4} \div 5 = \frac{1}{4} \times \frac{1}{5} = \frac{1}{20}$

Exercise 22A

1	$\frac{2}{3} \div \frac{9}{10}$	**2**	$\frac{1}{4} \div 2$	**3**	$\frac{2}{5} \div \frac{3}{4}$	**4**	$\frac{1}{4} \div 3$	**5**	$\frac{4}{9} \div 5$
6	$\frac{3}{7} \div \frac{4}{5}$	**7**	$\frac{3}{7} \div \frac{1}{2}$	**8**	$\frac{7}{20} \div \frac{2}{5}$	**9**	$\frac{3}{11} \div \frac{1}{3}$	**10**	$\frac{4}{7} \div \frac{6}{7}$
11	$\frac{7}{10} \div \frac{2}{5}$	**12**	$\frac{9}{3} \div \frac{15}{2}$	**13**	$\frac{3}{10} \div \frac{1}{2}$	**14**	$\frac{9}{5} \div \frac{27}{10}$	**15**	$\frac{24}{5} \div \frac{16}{3}$
16	$\frac{2}{3} \div 6$	**17**	$\frac{32}{5} \div \frac{16}{15}$	**18**	$\frac{14}{3} \div \frac{28}{9}$	**19**	$\frac{9}{4} \div \frac{15}{8}$	**20**	$\frac{25}{2} \div \frac{35}{8}$

Exercise 22B

1	$\frac{1}{2} \div 3$	**2**	$\frac{4}{5} \div \frac{2}{3}$	**3**	$\frac{1}{5} \div 2$	**4**	$\frac{2}{5} \div \frac{1}{2}$	**5**	$\frac{4}{9} \div \frac{7}{12}$
6	$\frac{7}{8} \div 3$	**7**	$\frac{1}{2} \div \frac{2}{3}$	**8**	$\frac{2}{9} \div \frac{1}{2}$	**9**	$\frac{2}{3} \div \frac{8}{9}$	**10**	$\frac{1}{6} \div \frac{2}{3}$

11 $\frac{21}{25} \div \frac{3}{5}$ **12** $\frac{9}{2} \div \frac{15}{2}$ **13** $\frac{4}{9} \div \frac{2}{3}$ **14** $\frac{4}{3} \div \frac{20}{9}$ **15** $\frac{4}{9} \div 8$

16 $\frac{28}{9} \div \frac{14}{3}$ **17** $\frac{3}{4} \div 6$ **18** $\frac{18}{7} \div \frac{12}{5}$ **19** $\frac{8}{3} \div \frac{20}{9}$ **20** $\frac{35}{3} \div \frac{25}{9}$

23/ CONVERSION BETWEEN FRACTIONS AND DECIMALS

To convert a fraction to a decimal, divide the top number by the bottom number, then add on any whole numbers.

EXAMPLE

▶ Convert $2\frac{4}{5}$ into a decimal.

$4 \div 5 = 0.8$

$2\frac{4}{5} = 2 + 0.8 = 2.8$

To convert a decimal to a fraction, write the decimal part over the appropriate denominator (the number of zeros is the same as the number of digits in the decimal part), cancel if possible, and add on any whole numbers.

EXAMPLE

▶ Convert (a) 2.15 (b) 0.0105 into fractions.

(a) $0.15 = \frac{15}{100} = \frac{3}{20}$

So $2.15 = 2\frac{3}{20}$

(b) $0.0105 = \frac{105}{10\,000} = \frac{21}{2000}$

Exercise 23A

Convert the following fractions to decimals.

1 $\frac{1}{4}$ **2** $\frac{3}{8}$ **3** $\frac{1}{5}$ **4** $\frac{1}{16}$ **5** $\frac{9}{16}$

6 $\frac{7}{10}$ **7** $2\frac{3}{25}$ **8** $\frac{3}{20}$ **9** $10\frac{2}{5}$ **10** $4\frac{2}{5}$

11 $3\frac{3}{10}$ **12** $6\frac{1}{25}$ **13** $\frac{13}{20}$ **14** $4\frac{7}{40}$ **15** $\frac{15}{16}$

16 $2\frac{7}{20}$ **17** $\frac{3}{32}$ **18** $4\frac{9}{20}$ **19** $5\frac{19}{20}$ **20** $2\frac{11}{25}$

In the following questions give your answers to 4 decimal places.

21 $\frac{1}{3}$ **22** $\frac{5}{11}$ **23** $\frac{7}{12}$ **24** $\frac{1}{9}$ **25** $\frac{19}{30}$

26 $\frac{5}{6}$ **27** $\frac{1}{7}$ **28** $\frac{7}{9}$ **29** $\frac{1}{12}$ **30** $\frac{9}{11}$

Exercise 23B

Convert the following fractions to decimals.

1 $\frac{1}{2}$ **2** $\frac{1}{8}$ **3** $\frac{4}{5}$ **4** $\frac{1}{20}$ **5** $\frac{5}{16}$

6 $\frac{3}{10}$ **7** $3\frac{17}{100}$ **8** $4\frac{9}{10}$ **9** $\frac{9}{20}$ **10** $1\frac{7}{8}$

11 $2\frac{9}{25}$ **12** $\frac{13}{16}$ **13** $5\frac{2}{5}$ **14** $\frac{19}{20}$ **15** $4\frac{21}{40}$

16 $4\frac{7}{25}$ **17** $1\frac{13}{25}$ **18** $\frac{5}{32}$ **19** $5\frac{21}{25}$ **20** $7\frac{13}{40}$

In the following questions give your answers to 4 decimal places.

21	$\frac{2}{3}$	**22**	$\frac{3}{11}$	**23**	$\frac{5}{12}$	**24**	$\frac{4}{9}$	**25**	$\frac{6}{11}$
26	$\frac{13}{30}$	**27**	$\frac{5}{9}$	**28**	$\frac{2}{7}$	**29**	$\frac{10}{11}$	**30**	$\frac{1}{11}$

Exercise 23C

Convert the following decimals to fractions expressed in their lowest terms.

1	0.7	**2**	0.03	**3**	0.65	**4**	0.85	**5**	0.9
6	0.04	**7**	0.4	**8**	0.95	**9**	0.1	**10**	0.125
11	0.37	**12**	0.002	**13**	0.447	**14**	0.27	**15**	0.35
16	0.575	**17**	0.1275	**18**	0.842	**19**	0.24	**20**	0.96
21	3.225	**22**	0.735	**23**	0.955	**24**	1.52	**25**	0.25
26	6.85	**27**	0.56	**28**	0.935	**29**	2.2125	**30**	5.8

Exercise 23D

Convert the following decimals to fractions expressed in their lowest terms.

1	0.47	**2**	0.6	**3**	0.2	**4**	0.02	**5**	0.19
6	0.375	**7**	0.99	**8**	0.36	**9**	0.18	**10**	0.07
11	0.64	**12**	0.725	**13**	0.55	**14**	0.925	**15**	0.595
16	0.905	**17**	0.144	**18**	0.68	**19**	5.81	**20**	3.6875
21	0.835	**22**	2.44	**23**	0.16	**24**	3.55	**25**	4.98
26	0.735	**27**	2.4125	**28**	1.3125	**29**	0.12	**30**	2.05

24/ CONVERSION BETWEEN DECIMALS AND PERCENTAGES

To convert a decimal to a percentage, multiply by 100.
To convert a percentage to a decimal, divide by 100.

EXAMPLE

▶ Convert (a) 0.14 (b) 0.165 (c) 0.5575 to a percentage.

(a) $0.14 \times 100 = 14\%$ (b) $0.165 \times 100 = 16.5\%$ or $16\frac{1}{2}\%$

(c) $0.5575 \times 100 = 55.75\%$ or $55\frac{3}{4}\%$

EXAMPLE

▶ Convert (a) 23% (b) $12\frac{1}{2}\%$ (c) $32\frac{2}{3}\%$ to a decimal.

(a) $23 \div 100 = 0.23$ (b) $12\frac{1}{2} \div 100 = 12.5 \div 100 = 0.125$

(c) $32\frac{2}{3} \div 100 = 32.67 \div 100 = 0.3267$

Exercise 24A

Convert the following decimals to percentages.

1	0.05	**2**	0.03	**3**	0.135	**4**	0.2	**5**	0.0125
6	0.07	**7**	0.235	**8**	0.39	**9**	0.075	**10**	0.09
11	0.735	**12**	0.4	**13**	0.1125	**14**	0.91	**15**	0.07
16	0.375	**17**	0.115	**18**	0.57	**19**	0.81	**20**	0.205

Exercise 24B

Convert the following decimals to percentages.

1 0.1	**2** 0.09	**3** 0.985	**4** 0.7	**5** 0.43
6 0.99	**7** 0.3	**8** 0.215	**9** 0.325	**10** 0.12
11 0.89	**12** 0.37	**13** 0.73	**14** 0.235	**15** 0.71
16 0.0125	**17** 0.59	**18** 0.3175	**19** 0.97	**20** 0.815

Exercise 24C

Convert the following percentages to decimals.

1 31%	**2** 85%	**3** 10%	**4** 42%	**5** 16%
6 50%	**7** 57%	**8** 2%	**9** 96%	**10** 41%
11 $18\frac{1}{3}\%$	**12** $21\frac{3}{4}\%$	**13** $86\frac{1}{2}\%$	**14** 44%	**15** $15\frac{1}{4}\%$
16 62%	**17** $32\frac{1}{4}\%$	**18** $79\frac{2}{3}\%$	**19** $31\frac{3}{4}\%$	**20** $49\frac{1}{2}\%$

Exercise 24D

Convert the following percentages to decimals.

1 86%	**2** 60%	**3** 31%	**4** 3%	**5** 53%
6 30%	**7** 82%	**8** 42%	**9** 8%	**10** 90%
11 $54\frac{1}{4}\%$	**12** $4\frac{2}{3}\%$	**13** $17\frac{1}{2}\%$	**14** $29\frac{3}{4}\%$	**15** 69%
16 $59\frac{1}{3}\%$	**17** $51\frac{3}{4}\%$	**18** 72%	**19** $80\frac{1}{4}\%$	**20** $59\frac{1}{2}\%$

25/ CONVERSION BETWEEN FRACTIONS AND PERCENTAGES

To convert a fraction to a percentage, divide the top number by the bottom number (to change it to a decimal), then multiply by 100.

EXAMPLE

▶ Convert each of these fractions to a percentage: (a) $\frac{2}{5}$ (b) $\frac{3}{40}$.

(a) $2 \div 5 \times 100 = 40\%$

(b) $3 \div 40 \times 100 = 7.5\%$ or $7\frac{1}{2}\%$

To convert a percentage to a fraction, write the percentage over 100, and cancel. If necessary, any fractional percentages must be removed before cancelling.

EXAMPLE

▶ Convert the following percentages to fractions (a) 60% (b) $12\frac{1}{2}\%$.

(a) $60\% = \frac{60}{100} = \frac{6}{10} = \frac{3}{5}$

(b) $12\frac{1}{2}\% = \frac{12\frac{1}{2}}{100} = \frac{25}{200}$ (× 2 to remove fraction)

$= \frac{1}{8}$

Exercise 25A

Convert the following fractions to percentages.

1	$\frac{3}{5}$	**2**	$\frac{1}{4}$	**3**	$\frac{1}{2}$	**4**	$\frac{11}{50}$	**5**	$\frac{1}{20}$
6	$\frac{3}{100}$	**7**	$\frac{21}{50}$	**8**	$\frac{17}{50}$	**9**	$\frac{3}{20}$	**10**	$\frac{1}{10}$
11	$\frac{3}{8}$	**12**	$\frac{6}{25}$	**13**	$\frac{31}{50}$	**14**	$\frac{5}{8}$	**15**	$\frac{1}{80}$
16	$\frac{12}{25}$	**17**	$\frac{104}{200}$	**18**	$\frac{7}{9}$	**19**	$\frac{6}{7}$	**20**	$\frac{9}{80}$

Exercise 25B

Convert the following fractions to percentages.

1	$\frac{3}{10}$	**2**	$\frac{3}{4}$	**3**	$\frac{9}{50}$	**4**	$\frac{1}{100}$	**5**	$\frac{3}{40}$
6	$\frac{7}{100}$	**7**	$\frac{7}{10}$	**8**	$\frac{19}{40}$	**9**	$\frac{11}{20}$	**10**	$\frac{7}{8}$
11	$\frac{17}{25}$	**12**	$\frac{9}{10}$	**13**	$\frac{19}{100}$	**14**	$\frac{1}{8}$	**15**	$\frac{13}{40}$
16	$\frac{2}{11}$	**17**	$\frac{62}{200}$	**18**	$\frac{5}{12}$	**19**	$\frac{9}{16}$	**20**	$\frac{5}{21}$

Exercise 25C

Convert the following percentages to fractions.

1	30%	**2**	1%	**3**	5%	**4**	42%	**5**	15%
6	3%	**7**	75%	**8**	99%	**9**	64%	**10**	49%
11	56%	**12**	48%	**13**	16%	**14**	95%	**15**	68%
16	$62\frac{1}{2}\%$	**17**	$12\frac{1}{2}\%$	**18**	$16\frac{2}{3}\%$	**19**	$7\frac{1}{2}\%$	**20**	$8\frac{1}{3}\%$

Exercise 25D

Convert the following percentages to fractions.

1	10%	**2**	3%	**3**	55%	**4**	60%	**5**	7%
6	25%	**7**	41%	**8**	80%	**9**	77%	**10**	35%
11	24%	**12**	17%	**13**	45%	**14**	12%	**15**	31%
16	$2\frac{1}{2}\%$	**17**	$87\frac{1}{2}\%$	**18**	$37\frac{1}{2}\%$	**19**	$8\frac{1}{2}\%$	**20**	$9\frac{2}{3}\%$

26/ CALCULATING PERCENTAGES OF QUANTITIES

There are several tricks that can be used to calculate simple percentages. Here are two of them.

Recognising the fraction

If you can recognise the conversion of the percentage to a fraction, the calculation is much easier.

EXAMPLE

► Find 40% of 5 kg.

$40\% = \frac{2}{5}$

$\frac{2}{5}$ of $5\text{ kg} = \frac{2}{5} \times 5 = 2$

So 40% of 5 kg is 2 kg.

A more formal method

EXAMPLE

► Find 8% of £5.60.

$\frac{8}{100} \times £5.60 = \frac{£44.80}{100} = £0.448 = £0.45$ (to the nearest penny)

Exercise 26A

Work out.

1 8% of £225
2 10% of £220
3 25% of 180
4 15% of £380
5 6% of 125 kg
6 15% of £560
7 $12\frac{1}{2}\%$ of 2400 kg
8 36% of 150 tonnes
9 10% of 50p
10 $6\frac{1}{4}\%$ of 400
11 18% of 225 m
12 16% of 1275
13 10% of £17
14 $62\frac{1}{2}\%$ of £4.80
15 7% of £5
16 5% of £800
17 20% of £600
18 $33\frac{1}{3}\%$ of £4.50
19 16% of 80 kg
20 $11\frac{1}{2}\%$ of £150
21 17% of £2
22 32% of 55 m
23 $2\frac{1}{2}\%$ of 1200
24 32% of $11\frac{1}{4}$ m
25 40% of 30 g
26 10% of £22.20
27 75% of 20 km
28 80% of £8.40
29 17% of £2
30 2% of £15

Exercise 26B

Work out.

1 12% of 85 t
2 35% of £140
3 5% of £800
4 35% of 60 m
5 15% of 250 g
6 40% of 120 kg
7 15% of £660
8 25% of 15 m
9 14% of 85 m
10 10% of 500
11 18% of £6.50
12 15% of £800
13 $17\frac{1}{2}\%$ of 280
14 $33\frac{1}{3}\%$ of £9.75
15 15% of £40
16 10% of £420
17 24% of 45 kg
18 35% of £42
19 16% of $12\frac{1}{2}$ kg
20 60% of 18 kg
21 15% of 1280
22 10% of 400
23 24% of $6\frac{1}{4}$ g
24 15% of £800
25 13% of £10
26 60% of 50
27 40% of 10 ml
28 20% of 50 g
29 11% of £4
30 $33\frac{1}{3}\%$ of £66

27/ FRACTIONAL CHANGES

A number can be increased or decreased by a fractional amount.

EXAMPLE

▶ Increase £12 by $\frac{1}{3}$.

$\frac{1}{3}$ of £12 = £12 × $\frac{1}{3}$ = $\frac{£12}{3}$ = £4

The increased amount is therefore £12 + £4 = £16.

EXAMPLE

▶ Decrease £180 by $\frac{2}{5}$.

$\frac{2}{5}$ of £180 = $\frac{2}{5}$ × £180 = £72

The decreased amount is therefore £180 – £72 = £108.

Exercise 27A

1 Increase 21 by $\frac{1}{7}$.

2 Increase 24 by $\frac{1}{6}$.

3 Decrease 30 by $\frac{1}{6}$.

4 Increase 18 by $\frac{1}{3}$.

5 Decrease 56 by $\frac{1}{4}$.

6 Increase 24 by $\frac{2}{3}$.

7 Decrease 36 by $\frac{1}{6}$.

8 Decrease 20 by $\frac{2}{5}$.

9 Increase 12 by $\frac{3}{4}$.

10 Decrease 30 by $\frac{4}{5}$.

11 Increase 80 by $\frac{7}{8}$.

12 Decrease 14 by $\frac{5}{7}$.

13 Increase 40 by $\frac{1}{8}$.

14 Increase 64 by $\frac{1}{8}$.

15 Decrease 20 m by $\frac{3}{5}$.

16 Increase 50 l by $\frac{9}{10}$.

17 Decrease \$45 by $\frac{1}{9}$.

18 Decrease 48 gal by $\frac{7}{16}$.

19 Decrease 18 m by $\frac{4}{9}$.

20 Increase 88 g by $\frac{3}{8}$.

21 Increase 63 l by $\frac{4}{9}$.

22 Decrease 35 m by $\frac{3}{7}$.

23 Decrease \$16 by $\frac{5}{8}$.

24 Decrease 121 cm by $\frac{5}{11}$.

25 Increase 45 m by $\frac{7}{9}$.

26 Increase £1 by $\frac{9}{10}$.

27 Increase 48 by $\frac{7}{12}$.

28 Decrease 60p by $\frac{11}{12}$.

29 Decrease £22.95 by $\frac{2}{3}$.

30 Increase £25.68 by $\frac{3}{8}$.

Exercise 27B

1 Increase 8 by $\frac{1}{2}$.

2 Decrease 30 by $\frac{1}{5}$.

3 Increase 36 by $\frac{5}{6}$.

4 Decrease 21 by $\frac{2}{7}$.

5 Decrease 24 by $\frac{1}{3}$.

6 Increase 14 by $\frac{2}{7}$.

7 Decrease 40 by $\frac{3}{8}$.

8 Decrease 20 by $\frac{3}{5}$.

9 Decrease 18 by $\frac{2}{3}$.

10 Increase 24 by $\frac{3}{4}$.

11 Increase 64 by $\frac{5}{8}$.

12 Decrease 12 by $\frac{1}{4}$.

13 Decrease 56 by $\frac{3}{4}$.

14 Increase 30 by $\frac{5}{6}$.

15 Increase £48 by $\frac{9}{16}$.

16 Increase 18 by $\frac{1}{9}$.

17 Decrease 35 by $\frac{2}{7}$.

18 Decrease 45 by $\frac{5}{9}$.

19 Increase 80 by $\frac{5}{8}$.

20 Decrease 50 l by $\frac{7}{10}$.

21 Decrease 121 g by $\frac{9}{11}$.

22 Increase \$45 by $\frac{2}{9}$.

23 Increase £1 by $\frac{3}{10}$.

24 Increase £20 by $\frac{4}{5}$.

25 Decrease 180 by $\frac{5}{12}$.

26 Decrease 88 mm by $\frac{1}{8}$.

27 Increase £63 by $\frac{8}{9}$.

28 Decrease 48 cm by $\frac{5}{12}$.

29 Increase £6.55 by $\frac{2}{5}$.

30 Decrease £15.90 by $\frac{3}{10}$.

28/ ONE NUMBER AS A FRACTION OF ANOTHER

EXAMPLE

▶ Write £15 as a fraction of £75.

$$\frac{15}{75} = \frac{1}{5}$$

EXAMPLE

▶ A computer costs £120. A computer game costs £20. Write the cost of the game as a fraction of the cost of the computer.

$$\frac{£20}{£120} = \frac{1}{6}$$

Remember: Write the fraction in its lowest terms by cancelling where possible.

Exercise 28A

Write the first quantity as a fraction of the second.

1 10p, 80p
2 40 g, 80 g
3 30, 130
4 10 cm, 85 cm
5 12 ml, 144 ml
6 60p, £1.40
7 5 mm, 85 mm
8 40 km, 120 km
9 £30, £35
10 70 g, 130 g
11 45 t, 120 t
12 5 miles, 135 miles
13 80 hours, 140 hours
14 15 m.p.h., 75 m.p.h.
15 10 kg, 85 kg
16 The cost of a jotter at 45p, compared with the cost of an art pad at £1.20
17 30 miles travelled in one hour, compared with 180 miles travelled in one day
18 15 parts made in a day, compared with 115 parts made in a week
19 16p for a pencil, compared with £2.50 for a pen
20 4 faulty chips from a batch of 200

Exercise 28B

Write the first quantity as a fraction of the second.

1 30p, 70p
2 60 g, 90 g
3 10 mm, 35 mm
4 40p, £1.20
5 5 km, 45 km
6 50 cm, 140 cm
7 £30, £60
8 50 kg, 130 kg
9 20 hours, 35 hours
10 25 ml, 85 ml
11 5p, 75p
12 30 g, 120 g
13 60 t, 75 t
14 30 km/h, 120 km/h
15 25p, £2.50
16 35 people smoking in a railway carriage as a fraction of the 165 non-smoking
17 The 8-g weight of one bird's egg compared with the 50-g weight of another bird's egg
18 A 75p bus fare compared with a £1.80 bus fare
19 The 32p cost of a manual sharpener compared with £1.80 for an electric sharpener
20 2 faulty components from a batch of 150

29/ PERCENTAGE CHANGE

A percentage change can be either an increase *or* a decrease by a percentage. There are two common methods used to calculate a percentage change.

EXAMPLE

▶ Decrease 150 by 35%.

Method 1

35% of 150 $= 150 \times \frac{35}{100}$

$= 52.5$

A decrease requires a subtraction:

$150 - 52.5 = 97.5$

Method 2

A decrease of 35% is a reduction from 100% to 65%:

65% of 150 $= 150 \times \frac{65}{100} = 97.5$

EXAMPLE

▶ A new cooker costs £289 plus VAT at $17\frac{1}{2}$%. Find the total cost.

Method 1

$17\frac{1}{2}$% of £289 $= 289 \times \frac{17.5}{100}$

$= 50.575$

$=$ £50.58 (to the nearest penny)

An increase requires an addition:

£289 + £50.58 = £339.58

Method 2

An increase of $17\frac{1}{2}$% means 100% becomes $117\frac{1}{2}$%:

£289 $\times \frac{117.5}{100} = 339.575$

$=$ £339.58 (to the nearest penny)

Exercise 29A

1 Increase 300 by 5%.
2 Decrease 640 by 25%.
3 Decrease £240 by 4%.
4 Increase £1 by 20%.
5 Decrease 975 by 36%.
6 Increase £41 by $7\frac{1}{2}$%.
7 Increase £60 by $\frac{1}{2}$%.
8 Decrease 80 by 10%.
9 Decrease 280 ml by $17\frac{1}{2}$%.
10 Increase £420 by 85%.
11 Decrease 240 m by 53%.
12 Increase £250 by 30%.
13 Increase 32 km by $12\frac{1}{2}$%.
14 Decrease £1.80 by $12\frac{1}{2}$%.
15 Decrease 25 g by 90%.
16 Increase 800 kg by 40%.
17 Increase 48 g by $6\frac{1}{4}$%.
18 Decrease £3.00 by 5%.
19 Increase 880 mm by 80%.
20 Decrease £6.40 by 25%.
21 Decrease 50p by 16%.
22 Increase £41 by $7\frac{1}{2}$%.
23 Increase 800 m by 64%.
24 Decrease £7.40 by $2\frac{1}{2}$%.
25 Decrease £8.85 by $7\frac{1}{2}$%.
26 Linda has her £12 800 salary increased by $5\frac{1}{2}$%. What is her new salary?
27 A meal for four costs £75.80 plus $17\frac{1}{2}$% VAT. What is the total cost of the meal?
28 A £48 coat is reduced by 30% in a sale. What is the new price of the coat?
29 The 60 000 population of a town has increased this year by 6%. What is the population now?
30 A man pays 25% tax on earnings of £3500. How much has he left after paying the tax?

Exercise 29B

1 Increase 350 by 20%.
2 Decrease £10 by 5%.
3 Increase £40 by 15%.
4 Decrease 500 by 16%.
5 Increase £240 by 5%.
6 Increase £480 by 9%.
7 Increase £40 by $\frac{1}{8}$%.
8 Decrease £1.25 by 68%.
9 Decrease 600 cm by 27%.
10 Increase 1250 g by 85%.
11 Decrease 3000 ml by 86%.
12 Decrease £9.50 by $6\frac{1}{2}$%.

13 Decrease £48 by 17%.
14 Increase 4.5 km by 10%.
15 Decrease £2.50 by 17%.
16 Decrease £2.00 by $13\frac{3}{4}$%.
17 Increase 640 g by $62\frac{1}{2}$%.
18 Increase 900 km by 31%.
19 Decrease £3.00 by $12\frac{1}{2}$%.
20 Increase 96 ml by $18\frac{3}{4}$%.
21 Decrease £3.50 by 40%.
22 Decrease £2.80 by 45%.
23 Increase £7.50 by 75%.
24 Increase £15.50 by 35%.
25 Increase £35 by $17\frac{1}{2}$%.
26 A dining-room suite costs £625, but is reduced by 15% in a sale. What is the sale price?
27 A garage offers a 20% reduction on a £180 car service. How much will you pay?
28 A table is advertised at £88 plus $17\frac{1}{2}$% VAT. What is the purchase price of the table?
29 A woman has been offered a $22\frac{1}{2}$% discount on a £10 475 car. How much will she have to pay for it?
30 Mortgage repayments of £230 are to be increased by $4\frac{1}{2}$%. What will the new payment be?

30/ ONE NUMBER AS A PERCENTAGE OF ANOTHER

A percentage is used to show by how much a number or quantity has changed, or to show the proportional difference between two numbers.

EXAMPLE

► Express (a) 12 as a percentage of 60 (b) 7 as a percentage of 56.

(a) $\frac{12}{60} \times 100 = 20\%$

(b) $\frac{7}{56} \times 100 = 12.5\%$ or $12\frac{1}{2}\%$

EXAMPLE

► In a class of 30 pupils 12 are boys. What percentage are (a) boys (b) girls?

(a) $\frac{12}{30} \times 100 = 40\%$

(b) $100\% - 40\% = 60\%$

Remember: Whenever comparisons are made between two numbers they should always have the same units.

Exercise 30A

Write the first number as a percentage of the second.

1 30, 100
2 3, 24
3 80, 1000
4 5p, £1
5 60, 200
6 750, 2000
7 36 mm, 225 mm
8 £37, £50
9 15, 200
10 135, 400
11 450 mm, 1.5 m
12 £6, £300
13 25 mm, 75 cm
14 £18.75, £125
15 34 cm, 85 cm
16 £8.40, £12
17 2.5 km, 4 km
18 225, 600
19 80, 150
20 $7\frac{1}{2}$, 25
21 650 g, 1.5 kg
22 £8.50, £62.50
23 £2.50, £75
24 £4.20, £24
25 11 mm, 16 mm
26 In a road survey 25 out of 250 vehicles were buses. What percentage is this?
27 Sarah gained 39 marks out of 50 from a maths test. Write this as a percentage.
28 A class had 242 attendances out of 250. What was the percentage attendance?
29 A population has increased by 30 from 1800. What is the percentage increase?
30 During the 30 days of November it rained on 11 days. What percentage of days in the month were free from rain?

Exercise 30B

Write the first number as a percentage of the second.

1	30, 60	**2**	10, 200	**3**	850 mm, 1 m	**4**	84, 250
5	58, 725	**6**	30, 200	**7**	174, 725	**8**	18 mm, 225 mm
9	4.8 km, 24 km	**10**	98 ml, 350 ml	**11**	£8.75, £25	**12**	350, 625
13	63, 840	**14**	£9.25, £50	**15**	£37.50, £125	**16**	10, 60
17	25p, £2	**18**	10p, £1.60	**19**	5, 60	**20**	15 m, 75 m
21	70p, £10.50	**22**	125 g, 400 g	**23**	£5, £7.50	**24**	£2.25, £15
25	20 mm, 32 mm						

26 Martin gained 57 out of 60 marks for an art test. Write this as a percentage.

27 The cost of a computer has increased by £150 from £1600. What is the percentage increase?

28 A packet of stamps contains 19 first-class and 31 second-class stamps. What percentage of the stamps in the packet are first-class?

29 A group of 20 men and women have jointly won a lottery prize. What percentage of the winnings will each person receive?

30 During a season a football team and a reserve team score 51 and 34 goals respectively. What percentage of the total number of goals were scored by the reserve team?

31/ RATIO

A ratio is a comparison of two numbers or quantities. Ratios are normally expressed in their simplest form, as whole numbers.

EXAMPLE

▶ Simplify (a) 14 : 32 (b) 1 mm : 5 cm (c) $3\frac{1}{2} : 1\frac{1}{4}$.

(a) 14 : 32 = 7 : 16 (Cancel by 2.)
(b) 1 mm : 5 cm = 1 : 50 (Change to the same units: mm.)
(c) $3\frac{1}{2} : 1\frac{1}{4} = 14 : 5$ (Multiply by 4 to remove the fractions.)

Ratios expressed in the form 1 : *n* are called **unitary** ratios. The number *n* could be a whole number, a fraction, or a decimal.

EXAMPLE

▶ Express in the form 1 : *n* (a) 5 : 3 (b) 5 m to $3\frac{1}{2}$ m.

(a) 5 : 3 = 1 : 3 ÷ 5 = 1 : 0.6 (b) 5 m to $3\frac{1}{2}$ m = 1 : 3.5 ÷ 5 = 1 : 0.7

Exercise 31A

Simplify.

1	9 : 12	**2**	5 : 25	**3**	4 : 6	**4**	21 : 90
5	35 : 10	**6**	8 : 4	**7**	12 : 42	**8**	21 : 35
9	$\frac{1}{2} : 3$	**10**	$\frac{1}{8} : \frac{1}{2}$	**11**	$3 : \frac{2}{5}$	**12**	80p : £1.50
13	600 m : 2 km	**14**	$\frac{2}{3} : \frac{5}{6}$	**15**	825 mm : 2.5 m	**16**	6 : 9
17	£1 : 30p	**18**	$\frac{7}{8} : \frac{3}{4}$	**19**	6 cm : 90 mm	**20**	90p : £1.10

21 16 kg : 32 g   22 35 cm : 50 mm

Express these ratios in the form 1 : *n*.

23 4 : 5   24 2 : 10   25 5 : 6   26 12 : 48
27 8 : 6   28 2 : 3   29 3 : 10   30 5 : 8

Exercise 31B

Simplify.

1 6 : 18   2 7 : 21   3 40 : 80   4 180 : 270
5 12 : 30   6 15 : 5   7 36 : 63   8 $\frac{1}{8}$: 2
9 1 : $\frac{1}{2}$ 10 $\frac{1}{4}$: $\frac{2}{3}$ 11 $\frac{3}{4}$: $2\frac{1}{2}$ 12 $\frac{2}{3}$: 1
13 14 : 12   14 £7.25 : £10   15 20 : 36   16 850 g : 1 kg
17 $\frac{1}{4}$: $\frac{3}{8}$ 18 1500 m : 3 km   19 £2 : 75p   20 £2.40 : 48p
21 250 m : 0.5 km   22 £14 : 70p

Express these ratios in the form 1 : *n*.

23 4 : 3   24 4 : 2   25 2 : 15   26 5 : 1
27 4 : 31   28 5 : 3   29 9 : 10   30 3 : 2

32/ USING RATIOS

EXAMPLE

▶ Find the value of x in (a) $1 : 8 = 3 : x$ (b) $7 : x = 35 : 45$.

(a) $1 : 8 = 3 : x$ (1→3, multiplication by 3)
So, $1 : 8 = 3 : (8 \times 3)$
$1 : 8 = 3 : 24$
So, $x = 24$

(b) $7 : x = 35 : 45$ (7→35, multiplication by 5)
So, $7 : (45 \div 5) = 35 : 45$ (division by 5 since moving backwards)
$7 : 9 = 35 : 45$
So, $x = 9$

EXAMPLE

▶ In a class the ratio of boys to girls is 1 : 2. There are nine boys. How many girls are there?

$1 : 2 = 9 : x$
$1 : 2 = 9 : 18$
The number of girls is 18.

Exercise 32A

Find the missing number in each question.

1 $1 : 4 = 3 : x$ 2 $1 : 9 = x : 27$ 3 $1 : 6 = 5 : x$ 4 $3 : x = 9 : 12$
5 $2 : 5 = x : 10$ 6 $1 : 6 = 5 : x$ 7 $3 : x = 1 : 4$ 8 $x : 2 = 35 : 10$
9 $4 : 9 = x : 27$ 10 $x : 20 = 3 : 4$ 11 $1 : x = 3 : 21$ 12 $3 : 15 = x : 30$

13 $x:9 = 4:36$ **14** $1:8 = 3:x$ **15** $1:x = 5:25$ **16** $5:x = 20:45$

17 $x:5 = 12:15$ **18** $7:8 = 35:x$ **19** $4:21 = 8:x$ **20** $3:13 = x:39$

21 Two lengths are in the ratio 3 : 7. The second length is 42 cm. Find the first length.

22 In a rectangle the ratio of the width to the length is 7 : 8. The width is 21 cm. Find the length.

23 In a town the number of males to the number of females is 40 : 44. There are 9640 males. How many females are there?

24 An alloy contains iron and copper in the ratio 5 : 1. A block of this alloy contains 30 kg of iron. What weight of copper does it contain?

25 The ratio of the number of cats to the number of dogs owned by the children in a year group in a school is 5 : 3. There are 85 cats. How many dogs are there?

26 In making concrete you need sand and cement in the ratio 4 : 1. There has been a delivery of 50 kg of cement. What weight of sand is needed?

27 The ratio of the number of blue flowers to the number of white flowers in a garden is 6 : 13. There are 144 blue flowers. How many white flowers are there?

28 Every 5 in 100 silicon chips made at a factory are faulty. Of 480 silicon chips made in a batch, how many are expected to be faulty?

29 The ratio of cars to lorries passing a point on a road during one hour is 9 : 2. There were 16 lorries. How many cars were there?

30 Every fifth person entering a football ground is female. In one afternoon there were 12 680 males. How many females were there?

Exercise 32B

Find the missing number in each question.

1 $6:5 = x:10$ **2** $1:6 = x:42$ **3** $1:3 = x:18$ **4** $3:2 = 18:x$

5 $x:6 = 12:18$ **6** $2:5 = x:10$ **7** $3:4 = x:20$ **8** $3:x = 4:12$

9 $8:x = 1:2$ **10** $6:1 = 42:x$ **11** $1:x = 2:18$ **12** $3:8 = x:40$

13 $2:5 = 6:x$ **14** $x:7 = 12:42$ **15** $3:10 = x:80$ **16** $7:x = 35:45$

17 $1:15 = x:60$ **18** $x:8 = 15:24$ **19** $6:x = 24:28$ **20** $9:10 = 27:x$

21 The ratio of boys to girls in a PE class is 4 : 5. There are 25 girls in the class. How many boys are there?

22 The speed of two boats is in the ratio 9 : 4. The speed of the second boat is 20 km/h. What is the speed of the first boat?

23 Three in every ten trains are late arriving at a station. On one particular day 24 trains were late. How many trains arrived on time?

24 Two lengths of wood are in the ratio 4 : 7. The shorter length is 16 cm. What is the longer length?

25 The ratio of the perimeter of a triangle to its shortest side is 10 : 3. The perimeter is 35 cm. What is the length of the shortest side?

26 On a housing estate the ratio of semi-detached houses to detached houses is 5 : 3. There are 36 detached houses on the estate. How many semi-detached houses are there?

27 Two soap packets contain powder in the ratio 4 : 9. The larger packet contains 3 kg of powder. What amount of powder does the smaller packet contain?

28 The ratio of the lengths of two rectangles is 6 : 5. The length of the second is 7.5 cm. What is the length of the first?

29 In a survey the ratio of people who drink coffee to the people who drink tea is 10 : 7. If 49 people stated they preferred tea, how many people preferred coffee?

30 At a garage four cars out of every ten, on average, failed the MOT test. During one week 65 cars were tested. How many were expected to fail?

33/ DIVISION INTO PARTS USING A RATIO

Ratios can be used to divide numbers or quantities into parts.

EXAMPLE

▶ Peter and Shreena have won a £5000 prize in a lottery. They are to share the winnings in the ratio 9 : 11. How much would they each receive?

The ratio 9 : 11 means there are 20 parts altogether.
1 part = £5000 ÷ 20 = £250
Peter's share: 9 parts is £250 × 9 = £2250
Shreena's share: 11 parts is £250 × 11 = £2750

Exercise 33A

Divide each of the following numbers and quantities in the ratio given.

1 35; 3 : 2	**2** 30; 2 : 1	**3** 112; 4 : 3	**4** 400; 12 : 8
5 40; 5 : 3	**6** 374; 5 : 6	**7** £4.50; 4 : 5	**8** 9 m; 5 : 1
9 250; 12 : 13	**10** £6.50; 1 : 4	**11** 18 m; 5 : 1	**12** £33.60; 9 : 15
13 £12.24; 1 : 7	**14** £12.00; 7 : 13	**15** £6.20; 2 : 3	**16** 76 kg; 3 : 5
17 £24.80; 2 : 3	**18** £56.96; 1 : 2 : 5	**19** 39.45 g; 4 : 5 : 6	**20** 81; 8 : 9 : 10
21 18.4 *l*; 2 : 3 : 5	**22** 1200; 2 : 3 : 3	**23** £130.20; 10 : 12 : 20	**24** 669.6 kg; 3 : 4 : 5

Exercise 33B

Divide each of the following numbers and quantities in the ratio given.

1 200; 3 : 2	**2** 60; 8 : 4	**3** 225; 4 : 5	**4** 224; 4 : 3
5 660; 5 : 6	**6** 80p; 3 : 7	**7** 6 kg; 1 : 4	**8** 108; 6 : 3
9 £8.56; 1 : 3	**10** £6; 7 : 13	**11** £69.16; 5 : 8	**12** £15.12; 3 : 4
13 23.4 *l*; 1 : 5	**14** 47.1 m; 1 : 2	**15** 162.4 kg; 1 : 6	**16** £23.40; 1 : 5
17 £51.92; 2 : 4 : 5	**18** £1.60; 1 : 4 : 5	**19** £90; 7 : 13 : 16	**20** 31.05 kg; 1 : 4 : 4
21 26.28 m; 2 : 3 : 4	**22** 144; 9 : 8 : 7	**23** 34.65 m; 2 : 4 : 5	**24** 77.13 km; 1 : 4 : 4

REVISION

Exercise B

1 Find the missing numbers.

(a) $\frac{1}{8} = \frac{2}{?} = \frac{?}{24} = \frac{4}{?} = \frac{?}{48}$ (b) $\frac{7}{12} = \frac{?}{24} = \frac{?}{36} = \frac{35}{?} = \frac{56}{?}$

2 Work out. (a) $\frac{1}{5}$ of £5.20 (b) $\frac{3}{10}$ of 40 kg (c) $\frac{5}{6}$ of £12

3 Cancel. (a) $\frac{12}{32}$ (b) $\frac{75}{175}$ (c) $\frac{48}{80}$

4 Change into improper fractions. (a) $3\frac{1}{4}$ (b) $4\frac{4}{5}$ (c) $8\frac{1}{3}$

5 Change into fractions. (a) 0.85 (b) 0.375 (c) 2.65
(d) 63% (e) 65% (f) $7\frac{1}{2}$%

6 Change into decimals.

(a) $\frac{5}{16}$ (b) $3\frac{2}{5}$ (c) $2\frac{7}{40}$ (d) 63% (e) $37\frac{1}{2}$% (f) $12\frac{4}{5}$%

7 Change into percentages.

(a) 0.07 (b) 0.665 (c) 1.0325 (d) $\frac{7}{20}$ (e) $\frac{5}{8}$ (f) $\frac{13}{16}$

8 Change into mixed numbers.

(a) $\frac{13}{4}$ (b) $\frac{34}{10}$ (c) $\frac{27}{5}$

9 Work out.

(a) $\frac{2}{5} + \frac{4}{5}$ (b) $\frac{5}{8} + \frac{3}{4}$ (c) $1\frac{3}{4} + 2\frac{7}{8}$ (d) $3 - \frac{3}{4}$ (e) $\frac{7}{8} - \frac{5}{16}$

(f) $4\frac{3}{4} - 2\frac{1}{8}$ (g) $\frac{3}{4} \times 3$ (h) $\frac{3}{5} \times \frac{7}{8}$ (i) $\frac{7}{8} \div \frac{2}{5}$ (j) $\frac{5}{12} \div 3$

10 Work out (a) 15% of £23.00 (b) $12\frac{1}{2}$% of 48 kg.

11 (a) Increase 40 by $\frac{5}{8}$. (b) Decrease £20 by $\frac{3}{5}$. (c) Decrease £6.00 by $\frac{7}{12}$.

(d) Increase \$400 by 15%. (e) Decrease 72 cm by $62\frac{1}{2}$%. (f) Increase 96 ml by 25%.

12 Write (a) 45 m.p.h. as a fraction of 70 m.p.h. (b) 30p as a fraction of £2.50.

13 Write (a) 75p as a percentage of £2 (b) 350 kg as a percentage of 625 kg.

14 Simplify (a) 9 : 21 (b) 60 : 270 (c) $\frac{1}{2}$: 3.

15 Divide (a) 80p in the ratio 3 : 7 (b) £4.50 in the ratio 2 : 3 : 4.

Exercise BB

1 'Time and a quarter' means that an extra quarter of a pay-rate is added on for overtime. Find the time-and-a-quarter overtime rate if the basic rate is £5.80.

2 A pipe which is 80 cm long has its length extended by $\frac{2}{5}$ of its original length. What is its new length?

3 A man earns 8% commission on all that he sells. He sells £508 of insurance. What will be his commission?

4 Calculate the $17\frac{1}{2}$% VAT due on a building invoice of £2040.

5 A landlord will pay 20% of a telephone bill of £28.40. How much will the landlord charge the person in the flat?

6 Find the cost of a car exhaust system priced at £86 plus $17\frac{1}{2}$% VAT.

7 A £25 train ticket is to be increased by $5\frac{1}{2}$%. What is its new price?

8 A £425 washing machine has its price reduced by 15% in a sale. What is the sale price?

9 A £12 998 car has its price reduced by 18%. How much does it now cost?

10 A clarinet costs £150 plus $17\frac{1}{2}$% VAT. What is the total cost?

11 A village population of 2700 reduces by 8% in a year. What is the new population?

12 William gained 13 marks out of 25 for a biology test. Write this as a percentage.

13 A class had 192 attendances out of 200. What is the percentage attendance?

14 Sally has spent 90p out of £4 pocket money. What percentage is this?

15 A woman earns £480 per month. She is awarded an increase of £31.20. What is the percentage increase?

16 Divide £1 between Bill and Ben so that Bill receives four times as much as Ben.

17 Bronze is formed by mixing copper, tin and zinc in the ratio 95 : 4 : 1 by mass. Find the mass of each metal in 2 kg of bronze.

18 Three boys on a tour to Austria have £50, £70 and £80 pocket money which they change into 11 400 Austrian schillings. How should this be divided up amongst them?

Algebra

34/ CONTINUING A NUMBER SEQUENCE

Number sequences can follow a pattern. There are many different types of number pattern in sequences. The most common patterns in number sequences can be investigated using a **difference method.**

EXAMPLE

▶ State the next two terms in the sequence: 5, 7, 9, 11.

5		7		9		11	
	2		2		2		← These are the differences between each pair of numbers in the sequence.

The second row gives the pattern: add on 2 each time.
The next two numbers are: 11 + 2 = *13*, 13 + 2 = *15*.

EXAMPLE

▶ State the next two terms in the sequence: 8, 10, 14, 20.

8			10			14			20			*28*			*38*	
	2			4			6			*8*			*10*			← These two rows explain the pattern. This pattern can then be continued to give the next two terms in the sequence: 28 and 38.
		2			2			*2*			*2*					←

Exercise 34A

State the next two terms in each sequence.

1 4, 6, 8, 10, ..., ...
2 20, 31, 42, ..., ...
3 11, 15, 19, 23, ..., ...
4 22, 29, 36, 43, ..., ...
5 15, 23, 31, 39, ..., ...
6 1, 12, 23, 34, ..., ...
7 9, 15, 21, 27, ..., ...
8 80, 71, 62, 53, ..., ...
9 53, 46, 39, 32, ..., ...
10 31, 27, 23, 19, ..., ...
11 3, 5, 8, 12, ..., ...
12 7, 8, 11, 16, ..., ...
13 5, 7, 11, 17, ..., ...
14 4, 9, 15, 22, ..., ...
15 10, 13, 18, 25, ..., ...
16 9, 11, 16, 24, ..., ...
17 15, 16, 21, 30, ..., ...
18 21, 23, 27, 35, ..., ...
19 10, 13, 19, 28, ..., ...
20 4, 9, 16, 25, ..., ...
21 5, 15, 24, 32, ..., ...
22 7, 11, 19, 31, ..., ...
23 16, 32, 46, 58, ..., ...
24 4, 9, 19, 34, ..., ...
25 12, 32, 49, 63, ..., ...
26 3, 7, 13, 21, ..., ...
27 15, 18, 26, 39, ..., ...
28 9, 12, 17, 24, ..., ...
29 7, 17, 25, 31, ..., ...
30 23, 27, 37, 54, ..., ...

Exercise 34B

State the next two terms in each sequence.

1 9, 14, 19, 24, ..., ...
2 16, 25, 34, 43, ..., ...
3 17, 20, 23, 26, ..., ...
4 17, 23, 29, 35, ..., ...
5 17, 20, 23, 26, ..., ...
6 2, 6, 10, 14, ..., ...
7 9, 16, 23, 30, ..., ...
8 79, 74, 69, 64, ..., ...
9 20, 17, 14, 11, ..., ...

10 32, 26, 20, 14, ..., ...
11 2, 4, 8, 14, ..., ...
12 4, 7, 12, 19, ..., ...
13 9, 13, 20, 30, ..., ...
14 10, 12, 17, 25, ..., ...
15 12, 16, 24, 36, ..., ...
16 8, 13, 23, 38, ..., ...
17 7, 16, 28, 43, ..., ...
18 11, 14, 22, 35, ..., ...
19 8, 20, 30, 38, ..., ...
20 10, 28, 44, 58, ..., ...
21 14, 21, 29, 38, ..., ...
22 7, 9, 13, 21, ..., ...
23 9, 17, 24, 30, ..., ...
24 5, 8, 15, 26, ..., ...
25 6, 13, 23, 36, ..., ...
26 12, 17, 26, 39, ..., ...
27 8, 28, 45, 59, ..., ...
28 11, 14, 19, 27, ..., ...
29 15, 27, 44, 65, ..., ...
30 22, 50, 72, 89, ..., ...

35/ MAKING PREDICTIONS AND GENERALISING IN A NUMBER SERIES

A **rule** is a short-cut, using calculation methods, to find later terms more easily.

EXAMPLE

► A sequence of numbers is: 1st 8, 2nd 9, 3rd 10, 4th 11.
(a) Find a rule to describe this series.
(b) Use the rule to find the 10th and 15th terms in the series.

(a) It is helpful to write the series in a table:

Term	1	2	3	4
Number	8	9	10	11

$1 \rightarrow 8$
$2 \rightarrow 9$
$3 \rightarrow 10$ In each case 7 is added.
$4 \rightarrow 11$ The rule is: 'Add 7.'

(b) The rule is 'Add 7', so:
10th term = 10 + 7 = 17
15th term = 15 + 7 = 22

EXAMPLE

► A sequence of numbers is: 3rd 10, 4th 13, 5th 16, 6th 19.
(a) Find a rule to describe this series.
(b) Use the rule to find the 20th and 50th term in the series.

(a)

Term	3	4	5	6
Number	10	13	16	19

$3 \rightarrow 10$
$4 \rightarrow 13$ In each case the first number is multiplied by 3,
$5 \rightarrow 16$ and then 1 is added.
$6 \rightarrow 19$ The rule is: 'Times 3 and add 1.'

(b) The rule is 'Times 3 and add 1', so:
20th term = $(20 \times 3) + 1 = 61$
50th term = $(50 \times 3) + 1 = 151$

Exercise 35A

In each question four terms of a series of numbers are given.
(a) Write down a description of the rule for the series. (b) Find the terms indicated.

1	1st 6	2nd 7	3rd 8	4th 9	State the 10th and 15th terms.
2	1st 9	2nd 10	3rd 11	4th 12	State the 10th and 20th terms.
3	2nd 0	3rd 1	4th 2	5th 3	State the 15th and 20th terms.
4	4th 0	5th 1	6th 2	7th 3	State the 20th and 25th terms.
5	1st 13	2nd 14	3rd 15	4th 16	State the 10th and 20th terms.
6	5th 0	6th 1	7th 2	8th 3	State the 20th and 30th terms.
7	1st 3	2nd 5	3rd 7	4th 9	State the 15th and 20th terms.
8	1st 7	2nd 9	3rd 11	4th 13	State the 10th and 20th terms.
9	2nd 0	3rd 2	4th 4	5th 6	State the 10th and 20th terms.
10	1st 8	2nd 11	3rd 14	4th 17	State the 10th and 20th terms.
11	1st 1	2nd 4	3rd 7	4th 10	State the 10th and 15th terms.
12	1st 5	2nd 9	3rd 13	4th 17	State the 10th and 20th terms.
13	2nd 1	3rd 4	4th 7	5th 10	State the 15th and 20th terms.
14	1st 2	2nd 7	3rd 12	4th 17	State the 15th and 20th terms.
15	1st 11	2nd 13	3rd 15	4th 17	State the 15th and 25th terms.
16	1st 8	2nd 12	3rd 16	4th 20	State the 20th and 30th terms.
17	1st 1	2nd 3	3rd 5	4th 7	State the 15th and 30th terms.
18	1st 0	2nd 3	3rd 6	4th 9	State the 20th and 30th terms.
19	1st 8	2nd 10	3rd 12	4th 14	State the 15th and 20th terms.
20	4th 1	5th 3	6th 5	7th 7	State the 20th and 30th terms.
21	1st 10	2nd 14	3rd 18	4th 22	State the 15th and 25th terms.
22	1st 2	2nd 6	3rd 10	4th 14	State the 20th and 30th terms.
23	1st 9	2nd 12	3rd 15	4th 18	State the 20th and 30th terms.
24	1st 4	2nd 9	3rd 14	4th 19	State the 20th and 40th terms.
25	1st 7	2nd 15	3rd 23	4th 31	State the 20th and 40th terms.
26	1st 7	2nd 12	3rd 17	4th 22	State the 30th and 50th terms.
27	1st 9	2nd 15	3rd 21	4th 27	State the 20th and 50th terms.
28	1st 5	2nd 8	3rd 11	4th 14	State the 20th and 50th terms.
29	1st 19	2nd 18	3rd 17	4th 16	State the 10th and 15th terms.
30	1st 28	2nd 26	3rd 24	4th 22	State the 10th and 15th terms.

Exercise 35B

In each question four terms of a series of numbers are given.
(a) Write down a description of the rule for the series. (b) Find the terms indicated.

1	1st 10	2nd 11	3rd 12	4th 13	State the 10th and 15th terms.
2	1st 5	2nd 6	3rd 7	4th 8	State the 10th and 20th terms.
3	1st 0	2nd 1	3rd 2	4th 3	State the 10th and 20th terms.
4	3rd 0	4th 1	5th 2	6th 3	State the 15th and 20th terms.
5	1st 12	2nd 13	3rd 14	4th 15	State the 10th and 20th terms.
6	6th 0	7th 1	8th 2	9th 3	State the 20th and 30th terms.
7	1st 6	2nd 10	3rd 14	4th 18	State the 15th and 20th terms.
8	1st 4	2nd 6	3rd 8	4th 10	State the 20th and 30th terms.
9	3rd 0	4th 2	5th 4	6th 6	State the 15th and 20th terms.
10	1st 6	2nd 9	3rd 12	4th 15	State the 10th and 20th terms.

11	1st 7	2nd 11	3rd 15	4th 19	State the 10th and 15th terms.
12	1st 2	2nd 5	3rd 8	4th 11	State the 10th and 20th terms.
13	1st 0	2nd 2	3rd 4	4th 6	State the 15th and 20th terms.
14	1st 9	2nd 11	3rd 13	4th 15	State the 20th and 30th terms.
15	1st 6	2nd 10	3rd 14	4th 18	State the 20th and 30th terms.
16	2nd 2	3rd 5	4th 8	5th 11	State the 10th and 20th terms.
17	2nd 1	3rd 3	4th 5	5th 7	State the 15th and 25th terms.
18	1st 8	2nd 13	3rd 18	4th 23	State the 20th and 30th terms.
19	1st 3	2nd 7	3rd 11	4th 15	State the 15th and 20th terms.
20	1st 1	2nd 6	3rd 11	4th 16	State the 20th and 30th terms.
21	1st 0	2nd 4	3rd 8	4th 12	State the 15th and 25th terms.
22	1st 9	2nd 13	3rd 17	4th 21	State the 20th and 30th terms.
23	1st 1	2nd 3	3rd 5	4th 7	State the 20th and 30th terms.
24	1st 6	2nd 11	3rd 16	4th 21	State the 20th and 40th terms.
25	1st 7	2nd 10	3rd 13	4th 16	State the 20th and 40th terms.
26	1st 6	2nd 13	3rd 20	4th 27	State the 30th and 50th terms.
27	1st 3	2nd 8	3rd 13	4th 18	State the 20th and 50th terms.
28	1st 8	2nd 14	3rd 20	4th 26	State the 20th and 50th terms.
29	1st 24	2nd 23	3rd 22	4th 21	State the 10th and 15th terms.
30	1st 38	2nd 36	3rd 34	4th 32	State the 10th and 15th terms.

36/ SERIES FROM DIAGRAMS

Number patterns also exist in diagrams.

EXAMPLE

▶ This diagram shows how a pattern develops. It shows the first three stages in the pattern. Write down a rule which will help you calculate the number of sticks in each stage of the diagram.

Stage 1 Stage 2 Stage 3

Summarise this information in a table.

Diagram stage	1	2	3	
Number of sticks	2	3	4	

Comparing the top row with the bottom row (as before in number patterns) helps state the rule: 'The number of sticks is found by adding 1 to the diagram stage.'

Exercise 36A

In each question a diagram shows the first three stages in a pattern. Write down a rule for each pattern.

1 The number of stone slabs to make a patio.

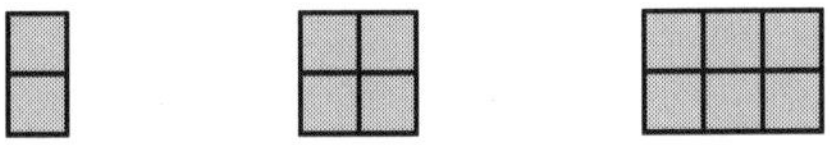

1 2 3

2 The number of bricks.

1 2 3

3 The number of sticks.

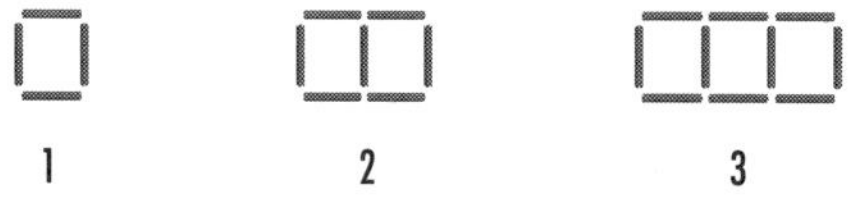

4 The perimeter of each shape.

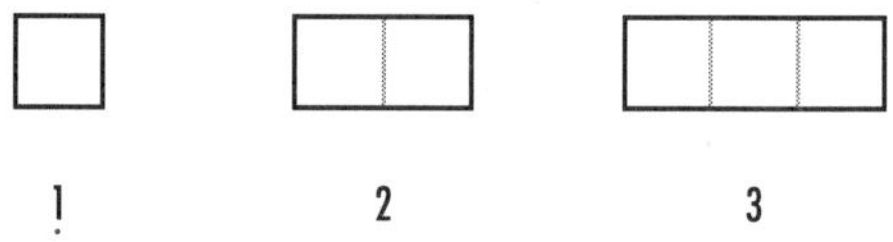

5 The number of sticks.

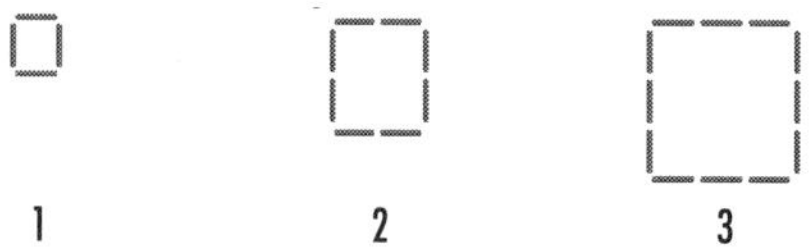

6 The number of sticks.

7 The number of 'x' points.

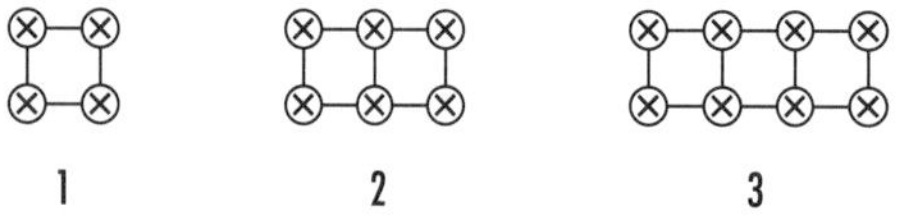

8 The number of white slabs.

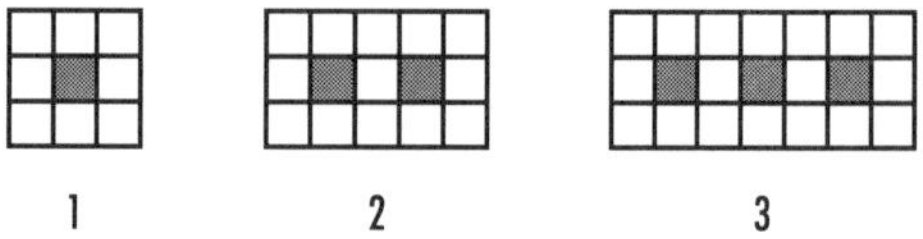

9 The number of 'x' points.

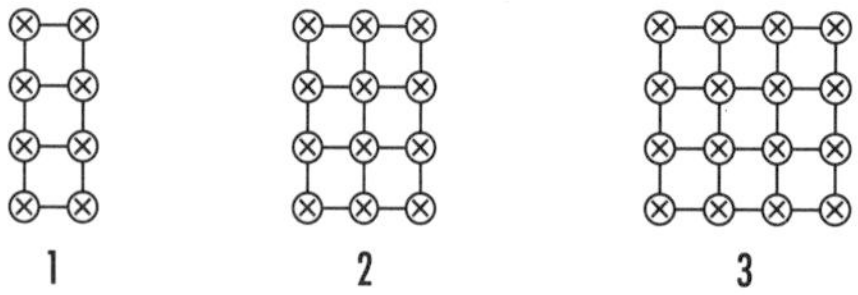

10 The number of sticks.

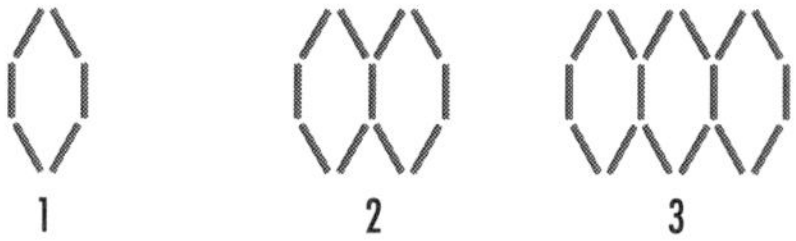

11 The number of dots.

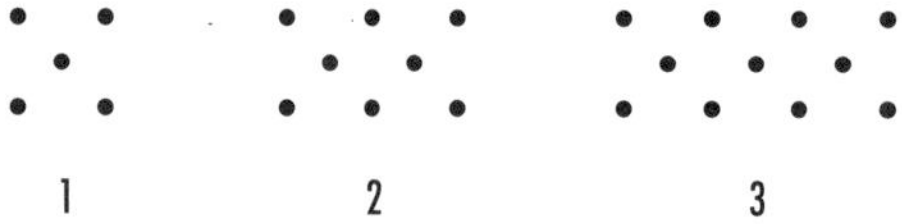

12 The number of regions inside.

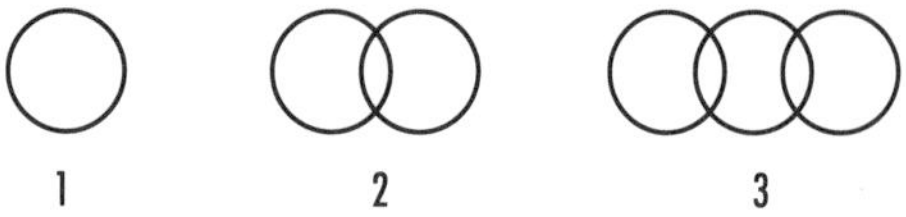

13 The number of sticks.

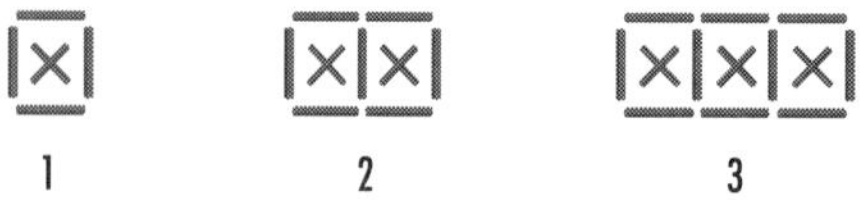

14 The number of sticks.

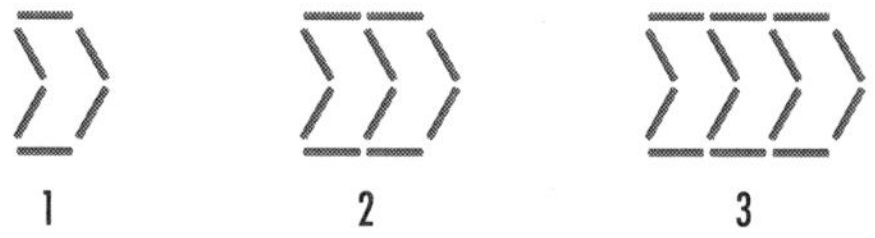

15 The number of sticks.

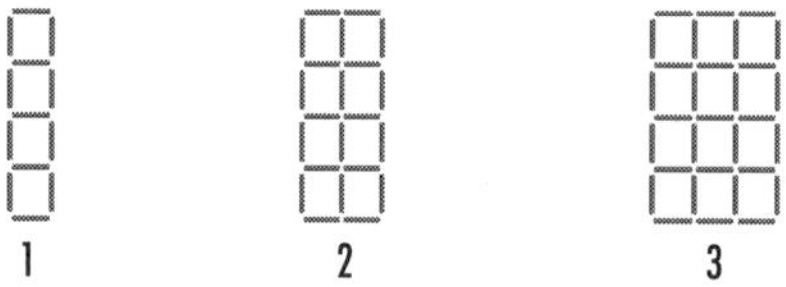

Exercise 36B

In each question a diagram shows the first three stages in a pattern. Write down a rule for each pattern.

1 The number of stone slabs to make a patio.

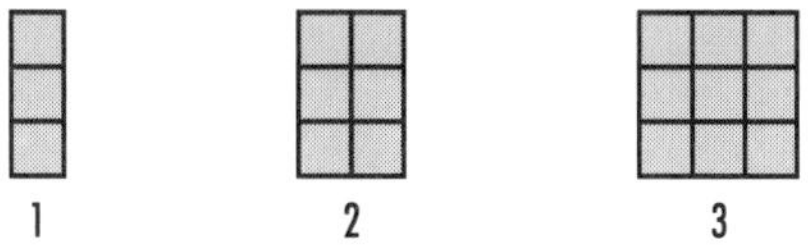

2 The number of 'x' points.

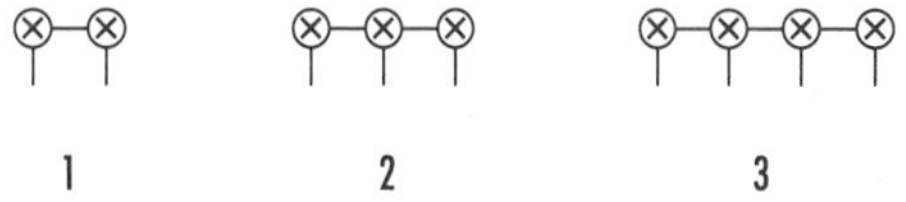

3 The number of dots in each shape.

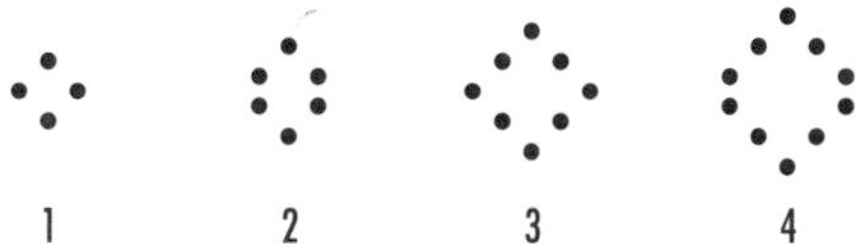

4 The number of 'x' points.

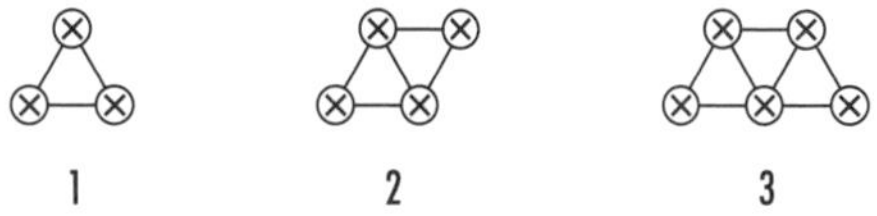

5 The number of sticks.

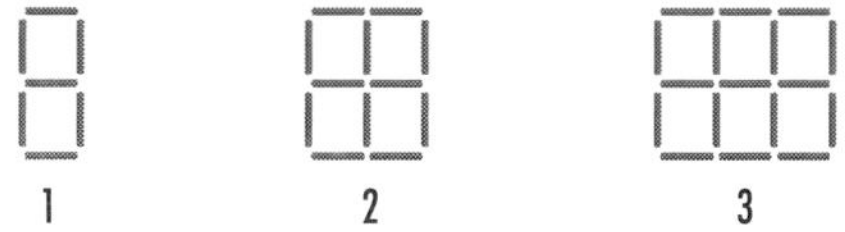

6 The number of 'x' points.

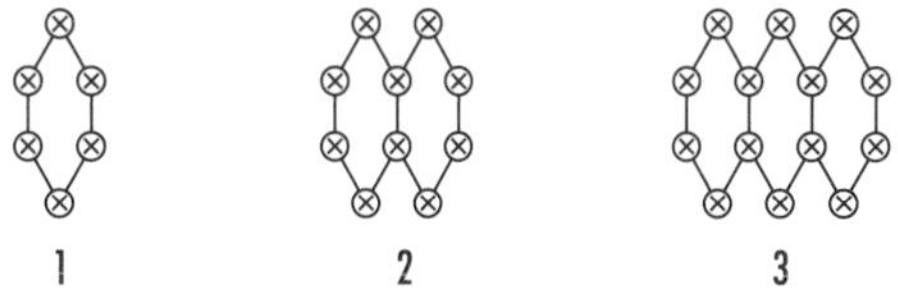

7 The number of sticks.

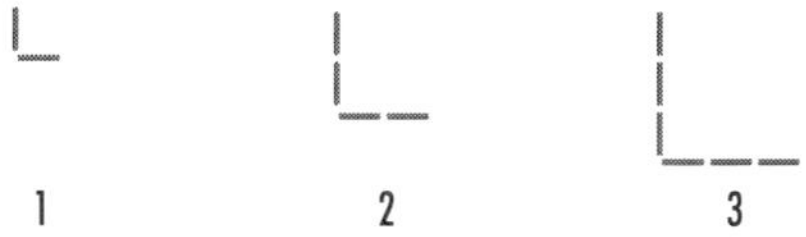

8 The number of dotted lines in the shape.

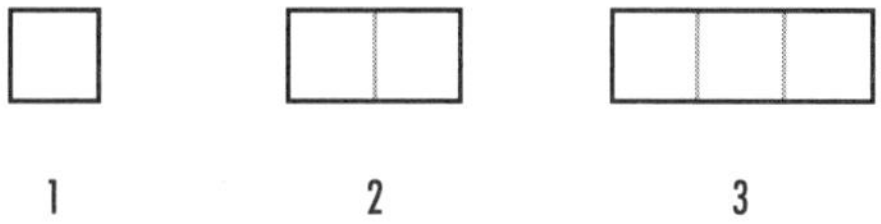

9 The number of 'x' points.

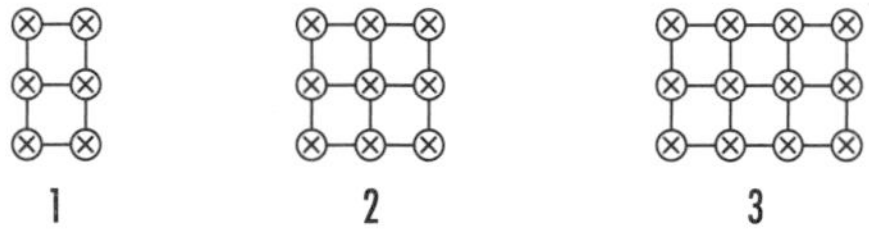

10 The number of sticks.

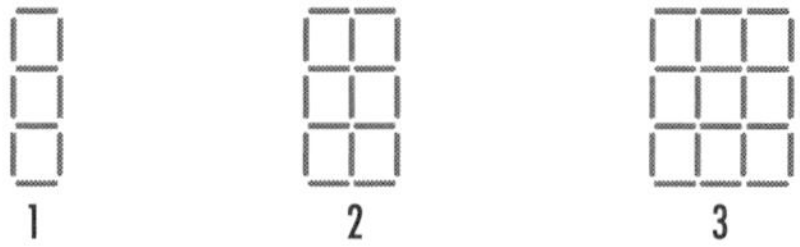

11 The number of white slabs.

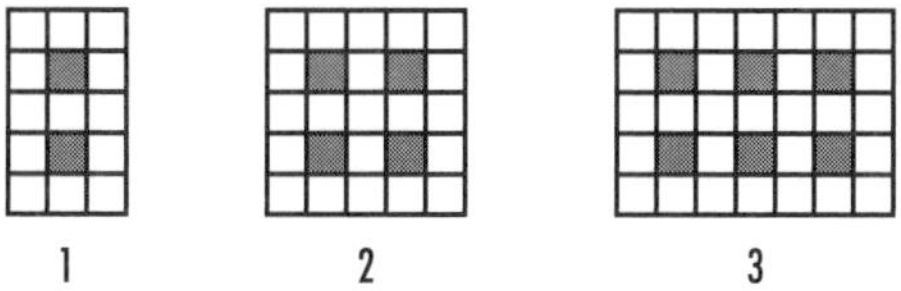

12 The perimeter of each shape.

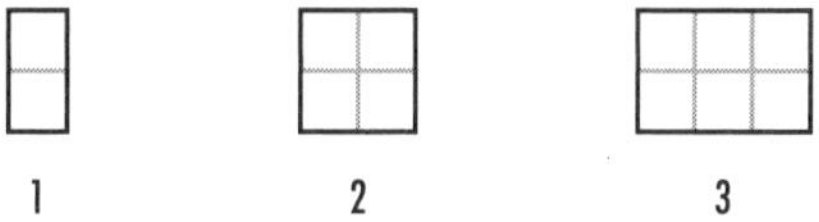

13 The number of dots.

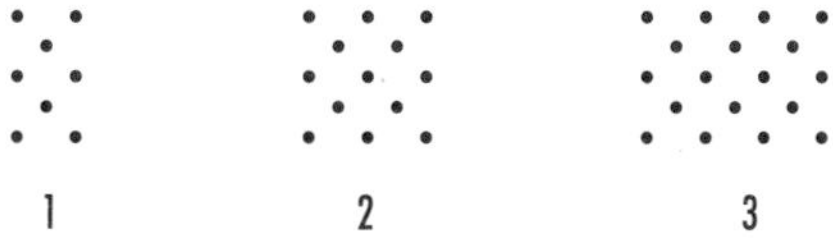

14 The number of sticks.

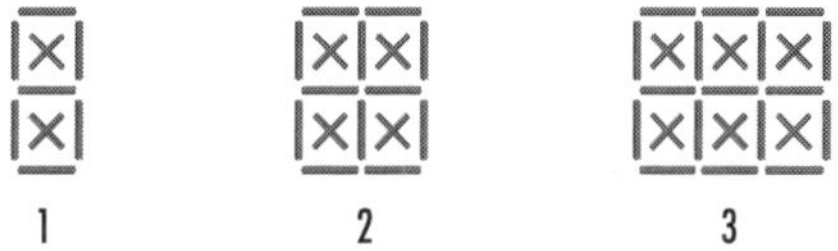

15 The number of '+' points.

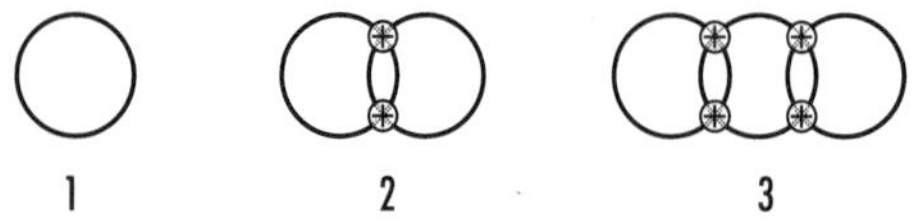

37/ COLLECTING LIKE TERMS (1)

$a + a + a + a = 4a$

$4c + 2c = 6c$

$6x - 5x = x$

$b + b + b = 3b$

$5d - 3d = 2d$

$a + 2b + 2a - 3c = 3a + 2b - 3c$

EXAMPLE

▶ Simplify (a) $2a + 7b - 3b + 2a$ (b) $7x + 3y - 3x + x - 4w$.

(a) $2a + 7b - 3b + 2a = 4a + 4b$

(b) $7x + 3y - 3x + x - 4w = 5x + 3y - 4w$

Exercise 37A

Simplify.

1 $x + x + x$
2 $y + y$
3 $w + w + w + w$
4 $d + d - d + d - d$
5 $f + f - f - f$
6 $g + g + g - g + g$
7 $2a + a + 3a$
8 $4a - a + 2a$
9 $d + 3d + 6d$
10 $4b + 3b + 2b$
11 $5y - y + 2y$
12 $3a + 4a + 5a$
13 $c + 2c - c + 3c$
14 $3x - x + 3x - x$
15 $m + 2m + 3n$
16 $2a + 4b + 5a + 2b$
17 $a + 2b + a$
18 $s + 2t + s - t - s$
19 $3c + 3b - 3c + b$
20 $7y + 2w - 6y + w$
21 $2a + 4b + a + 2b$
22 $5c + 3a - c + 3b - 2a$
23 $8m + 6n - 2m + 3n$
24 $8x - 4x + y + 6y - 4x$
25 $6a + b - 3a + 2b$
26 $5x + 3y - 2x - y$
27 $4b + 4c - 3b + 2a - 3c$
28 $6p + q - 5p + 2q$
29 $3a + b + 2c - a - b$
30 $s + 7t + 4s - 3t$

Exercise 37B

Simplify.

1 $a + a + a + a$
2 $b + b$
3 $c + c + c$
4 $e + e - e + e + e$
5 $y + y + y$
6 $x + x - x + x - x$
7 $6w - 2w - w$
8 $5c + 2c + c$
9 $6e + 2e - 7e + e$
10 $3a - 2a + 4a$
11 $3f + 5f - 4f$
12 $5b + 2b + b$
13 $2x + 4x - 3x$
14 $6w + 8w - 3w + w$
15 $x + x + 2y + y$
16 $4b + c + 2b + c$
17 $x + x + x + y + 2y + x$
18 $2a + b + 3a - b$
19 $3x - x + 3y + y$
20 $8a + 3b + a - b$
21 $3a + 2c + 3c + a$
22 $6a + 3y + 3x + 4y$
23 $s + 2s + 3t - 2t + s$
24 $6p + 2q - 3p + 2q$
25 $x + y + 2y + 4x + 2y$
26 $5a + 2b - b + 3a - b$
27 $5x + 4y - 2x - 2y$
28 $5c + 2a - c + 3a$
29 $2a + 3b - a + 4c - c$
30 $7a + 2b + 4c - 6a + 3b$

38/ COLLECTING LIKE TERMS (2)

As ab is the same as ba, $3ab + 4ba = 7ab$.

EXAMPLE

▶ Simplify (a) $5a^2 + 4a^3 - 3a^2 + 6ab$ (b) $4ab^2c + 5abc^2 - 3ab^2c + 2abc^2$.

(a) $5a^2 + 4a^3 - 3a^2 + 6ab = 4a^3 + 2a^2 + 6ab$

(b) $4ab^2c + 5abc^2 - 3ab^2c + 2abc^2 = ab^2c + 7abc^2$

Note: a^2 and a^3 cannot be added, but $a^2 + a^2 = 2a^2$ since terms with similar powers can be combined.

Exercise 38A

Simplify.

1 $x + 2x + x^2 + 3x^2$
2 $xy + 2cd + 3xy - cd$
3 $11ab + 14ba + 3ab$
4 $3x^2 + x + 2x^2$
5 $14a^3 + 4a^3 - 7a^3$
6 $3x + 3y + 4y^2 - 2y$
7 $12x^2 + 10x^3 + 7x^4 - 2x^2$
8 $5x^2y^2 + 3x^2y^2 - 4x^2y^2$
9 $4a^2y^2 + 2ay^2 + 6a^2y^2$
10 $6a + 2a^2 + 4a^3 + 10a$
11 $5xyuv - 3xyuv + 2xyuv$
12 $6a^2 + 15a^2 - 5a^2 + 3a^2$
13 $9mn + 6mn - 4mn - 3mn$
14 $4ab + 4b - 3ab + 2b$
15 $3xyw - xyw + 4xyw$
16 $14a^2 + 3a^2 + 4a^3 + 2a^3$
17 $9abc + 5ab - 2a + 2ab$
18 $4xy + 18xy + 17xy - 23xy$
19 $4a + a^5 + 3a^2 - a$
20 $3x^2 - 2x^5 - x^3 + x^2$
21 $5x^3 - 6 + 2x^3 - x^2$
22 $3x^2 + 2x - 3 + 6x - 2x^2$
23 $9a^3 - 5a^3 - a^4 - a$
24 $6t^2 + 2 + 9t^4 - 2t^2 + 4$
25 $pqr^2 + pqr + 2pqr + pqr^2$
26 $3x^3 - 2x^2 + x^3 + 2x^2$
27 $5abc + 13 - 2abc - 9$
28 $4def + 3de^2f - 2def + def^2$
29 $2a^3 + a^2 + 6a + 3a^3$
30 $a^3 + 2a^4 + 3a^5 - a^2 - a^3$

Exercise 38B

Simplify.

1 $xy + 2y + 3xy + 4y$
2 $7xy + 2yx - 3xy$
3 $7x + 3y + 2y^2 + 3x$
4 $5x^3 + 3x^2 - 2x^3 + 2x^2$
5 $10x^2 + x + 3x^2 + 2x$
6 $2a^2y^2 + ay^2 + 2a^2y^2$
7 $cd + 3cd + d - cd$
8 $5a + a^2 + 3a^3 + 9a$
9 $4abcd + 3abcd - 2abcd$
10 $6cd^2 + 4cd^2 - 5cd^2$
11 $10mn - 4mn - 3mn + 5mn$
12 $7xy + 3x - 2xy + 2x$
13 $10p^2 + 3p^2 + 4p^3 - 2p^2$
14 $9pqr - 4pqr + 3pqr$
15 $2a + a^5 + 3a^2 - a$
16 $2xy + 3xy - 4xy + 5xy$
17 $9a^2 + 6a^2 - 3a^2 - 5a^2$
18 $10a + 4a^3 + 2a^3 - 7a$
19 $2x^2 - 3x^5 - 2x^3 - x^2$
20 $8pqr - 3pq + 5p - 3pqr$
21 $2x^3 - 7 + 4x^3 - 2x^4$
22 $10a^3 - 7a^3 - 2a^4 - a$
23 $4x^2 + 2x - 3 + 4x - 2x^2$
24 $a^2bc + 3abc + 2a^2bc$
25 $6t^2 + 4 + 10t^3 - 2t - 4$
26 $4x^3 - 2x^2 + x^3 - x^2$
27 $3stuv + 2stuv - stuv$
28 $5a^3 - a^2 + 6a - 3a^3$
29 $3a^3 + 5a^4 + 3a^5 - 2a^2 - 2a^3$
30 $4pqr + 2pq^2r - 2pqr + pqr^2$

39/ MULTIPLICATION AND DIVISION IN ALGEBRA

$2a$ means $2 \times a$

a^2 means $a \times a$

ab means $a \times b$

$2ab$ means $2 \times a \times b$

$3a^2$ means $3 \times a \times a$

$a \div b$ can be written $\frac{a}{b}$

$a \div 2$ can be written as $\frac{a}{2}$ or $\frac{1}{2}a$

$2a \div 3b$ can be written $\frac{2a}{3b}$

$2a \div 4b$ can be written as $\frac{2a}{4b}$, and then cancelled to $\frac{a}{2b}$

Note: Letters in expressions are normally written in alphabetical order.

EXAMPLE

► Simplify (a) $a \times b \times c$ (b) $2d \times 4d$ (c) $w \div y$ (d) $4b \div 8c$.

(a) $a \times b \times c = abc$

(b) $2d \times 4d = 8d^2$

(c) $w \div y = \frac{w}{y}$

(d) $4b \div 8c = \frac{4b}{8c} = \frac{b}{2c}$

Exercise 39A

Simplify.

1 $b \times b$	**2** $4 \times f$	**3** $b \div c$	**4** $g \times h$	**5** $m \times n$
6 $x \div y$	**7** $a \div 3$	**8** $a \times 3$	**9** $5 \div k$	**10** $d^2 \div e$
11 $f \div d^2$	**12** $p \times q \times r$	**13** $3 \times f \times g$	**14** $5 \times u \times v$	**15** $d \times e \times f$
16 $a \times b \div 4$	**17** $b \times b \div c$	**18** $3 \times j \div k$	**19** $4 \div r$	**20** $t \div 5$
21 $c \times c \times d$	**22** $d \times d \div f$	**23** $g \times h \div i$	**24** $6 \times c \div 4$	**25** $3 \times s \times 4 \times t$
26 $4 \times j \times k \times l$	**27** $4 \times b \div 5$	**28** $f \times f \div g$	**29** $1 \div a^2$	**30** $3 \times t \times 4 \times t$

Exercise 39B

Simplify.

1 $a \times b$	**2** $f \div c$	**3** $b^2 \div d$	**4** $t \div 5$	**5** $7 \div q$
6 $y \div w$	**7** $3 \times r \times r$	**8** $7 \times t$	**9** $c \times c$	**10** $k \times y$
11 $m \times n$	**12** $c \times d \times e$	**13** $4 \times s \times t$	**14** $8 \times k \times k$	**15** $3 \times q \times r$
16 $g^2 \div e$	**17** $a \times b \div 4$	**18** $9 \div q^2$	**19** $f \times f \div h$	**20** $j \times m \div 3$
21 $q \times w \times e \times r$	**22** $a \times s \times d \times f$	**23** $1 \div t$	**24** $7 \times d \div e$	**25** $5 \times s \times s$
26 $3 \times f \times g \times h$	**27** $3 \times f \times f \times g$	**28** $y \times y \times y$	**29** $9 \times q \div r$	**30** $7 \times s \times t \times u$

40/ MULTIPLYING OUT BRACKETS

$2(x + 3)$ means 'two lots of $(x + 3)$'.
$2(x + 3) = 2x + 6$

EXAMPLE

▶ Multiply out (a) $4(b - 3)$ (b) $3(3p - 4q)$.

(a) $4(b - 3) = 4 \times b - 4 \times 3 = 4b - 12$

(b) $3(3p - 4q) = 3 \times 3p - 3 \times 4q = 9p - 12q$

Exercise 40A

Multiply out the brackets.

1	$3(x - 1)$	**2**	$4(a - 2)$	**3**	$2(a + 4)$	**4**	$6(x - 3)$	**5**	$5(x + y)$
6	$2(a - b)$	**7**	$3(x - y)$	**8**	$7(a + b)$	**9**	$6(6 + d)$	**10**	$5(c + 6)$
11	$2(3x + 6)$	**12**	$2(3x - 4)$	**13**	$5(2x - 3)$	**14**	$5(2x - 3)$	**15**	$7(x + 2)$
16	$4(2x + 3)$	**17**	$5(p + 2q)$	**18**	$4(x + 5)$	**19**	$2(3x - 2y)$	**20**	$3(2x - 5)$
21	$2(3x - 2)$	**22**	$3(3x + 4)$	**23**	$2(3x - 4)$	**24**	$4(4x + 7)$	**25**	$4(5x - 3)$
26	$4(4x - 3)$	**27**	$2(2x + 13)$	**28**	$8(x + y)$	**29**	$3(3x + 2)$	**30**	$3(5x - 2)$

Exercise 40B

Multiply out the brackets.

1	$2(y - 4)$	**2**	$3(r + 3)$	**3**	$5(x + y)$	**4**	$6(a + b)$	**5**	$4(p + q)$
6	$3(s - t)$	**7**	$2(p - q)$	**8**	$5(t + s)$	**9**	$4(s - 3)$	**10**	$3(p + 3)$
11	$3(2x + 9)$	**12**	$4(x + 1)$	**13**	$2(5x + 7)$	**14**	$3(3x + 2)$	**15**	$5(4x + 1)$
16	$3(3x + 2)$	**17**	$4(3x + 6)$	**18**	$3(7s + u)$	**19**	$2(6m - 15n)$	**20**	$3(5f - 2e)$
21	$8(3x - 2)$	**22**	$4(3x + 5)$	**23**	$3(2x - 1)$	**24**	$2(2x - 3)$	**25**	$5(2x - 1)$
26	$2(5x + 1)$	**27**	$3(6x + 5y)$	**28**	$4(3x - 1)$	**29**	$5(3x + 2)$	**30**	$3(2x + 5y)$

41/ SIMPLIFYING WITH BRACKETS

Multiplying out the brackets may produce terms which can then be collected together.

EXAMPLES

▶ $2(x + 2y) + 3(x + y)$
$= 2x + 4y + 3x + 3y$
$= 5x + 7y$

$3q + 8r - 2(q + 3r)$
$= 3q + 8r - 2q - 6r$
$= q + 2r$

$4d - 3(e - 2d)$
$= 4d - 3e + 6d$
$= 10d - 3e$

Note: '–' outside and '–' inside = '+', so $-3 \times -d = +6d$.

Exercise 41A

Multiply out the brackets and simplify.

1	$6(2m + n) + 2(n - 3m)$	**2**	$5(p + 2q) + 2(p - 3q)$	**3**	$4(2x + y) + 2(3x - 2y)$
4	$2(3x + 4y) + 3(5x + 2y)$	**5**	$3(d + e) + 2(3d + 2e)$	**6**	$6(5m + 2n) + 2(6n - 12m)$
7	$4(2c + 3d) + 2(3c + d)$	**8**	$4d + 3e + 2(e - 2d)$	**9**	$6(x + 2y) + 12x - 5y$
10	$4(d + e) - 3d - e$	**11**	$6x + 2y + 3(5y - 2x)$	**12**	$3(6q + 4r) + 4(q - r)$

13 $3a + 8b + 2(a - 3b)$
14 $2(3p + 2q) + 3(p - q)$
15 $3c + 8d + 2(c - 3d)$
16 $3(5x + 4) - 3x - 10$
17 $6(x + y) + 2(y - 2x)$
18 $2(3 + x) + 3(2x + 4)$
19 $3(2c + 4) + 2(c - 3)$
20 $7(2x + 3) + 4(3x - 2)$
21 $2(3a + b + 4c) + 3(c + 4b - 2a)$
22 $3d + 9e + 3(e - d - f)$
23 $7 - 2(x - 5)$
24 $2x + 5(3x - 4)$
25 $4 - 5(2k - 3)$
26 $3(d + 4) - 2(3 - 2d)$
27 $5(2y - 8) - 3(2 - 5y)$
28 $5(4b - 5) - (4 - 2b)$
29 $5(4b - 2a) - 3(2a - 3b)$
30 $3(2x + 5y) - 2(2x - y)$

Exercise 41B

Multiply out the brackets and simplify.

1 $3(7e + f) + 2(e + 5f)$
2 $8(2a + 3b) + 2(b - 3a)$
3 $2(p + 3q) + 5(p - q)$
4 $2(y + 2w) + 3(y - w)$
5 $4(5s + t) + 3(s - t)$
6 $5(p + 2q) + 3(2p - 2q)$
7 $4(2a + 3b) + 5(b - a)$
8 $5(4m + 3n) + 3(2m - 3n)$
9 $8(3g + 5h) - 14g - 3h$
10 $5(a + 6b) - 25b + 5a$
11 $3(2c + d) - 4c + 2d$
12 $8x + 4y + 5(y - x)$
13 $5(s + 3t) + s - 7t$
14 $8(2x + 1) - x - 7$
15 $5(p + 2q) + 2(p - 3q)$
16 $5(3q + 2r) + 3(r - 5q)$
17 $2(7s + 8) + 4$
18 $p + 2q + 3r + 2(p + 2q + r)$
19 $4(6x + 3) + 5(3 - 2x)$
20 $4(p + 3) + 2(2p - 4)$
21 $4(a + 2b + 3c) + 2(c - 4b - 2a)$
22 $2(3w + x + 4y) + 3(y + 4x - 2w)$
23 $6g + 7h + 2(h - g - d)$
24 $3t + 6(3t - 5)$
25 $3m - 4(5 - 3m)$
26 $2(3f + 5) - 2(4 + 3f)$
27 $7(a - 2) - (2a + 3)$
28 $2(6q + 7) - 3(3p - 4q)$
29 $4(3s + 5t) - 3(2s - 3t)$
30 $3(p - 2q) - (3p - 6q)$

REVISION

Exercise C

1 Simplify.
(a) $d + d + d + d + d$
(b) $8x + 2x - 5x + x$
(c) $3f + 4g + 5f + 2g$
(d) $7x - 4x + y + 6y - 3x$
(e) $y + 2y^2 + 3y + 3y^2$
(f) $7a^2 + 4a^2 - 6a^2 + a^2$
(g) $2pqr^2 + pq^2r + pqr^2 + pq^2r$
(h) $4d^3 + d + d^2 - d^3 + 3d + 4d^2$
(i) $a \times a \times a$
(j) $b \times b \times c \div 3$
(k) $3 \times p \times q \times r$
(l) $d \times e \div f$

2 Multiply out any brackets, and simplify where possible.
(a) $3(x + 2)$
(b) $4(3x - 2)$
(c) $5(2d - e)$
(d) $6(3f + 5g)$
(e) $3(4x + 5y) + 2(2x + 3y)$
(f) $4(3c - d) - 7c + 4d$
(g) $3t + 2(t - 3)$
(h) $5(4m + 2n) - 2(5m - 3n)$

Exercise CC

1 Find the next two terms in each of the following number series.
(a) 4, 12, 20, 28
(b) 20, 17, 14, 11
(c) 7, 9, 13, 19
(d) 2, 3, 6, 11
(e) 9, 12, 18, 27
(f) 6, 11, 17, 25

2 In each of the following questions,
(i) find a rule to describe the sequence or pattern,
(ii) use the rule to find the 10th and 20th number in the sequence.

(a)	1st 4	2nd 7	3rd 10	4th 13
(b)	3rd 4	4th 6	5th 8	6th 10
(c)	1st 7	2nd 8	3rd 9	4th 10
(d)	3rd 6	4th 9	5th 12	6th 15
(e)	1st 1	2nd 5	3rd 9	4th 13
(f)	1st 29	2nd 28	3rd 27	4th 26

(g) The number of sticks in each diagram.

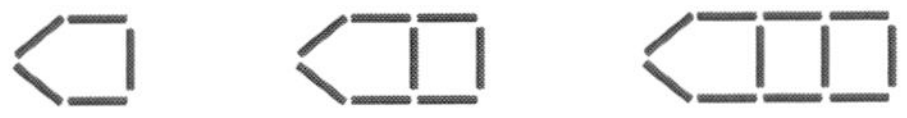

1 2 3

(h) The number of squares in each diagram.

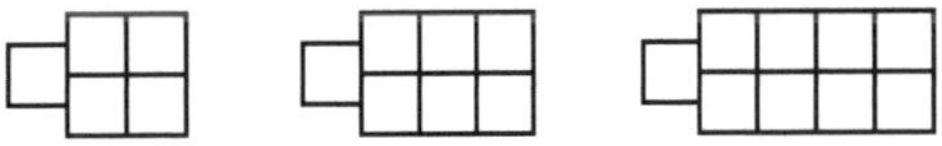

1 2 3

42/ SOLVING SIMPLE EQUATIONS (1)

To solve an equation, collect the numbers on one side of the equation and the unknowns on the other side. This can be done by adding or subtracting the same term from both sides, or using the simple rule of '*Cross the bridge and change the sign*'.

EXAMPLE

▶ Solve the equation $x + 5 = 12$.

This means:

$x = 12 - 5$

$= 7$

When a term is moved from one side of the equation to the other, the sign of that term is changed.

EXAMPLE

▶ Solve the equation $12 - x = 3$.

$12 - 3 = x$

$x = 9$

Exercise 42A

Solve the equations.

1 $x + 4 = 7$	**2** $x + 9 = 11$	**3** $x - 3 = 6$	**4** $5 + x = 13$
5 $x + 7 = 11$	**6** $12 - x = 5$	**7** $x - 5 = 4$	**8** $x + 3 = 11$
9 $x + 7 = 13$	**10** $9 + x = 13$	**11** $12 - x = 3$	**12** $x + 3 = 15$
13 $19 - x = 5$	**14** $x + 4 = 23$	**15** $20 - x = 3$	**16** $x + 5 = 23$
17 $x + 9 = 25$	**18** $25 - x = 3$	**19** $x + 3 = 21$	**20** $17 - x = 0$
21 $23 - x = 5$	**22** $x + 9 = 24$	**23** $15 - x = 7$	**24** $25 - x = 5$
25 $x + 4 = 11$	**26** $20 - x = 8$	**27** $x + 4 = 22$	**28** $x + 7 = 12$
29 $18 - x = 4$	**30** $18 - x = 9$		

Exercise 42B

Solve the equations.

1 $x + 6 = 10$	**2** $x - 2 = 5$	**3** $x + 3 = 9$	**4** $x - 1 = 4$
5 $10 - x = 7$	**6** $6 + x = 14$	**7** $x - 3 = 5$	**8** $x + 6 = 13$
9 $7 - x = 5$	**10** $6 + x = 10$	**11** $x + 5 = 14$	**12** $x - 4 = 14$
13 $5 + x = 22$	**14** $14 - x = 0$	**15** $25 - x = 7$	**16** $x + 4 = 19$
17 $x + 5 = 17$	**18** $4 + x = 25$	**19** $x - 7 = 8$	**20** $x + 4 = 21$
21 $x + 9 = 23$	**22** $24 - x = 7$	**23** $25 - x = 3$	**24** $x + 5 = 17$
25 $x + 10 = 20$	**26** $15 - x = 6$	**27** $x + 8 = 14$	**28** $7 + x = 20$
29 $x + 10 = 18$	**30** $10 - x = 3$		

43/ SOLVING SIMPLE EQUATIONS (2)

If an equation contains single terms that include the unknown the equation needs to be changed so that the unknown is left on its own. This is done by either multiplying both sides of the equation by a quantity, or dividing both sides by a quantity.

EXAMPLES

▶ $7x = 28$

$\frac{\not{7}x}{\not{7}} = \frac{28}{7}$

$x = 28 \div 7 = 4$

$x = 34$

$\frac{\not{4}x}{\not{4}} = \frac{34}{4}$

$x = 34 \div 4 = 8.5$

In each case both sides of the equation are divided by the number in front of the *x* term (called the **coefficient** of *x*).

EXAMPLES

▶ $\frac{x}{5} = 4$

$\not{5} \times \frac{x}{\not{5}} = 4 \times 5$

$x = 20$

$\frac{x}{7} = 9$

$\not{7} \times \frac{x}{\not{7}} = 9 \times 7$

$x = 63$

In each case both sides of the equation are multiplied by the number dividing into *x*. This leaves the *x* term on its own.

Exercise 43A

Solve the equations.

1 $3x = 18$	**2** $5x = 10$	**3** $9x = 27$	**4** $\frac{x}{3} = 2$	**5** $8x = 72$
6 $\frac{x}{7} = 4$	**7** $5x = 10$	**8** $9x = 45$	**9** $7x = 63$	**10** $8x = 56$
11 $\frac{x}{2} = 16$	**12** $\frac{x}{5} = 9$	**13** $\frac{x}{8} = 7$	**14** $5x = 25$	**15** $\frac{x}{6} = 2$
16 $9x = 18$	**17** $2x = 34$	**18** $\frac{x}{6} = 7$	**19** $8x = 48$	**20** $\frac{x}{2} = 4$
21 $7x = 49$	**22** $9x = 36$	**23** $\frac{x}{7} = 5$	**24** $2x = 38$	**25** $4x = 28$
26 $\frac{x}{5} = 3$	**27** $6x = 6$	**28** $\frac{x}{5} = 8$	**29** $6x = 0$	**30** $\frac{x}{4} = 7$

Exercise 43B

Solve the equations.

1 $2x = 10$	**2** $4x = 16$	**3** $7x = 14$	**4** $\frac{x}{3} = 2$	**5** $\frac{x}{5} = 4$
6 $4x = 24$	**7** $3x = 15$	**8** $7x = 21$	**9** $\frac{x}{3} = 7$	**10** $8x = 32$
11 $\frac{x}{4} = 9$	**12** $12x = 24$	**13** $\frac{x}{8} = 1$	**14** $7x = 7$	**15** $9x = 72$

16 $\frac{x}{9} = 2$	**17** $3x = 3$	**18** $\frac{x}{7} = 8$	**19** $\frac{x}{2} = 7$	**20** $9x = 81$
21 $\frac{x}{2} = 3$	**22** $\frac{x}{5} = 7$	**23** $7x = 7$	**24** $\frac{x}{6} = 4$	**25** $4x = 44$
26 $\frac{x}{4} = 8$	**27** $\frac{x}{8} = 3$	**28** $8x = 16$	**29** $\frac{x}{3} = 5$	**30** $9x = 27$

44/ SOLVING HARDER EQUATIONS

To solve an equation:
(a) collect numbers on one side of the equation and terms involving the unknown on the other side,
(b) multiply or divide both sides by the same quantity to ensure the unknown is on its own.

EXAMPLE

▶ Solve the equations (a) $2x + 3 = 13$ (b) $5x - 4 = 11$.

(a)
$$2x + 3 = 13$$
$$2x = 13 - 3$$
$$2x = 10$$
$$x = \frac{10}{2} = 5$$

(b)
$$5x - 4 = 11$$
$$5x = 11 + 4$$
$$5x = 15$$
$$x = \frac{15}{5} = 3$$

Exercise 44A

Solve the equations.

1 $2x + 1 = 5$	**2** $3x + 5 = 14$	**3** $3x + 1 = 16$	**4** $2x - 3 = 11$
5 $7x + 4 = 18$	**6** $5x + 7 = 42$	**7** $2x + 8 = 26$	**8** $3x - 5 = 4$
9 $2x + 3 = 5$	**10** $4x - 1 = 7$	**11** $4x - 3 = 29$	**12** $2x + 3 = 7$
13 $6x - 7 = 23$	**14** $8x + 9 = 17$	**15** $2x - 1 = 9$	**16** $6x + 8 = 50$
17 $2x - 5 = 13$	**18** $7x + 4 = 11$	**19** $9x - 4 = 23$	**20** $3x - 8 = 4$
21 $8x - 12 = 36$	**22** $6x - 3 = 39$	**23** $4x - 3 = 5$	**24** $4x - 2 = 18$
25 $10x + 2 = 42$	**26** $4x - 5 = 31$	**27** $6x - 2 = 40$	**28** $5x + 4 = 44$
29 $4x + 3 = 27$	**30** $6x - 7 = 5$		

Exercise 44B

Solve the equations.

1 $4x + 3 = 31$	**2** $2x + 3 = 19$	**3** $2x - 4 = 6$	**4** $2x - 3 = 5$
5 $3x - 2 = 13$	**6** $2x + 4 = 8$	**7** $10x - 7 = 3$	**8** $4x - 3 = 17$
9 $4x + 2 = 30$	**10** $4x + 7 = 23$	**11** $7x - 4 = 45$	**12** $10x + 7 = 37$
13 $4x + 3 = 11$	**14** $7x - 2 = 5$	**15** $2x + 5 = 21$	**16** $2x + 9 = 23$
17 $4x + 5 = 25$	**18** $9x - 14 = 40$	**19** $6x + 11 = 23$	**20** $6x - 1 = 35$
21 $2x + 8 = 26$	**22** $8x - 7 = 17$	**23** $2x + 4 = 22$	**24** $2x + 1 = 15$
25 $6x - 1 = 17$	**26** $3x + 1 = 25$	**27** $6x + 3 = 45$	**28** $4x - 2 = 34$
29 $7x - 4 = 38$	**30** $5x + 2 = 22$		

45/ EQUATIONS WITH BRACKETS

To solve equations involving brackets, first multiply out the brackets. Then proceed as before.

EXAMPLE

▶ Solve the equations (a) $2(x + 4) = 14$ (b) $3(2x - 5) = 21$.

(a) $2(x + 4) = 14$
$2x + 8 = 14$
$2x = 14 - 8$
$2x = 6$
$x = 3$

(b) $3(2x - 5) = 21$
$6x - 15 = 21$
$6x = 21 + 15$
$6x = 36$
$x = 6$

Exercise 45A

Solve the equations.

1 $2(2x + 3) = 18$	**2** $2(x + 3) = 18$	**3** $3(x + 3) = 24$	**4** $2(2x - 3) = 18$
5 $4(x - 1) = 8$	**6** $3(2x - 1) = 9$	**7** $2(5x + 3) = 36$	**8** $2(x - 3) = 2$
9 $2(4x + 3) = 46$	**10** $2(4x + 1) = 18$	**11** $4(2x + 1) = 52$	**12** $3(3x + 2) = 15$
13 $3(2x + 3) = 21$	**14** $4(3x - 1) = 44$	**15** $4(x + 5) = 40$	**16** $5(2x - 5) = 55$
17 $2(5x + 7) = 74$	**18** $2(x - 2) = 2$	**19** $2(2x - 3) = 10$	**20** $2(5x - 9) = 12$
21 $2(3x + 6) = 24$	**22** $3(3x + 2) = 69$	**23** $3(6x - 1) = 69$	**24** $2(4x + 1) = 50$
25 $3(x - 9) = 0$	**26** $4(3x + 6) = 48$	**27** $2(2x - 7) = 18$	**28** $2(2x + 1) = 30$
29 $6(3x + 2) = 48$	**30** $3(5x - 2) = 129$		

Exercise 45B

Solve the equations.

1 $2(3x + 5) = 22$	**2** $3(2x + 1) = 27$	**3** $3(x - 1) = 0$	**4** $2(2x - 7) = 2$
5 $2(x - 4) = 4$	**6** $3(x + 4) = 27$	**7** $3(3x + 1) = 21$	**8** $5(3x - 1) = 10$
9 $4(x + 1) = 28$	**10** $4(2x + 3) = 76$	**11** $3(3x + 4) = 75$	**12** $7(x + 2) = 49$
13 $3(x - 2) = 12$	**14** $3(6x + 4) = 138$	**15** $5(3x + 2) = 55$	**16** $6(6x - 7) = 102$
17 $4(2x - 1) = 12$	**18** $5(4x + 1) = 65$	**19** $5(2x - 3) = 25$	**20** $2(5x + 1) = 52$
21 $3(2x + 9) = 45$	**22** $4(5x - 6) = 16$	**23** $5(2x - 1) = 35$	**24** $3(x - 8) = 0$
25 $7(5x - 3) = 84$	**26** $5(2x - 3) = 75$	**27** $3(4x - 7) = 39$	**28** $7(2x + 3) = 147$
29 $3(7x + 5) = 57$	**30** $2(3x - 4) = 28$		

46/ SUBSTITUTION

Remember: ab means $a \times b$
$2a$ means $2 \times a$
$2abc$ means $2 \times a \times b \times c$
$\frac{a}{b}$ means $a \div b$
a^2 means $a \times a$

In these exercises the value of each letter is given. The purpose is to find the value of an expression, or formula, if the given values are substituted into that expression or formula.

EXAMPLE

▶ Using $a = 2$, $b = 3$, $c = 4$ and $d = 5$, find the values of (i) $3b$ (ii) c^2 (iii) $b + c$ (iv) $3(a + b)$ (v) $\frac{3a}{b}$.

(i) $3b = 3 \times b = 3 \times 3 = 9$ (ii) $c^2 = c \times c = 4 \times 4 = 16$

(iii) $b + c = 3 + 4 = 7$ (iv) $3(a + b) = 3(2 + 3) = 3 \times 5 = 15$

(v) $\frac{3a}{b} = 3 \times \frac{a}{b} = 3 \times \frac{2}{3} = \frac{6}{3} = 2$

Exercise 46A

Use $w = 3$, $x = 4$ and $y = 5$ to calculate the value of the following.

1 $2w$	**2** $3x$	**3** $4y$	**4** $w + x$	**5** $y + w$
6 $x - w$	**7** wx	**8** $y - w$	**9** xy	**10** $\frac{40}{y}$
11 $\frac{32}{x}$	**12** $2w + 3x$	**13** $3y - 3w$	**14** $2(x + y)$	**15** w^2
16 $3(y - w)$	**17** y^2	**18** $wx - y$	**19** $xy - 4$	**20** $6(w + y)$

Exercise 46B

Use $a = 3$, $b = 4$, $c = 2$ and $d = 5$ to calculate the value of the following.

1 $3a$	**2** $4c$	**3** $2d$	**4** $5bc$	**5** $3ad$
6 $a + b$	**7** $c + d$	**8** $ab + 3$	**9** $cd + ab$	**10** $3(a + b)$
11 b^2	**12** $\frac{24}{c}$	**13** $\frac{18}{a}$	**14** d^2	**15** $\frac{ab}{c}$
16 $2(b - a)$	**17** $3(ab - cd)$	**18** $ad - bc$	**19** $5(c + d)$	**20** $4(b + c)$

Exercise 46C

1	$W = 3a + 2b$	Find the value of W when (a) $a = 1$, $b = 4$ (b) $a = 3$, $b = 2$.
2	$C = 4T - V$	Find the value of C when (a) $T = 5$, $V = 2$ (b) $T = 3$, $V = 1$.
3	$d = xy$	Find the value of d when (a) $x = 2$, $y = 3$ (b) $x = 0$, $y = 4$.
4	$D = 2B + 3C$	Find the value of D when (a) $B = 7$, $C = 4$ (b) $B = 6$, $C = 5$.
5	$S = AB$	Find the value of S when (a) $A = 1$, $B = 0$ (b) $A = 2$, $B = 5$.
6	$y = 5c - d$	Find the value of y when (a) $c = 3$, $d = 1$ (b) $c = 9$, $d = 7$.
7	$h = 40 + 3y$	Find the value of h when (a) $y = 5$ (b) $y = 7$.
8	$C = 3(x + y)$	Find the value of C when (a) $x = 3$, $y = 9$ (b) $x = 1$, $y = 8$.
9	$x = 3b - 2c$	Find the value of x when (a) $b = 7$, $c = 8$ (b) $b = 4$, $c = 3$.
10	$r = \frac{1}{2}(a + b)$	Find the value of r when (a) $a = 9$, $b = 5$ (b) $a = 7$, $b = 3$.
11	$t = 3p + 4q$	Find the value of t when (a) $p = 4$, $q = 2$ (b) $p = 2$, $q = 9$.
12	$V = \frac{W}{4}$	Find the value of V when (a) $W = 8$ (b) $W = 14$.
13	$C = 3L + 2R$	Find the value of C when (a) $L = 4$, $R = 1$ (b) $L = 7$, $R = 2$.
14	$X = \frac{1}{2}CD$	Find the value of X when (a) $C = 4$, $D = 1$ (b) $C = 3$, $D = 9$.
15	$M = P + 10$	Find the value of M when (a) $P = 3$ (b) $P = 7$.

16 $p = 15 + 3q$ Find the value of p when (a) $q = 2$ (b) $q = 8$.
17 $C = 4(x + y)$ Find the value of C when (a) $x = 3, y = 8$ (b) $x = 9, y = 4$.
18 $f = \frac{g}{10}$ Find the value of f when (a) $g = 80$ (b) $g = 55$.
19 $A = \frac{B}{C}$ Find the value of A when (a) $B = 32, C = 4$ (b) $B = 75, C = 5$.
20 $D = 2r^2$ Find the value of D when (a) $r = 3$ (b) $r = 7$.

Exercise 46D

1 $C = 30 + 2x$ Find the value of C when (a) $x = 1$ (b) $x = 5$.
2 $B = 3A - D$ Find the value of B when (a) $A = 2, D = 5$ (b) $A = 8, D = 7$.
3 $a = \frac{1}{2}bh$ Find the value of a when (a) $b = 4, h = 2$ (b) $b = 6, h = 7$.
4 $E = 2A + 3B$ Find the value of E when (a) $A = 7, B = 3$ (b) $A = 3, B = 8$.
5 $t = 2p + 7h$ Find the value of t when (a) $p = 2, h = 3$ (b) $p = 1, h = 2$.
6 $g = 10 + 2t$ Find the value of g when (a) $t = 3$ (b) $t = 6$.
7 $q = r + 40$ Find the value of q when (a) $r = 2$ (b) $r = 7$.
8 $x = 3s - 2t$ Find the value of x when (a) $s = 8, t = 3$ (b) $s = 5, t = 6$.
9 $T = 2(a + b)$ Find the value of T when (a) $a = 9, b = 6$ (b) $a = 8, b = 1$.
10 $b = \frac{c}{3}$ Find the value of b when (a) $c = 15$ (b) $c = 63$.
11 $y = 4c - 2d$ Find the value of y when (a) $c = 4, d = 1$ (b) $c = 8, d = 6$.
12 $e = 4(f + g)$ Find the value of e when (a) $f = 2, g = 8$ (b) $f = 9, g = 3$.
13 $H = 3L + 2T$ Find the value of H when (a) $L = 1, T = 3$ (b) $L = 9, T = 2$.
14 $c = \frac{d}{5}$ Find the value of c when (a) $d = 30$ (b) $d = 65$.
15 $Z = \frac{a}{b}$ Find the value of Z when (a) $a = 28, b = 7$ (b) $a = 32, b = 8$.
16 $w = 2p - q$ Find the value of w when (a) $p = 6, q = 3$ (b) $p = 1, q = 2$.
17 $k = \frac{m}{100}$ Find the value of k when (a) $m = 300$ (b) $m = 50$.
18 $n = mgh$ Find the value of n when (a) $m = 1, g = 5, h = 3$ (b) $m = 1, g = 0, h = 5$.
19 $W = \frac{1}{2}XY$ Find the value of W when (a) $X = 3, Y = 1$ (b) $X = 9, Y = 6$.
20 $b = a^2 + c^2$ Find the value of b when (a) $a = 3, c = 4$ (b) $a = 12, c = 13$.

47/ WRITING ALGEBRAIC EXPRESSIONS

Sometimes an actual number answer is not needed. There are times when an expression shows how to obtain a value later when more information is available.

EXAMPLE

► How many months are there in n years?

There are 12 months in one year.
There are 12×2 months in two years.
There are $12 \times n$ or $12n$ months in n years.

EXAMPLE

▶ What capacity is left in a 200-litre tank after c litres have been drained off?

The capacity c must be subtracted from the original capacity.
Remaining capacity = $200 - c$ litres.

EXAMPLE

▶ Diane has £x. Dierdre has twice as much as Diane. Dorothy has £35. How much do they have altogether?

They have: £x + £$2x$ + £35 = £$(3x + 35)$

Exercise 47A

Write down an expression for each of the following.

1 x more than 8
2 7 less than d
3 8 times k
4 5 divided by f
5 3 times g
6 6 less than c
7 p divided by q
8 the total of s and t
9 a times b
10 j divided by 9
11 3 times r
12 b more than 18
13 x more than y
14 v taken away from s
15 4 more than t

Write the answers to the following questions as algebraic expressions.

16 How many centimetres are there in d metres?
17 The cost of one book is b pence. How much will five books cost?
18 What is £$2x$ in pence?
19 A man has £m in the bank. He takes £n out. How much is left?
20 What is the cost of two articles if one costs t pence?
21 A piece of wood w cm long has v cm cut off. What length is left?
22 How many seconds are there in t minutes?
23 There are 48 people on a bus. If w people get off, how many are left on the bus?
24 Two letters cost f pence and s pence to post. What is the total cost of the two stamps needed?
25 A lorry weighs T tonnes. It is loaded with W tonnes of concrete. What is the total weight?
26 A computer costs £c. What is the total cost of n computers?
27 How many hours are there in d days?
28 Three friends have £p, £q and £r in savings. What is the total amount they have saved?
29 Remi earns £4 per hour. How much does he earn in h hours?
30 What is the total weight of n nails weighing g grams each?

Exercise 47B

Write down an expression for each of the following.

1 y more than 10
2 6 less than f
3 7 divided by m
4 e times f
5 4 less than q
6 q less than 4
7 t more than s
8 x divided by 3
9 15 more than t
10 the total of g and h
11 10 divided by d
12 4 more than n
13 1 divided by y
14 3 times h
15 m taken away from n

Write the answers to the following questions as algebraic expressions.

16 What is £x in pence?
17 How many grams are there in f kilograms?

18 What is the total cost of five articles if one article costs m pence?
19 The cost of one book is y pence. How much will 12 books cost?
20 In a game you start with m counters, but lose n counters. How many counters do you now have?
21 Bus tickets cost x pence on Monday and y pence on Tuesday. What is the total cost of the bus tickets?
22 Julie is 18 years old. How old will she be in y years?
23 A bag has T pens in it. Three are removed. How many pens are left in the bag?
24 There are g girls and b boys in a class. What is the total number of pupils in the class?
25 A class has p pupils in it. One day three pupils were absent. How many pupils were present?
26 Garden chairs cost £g. What is the total cost of n chairs?
27 A piece of string is K metres long. T metres are cut off. What is the length of the remaining string?
28 How many minutes are there in h hours?
29 A man is 40 years old. How old will he be in x years time?
30 A question number is n. What is the number of the next question?

48/ WRITING EQUATIONS

An **equation** is a way of describing a situation mathematically. It can be solved to find the answer to a problem.
The equation can often be written down and then solved later when a practical situation arises. Sometimes the answer to the problem may be obvious, or it can be found by trial and error.

EXAMPLE

▶ When a number is doubled and 5 added, the result is 17. Find the number.

Let x be the number. Then $2x + 5 = 17$

$$2x = 17 - 5$$
$$2x = 12$$
$$x = 6$$

EXAMPLE

▶ Three people are in a store. Tina spends £x. Mary spends twice as much as Tina. Sean spends twice as much as Mary. Altogether they spend £42. How much do they each spend?

Tina: £x Mary: £$x \times 2$ = £$2x$ Sean: £$2x \times 2$ = £$4x$

£x + £$2x$ + £$4x$ = £42

$$7x = 42$$
$$x = 6$$

So Tina spends £6, Mary spends £12 and Sean spends £24.

EXAMPLE

▶ Find x.

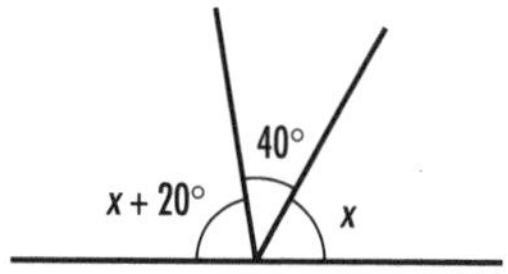

Altogether the angles add up to 180°.

$$x + 20° + 40° + x = 180°$$
$$2x + 60° = 180°$$
$$2x = 180° - 60°$$
$$2x = 120°$$
$$x = 60°$$

Exercise 48A

Write down an equation for each of the following problems, and solve it.

1 A number is doubled, and 8 is added. The result is 26.
2 A number is trebled, and 4 is taken away. The result is 29.
3 A number is doubled, and 7 is added. The result is 17.
4 A number is multiplied by 4, and 8 is taken away. The result is 20.
5 A number is trebled, and 6 is added. The result is 21.
6 A number has 5 added to it. The answer is then multiplied by 3. The result is 39.
7 A number is multiplied by 4, and 2 is added. The result is 10.
8 A number is trebled, and 8 is taken away. The result is 10.
9 A number is multiplied by 2, and 4 is taken away. The result is 2.
10 A number is multiplied by 4, and 2 is taken away. The result is 10.
11 William has £x. John has £12 more than William. They have £20 altogether. Find x.
12 Lisa has walked for x km. Her sister Katy has walked for twice this distance. Altogether they have walked 42 km. Find x.
13 Paul has collected x pebbles. Maralyn has collected 18 more pebbles than Paul. Altogether they have 82 pebbles. Find x.
14 A small coach carries x passengers. A large coach carries 21 more passengers than the smaller coach. Together they can carry 91 passengers. How many passengers can be carried by the larger coach?
15 A painting costs £x. A print of the painting costs a third of the cost of the painting. To buy both would cost £436. Find x.
16 Three people go shopping. Jenny spends £x. Shreena spends twice as much as Jenny. Marie spends three times as much as Jenny. They spend £126 altogether. Find x.
17 Darren has x stamps. Jim has three times as many stamps as Darren. Ali has four times as many stamps as Darren. Altogether they have 32 stamps. Find x.
18 Chris is x years old. His elder sister is six years older, whilst his younger brother is eight years younger. Altogether their ages add up to 37 years. Find x.
19 Three girls had x magazines each. They gave nine magazines to another girl, but still had 18 magazines left between them. Find x.
20 Eric, Liz and Tony collect drink cans. Liz has 23 more than Eric, and Tony has 41 more than Eric. Altogether they have 103. How many drink cans has Eric collected?

Write down an equation for each of the following diagrams, and use it to find the value of x.

21

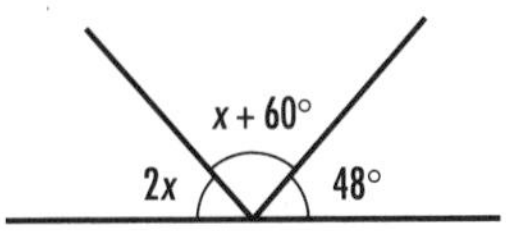

22

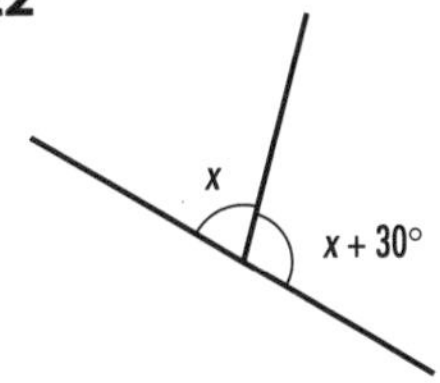

23

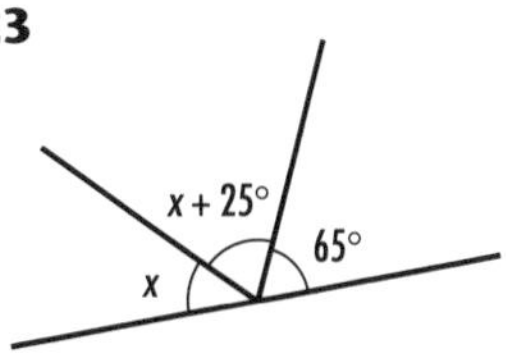

24

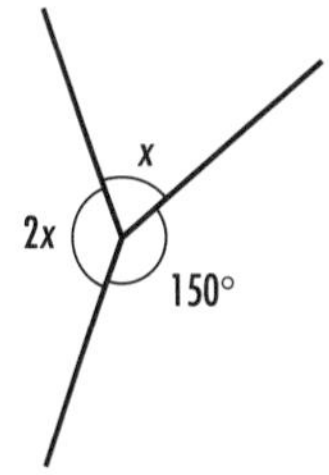

25

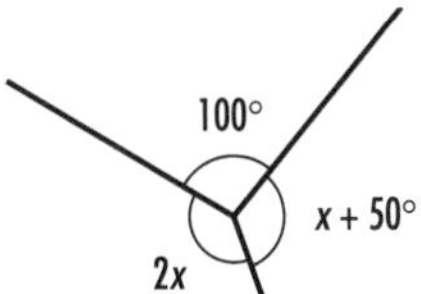

26

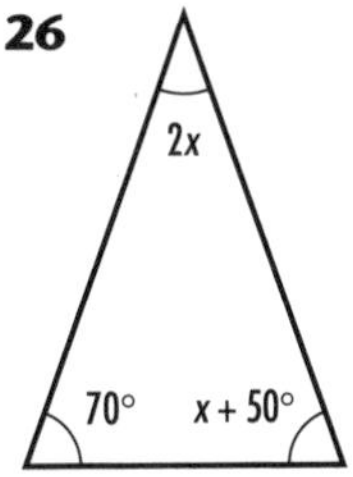

27

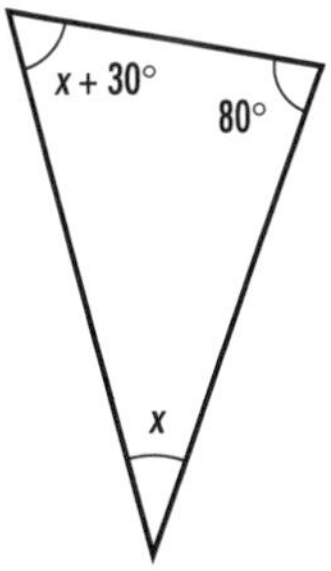

28

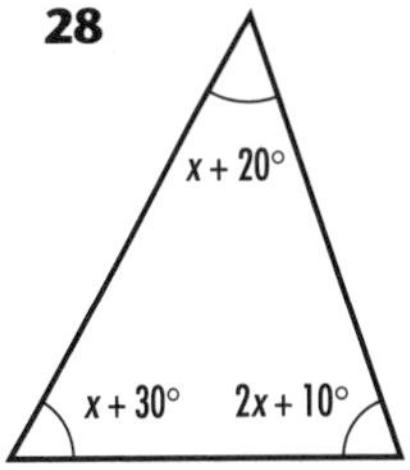

29

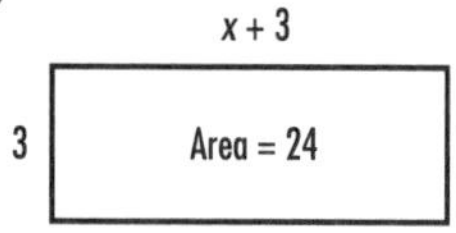

30

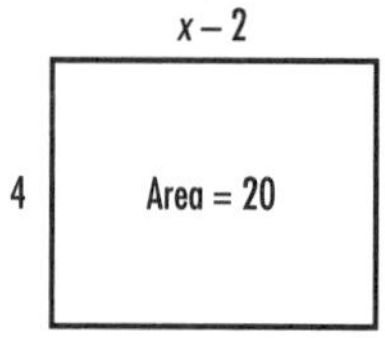

Exercise 48B

Write down an equation for each of the following problems, and solve it.

1 A number is trebled, and 5 is taken away. The result is 7.

2 A number is doubled, and 6 is taken away. The result is 12.

3 A number is trebled, and 7 is added. The result is 28.

4 A number is doubled, and 9 is added. The result is 25.

5 A number has 6 added, and then the answer is doubled. The result is 18.

6 A number is multiplied by 7, and then 2 is added. The result is 16.

7 A number is doubled, and 5 is added. The result is 9.

8 A number is multiplied by 6, and 1 is taken away. The result is 29.

9 A number is multiplied by 6, and 3 is added. The result is 15.

10 A number is multiplied by 7, and 4 is added. The result is 25.

11 Helen receives £x pocket money. Elaine receives £3.50 more pocket money. Together they receive £14.50. Find x.

12 Kevin travels 120 miles by car. His wife Jane travels x miles more during the same day. Together they have travelled 275 miles. Find x.

13 Brian has x pencils. Bert has three times as many pencils. Together they have 48 pencils. Find x.

14 Ahmed has borrowed x books. Beryl has borrowed half as many books as Ahmed. Together they have 15 books. Find x.

15 Daniel has spent £x, but his brother Harold has spent £14 more than this. Together they have spent £82. Find x.

16 Susie is x years old. Shamsa is three years older than Susie, but Jane is two years younger than Susie. Their ages add up to 43 years. Find x.

17 Bill and Simon each have x sweets. Remi has 10 sweets. Altogether they have 24 sweets. Find x.

18 There are two pieces of wood each x metres long. A third piece is 9 metres long. Altogether the three pieces are 31 metres long. How long is x metres?

19 Gemma has x pence. Julie has 20p more than Gemma. Josie has twice as much as Gemma. They have 80p altogether. Find x.

20 Ali has £x. Alan has three times as much as Ali. Adam has £6 more than Ali. They have £42 altogether. Find x.

Write down an equation for each of the following diagrams, and use it to find the value of x.

21

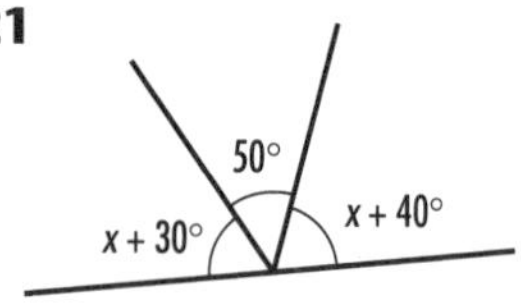

22

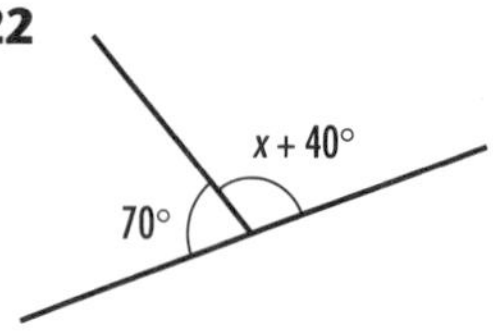

23

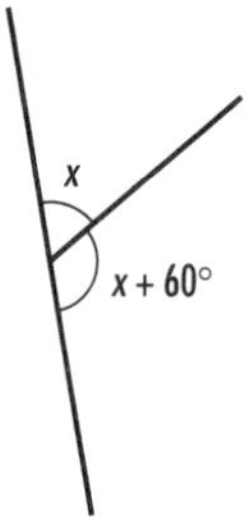

24

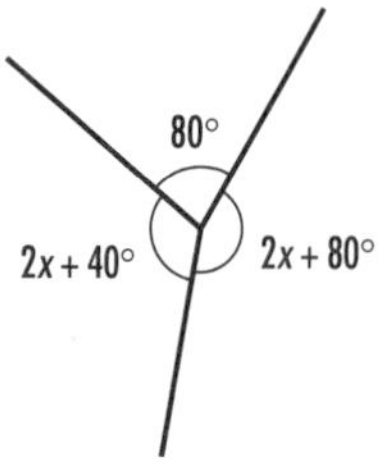

25

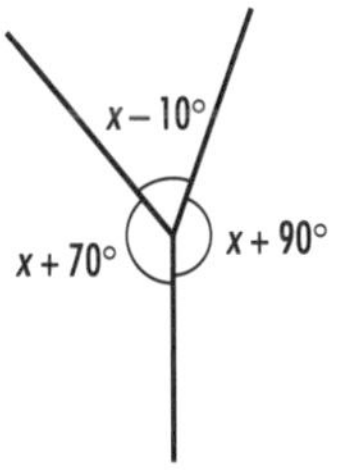

26

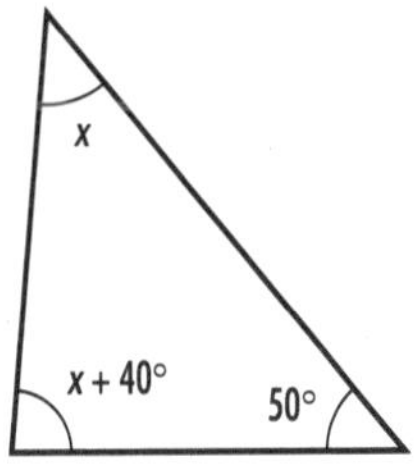

27

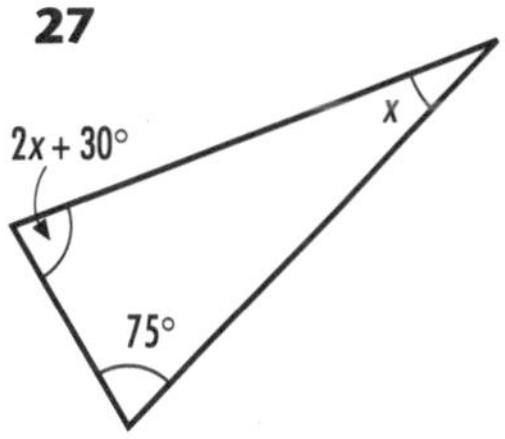

28

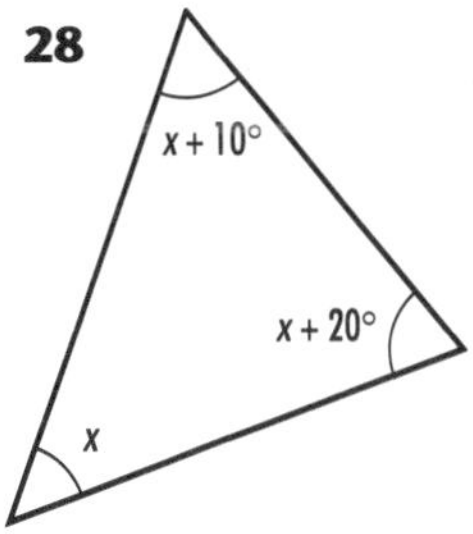

29

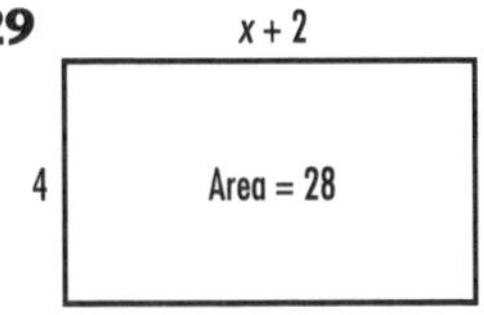

30

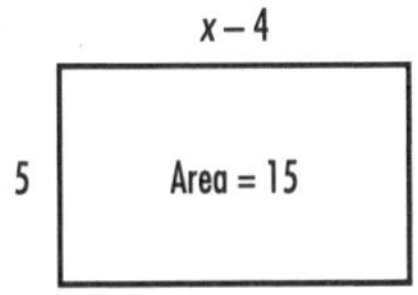

49/ TRIAL AND IMPROVEMENT

'Trial and improvement' is a recognised method of solving equations. The method is to try a possible answer; if this is not an exact answer, then try an answer which might be more accurate.

EXAMPLE

▶ Find a solution to the equation $x^2 + 2x = 7$.

Try $x = 1$: $1^2 + (2 \times 1) = 3$
Try $x = 2$: $2^2 + (2 \times 2) = 8$
A solution seems to be between $x = 1$ and $x = 2$, probably nearer 2.
Try $x = 1.8$: $(1.8)^2 + (2 \times 1.8) = 6.84$ – too small
Try $x = 1.9$: $(1.9)^2 + (2 \times 1.9) = 7.41$ – too big
As 6.84 is 0.16 below 7, and 7.41 is 0.41 above 7, it would seem reasonable to try a number nearer to 1.8 than 1.9, say 1.83.
Try $x = 1.83$: $(1.83)^2 + (2 \times 1.83) = 7.0089$ – very close
Try $x = 1.82$: $(1.82)^2 + (2 \times 1.82) = 6.9524$ – too small
Hence an approximate solution (to 2 decimal places) is 1.83.

The second solution to the quadratic equation can be found in the same way. This solution could be a larger positive number or even a negative number.

Exercise 49A

Solve these equations, to 2 decimal places, using the 'trial and improvement' process.
Note: The equations with x^2 have two solutions, whilst those with x^3 have only one.

1 $x^2 - 2x = 7$	**2** $x^2 + 2x = 5$	**3** $x^2 - 3x = 1$	**4** $x^2 + 4x = 6$
5 $2x^2 + 7x = 3$	**6** $x^3 + 1 = 14$	**7** $2x^2 + 4x = -1$	**8** $x^2 - 14x = -3$
9 $3x^2 - x = 6$	**10** $2x^2 - 10x = -3$	**11** $3x^2 - x = 3$	**12** $x^2 - x = 4$
13 $x^3 - 2 = 8$	**14** $x^2 + 2x = 2$	**15** $x^3 + 6 = 10$	**16** $x^2 + 3x = -1$
17 $x^3 - 5 = 4$	**18** $3x^2 + 7x = -3$	**19** $5x^2 - 17x = -10$	**20** $3x^2 + 10x = -2$

Exercise 49B

Solve these equations, to 2 decimal places, using the 'trial and improvement' process.
Note: The equations with x^2 have two solutions, whilst those with x^3 have only one.

1 $x^2 + 4x = 6$	**2** $x^2 - x = 1$	**3** $x^2 - 20 = 0$	**4** $2x^2 - 7x = -2$
5 $3x^2 - 11x = -7$	**6** $x^3 = 60$	**7** $2x^2 - 3x = 3$	**8** $3x^2 - 5x = -1$
9 $7x^2 - 12x = -3$	**10** $x^3 + 9 = 15$	**11** $2x^2 - 7x = 1$	**12** $5x^2 - 9x = 4$
13 $3x^2 + 12x = 3$	**14** $x^2 - 6x = 3$	**15** $x^2 - 9x = 12$	**16** $2x^2 - 15x = 3$
17 $x^3 - 1 = 6$	**18** $3x^2 - 10x = 4$	**19** $4x^2 + 11x = 8$	**20** $2x^2 + 8x = -3$

50/ DRAWING AND INTERPRETING CONVERSION GRAPHS

It is known that: 1 metre = 3.28 feet
2 metres = 6.56 feet
3 metres = 9.84 feet etc.

This information can be plotted on a graph of feet against metres.

In practice, plotting lots of points for a straight line can be a waste of time; two points are normally enough.

In the graph shown, 0 metres = 0 feet is plotted as (0, 0) and 10 metres = 32.8 feet is plotted as (10, 32.8). These two points are joined by a straight line. This line contains all the points of conversion between 0 metres and 10 metres. This is a **conversion graph**.

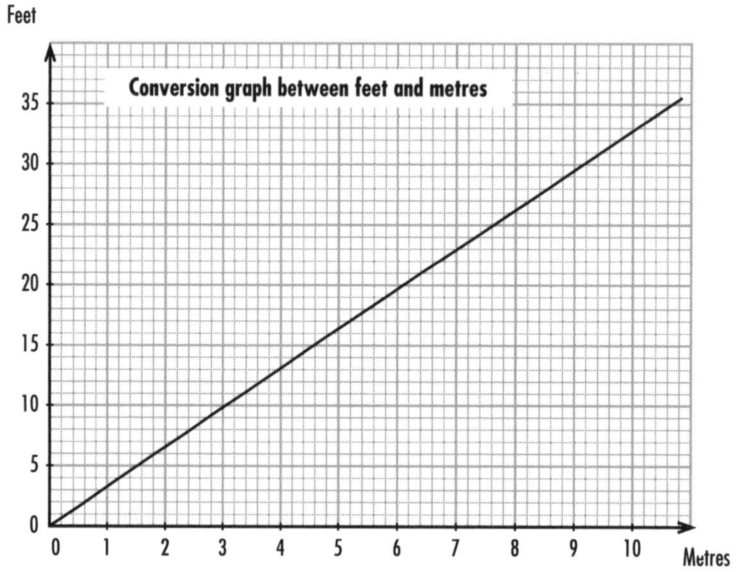

The conversion graph can be used to convert metres to feet and also to convert feet to metres. For example, you can read off that 5.5 metres is approximately 18 feet, and 10 feet is approximately 3 metres.

Exercise 50A

1 The graph converts pounds to tonnes, using a conversion of 1 t = 2205 lb.

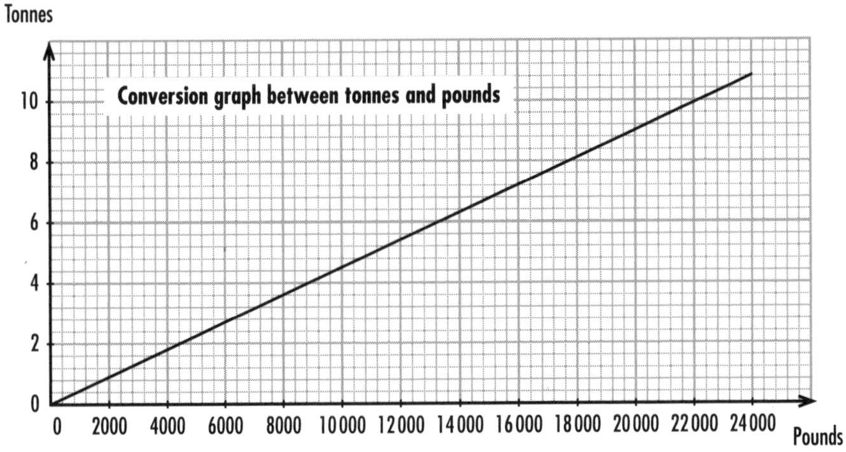

(a) Use the graph to convert the following to tonnes. Give your answers to the nearest 0.2 t.
6000 lb, 14 000 lb, 8500 lb, 18 600 lb

(b) Use the graph to convert the following to pounds. Give your answer to the nearest 200 lb.
9.6 t, 7.4 t, 4.2 t, 8.8 t

2 The graph converts pesetas to pounds, using an exchange rate of 190 pta = £1.

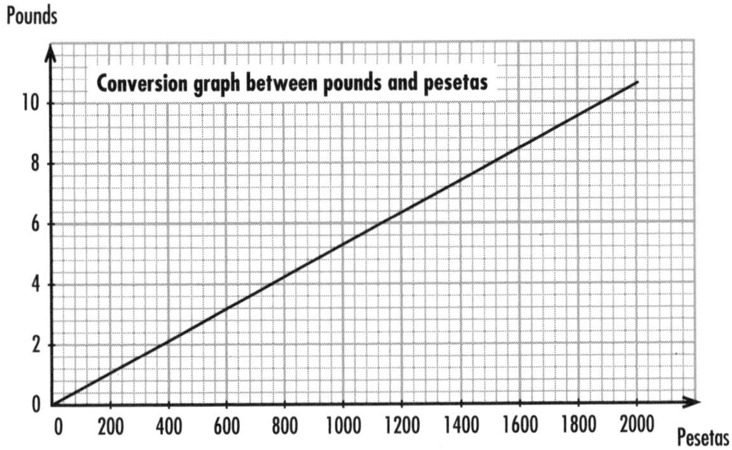

(a) Use the graph to convert the following to pounds. Give your answer to the nearest 20p.
300 pta, 1200 pta, 1680 pta, 640 pta

(b) Use your graph to convert the following to pesetas. Give your answer to the nearest 20 pta.
£7.20, £4.00, £2.60, £5.80

3 On graph paper draw a 15-cm horizontal axis using 1 cm to represent 10 schillings.
Draw a 10-cm vertical axis using 1 cm to represent £1.00.
Draw a conversion graph for pounds and Austrian schillings, using a conversion rate of £1 = 14.8 sch.

(a) Use your graph to convert the following to pounds. Give your answer to the nearest 10p.
30 sch, 56 sch, 120 sch, 98 sch

(b) Use your graph to convert the following to schillings. Give your answer to the nearest schilling.
£6.00, £2.50, £9.40, £7.60

4 On graph paper draw a 13-cm horizontal axis using 1 cm to represent 10 mm.
Draw a 10-cm vertical axis using 1 cm to represent 0.5 inch (in).
Draw a conversion graph for inches and millimetres, using a conversion rate of 1 in = 25.4 mm.
(a) Use your graph to convert the following to inches. Give your answer to the nearest 0.1 in.
30 mm, 72 mm, 95 mm, 44 mm
(b) Use your graph to convert the following to millimetres. Give your answer to the nearest millimetre.
4 in, 3.5 in, 0.8 in, 2.3 in

5 On graph paper draw a 15-cm horizontal axis using 1 cm to represent 25 fl. oz.
Draw a 10-cm vertical axis using 1 cm to represent 1 litre.
Draw a conversion graph for litres and fluid ounces, using a conversion rate of 1 *l* = 35.2 fl. oz.
(a) Use your graph to convert the following to litres. Give your answer to the nearest 0.1 *l*.
325 fl. oz, 40 fl. oz, 290 fl. oz, 190 fl. oz
(b) Use your graph to convert the following to fluid ounces. Give your answer to the nearest 5 fl. oz.
5 litres, 6.5 litres, 4.3 litres, 8.7 litres

6 On graph paper draw a 12-cm horizontal axis using 1 cm to represent 2 DM (German mark).
Draw a 10-cm vertical axis using 1 cm to represent £1.00.
Draw a conversion graph for pounds and German marks, using an exchange rate of £1 = 2.25 DM.
(a) Use your graph to convert the following to pounds. Give your answer to the nearest 10p.
5 DM, 23 DM, 10.40 DM, 18.80 DM
(b) Use your graph to convert the following to marks. Give your answer to the nearest 0.1 DM.
£1.50, £7.00, £9.80, £4.40

7 On graph paper draw a 13-cm horizontal axis using 1 cm to represent 25 cm.
Draw a 10-cm vertical axis using 1 cm to represent 1 ft.
Draw a conversion graph for feet and centimetres, using a conversion rate of 1 ft = 30.48 cm.
(a) Use your graph to convert the following to feet. Give your answer to the nearest 0.1 ft.
280 cm, 40 cm, 185 cm, 85 cm
(b) Use your graph to convert the following to centimetres. Give your answer to the nearest 5 cm.
4 ft, 8.5 ft, 6.7 ft, 3.3 ft

8 On graph paper draw a 10-cm horizontal axis using 1 cm to represent 500 g.
Draw a 10-cm vertical axis using 1 cm to represent 1 lb.
Draw a conversion graph for pounds and grams, using a conversion rate of 1 lb = 455 g.
(a) Use your graph to convert the following to pounds. Give your answer to the nearest 0.1 lb.
4400 g, 1700 g, 900 g, 3700 g
(b) Use your graph to convert the following to grams. Give your answer to the nearest 100 g.
7 lb, 6.3 lb, 2.4 lb, 4.6 lb

Exercise 50B

1 The graph converts grams to ounces, using a conversion of 1 oz = 28.4 g.

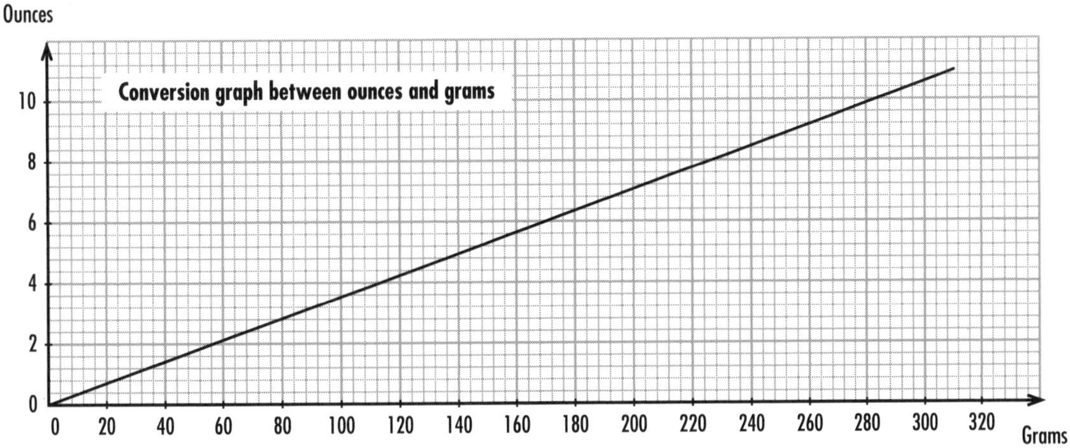

(a) Use the graph to convert the following to ounces. Give your answers to the nearest 0.2 oz.
80 g, 200 g, 124 g, 250 g

(b) Use the graph to convert the following to grams. Give your answer to the nearest 2 g.
4 oz, 8 oz, 6.4 oz, 3.6 oz

2 The graph converts cubic centimetres to cubic feet, using a conversion rate of 1 cubic foot = 28.3 cm^3.

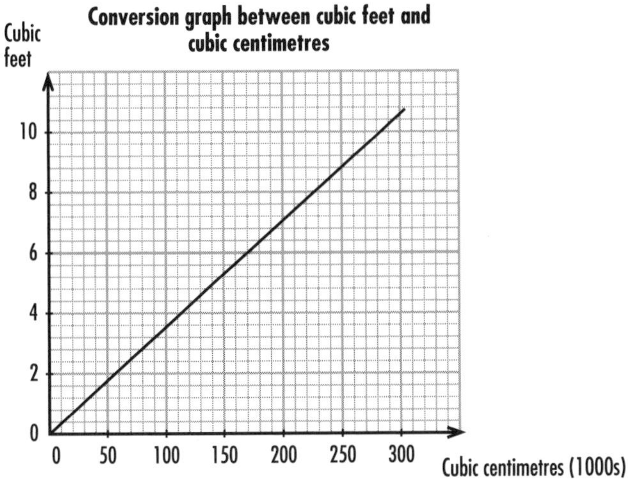

(a) Use the graph to convert the following to cubic feet. Give your answer to the nearest 0.2 cubic feet.
50 000 cm^3, 160 000 cm^3, 250 000 cm^3, 210 000 cm^3

(b) Use your graph to convert the following to cubic centimetres.
Give your answer to the nearest 5000 cm^3.
2 cubic feet, 9.4 cubic feet, 6.2 cubic feet, 3.6 cubic feet

3 On graph paper draw a 10-cm horizontal axis using 1 cm to represent 1 kg.
Draw a 10-cm vertical axis using 1 cm to represent 2.5 lb.
Draw a conversion graph for kilograms and pounds, using a conversion rate of 1 kg = 2.2 lb.
(a) Use your graph to convert the following to kilograms. Give your answer to the nearest 0.1 kg.
20 lb, 5.5 lb, 12.5 lb, 15.5 lb
(b) Use your graph to convert the following to pounds. Give your answer to the nearest 0.5 lb.
8 kg, 4.5 kg, 2.8 kg, 6.3 kg

4 On graph paper draw a 10-cm horizontal axis using 1 cm to represent 10 kr (kroner).
Draw a 10-cm vertical axis using 1 cm to represent £1.00.
Draw a conversion graph for pounds and Danish kroner, using an exchange rate of £1 = 8.56 kr.
(a) Use your graph to convert the following to pounds. Give your answer to the nearest 10p.
30 kr, 46 kr, 64 kr, 83 kr
(b) Use your graph to convert the following to kroner. Give your answer to the nearest 0.1 kr.
£2, £8.20, £6.40, £7.50

5 On graph paper draw a 12-cm horizontal axis using 1 cm to represent 25 ml.
Draw a 10-cm vertical axis using 1 cm to represent 1 fl. oz.
Draw a conversion graph for fluid ounces and millilitres, using a conversion rate of 1 fl. oz = 28.4 ml.
(a) Use your graph to convert the following to fluid ounces. Give your answer to the nearest 0.1 fl. oz.
275 ml, 40 ml, 120 ml, 210 ml
(b) Use your graph to convert the following to millilitres. Give your answer to the nearest 5 ml.
3 fl. oz, 6.5 fl. oz, 8.3 fl. oz, 4.7 fl. oz

6 On graph paper draw a 15-cm horizontal axis using 1 cm to represent $1.
Draw a 10-cm vertical axis using 1 cm to represent £1.
Draw a conversion graph for pounds and dollars, using a conversion rate of £1 = $1.45.
(a) Use your graph to convert the following to pounds. Give your answer to the nearest 10p.
$2, $8.50, $6.20, $12.80
(b) Use your graph to convert the following to dollars. Give your answer to the nearest 10 cents.
£4, £2.50, £7.60, £9.40

7 On graph paper draw a 10-cm horizontal axis using 1 cm to represent 5 *l*.
Draw a 10-cm vertical axis using 1 cm to represent 1 gal.
Draw a conversion graph for litres and gallons, using a conversion rate of 1 gal = 4.55 *l*.
(a) Use your graph to convert the following to gallons. Give your answer to the nearest 0.1 gal.
40 *l*, 15 *l*, 32 *l*, 25 *l*
(b) Use your graph to convert the following to litres. Give your answer to the nearest 0.5 *l*.
7 gal, 4.4 gal, 8.7 gal, 2.9 gal

8 On graph paper draw a 13-cm horizontal axis using 1 cm to represent 2 guilders.
Draw a 10-cm vertical axis using 1 cm to represent £1.
Draw a conversion graph for pounds and Dutch guilders, using an exchange rate of £1 = 2.45 guilders.
(a) Use your graph to convert the following to pounds. Give your answer to the nearest 10p.
5.00 guilders, 18.00 guilders, 9.40 guilders, 15.60 guilders
(b) Use your graph to convert the following to guilders. Give your answer to the nearest 0.5 guilder.
£3.00, £4.50, £8.60, £5.40

51/ READING POINTS IN ALL FOUR QUADRANTS

When finding the coordinates of a point find the x value (to the left or right) first and the y value (up or down) second.

EXAMPLE

▶ State the coordinates of the points in the diagram.

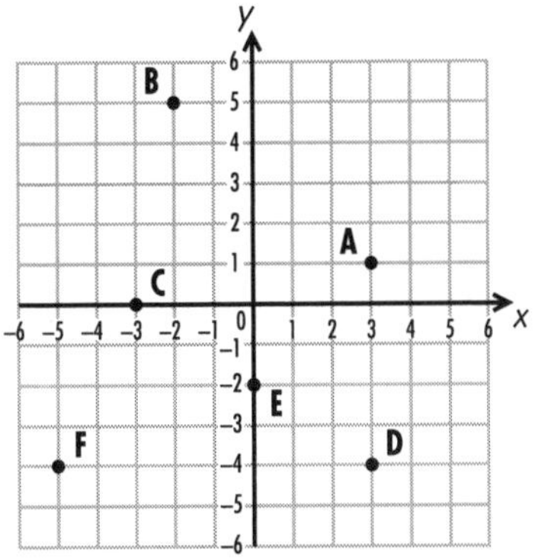

A = (3, 1) B = (–2, 5) C = (–3, 0)
D = (3, –4) E = (0, –2) F = (–5, –4)

Exercise 51A

Write down the coordinates of the points in each diagram.

1

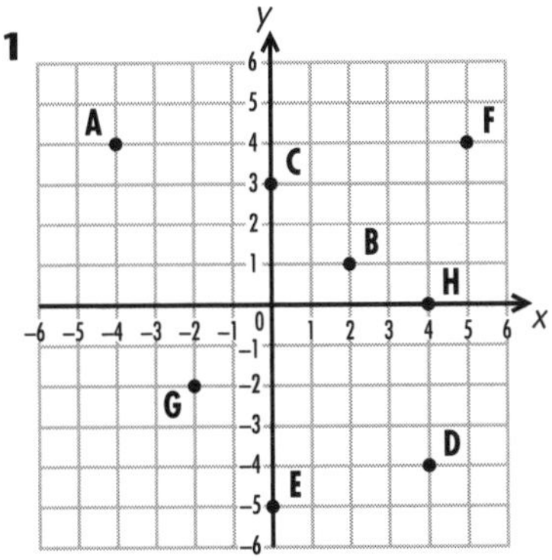

2

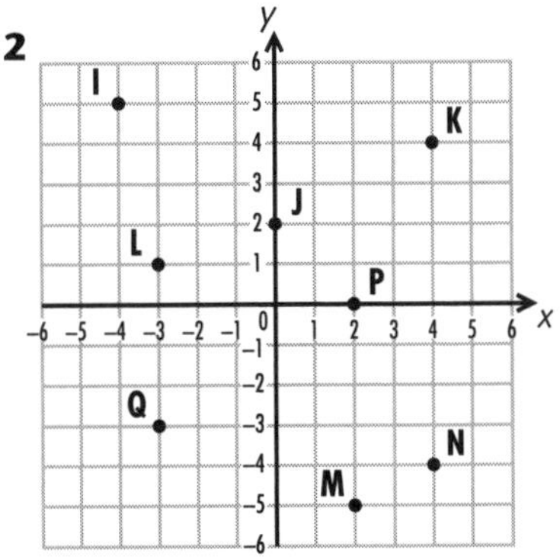

3

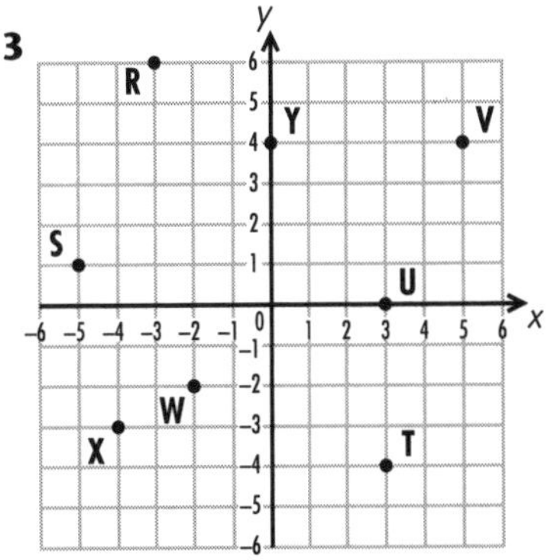

4

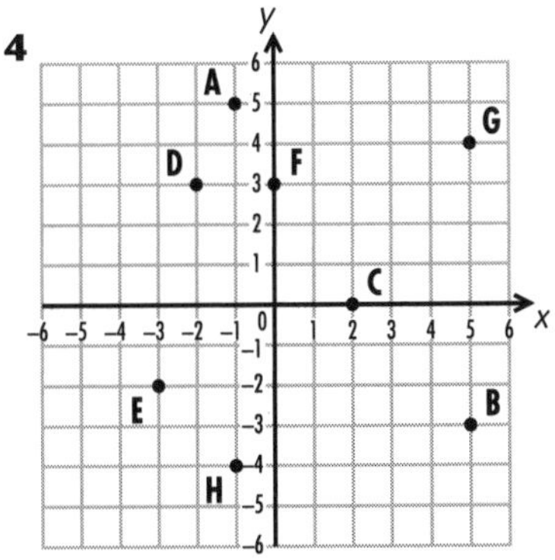

5

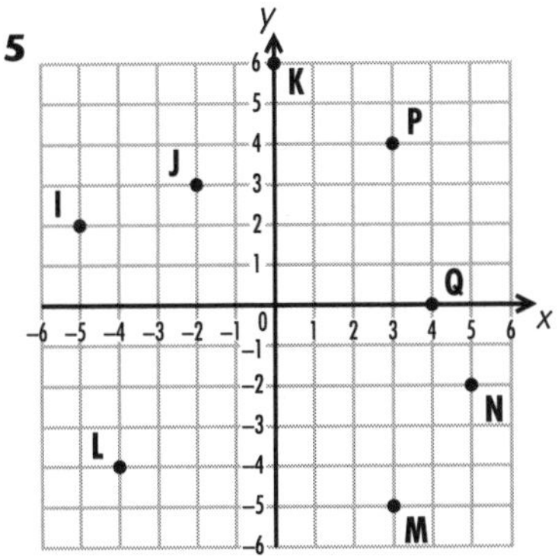

6

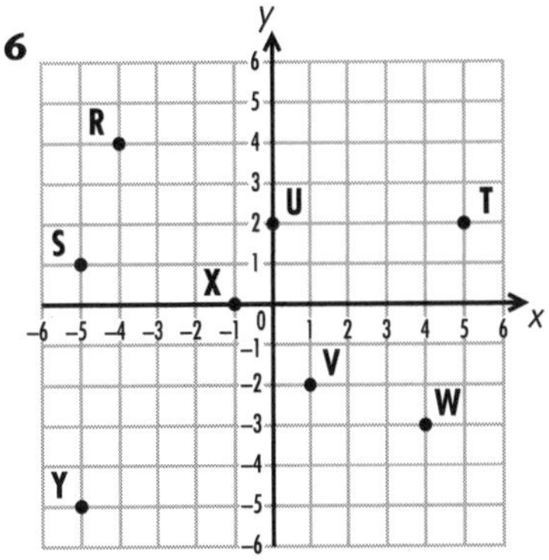

Exercise 51B

Write down the coordinates of the points in each diagram.

1

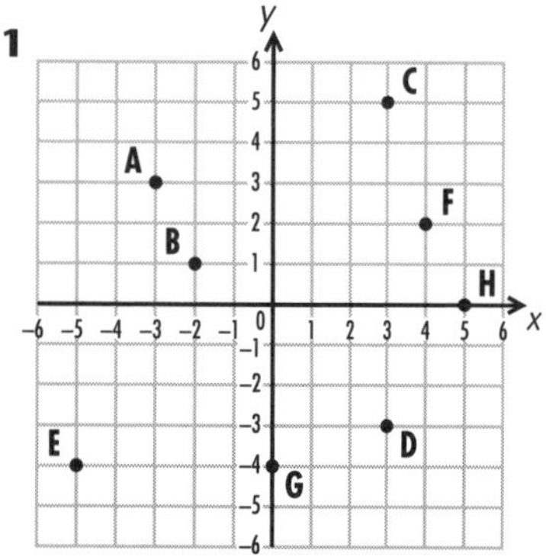

2

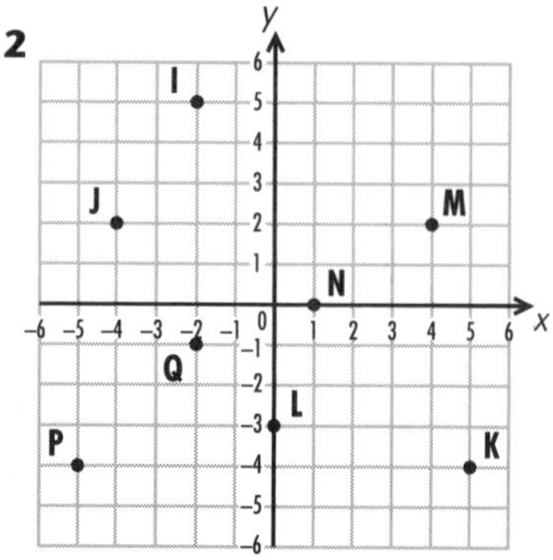

3

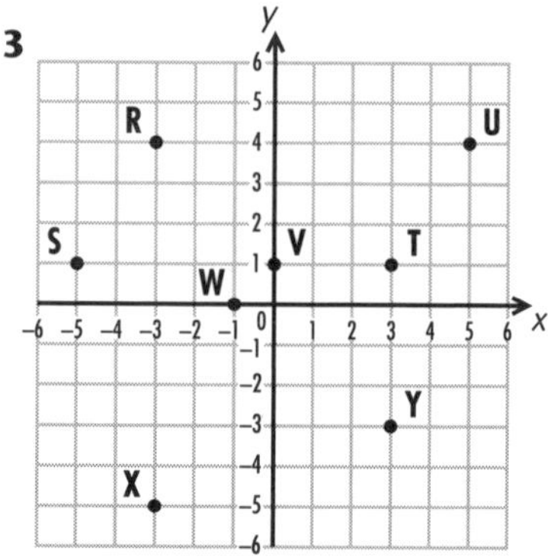

4

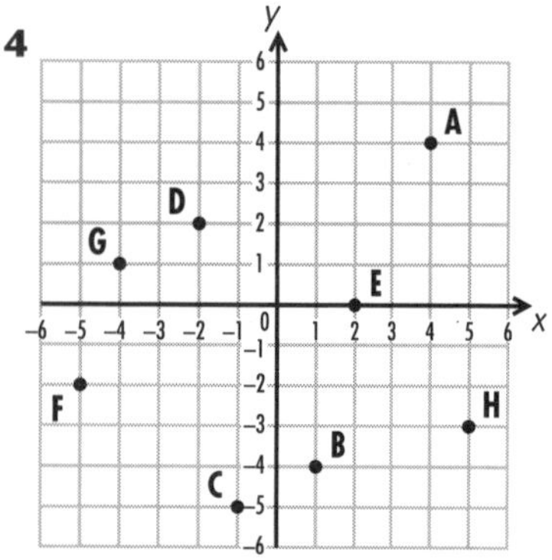

5

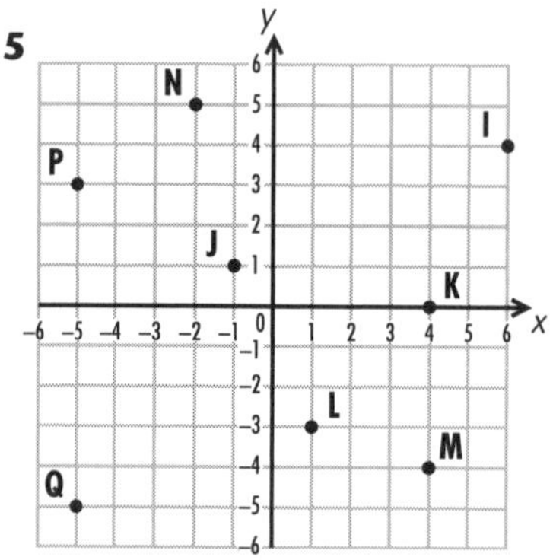

6

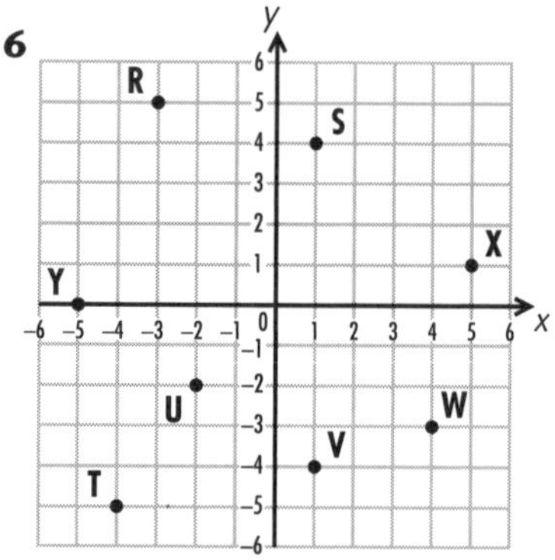

52/ PLOTTING POINTS IN ALL FOUR QUADRANTS

For each of these questions you will need to draw axes from –6 to +6 on squared paper.

EXAMPLE

► Plot and label these points.

A = (–4, 3) B = (4, 2) C = (–4, –2)

D = (3, –3) E = (0, 4) F = (–1, 0)

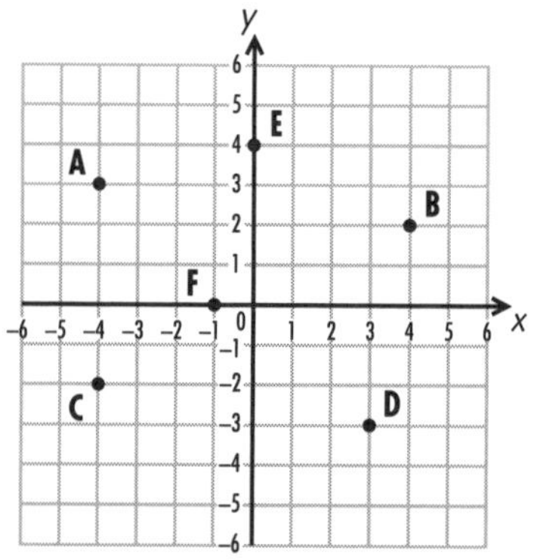

Exercise 52A

Draw axes from –6 to +6 for each question. Plot and label the points.

1 A = (–4, 5), B = (4, 4), C = (–2, –3), D = (2, 0), E = (–5, 1), F = (4, –4)
2 G = (–5, 1), H = (–1, 4), I = (1, 1), J = (–3, –4), K = (4, 0), L = (3, –4)
3 M = (–2, 6), N = (5, 4), P = (0, 2), Q = (–3, –4), R = (–5, 1), S = (3, –3)
4 T = (–2, 6), U = (4, 5), V = (–4, 2), W = (–4, –3), X = (4, –1), Y = (0, –5)
5 A = (0, 5), B = (–2, 1), C = (5, 2), D = (0, –3), E = (–5, 3), F = (4, –4)
6 G = (–5, 4), H = (1, –4), I = (–4, 0), J = (4, 4), K = (5, –2), L = (–4, –5)

Exercise 52B

Draw axes from –6 to +6 for each question. Plot and label the points.

1 M = (–5, 6), N = (–4, –4), P = (5, 3), Q = (–5, 0), R = (3, –3), S = (–2, 2)
2 T = (–5, 4), U = (–3, –3), V = (4, –4), W = (–4, 1), X = (4, 5), Y = (2, 0)
3 A = (–5, 1), B = (3, 4), C = (0, –4), D = (–4, –3), E = (–4, 5), F = (4, –2)
4 G = (–4, 4), H = (5, 1), I = (–2, –5), J = (2, 4), K = (–3, 0), L = (3, –5)
5 M = (–4, 2), N = (1, –5), P = (4, 0), Q = (2, 5), R = (–5, –4), S = (5, –3)
6 T = (–4, 3), U = (–3, –4), V = (1, –2), W = (3, 3), X = (–2, 0), Y = (5, –3)

Exercise 52C

Draw axes from –6 to +6 for each question. Plot the points and join them together, in the order stated, to draw various shapes.

1 (–4, –5), (–4, 5), (0, 0), (4, 5), (4, –5)
2 (3, 4), (–3, 4), (–3, 2), (3, –3), (3, –5), (–3, –5)
3 (3, 5), (4, 2), (4, –4), (–4, –4), (–4, 2), (–3, 5), (3, 5)
4 (3, 2), (3, 0), (0, 0), (0, –3), (–2, –3), (–2, 0), (–5, 0), (–5, 2), (–2, 2), (–2, 5), (0, 5), (0, 2), (3, 2)
5 (5, –1), (5, –5), (1, –5), (3, –4), (–4, 3), (–5, 1), (–5, 5), (–1, 5), (–3, 4), (4, –3), (5, –1)
6 (1, 1), (3, 2), (1, 3), (2, 4), (0, 5), (–2, 4), (–1, 3), (–3, 2), (–1, 1), (–4, –1), (–2, –3), (–5, –6), (0, –4), (5, –6), (2, –3), (4, –1), (1, 1)

Exercise 52D

Draw axes from –6 to +6 for each question. Plot the points and join them together, in the order stated, to draw various shapes.

1 (3, 5), (3, –4), (–4, 5), (–4, –4)
2 (–4, –5), (–4, 5), (1, 5), (2, 3), (2, 1), (1, –1), (–4, –1)
3 (2, 3), (0, 5), (–2, 3), (–2, –4), (–4, –6), (4, –6), (2, –4), (2, 3)
4 (4, 1), (4, 5), (0, 5), (2, 4), (–4, –2), (–3, –3), (3, 3), (4, 1)
5 (6, 3), (1, 5), (–4, 4), (–6, 1), (–3, –1), (–4, –5), (–1, –1), (3, –1), (5, –5), (5, –1), (6, 3)
6 (0, 6), (4, –1), (6, –1), (3, –4), (–3, –4), (–5, –1), (–3, –1), (0, 6) then join (–5, –1) to (6, –1)

53/ DRAWING GRAPHS

A simple function takes one number and changes it into another number according to a series of operations, or instructions. The way it does this can be shown as a graph, but first a table of values is needed to provide some coordinates for the graph.

EXAMPLE

► (a) Complete the table of values for the function $y = 2x - 1$.
(b) Draw the graph of $y = 2x - 1$.

(a) When $x = -2$, $y = (2 \times -2) - 1 = -5$
When $x = -1$, $y = (2 \times -1) - 1 = -3$
When $x = 0$, $y = (2 \times 0) - 1 = -1$
When $x = 1$, $y = (2 \times 1) - 1 = 1$, etc.

x	–2	–1	0	1	2	3	4
$y = 2x - 1$	–5	–3	–1	1	3	5	7

(b) These points can be plotted on a grid, and joined to make a straight-line graph.

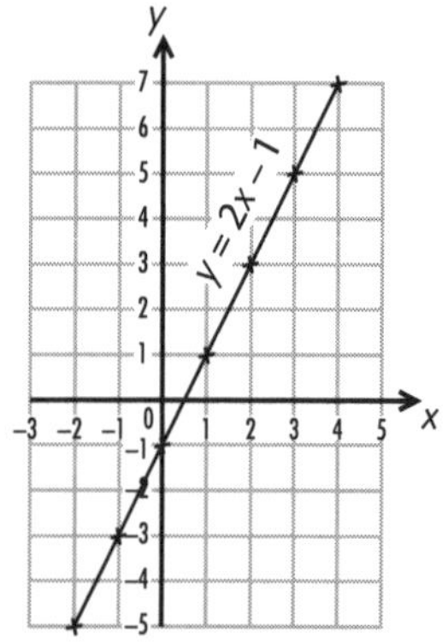

EXAMPLE

► (a) Complete the table of values for the function $y = 15 - 2x$.
(b) Draw the graph of $y = 15 - 2x$.

(a)

x	0	2	4	6	8
$y = 15 - 2x$	15	11	7	3	–1

(b) As the numbers in the table are large, you need to use a **scale** on the graph.

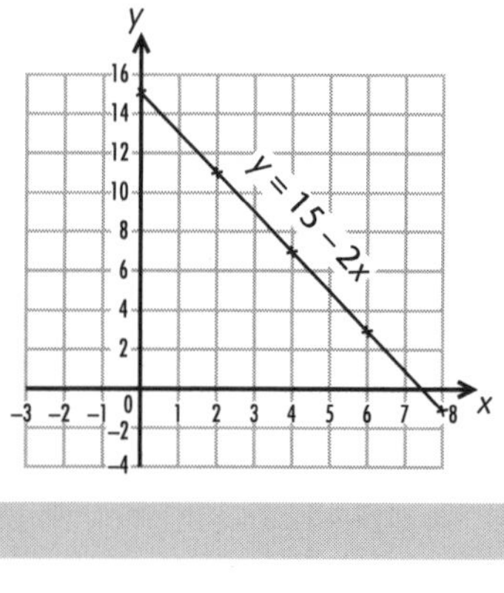

Exercise 53A

For each question:

(a) Copy and complete the table for the function shown.

(b) On graph or squared paper, draw and label the graph of the function.

1

x	−3	−2	−1	0	1	2	3
$y = x - 2$	−5			−2			

2

x	−3	−2	−1	0	1	2	3
$y = 2x + 2$			0				8

3

x	−3	−2	−1	0	1	2	3
$y = 3x$							

4

x	−2	−1	0	1	2	3	4
$y = 4x - 5$	−13			−1			

5

x	−2	−1	0	1	2	3	4
$y = 2x + 3$			3			9	

6

x	−3	−2	−1	0	1	2	3
$y = -2x$	6			0			

7

x	−3	−2	−1	0	1	2	3
$y = 2x + 6$		2				10	

8

x	−3	−2	−1	0	1	2	3
$y = 2x - 2$	−8				0		

9

x	−3	−2	−1	0	1	2	3	4
$y = 3x - 2$			−5		1			

10

x	−2	−1	0	1	2	3	4
$y = -x$	2						−4

11

x	−2	−1	0	1	2	3
$y = 4x - 2$						

12

x	−2	−1	0	1	2	3	4
$y = 10 - x$	12			9			

13

x	−2	−1	0	1	2	3	4
$y = 6 - 2x$		8				0	

14

x	−2	−1	0	1	2	3	4
$y = 2 - x$	4			1			

15

x	−2	0	2	4	6	8	10
$y = \frac{1}{2}x - 3$			−2			1	

Exercise 53B

In each question:

(a) Copy and complete the table for the function shown.

(b) On graph or squared paper, draw and label the graph of the function.

1

x	−3	−2	−1	0	1	2
$y = x + 3$	0			3		

2

x	−2	−1	0	1	2	3	4
$y = 2x + 4$		2				10	

3

x	−2	−1	0	1	2	3	4
$y = x - 1$							

4

x	−2	−1	0	1	2	3
$y = 3x - 4$		−7			2	

5

x	−2	−1	0	1	2	3
$y = 3x + 2$				5	8	

6

x	−2	−1	0	1	2	3	4
$y = 2x - 1$							

7

x	−3	−2	−1	0	1	2	3
$y = 2x$		−4					

8

x	−2	−1	0	1	2	3
$y = 3x - 1$	−7		−1			

9

x	−2	−1	0	1	2	3	4
$y = 2x - 3$				−1			

10

x	−2	−1	0	1	2	3	4
$y = 8 - x$	10			7			

11

x	−1	0	1	2	3	4	5	6
$y = 12 - 2x$			10	8				

12

x	–2	–1	0	1	2	3	4
$y = 4 - x$	6						0

13

x	–1	0	1	2	3	4	5
$y = 14 - 3x$			11		5		

14

x	–2	–1	0	1	2	3
$y = 4x - 1$						

15

x	–6	–4	–2	0	2	4	6
$y = \frac{1}{2}x + 2$	–1	0					

REVISION

Exercise D

Solve the following equations.

1 $x + 5 = 14$ **2** $3 + x = 10$ **3** $21 - x = 9$ **4** $x + 3 = 11$

5 $8x = 72$ **6** $\frac{x}{4} = 7$ **7** $7x = 7$ **8** $\frac{x}{8} = 6$

9 $4x - 2 = 22$ **10** $6x - 5 = 49$ **11** $3x + 1 = 22$ **12** $5x - 4 = 36$

13 $2(x - 3) = 10$ **14** $7(5x - 2) = 56$ **15** $3(3x + 2) = 33$ **16** $6(2x - 3) = 30$

17 Use the values $w = 3$, $x = 5$ and $y = 2$ to evaluate these expressions.
(a) x^2 (b) $xy - 3w$ (c) $2(x - y)$ (d) $\frac{39}{w}$

18 $A = 3r^2$ Find the value of A when (a) $r = 4$ (b) $r = 7$.

19 $P = 2(b + h)$ Find the value of P when (a) $b = 6$, $h = 2$ (b) $b = 4$, $h = 3$.

20 $V = 2n - 4$ Find the value of V when (a) $n = 7$ (b) $n = 15$.

21 $A = \frac{1}{2}bh$ Find the value of A when (a) $b = 14$, $h = 8$ (b) $b = 20$, $h = 6$.

22 Use a 'trial and improvement' method to find the solutions to these equations, to 2 decimal places.
(a) $x^2 - 2x = 300$ (b) $x^3 + 4 = 10$

23 Write down the coordinates of each of the points in the diagram.

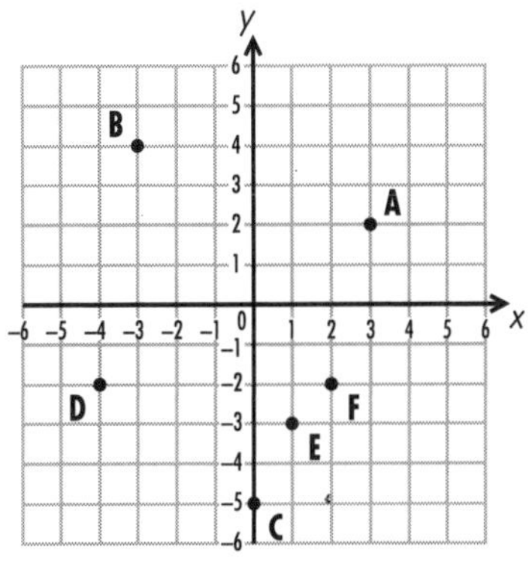

24 Draw axes from –6 to +6 on a squared grid, and plot the following points.
A = (3, 0), B = (1, 5), C = (–2, –3), D = (4, –1), E = (–2, 5), F = (0, –4)

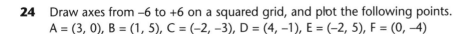

25 (a) Copy and complete the table of values for the function $y = 4x - 3$.

x	-2	-1	0	1	2	3
$y = 4x - 3$						

(b) On graph or squared paper, draw the graph of $y = 4x - 3$.

Exercise DD

1 In each of the questions (i) write down an equation for the problem (ii) solve the equation.

(a) When a number is doubled and 3 added, the result is 11.

(b) When a number is trebled and the answer is taken away from 20, the result is 11.

(c) Bill is a hill-walker. He is carrying a pack which weighs x kg. Mary has a pack twice the weight of Bill's, and Damien has a pack which weighs half that of Mary's. All three packs together weigh 100 kg. How heavy is Bill's pack?

(d) Three people go shopping. Clare spends £x. Sally spends twice as much as Clare. Kathy spends twice as much as Sally. Altogether they spend £35. How much has Clare spent?

(e)

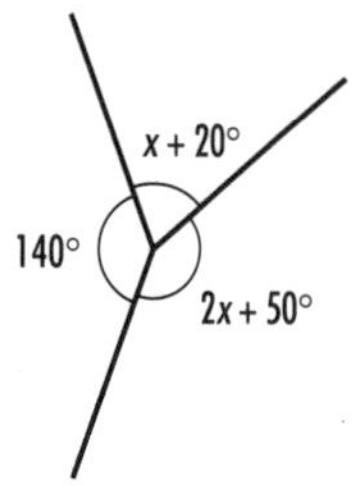

(f)

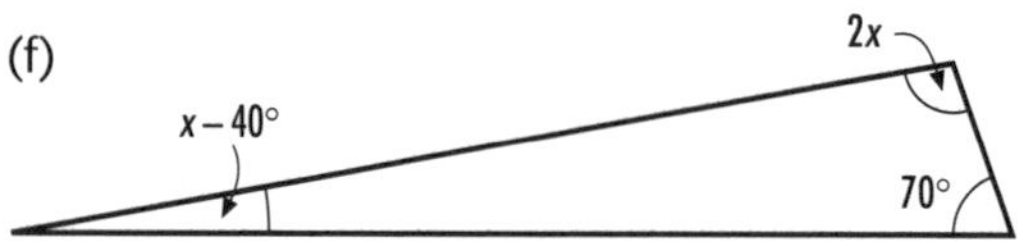

2 Write the expression that is:

(a) g times h (b) 4 less than t (c) x divided by 5 (d) 7 more than d

3 In each of the following questions, write the answer as an algebraic expression.

(a) What is the cost of 5 articles, if one article costs c pence?

(b) How many millimetres are there in x metres?

(c) Jerry is 40 years old. How old will he be in y years time?

4 On graph paper draw a 13-cm horizontal axis using 1 cm to represent 5 cm^2.
Draw a 10-cm vertical axis using 1 cm to represent 1 square inch.
Draw a conversion graph for square inches and square centimetres, using a conversion rate of 1 square inch = 6.45 cm^2.

(a) Use your graph to convert the following to square inches. Give your answer to the nearest 0.1 square inch.
58 cm^2, 11 cm^2, 33 cm^2, 22.5 cm^2

(b) Use your graph to convert the following to square centimetres. Give your answer to the nearest 0.5 cm^2.
8 square inches, 2.4 square inches, 6.5 square inches, 3.7 square inches

Shape, space and measures

54/ MEASURING AND IDENTIFYING ANGLES

Here are some words used to describe types of angles:

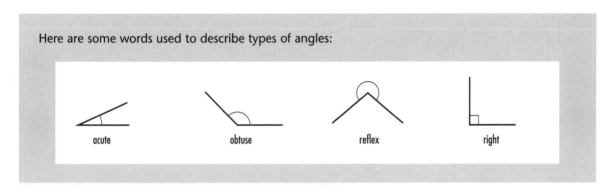

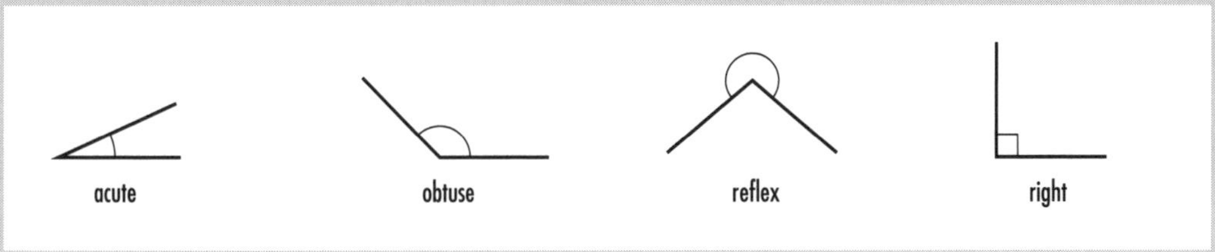

Exercise 54A

State the type of each of the following angles and measure each to the nearest degree.

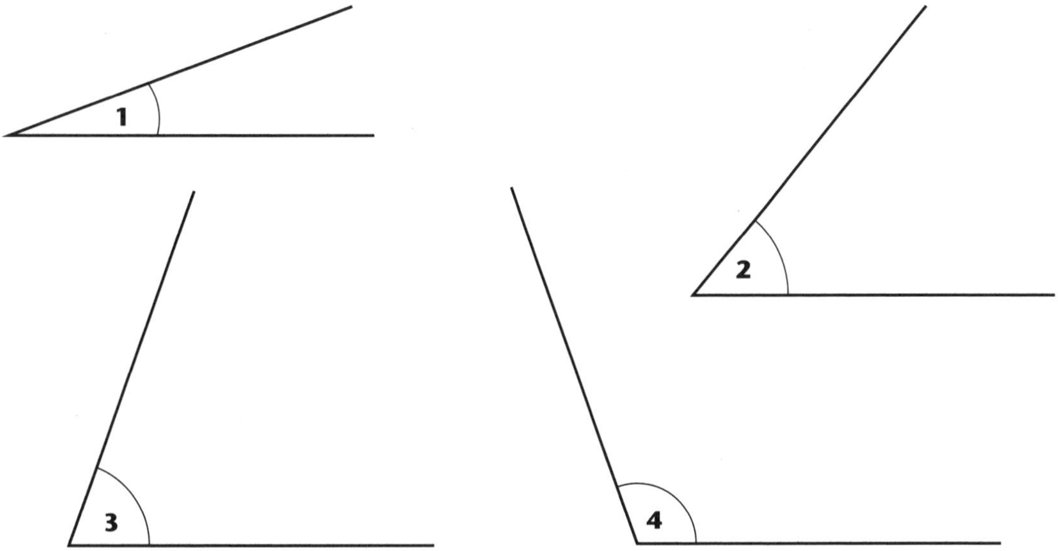

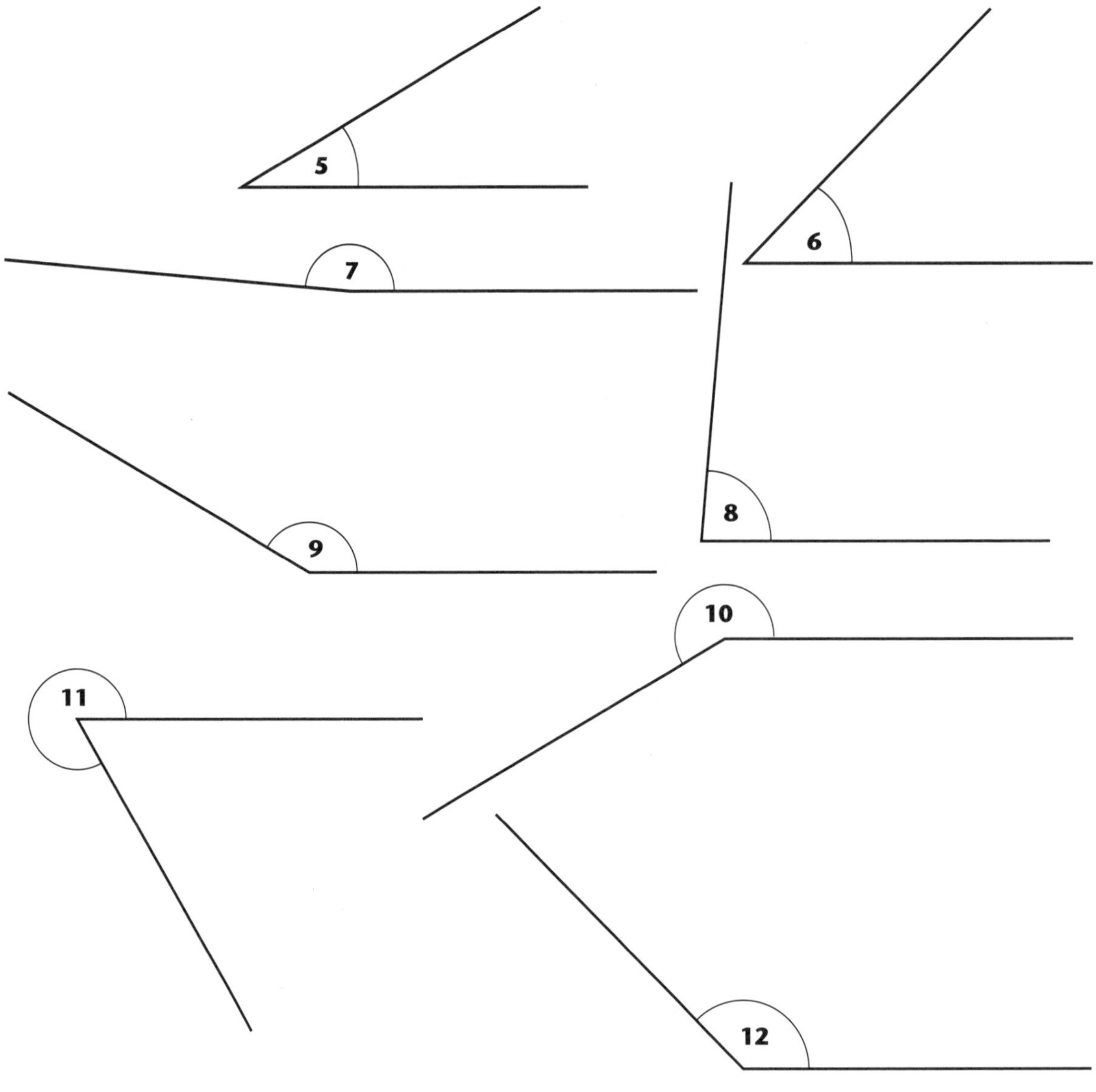

Exercise 54B

State the type of each of the following angles and measure each to the nearest degree.

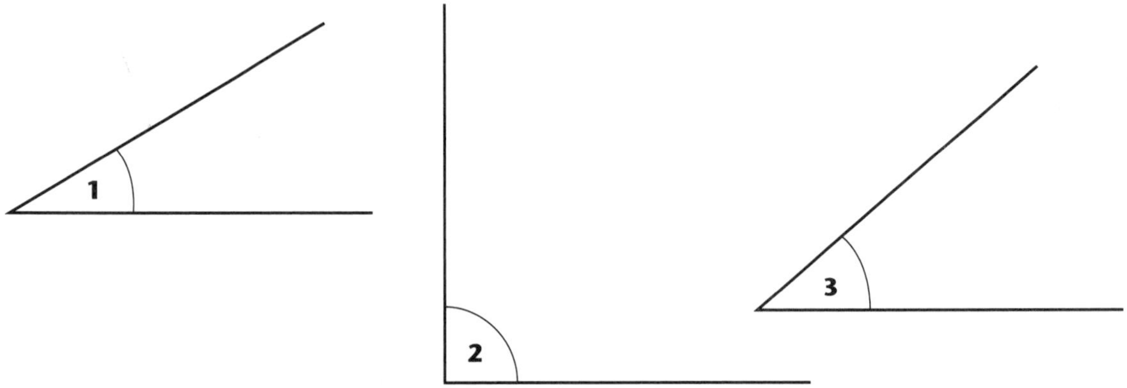

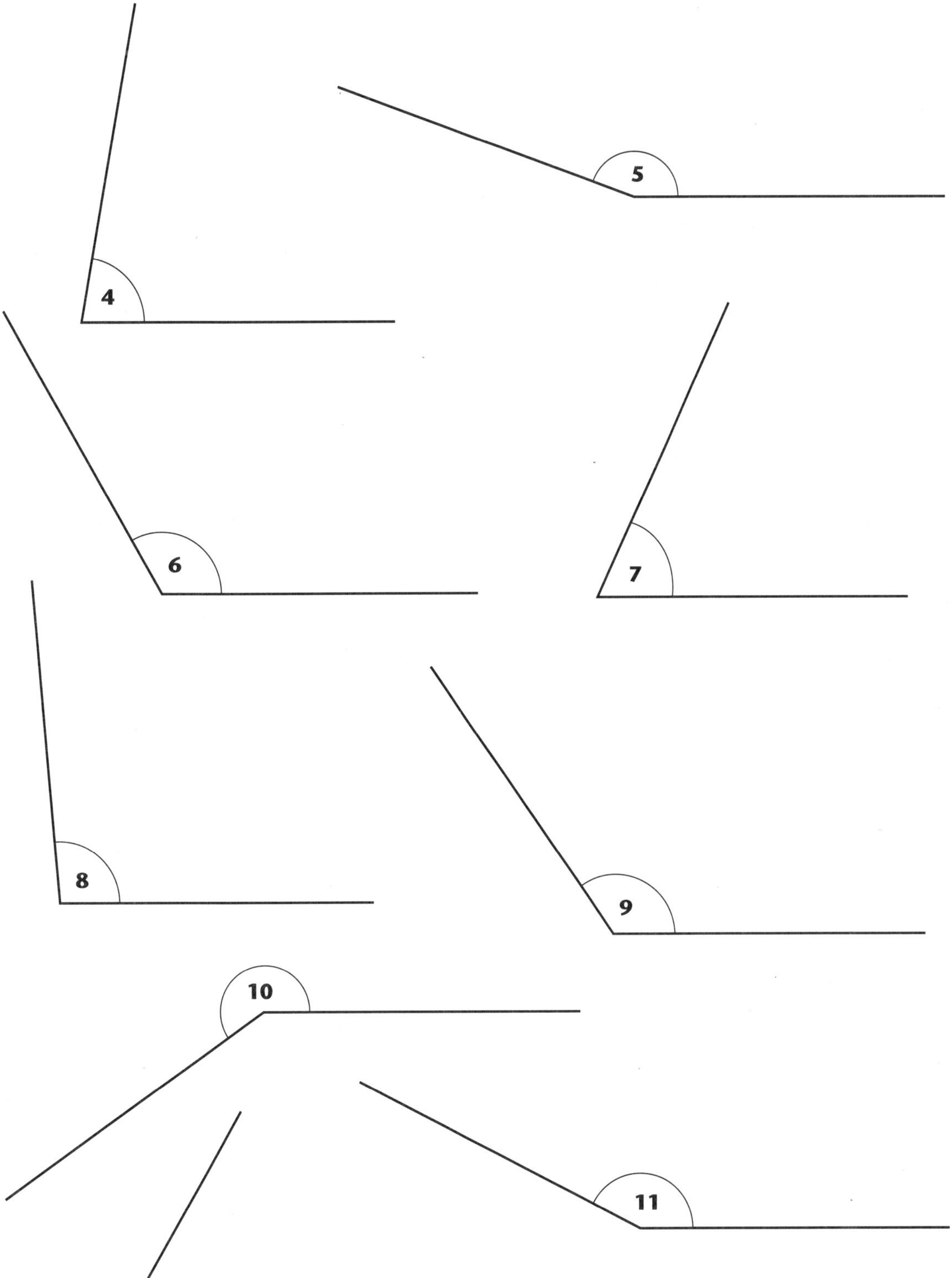
4
5
6
7
8
9
10
11
12

55/ DRAWING ANGLES

Exercise 55A

Draw each of the following angles as accurately as possible. Label each angle with its size and state its type.

1	30°	**2**	80°	**3**	50°	**4**	10°	**5**	110°
6	45°	**7**	85°	**8**	135°	**9**	67°	**10**	150°
11	240°	**12**	119°	**13**	225°	**14**	52°	**15**	254°
16	340°	**17**	170°	**18**	210°	**19**	123°	**20**	173°
21	28°	**22**	197°	**23**	160°	**24**	315°	**25**	144°
26	220°	**27**	180°	**28**	350°	**29**	130°	**30**	266°

Exercise 55B

Draw each of the following angles as accurately as possible. Label each angle with its size and state its type.

1	40°	**2**	15°	**3**	60°	**4**	90°	**5**	25°
6	75°	**7**	102°	**8**	120°	**9**	210°	**10**	300°
11	235°	**12**	140°	**13**	74°	**14**	95°	**15**	31°
16	105°	**17**	250°	**18**	189°	**19**	335°	**20**	270°
21	155°	**22**	55°	**23**	128°	**24**	275°	**25**	320°
26	200°	**27**	88°	**28**	236°	**29**	162°	**30**	290°

56/ ANGLES AT A POINT AND ON A STRAIGHT LINE

The angles at a point add up to 360°.
The total of the angles on a straight line is 180°.

EXAMPLE

▶ Calculate the angle marked *e*.

$90° + 45° + 110° + 60° = 305°$
$360° - 305° = 55°$
$e = 55°$

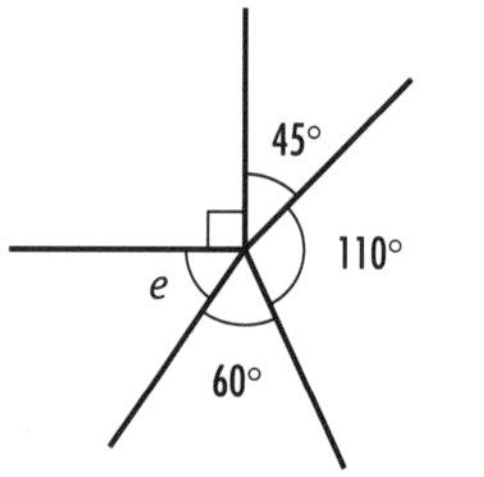

EXAMPLE

▶ Calculate the angle marked *f*.

$80° + 62° = 142°$
$180° - 142° = 38°$
$f = 38°$

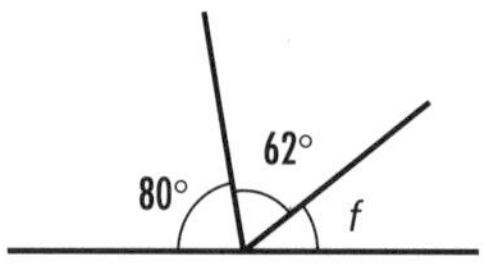

Exercise 56A

Calculate the size of each of the unknown angles marked with a letter in the diagrams.

1

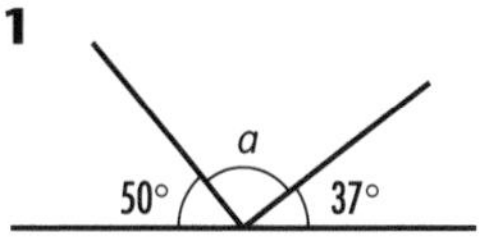

2

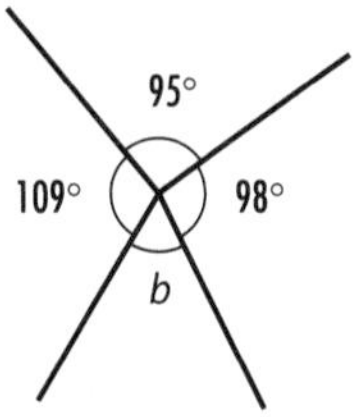

3

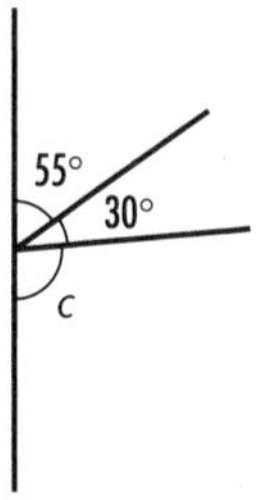

4

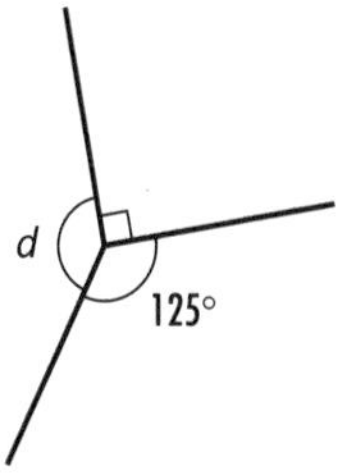

5

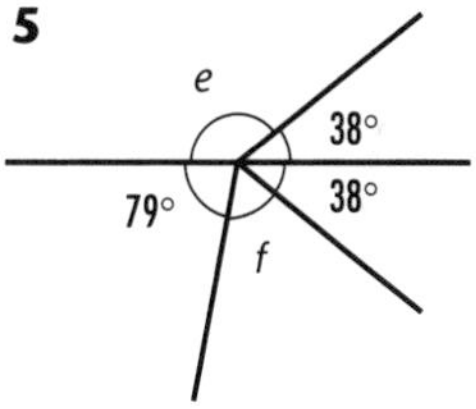

6

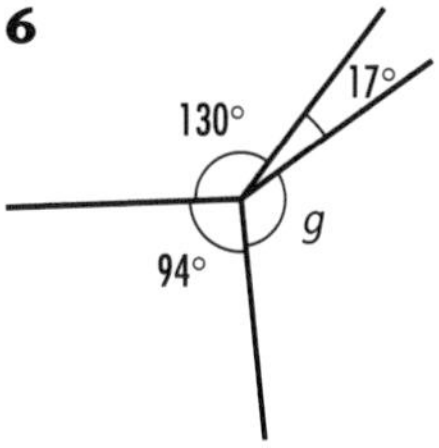

7

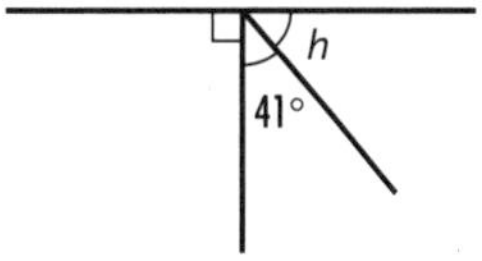

8

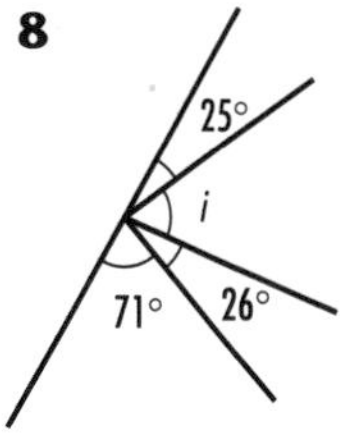

9

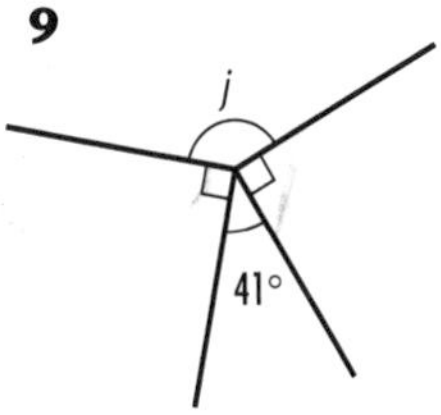

10

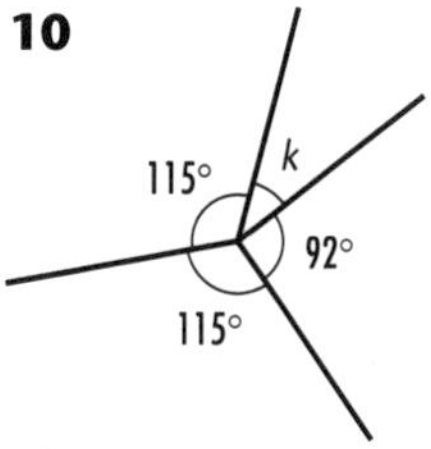

11

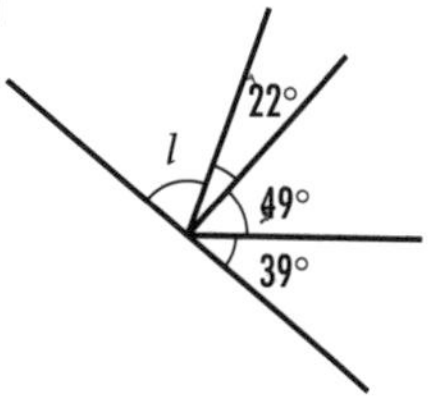

12

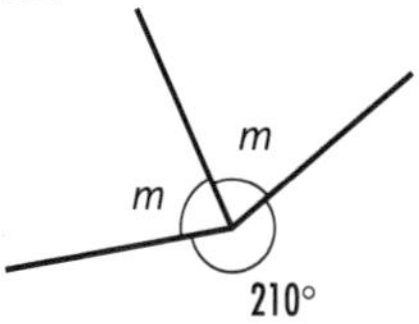

Exercise 56B

Calculate the size of each of the unknown angles marked with a letter in the diagrams.

1

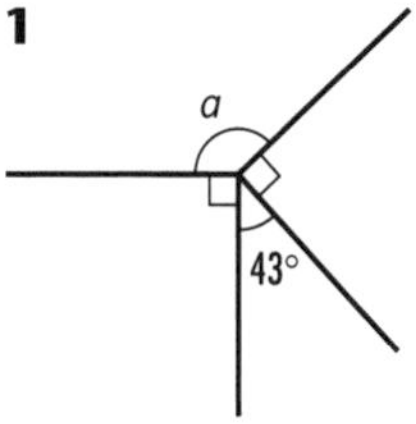

2

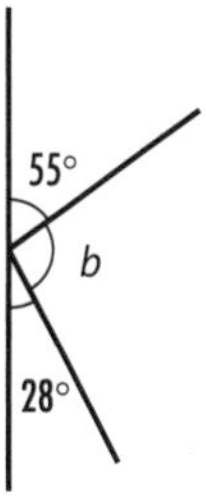

3

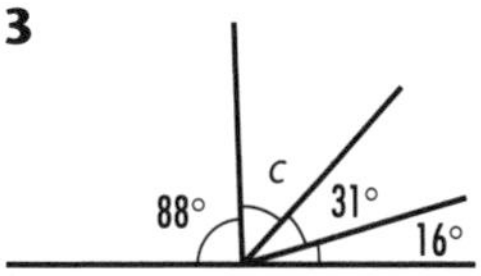

4

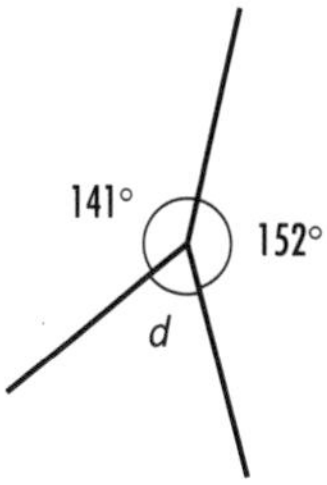

5

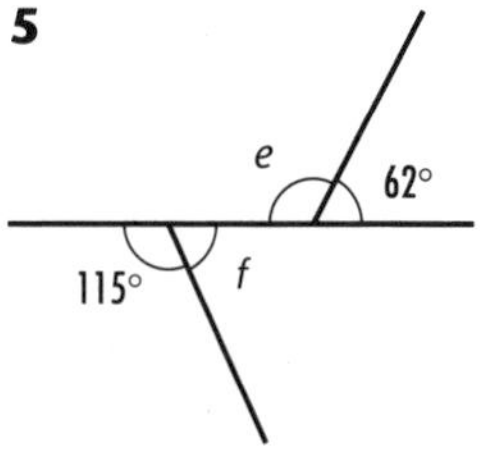

6

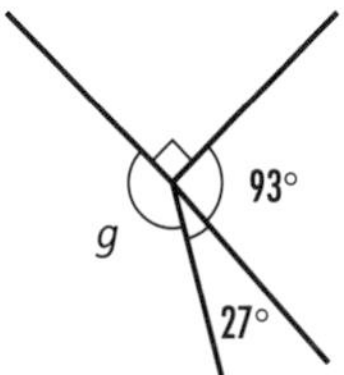

7

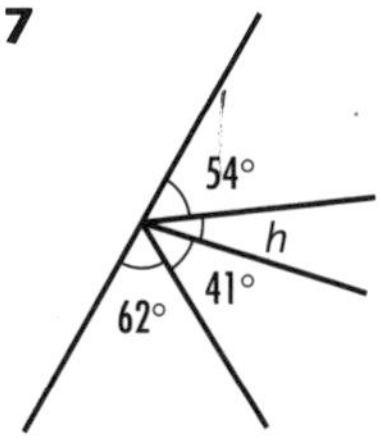

8

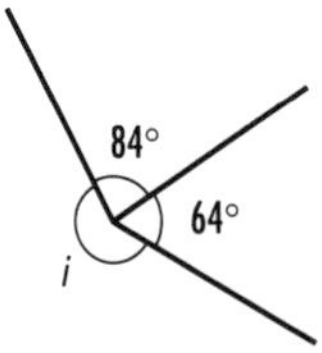

9

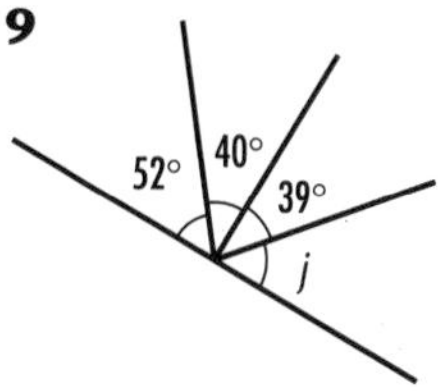

10

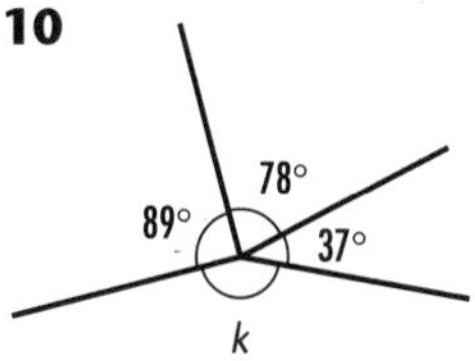

11

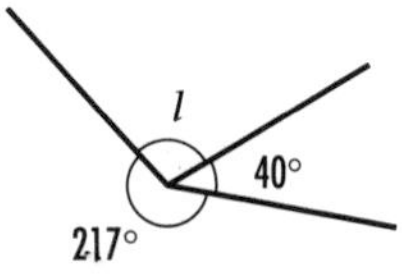

12

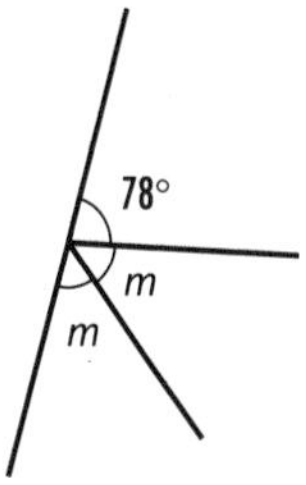

57/ FINDING THE UNKNOWN ANGLE IN A TRIANGLE

The sum of the angles in a triangle is 180°.
If two of the angles of a triangle are known then the third angle can be calculated by making the total 180°.

EXAMPLE

▶ Find the angle marked *a* in the diagram.

$35° + 57° = 92°$
$180° - 92° = 88°$
$a = 88°$

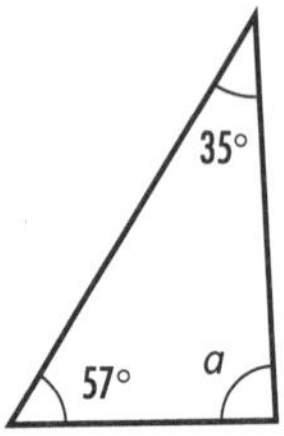

EXAMPLE

▶ Find the angles marked *b* and *c* in the diagram.

The sides are marked, which indicates that they are equal in length (the triangle is isosceles).
So $b = 42°$
$c = 180° - 42° - 42° = 96°$

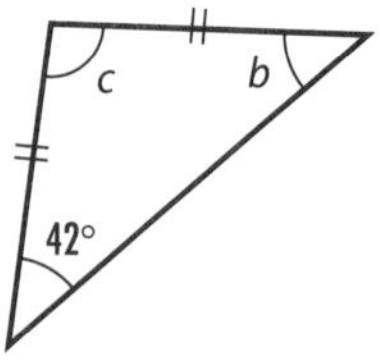

Exercise 57A

Calculate the size of each of the unknown angles marked with a letter in the diagrams.

1

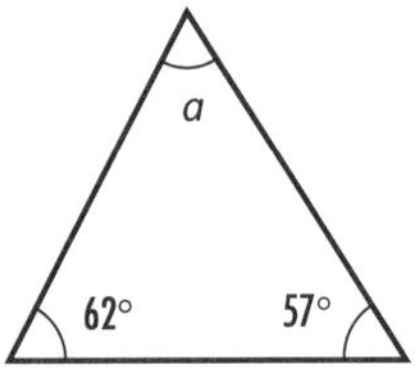

2

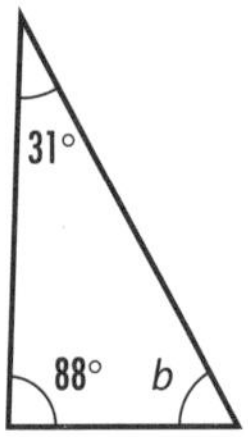

3

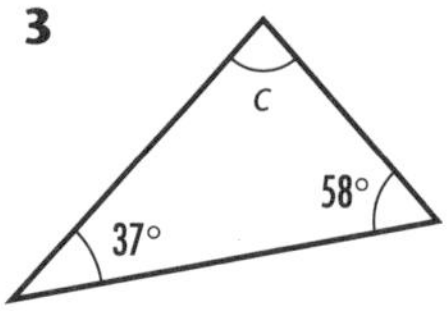

4

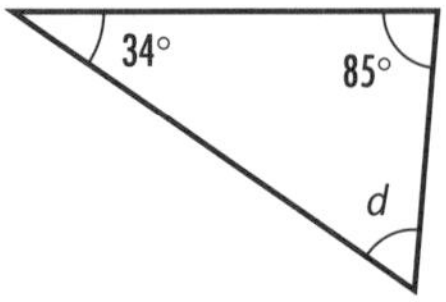

5

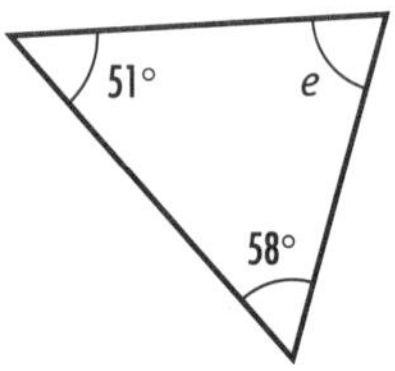

6

7

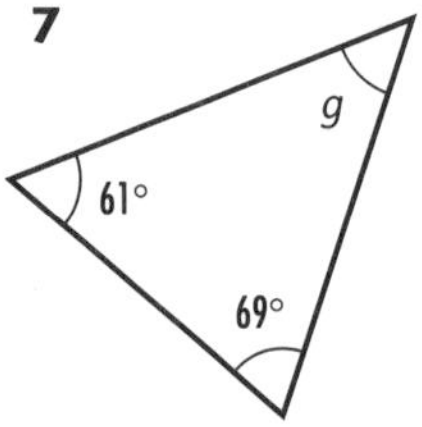

8

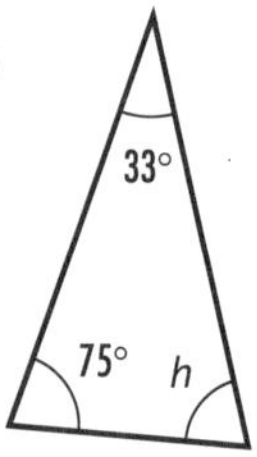

9

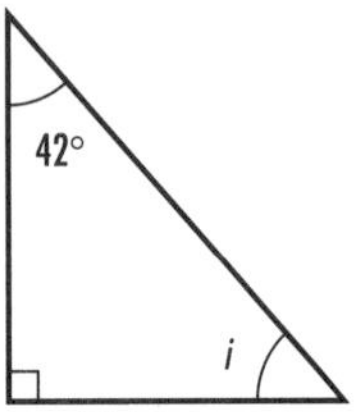

10

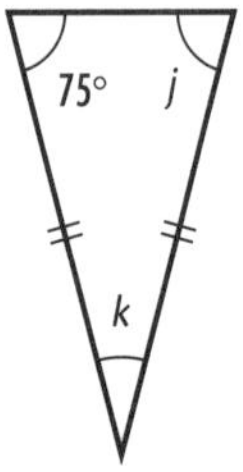

11

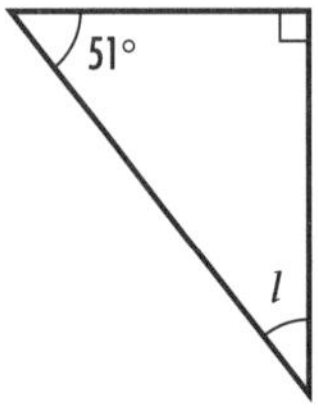

12

Exercise 57B

Calculate the size of each of the unknown angles marked with a letter in the diagrams.

1

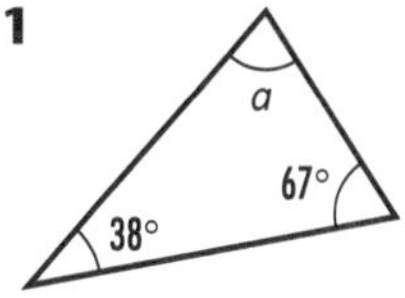

2

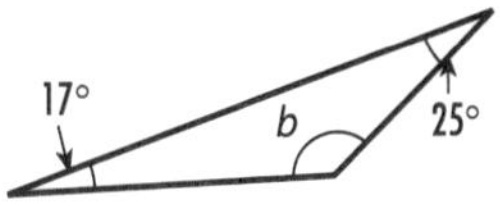

3

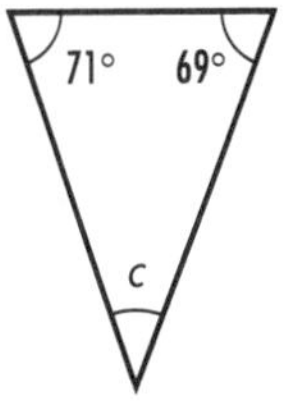

4

5

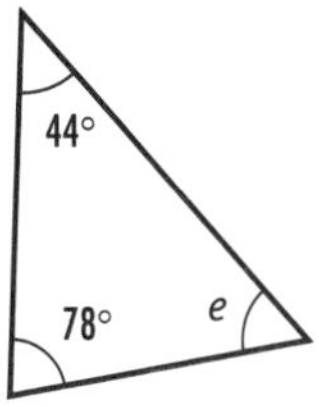

6

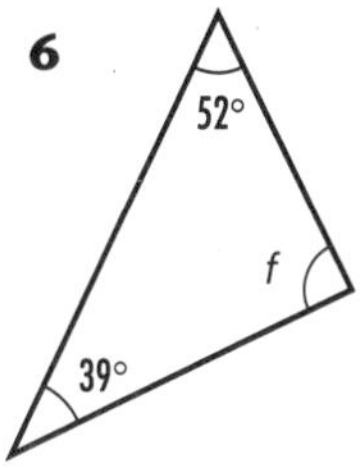

7

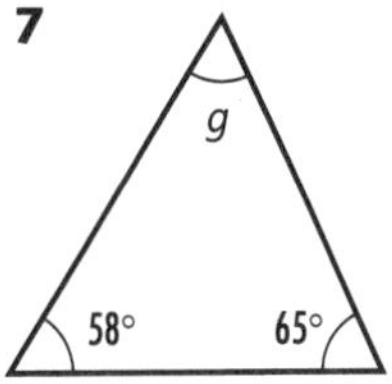

8

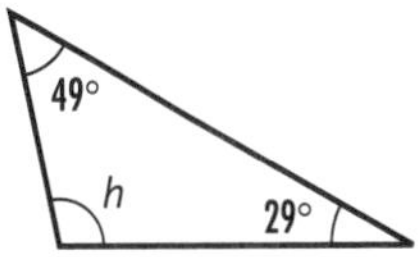

9

10

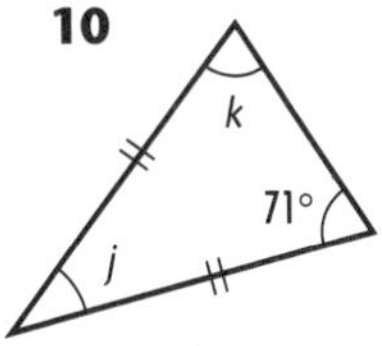

11

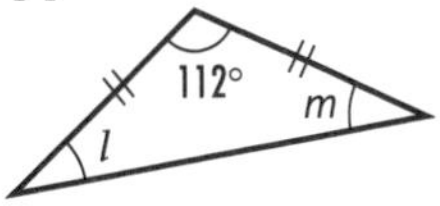

12

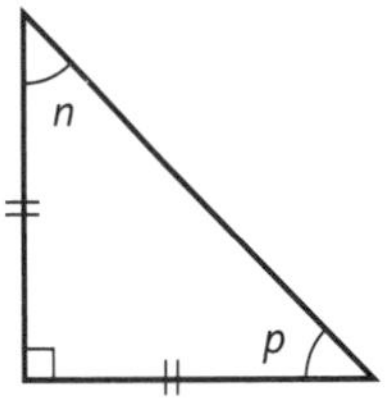

58/ SUM OF THE ANGLES IN A QUADRILATERAL

A quadrilateral is any shape with four straight sides. The angles in a quadrilateral add up to 360°.

EXAMPLE

▶ Calculate the angle marked *g*.

$58° + 115° + 75° = 248°$

$360° - 248° = 112°$

$g = 112°$

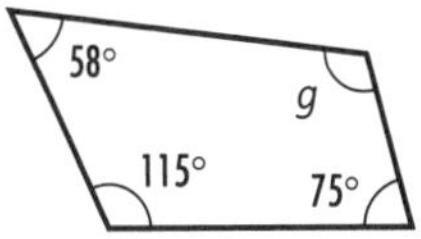

Exercise 58A

Calculate the size of the unknown angles marked with letters in the diagrams. The diagrams are not drawn to scale.

1

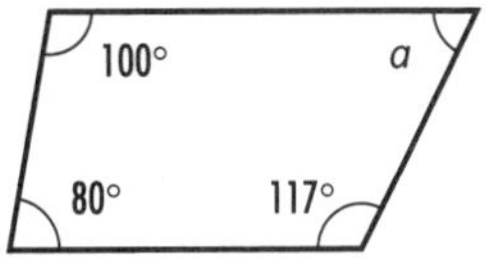

2

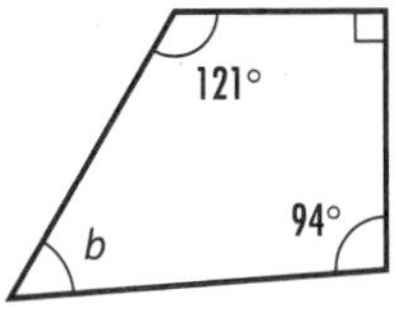

3

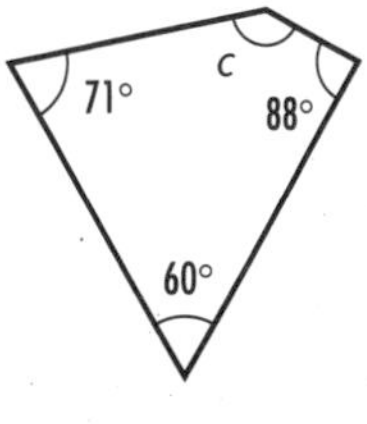

4

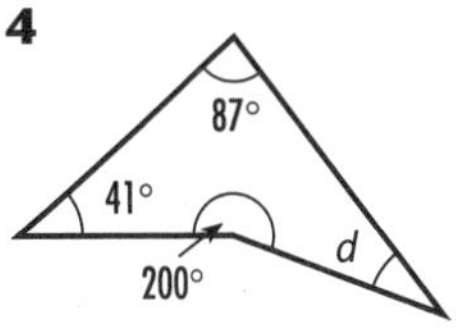

5

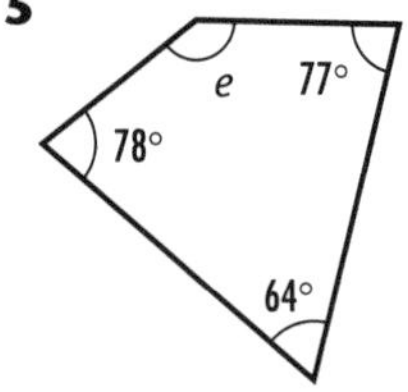

6

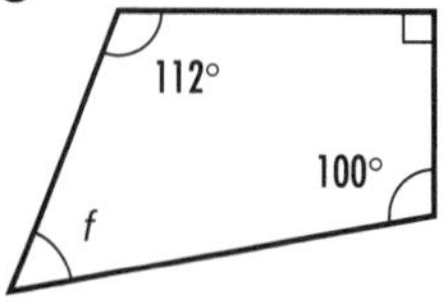

7

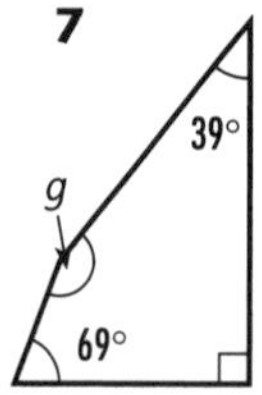

8

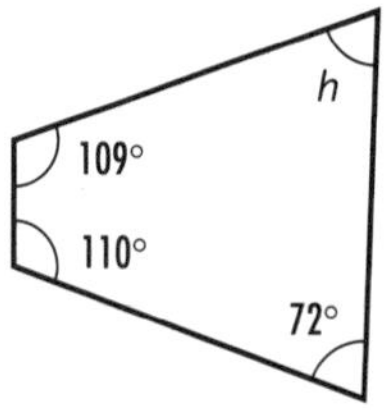

9

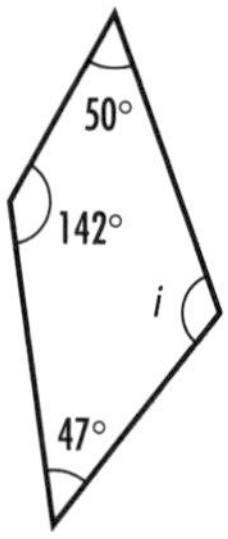

10

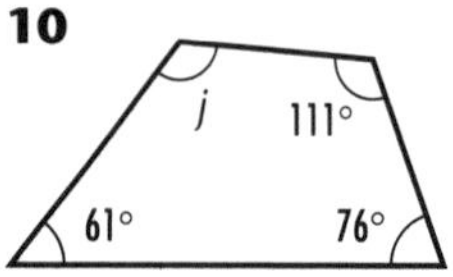

11

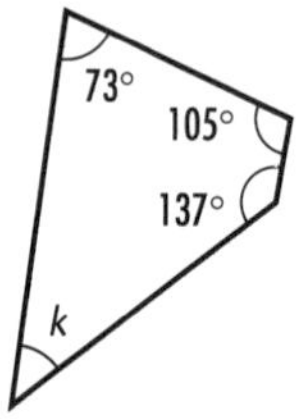

12

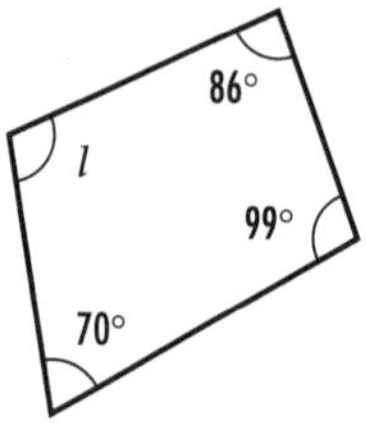

Exercise 58B

Calculate the size of the unknown angles marked with letters in the diagrams. The diagrams are not drawn to scale.

1

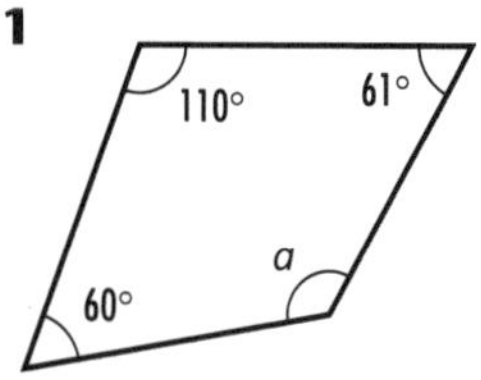

2

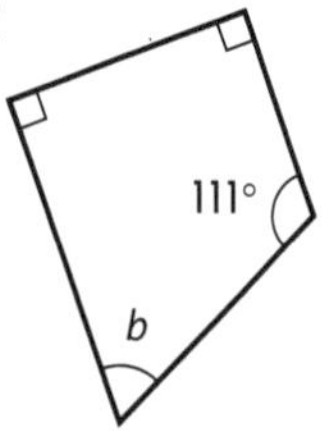

3

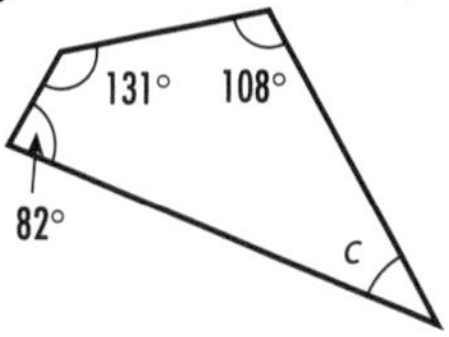

4

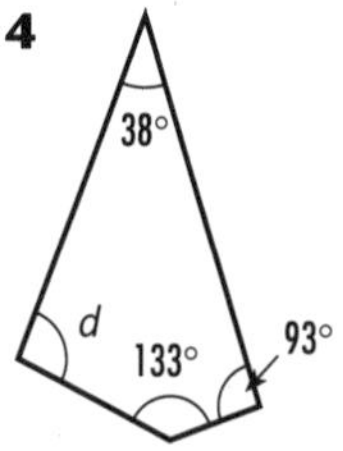

5

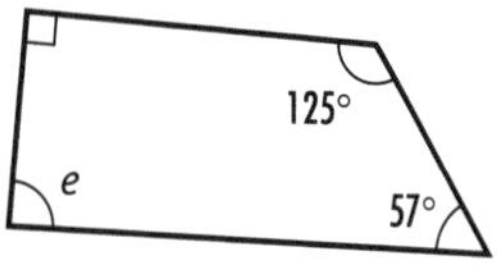

6

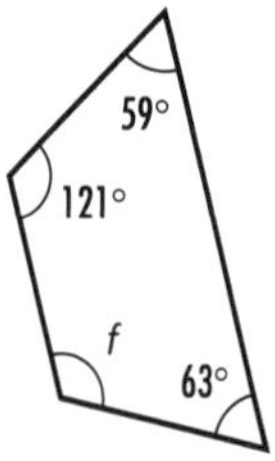

7

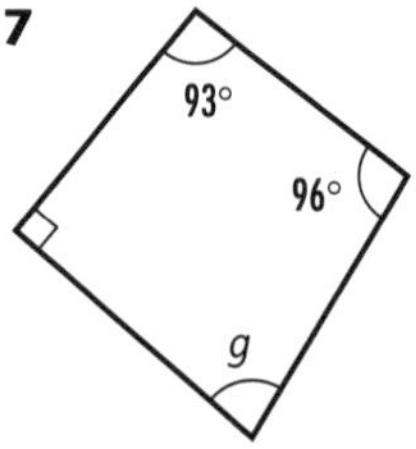

8

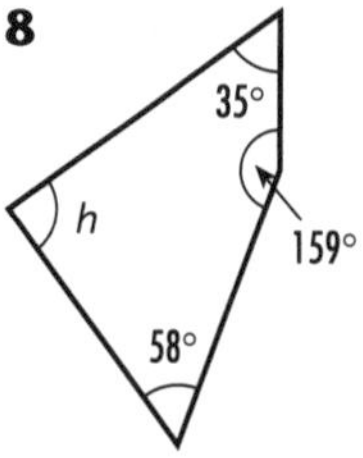

9

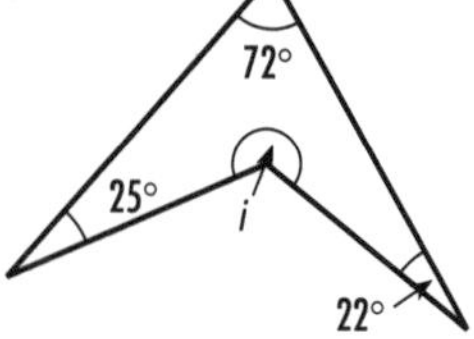

10

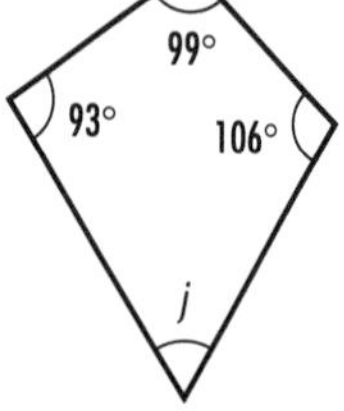

11

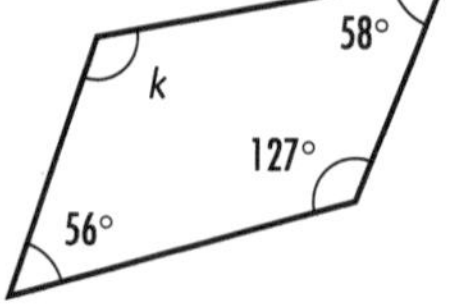

12

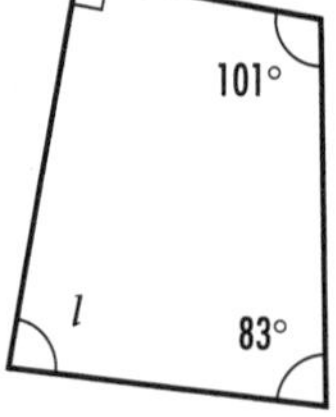

59/ ANGLES ON PARALLEL LINES

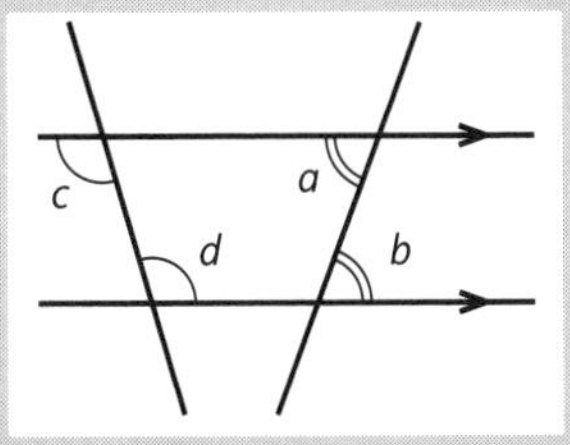

Alternate angles (often called **Z angles**) are equal.
a and *b* are alternate angles: $a = b$
c and *d* are alternate angles: $c = d$

Corresponding angles (often called **F angles**) are equal.
e and *f* are corresponding angles: $e = f$
g and *h* are corresponding angles: $g = h$

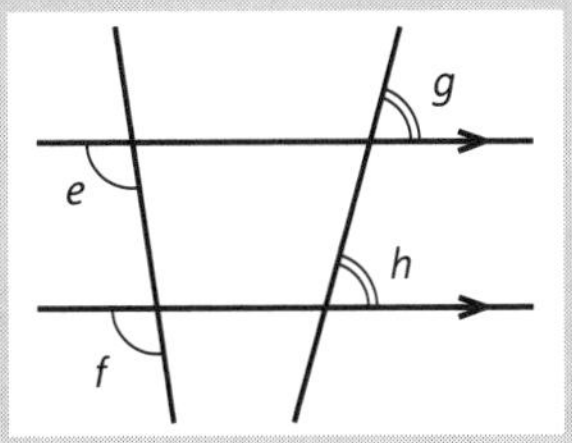

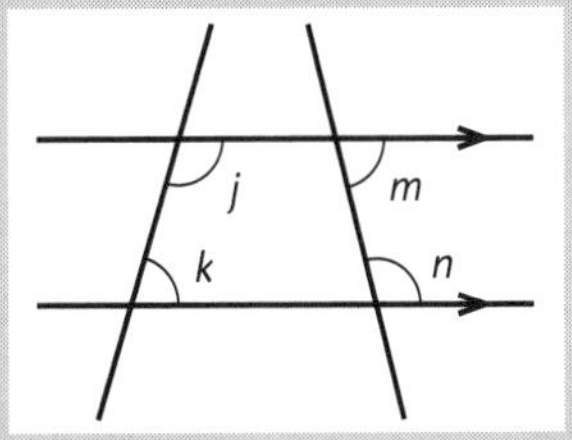

Supplementary angles (often called **allied angles**) are a pair of angles that add up to 180°. They are *not* equal in size (unless both are 90°).
j and *k* are supplementary angles: $j + k = 180°$
m and *n* are supplementary angles: $m + n = 180°$

Vertically opposite angles are equal.
p and *q* are vertically opposite angles: $p = q$
r and *s* are vertically opposite angles: $r = s$

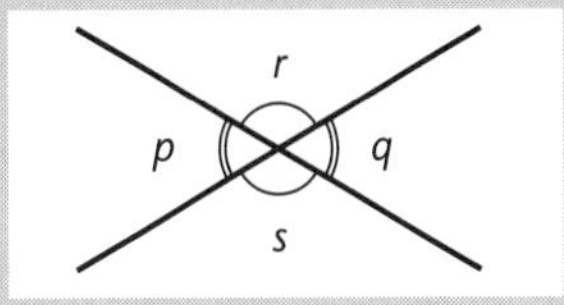

EXAMPLE

▶ State the sizes of angles *t*, *u* and *v*, giving reasons which refer to the angle marked 50°.

$t = 50°$ (alternate)
$u = 130°$ (supplementary)
$v = 50°$ (corresponding)

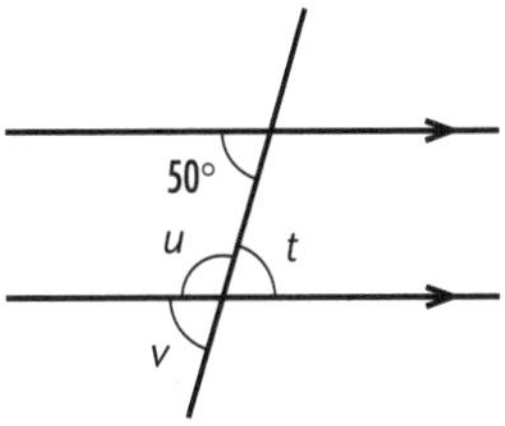

Exercise 59A

State the size of each of the angles marked with a letter, giving reasons which refer to the given angle.

1

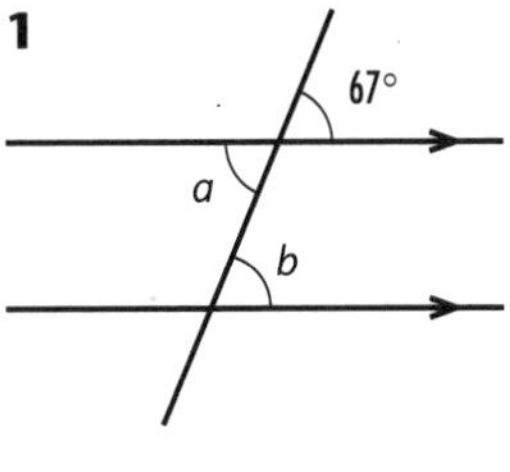

2

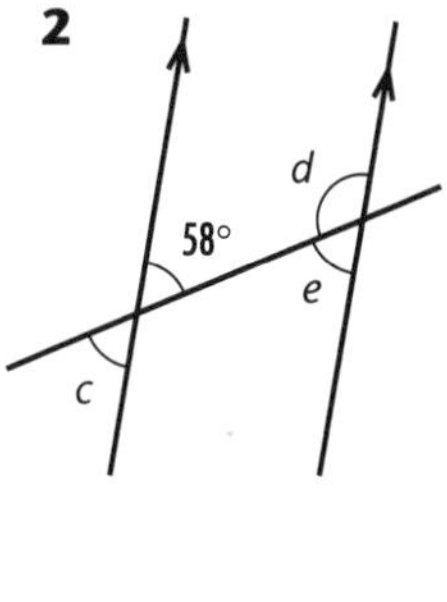

3

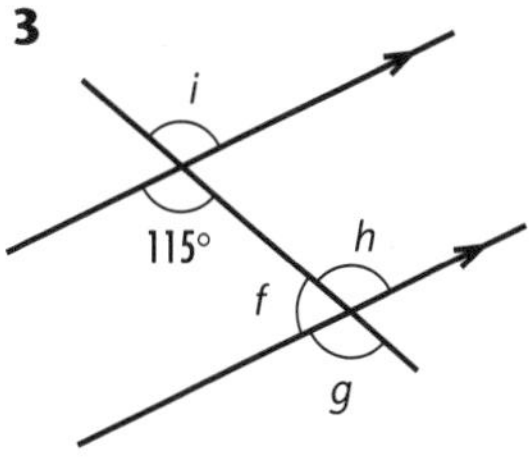

4

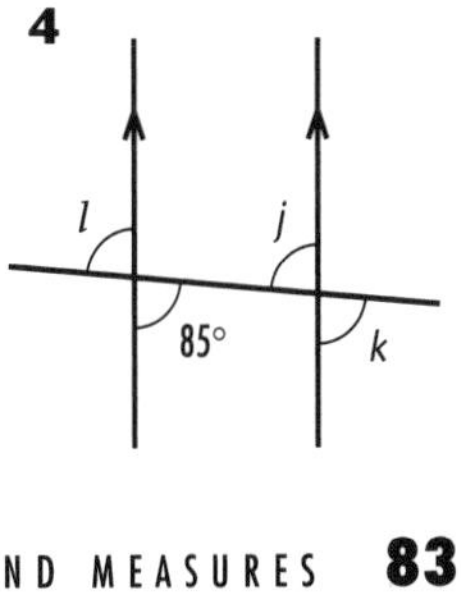

5

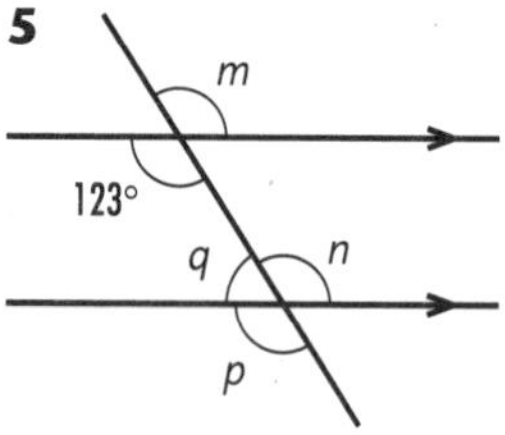

6

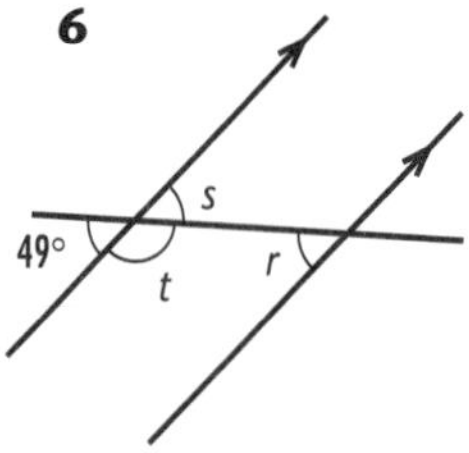

7

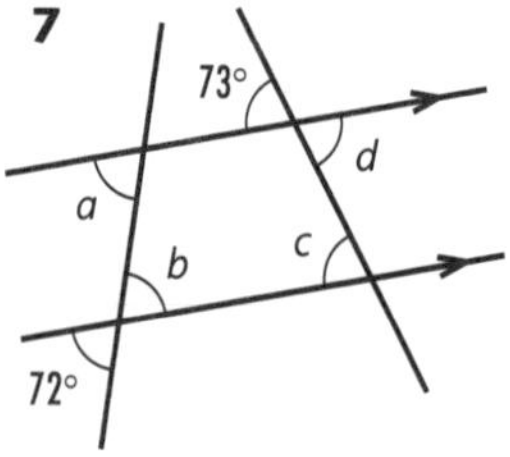

8

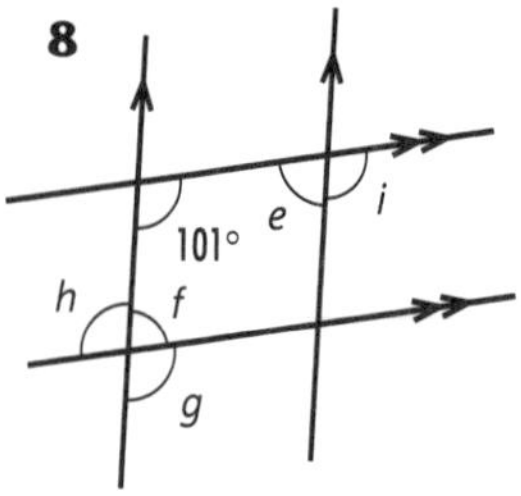

9

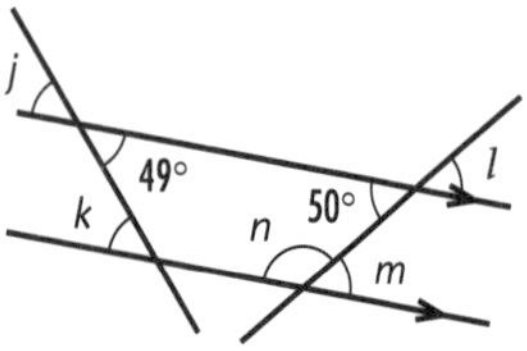

10

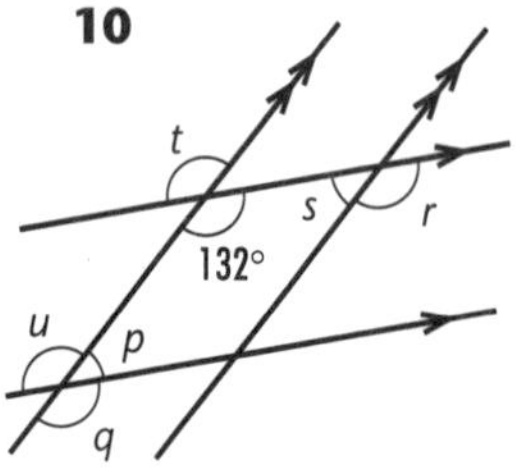

Exercise 59B

State the size of each of the angles marked with a letter, giving reasons which refer to the given angle.

1

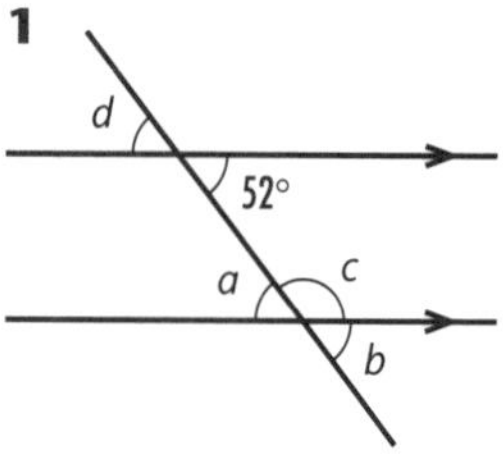

2

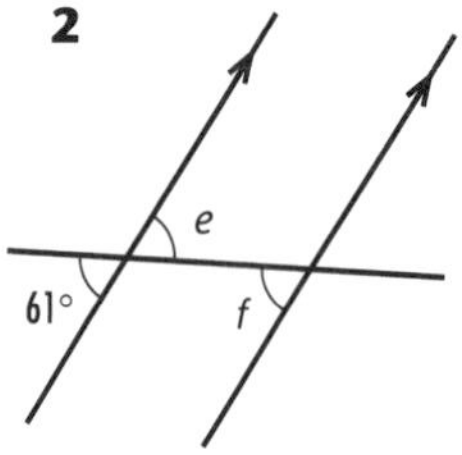

3

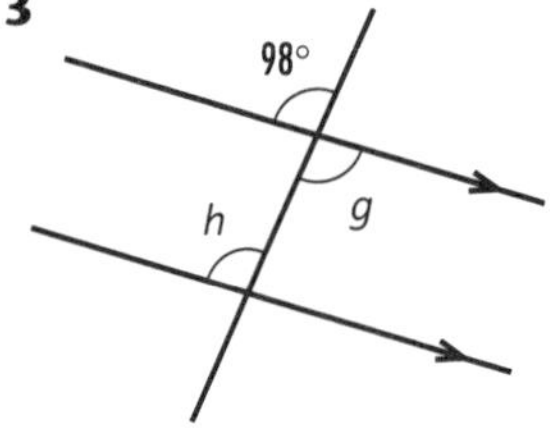

4

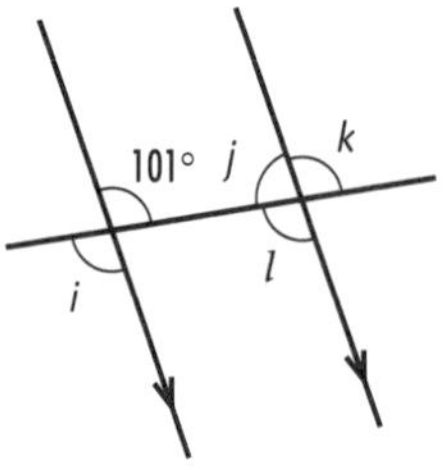

5

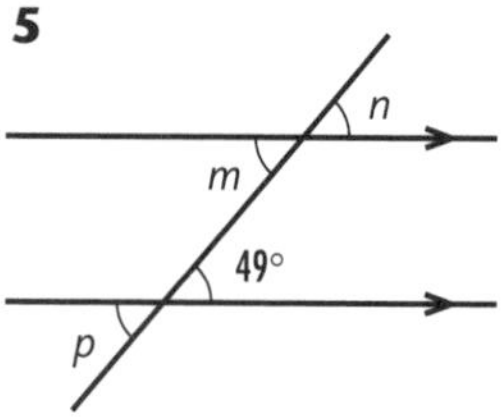

6

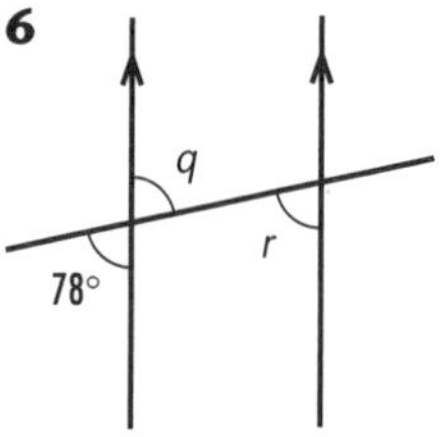

7

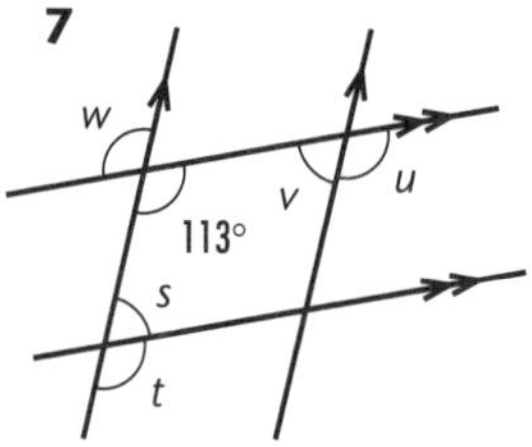

8

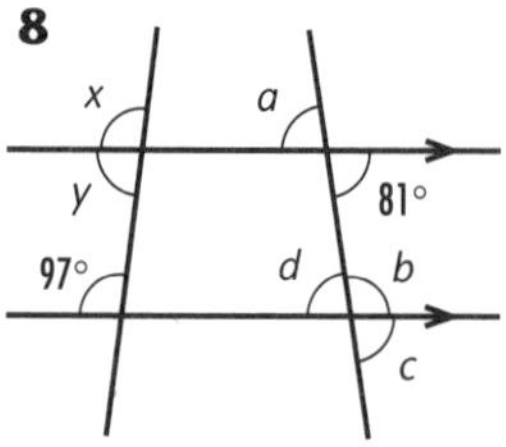

9

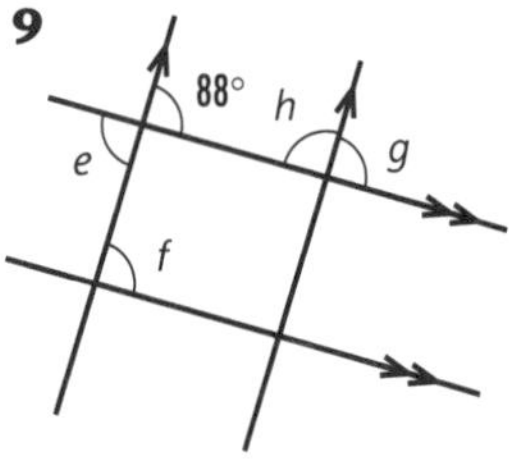

10

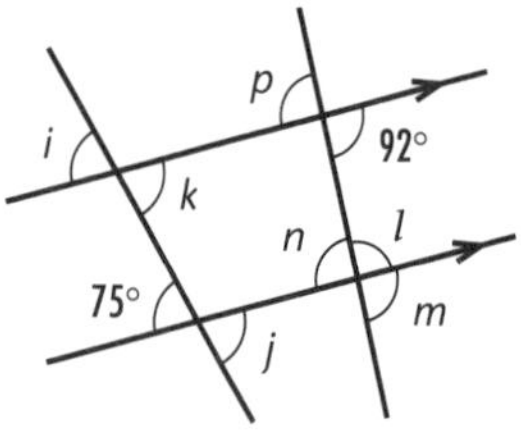

60/ RECOGNISING TRIANGLES, QUADRILATERALS AND POLYGONS

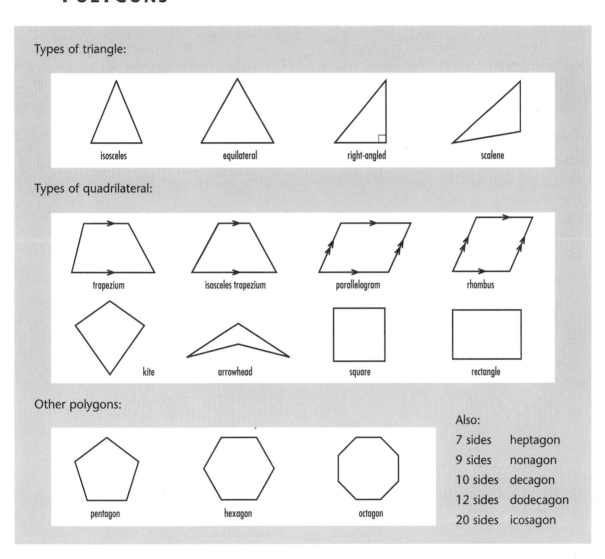

Types of triangle:

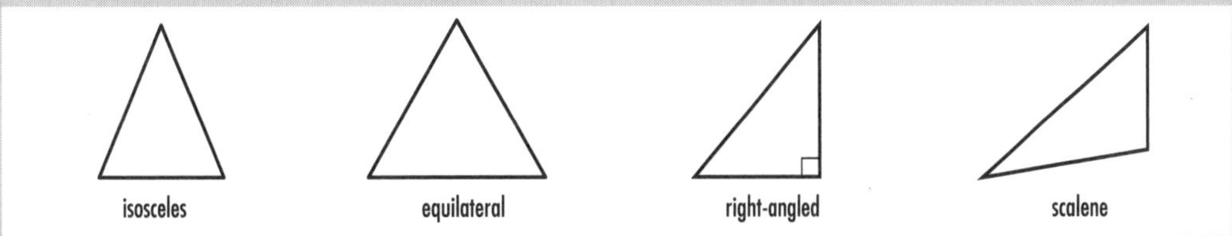

Types of quadrilateral:

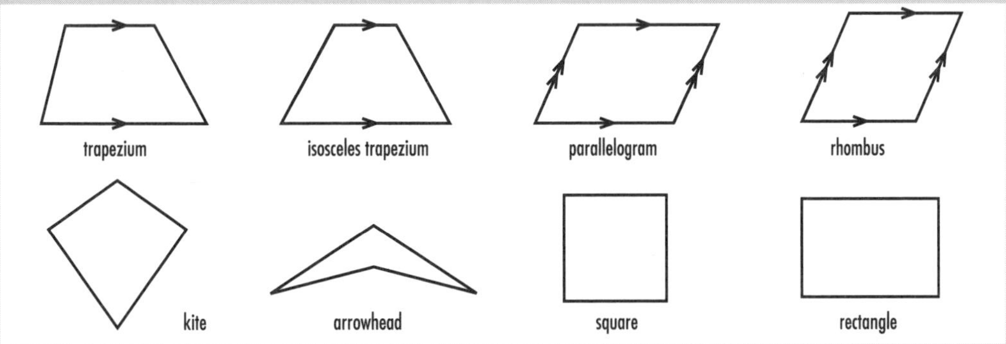

Other polygons:

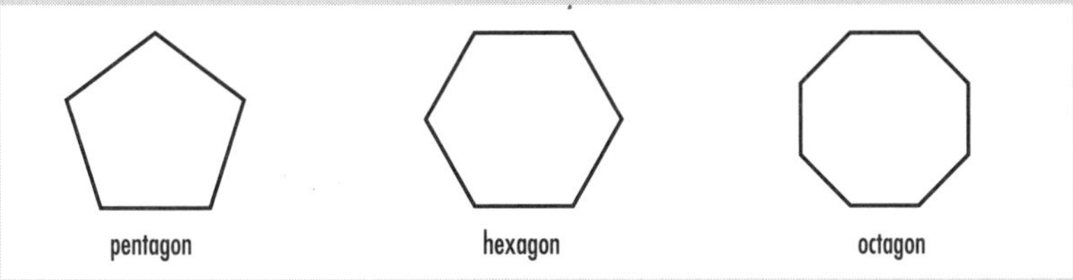

Also:

7 sides	heptagon
9 sides	nonagon
10 sides	decagon
12 sides	dodecagon
20 sides	icosagon

Exercise 60A

Choose the name from the list which *best* describes each of the shapes. None of the names is used more than once.

isosceles triangle   equilateral triangle   scalene triangle   right-angled triangle
rectangle   square   parallelogram   rhombus   trapezium   isosceles trapezium   kite
arrowhead   pentagon   hexagon   heptagon   octagon   nonagon   decagon

1

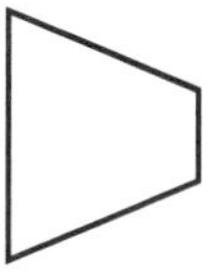

2

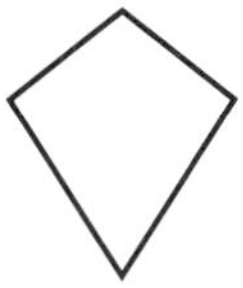

3

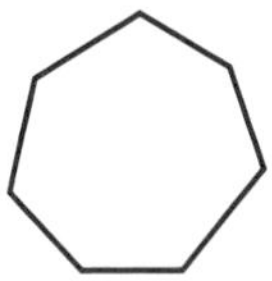

4

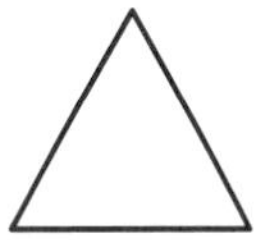

5

6

7

8

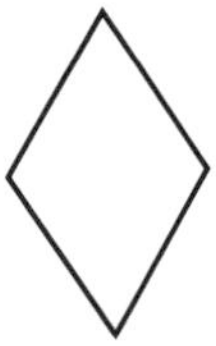

9

10

11

12

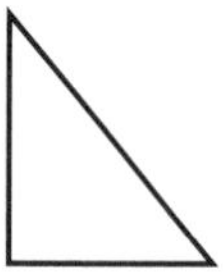

Exercise 60B

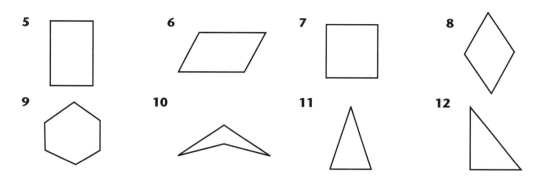

Choose the name from the list which *best* describes each of the shapes. None of the names is used more than once.

isosceles triangle equilateral triangle scalene triangle right-angled triangle
rectangle square parallelogram rhombus trapezium isosceles trapezium kite
arrowhead pentagon hexagon heptagon octagon nonagon decagon

1

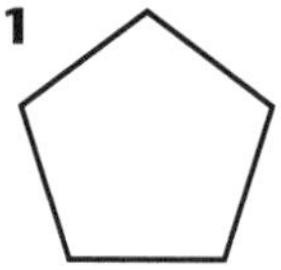

2

3

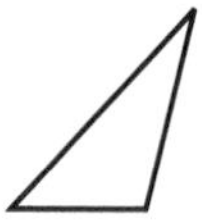

4

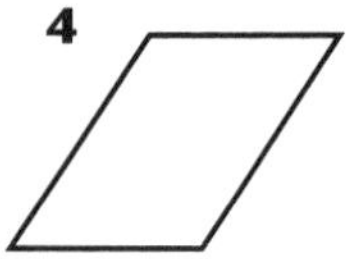

5

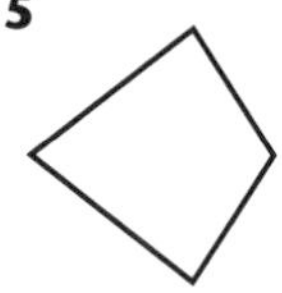

6

7

8

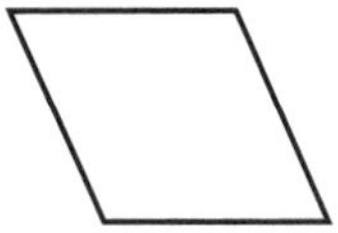

9

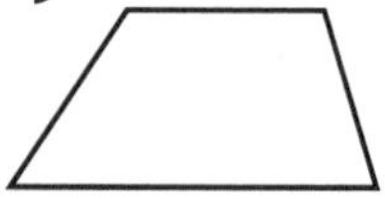

10

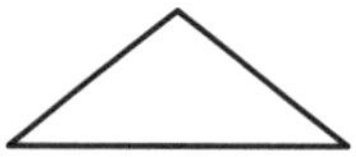

11

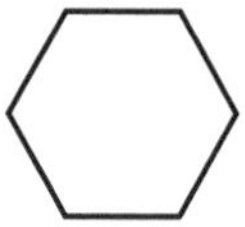

12

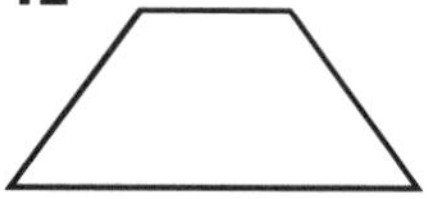

Exercise 60C

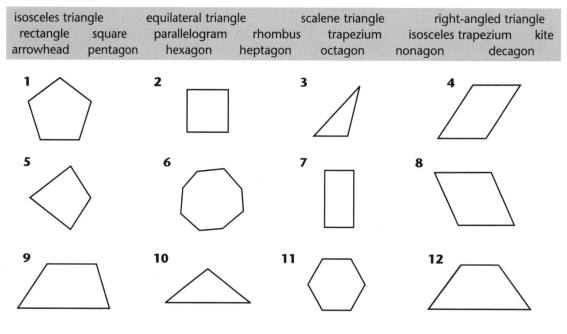

(This exercise is best attempted after the work on symmetry.)

Sketch the following shapes indicating parallel lines, equal lengths or equal angles.

1 Equilateral triangle
2 Kite
3 Isosceles triangle
4 Trapezium
5 Regular pentagon
6 Rhombus
7 Regular octagon
8 Parallelogram

In questions 9–12 give the *best* name for each shape described.

9 A quadrilateral with all sides equal but which does not necessarily have a right angle
10 A triangle with two sides that are equal in length
11 A quadrilateral with one line of symmetry and only one pair of parallel sides
12 A polygon with five sides

13 Is a rectangle also a parallelogram?
14 A square is a special rhombus. What makes it special?
15 Name a quadrilateral that has rotational symmetry but only has reflective symmetry in special cases.

Exercise 60D

(This exercise is best attempted after the work on symmetry.)

Sketch the following shapes indicating parallel lines, equal lengths or equal angles.

1 Right-angled triangle **2** Regular heptagon **3** Arrowhead **4** Rectangle
5 Scalene triangle **6** Square **7** Parallelogram **8** Regular hexagon

In questions 9–12 give the *best* name for each shape described.

9 A triangle with all sides of different length
10 A quadrilateral with only one pair of parallel sides
11 A quadrilateral with one axis of symmetry and a reflex angle
12 A polygon with six sides

13 Is a square a rhombus?
14 Name a quadrilateral with two pairs of parallel sides and a right angle
15 A square is a special case of a rectangle. What makes it special?

61/ ANGLES OF A REGULAR POLYGON

The **exterior angles** of a polygon add up to 360°.
A **regular** polygon has all its sides equal in size (and all its angles equal).
Each angle is $\frac{360}{n}$, where n is the number of sides of the polygon.

Each exterior angle in this regular octagon = 360° ÷ 8 = 45°.
Each pair of exterior and interior angles make a straight line (180°).
Interior angle = 180 – exterior angle
So, interior angle in the octagon = 180° – 45° = 135°

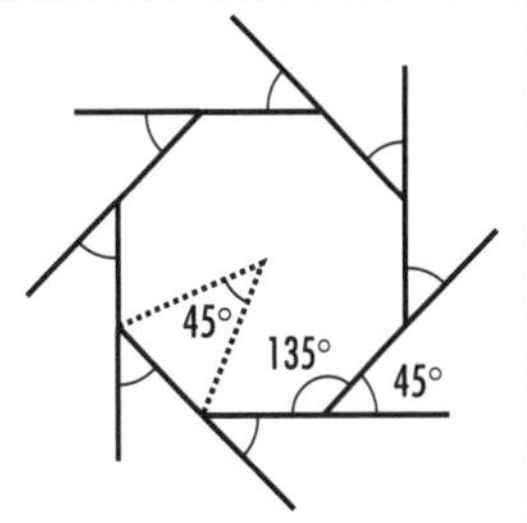

If a polygon is divided into triangles (from its centre), then the angle at the centre is the same as the exterior angle, that is $\frac{360°}{n}$.

EXAMPLE

▶ State the sizes of the angles marked *a*, *b* and *c*.

a = 360° ÷ 10 = 36°
b = 180° – 36° = 144°
c = 360° ÷ 10 = 36°

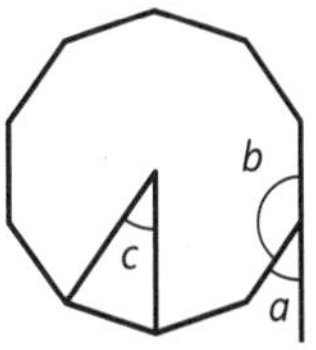

EXAMPLE

▶ A regular polygon has an interior angle of 135°. How many sides does it have?

Exterior angle = 180° – 135° = 45°

$$\frac{360°}{n} = 45°$$

$n = 8$

The polygon has 8 sides.

Exercise 61A

State the size of each unknown angle marked with a letter in the diagrams.

1

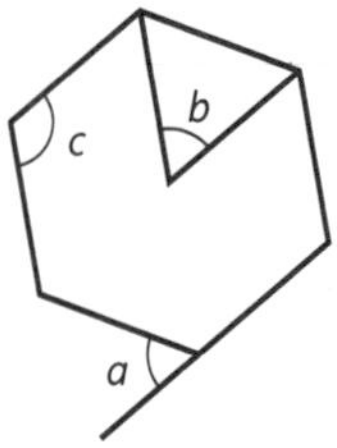

2

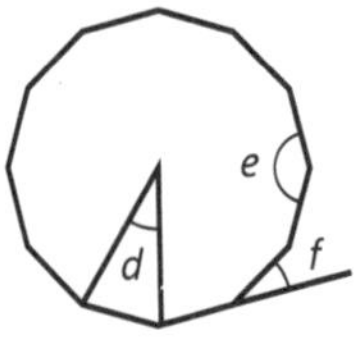

3

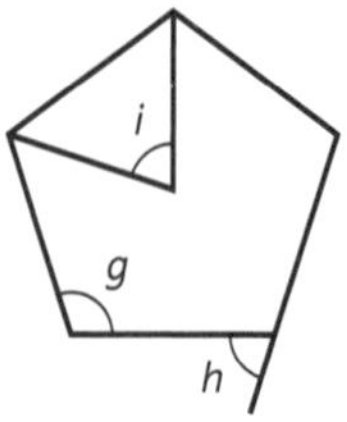

4

5 State (a) the exterior angle (b) the interior angle (c) the angle at the centre of a regular pentagon.

6 A regular polygon has an exterior angle of 20°. How many sides does it have and what is the size of each of its interior angles?

7 A regular polygon has an interior angle of 135°. What is the size of each of its exterior angles and how many sides does it have?

8 State (a) the exterior angle (b) the interior angle (c) the angle at the centre of a regular polygon with 15 sides.

9 A regular polygon has an interior angle of 144°. What is the size of the angle at its centre and how many sides does it have?

10 State (a) the exterior angle (b) the interior angle (c) the angle at the centre of a regular polygon with 20 sides.

Exercise 61B

State the size of each unknown angle marked with a letter in the diagrams.

1

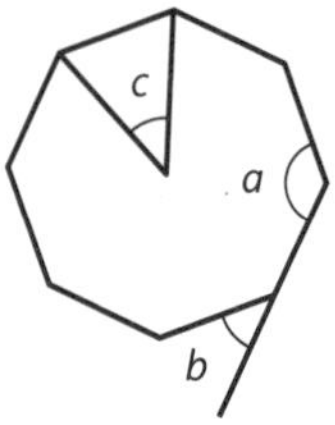

2

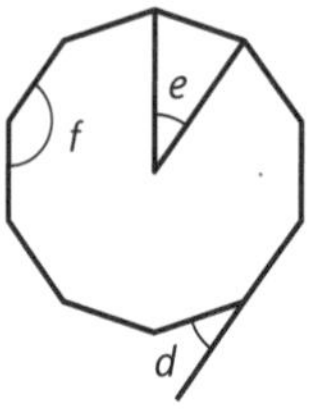

3

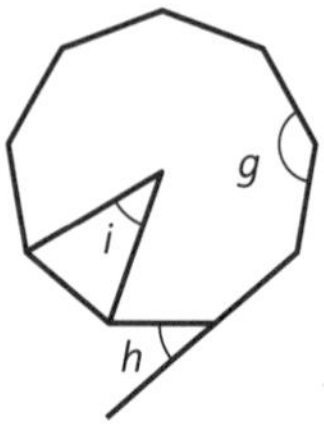

4

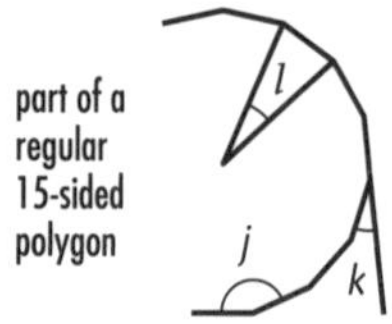

5 A regular polygon has an exterior angle of 15°. How many sides does it have and what is its interior angle?

6 State (a) the exterior angle (b) the interior angle (c) the angle at the centre of a regular octagon.

7 A regular polygon has an interior angle of 108°. What is its exterior angle and how many sides does it have?

8 State (a) the exterior angle (b) the interior angle (c) the angle at the centre of a regular polygon with 12 sides.

9 A regular polygon has an interior angle of 120°. What is the size of the angle at its centre and how many sides does it have?

10 State (a) the exterior angle (b) the interior angle (c) the angle at the centre of a regular polygon with 18 sides.

62/ FINDING UNKNOWN ANGLES IN VARIOUS SITUATIONS, WITH REASONS

In these exercises decide on the size of each of the unknown angles marked with a letter. Give a reason for each of your answers to show that you know why the angle is the size you have stated. You could choose from the following reasons:

Angles of a triangle	Angles on a straight line
Angles of a quadrilateral	Angles of a polygon
Angles at a point	Angles on parallel lines

Other information: for example, the base angles of an isosceles triangle are equal.

EXAMPLE

▶ The marked lengths are equal. State the size of each of the angles *a*, *b* and *c*.

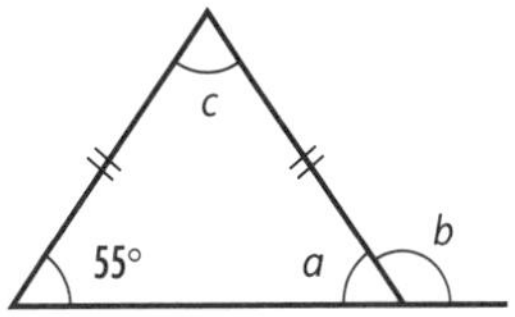

$a = 55°$ (base angles of an isosceles triangle)
$b = 180° - 55° = 125°$ (angles on a straight line)
$c = 180° - 55° - 55° = 70°$ (angles of a triangle)

EXAMPLE

▶ State the size of each of the angles *d*, *e* and *f*.

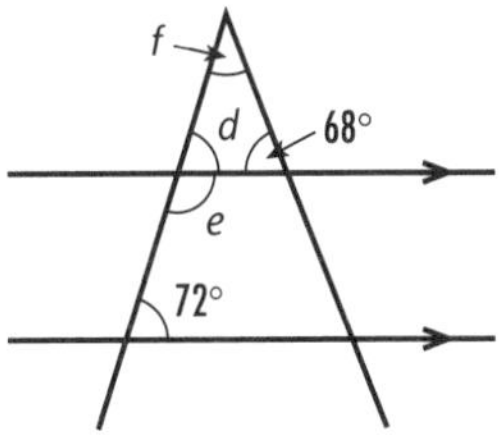

$d = 72°$ (corresponding angles)
$e = 180° - 72° = 108°$ (supplementary angles)
$f = 180° - 72° - 68° = 40°$ (angles in a triangle)

Exercise 62A

State, giving reasons, the size of each unknown angle marked with a letter in the diagrams.

1

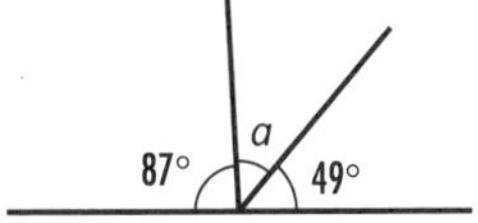

2

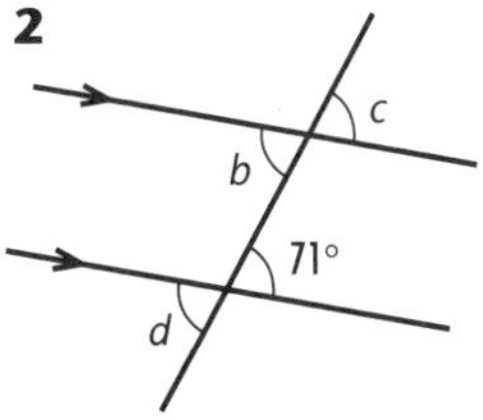

3

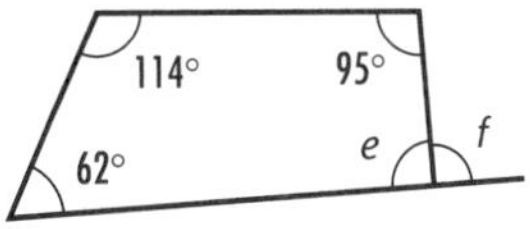

4

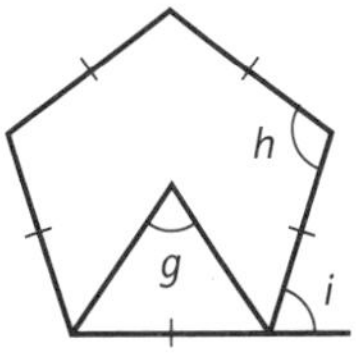

5

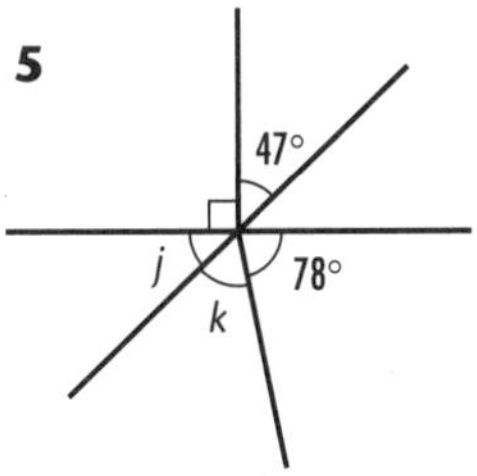

6

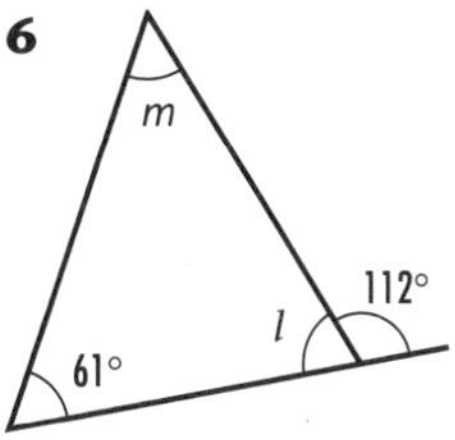

7

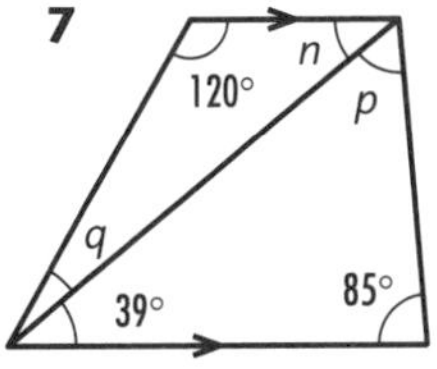

8

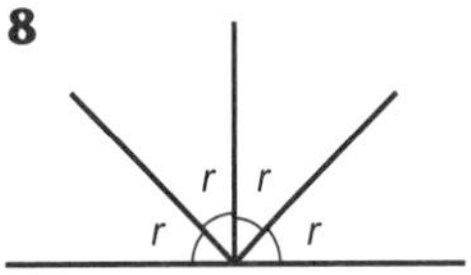

9

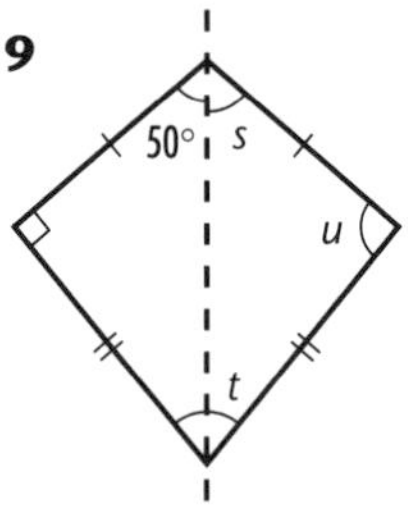

10

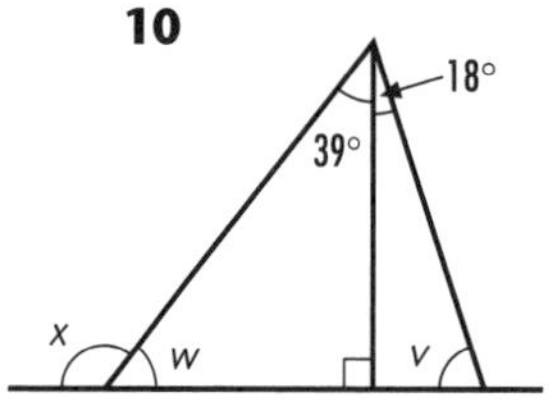

11

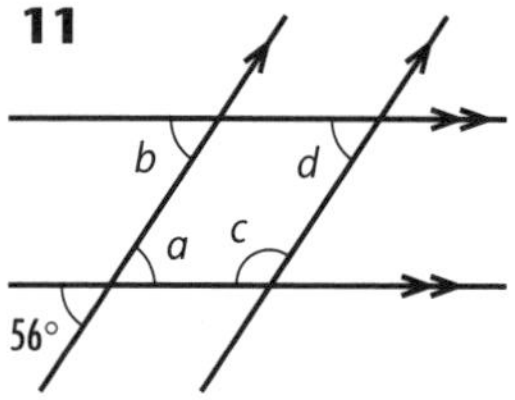

12

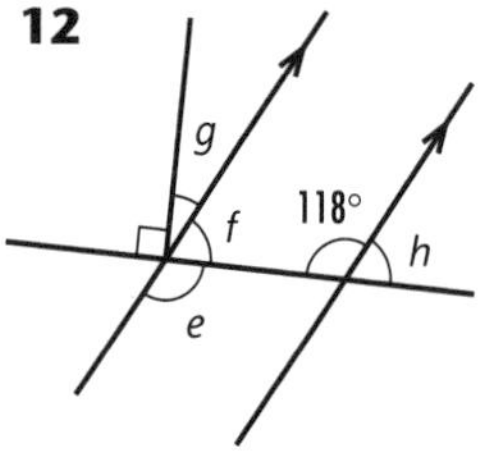

Exercise 62B

State, giving reasons, the size of each unknown angle marked with a letter in the diagrams.

1

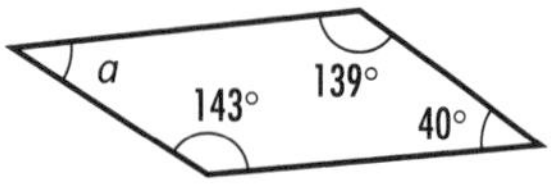

2

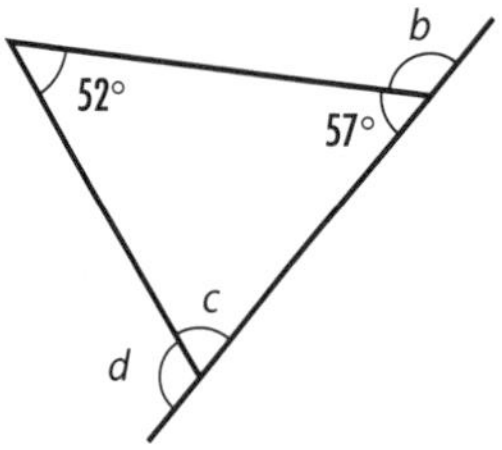

3

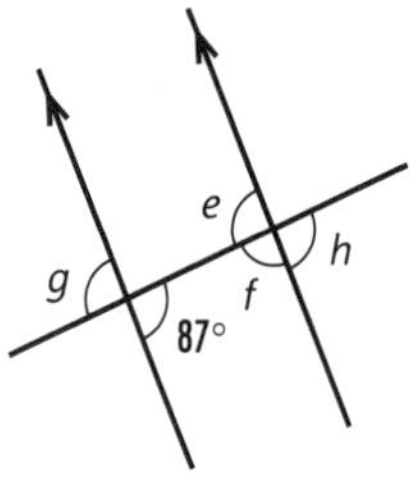

4

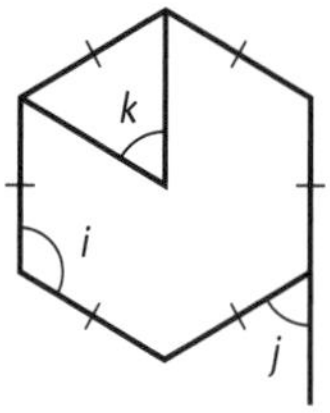

5

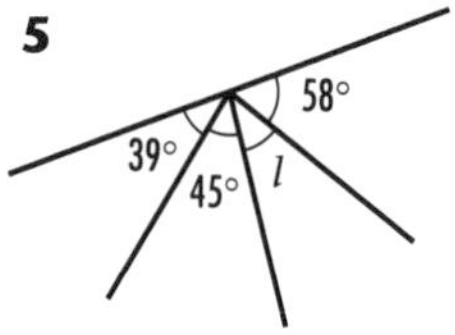

6

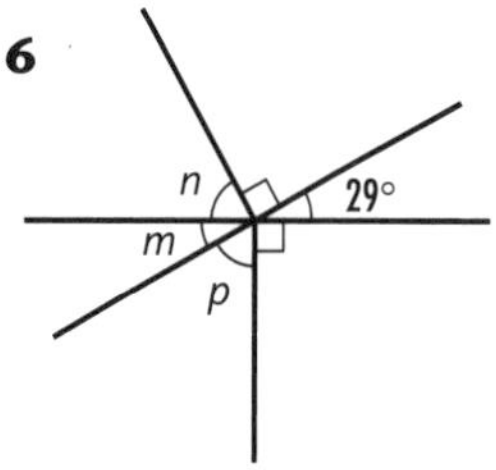

7

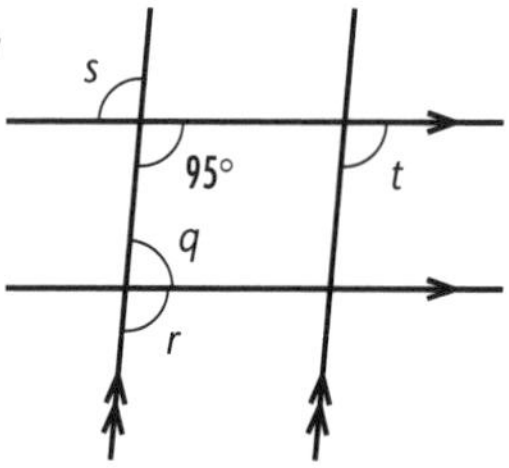

8

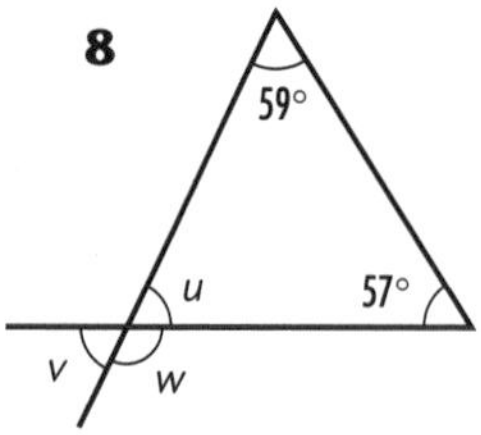

9

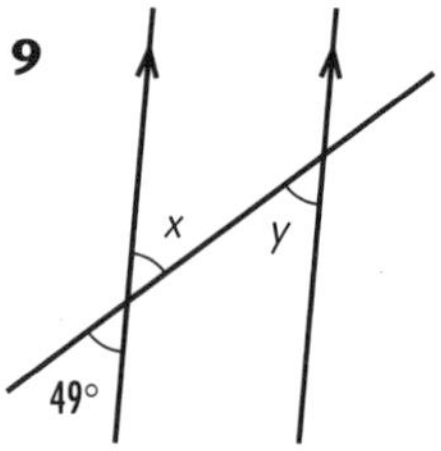

10

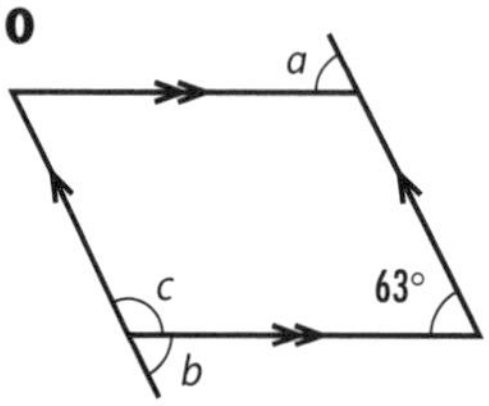

11

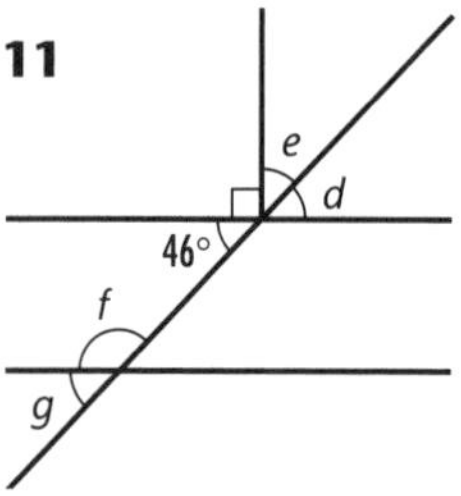

12

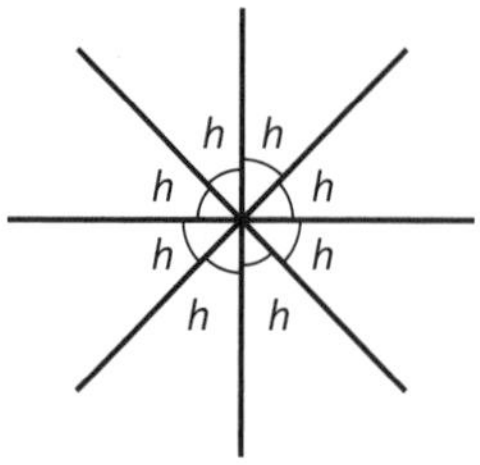

63/ RECOGNISING SYMMETRY

This shape has **reflective symmetry**.
The object is reflected to give the **image** on the other side of the **axis of reflection** (also called the mirror line or line of symmetry).

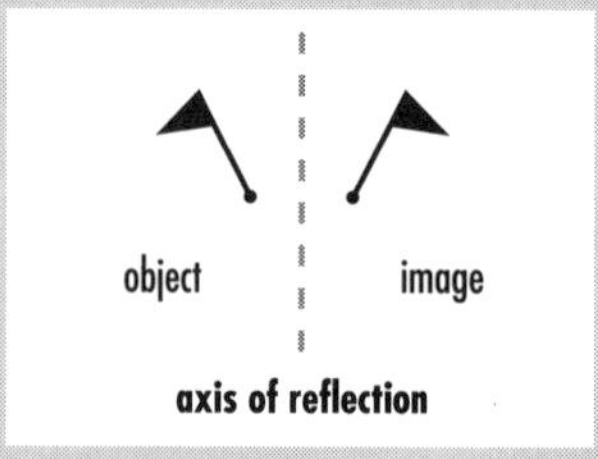

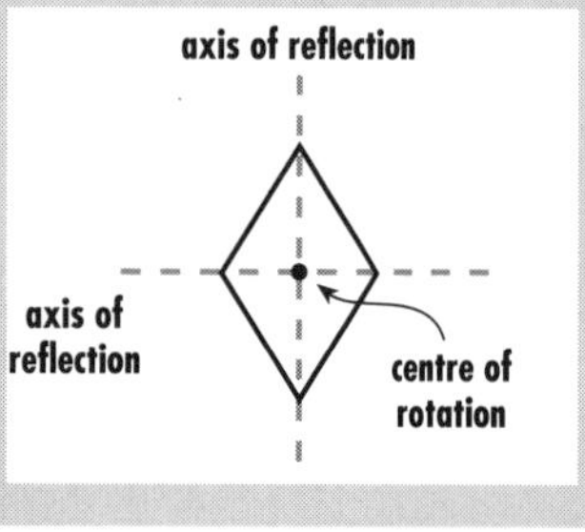

This shape has two axes of reflection. It also has **rotational symmetry** of **order 2**. That is, it can be turned about the **centre of rotation** and the shape will fit into itself in two different ways.

EXAMPLE

▶ 

Copy the diagram carefully and show any axes of reflection and any centre of rotation. If there is rotational symmetry, state the order.

The parallelogram has no reflective symmetry. (Many people think it has at first.) It has rotational symmetry of order 2.

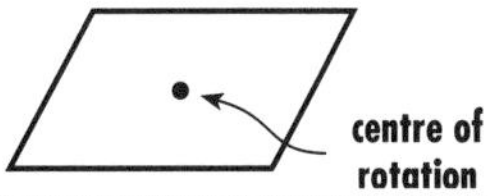

Exercise 63A

Draw an accurate diagram of each shape; show any axes of reflection and any centre of rotation. If there is rotational symmetry, state the order.

1 An isosceles triangle
2 A rhombus
3 An isosceles trapezium
4 A regular hexagon
5 A rectangle
6 A scalene triangle
7 A kite
8 A regular pentagon

Copy each diagram carefully; show any axes of reflection and any centre of rotation. If there is rotational symmetry, state the order.

9
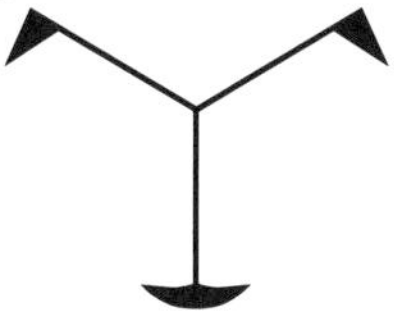

10
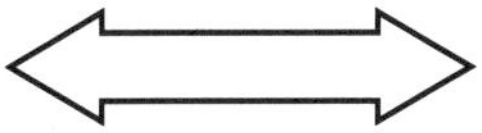

11
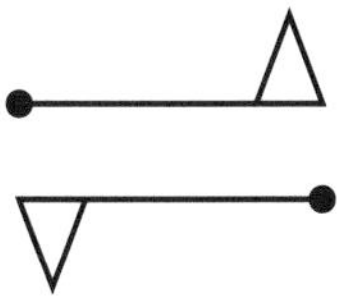

12
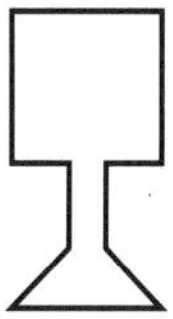

13

14
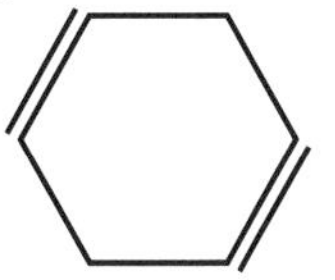

15
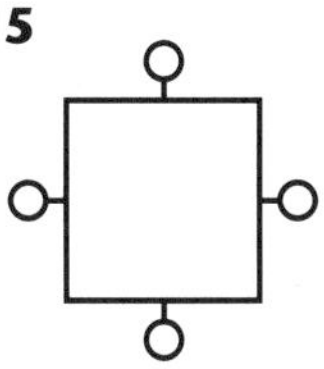

16
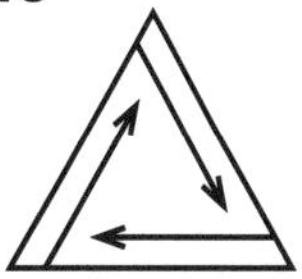

Exercise 63B

Draw an accurate diagram of each shape; show any axes of reflection and any centre of rotation. If there is rotational symmetry, state the order.

1 A square
2 An equilateral triangle
3 A trapezium (*not* an isosceles trapezium)
4 A regular octagon
5 A parallelogram
6 An arrowhead
7 A right-angled isosceles triangle
8 A regular heptagon

Copy each diagram carefully; show any axes of reflection and any centre of rotation. If there is rotational symmetry, state the order.

9

10

11
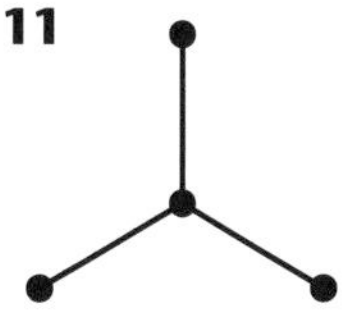

12
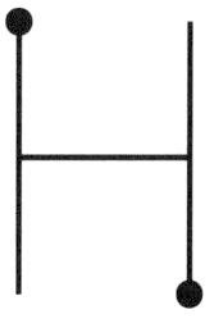

13

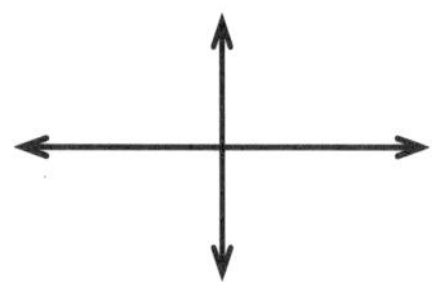

14

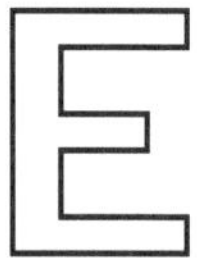

15

16

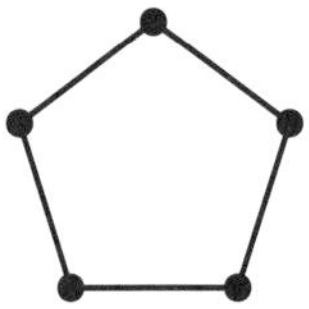

64/ **ROTATIONS AND REFLECTIONS**

In these questions you will be given an object and you will be required to draw the image after reflection or rotation.

EXAMPLE

► (a) Reflect the object in the axis of reflection. Label the image A.
(b) Rotate the object through 90° anticlockwise about the centre of rotation X. Label the image B.

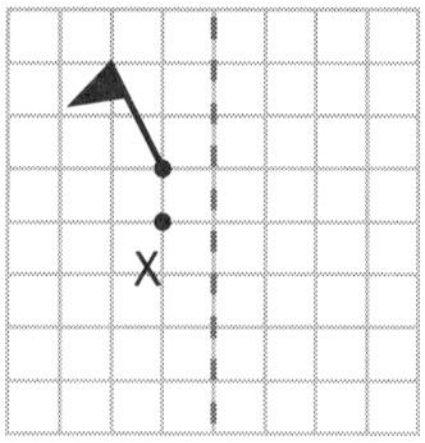

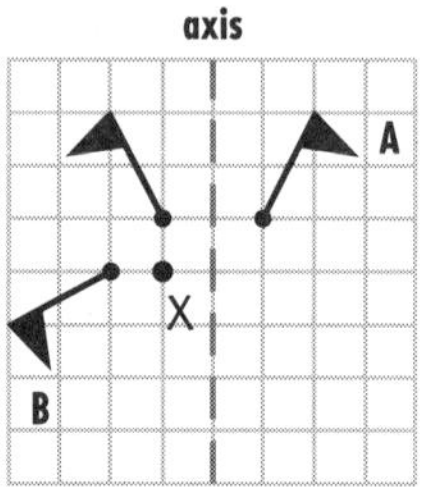

Note: You may find tracing paper useful, particularly with rotations. Trace the shape and then rotate the sheet of tracing paper about the centre of rotation.

Exercise 64A

In each question start by copying the diagram onto a suitable grid.

1 (a) Reflect the object in the axis of reflection. Label the image A.
(b) Rotate the object through 90° clockwise about the centre of rotation X. Label the image B.

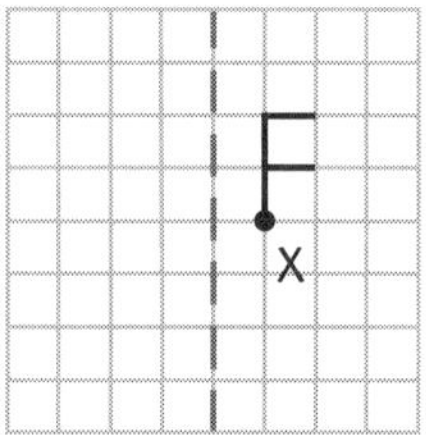

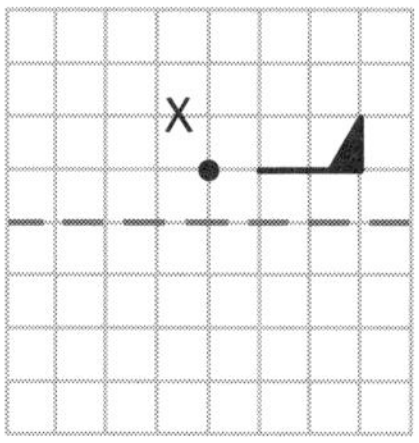

2 (a) Reflect the object in the axis of reflection. Label the image C.
(b) Rotate the object through 90° clockwise about the centre of rotation X. Label the image D.

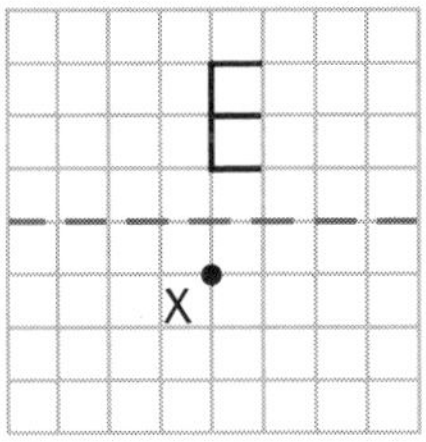

3 (a) Reflect the object in the axis of reflection.
Label the image E.
(b) Rotate the object through 90° clockwise about the centre of rotation X.
Label the image F.

4 (a) Reflect the object in the axis of reflection.
Label the image G.
(b) Rotate the object through 180° about the centre of rotation X.
Label the image H.

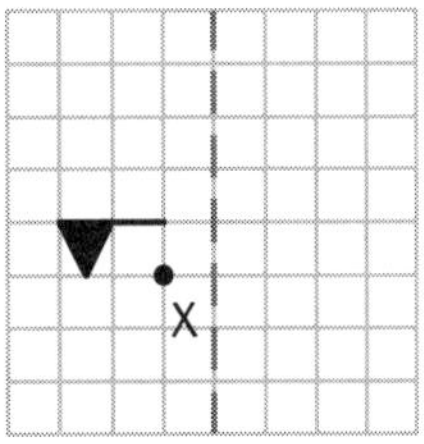

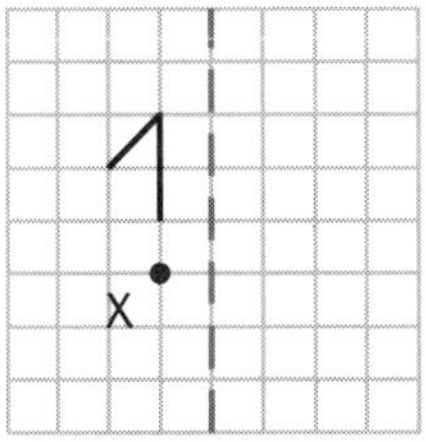

5 (a) Reflect the object in the axis of reflection.
Label the image I.
(b) Rotate the object through 90° anticlockwise about the centre of rotation X.
Label the image J.

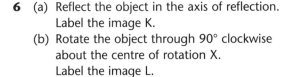

6 (a) Reflect the object in the axis of reflection.
Label the image K.
(b) Rotate the object through 90° clockwise about the centre of rotation X.
Label the image L.

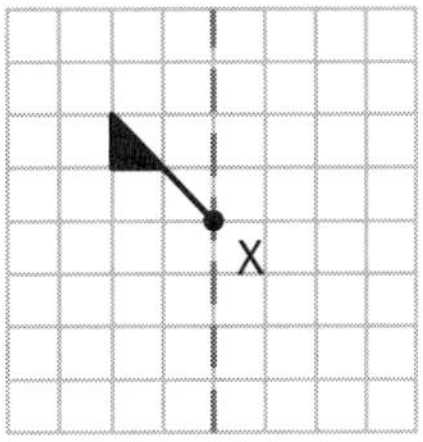

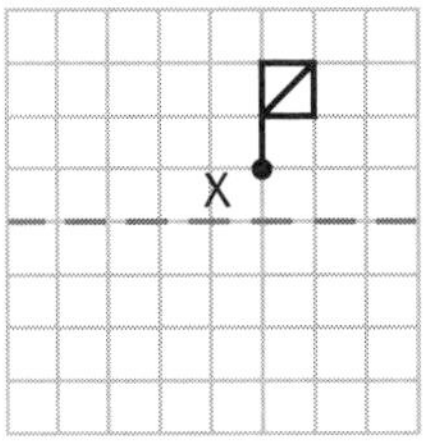

7 (a) Reflect the object in the axis of reflection.
Label the image M.
(b) Rotate the object through 270° anticlockwise about the centre of rotation X.
Label the image N.

8 (a) Reflect the object in the axis of reflection.
Label the image P.
(b) Rotate the object through 180° about the centre of rotation X.
Label the image Q.

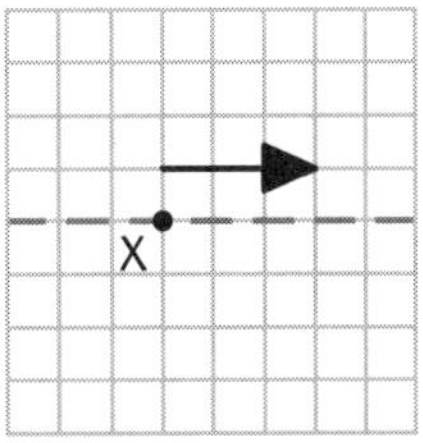

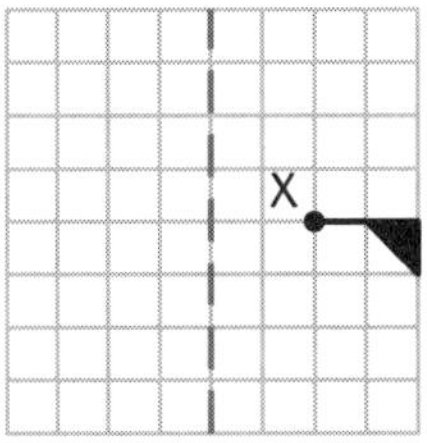

9 (a) Reflect the object in the axis of reflection.
Label the image R.
(b) Rotate the object through 45° anticlockwise about the centre of rotation X.
Label the image S.

10 (a) Reflect the object in the axis of reflection. Label the image T.
(b) Rotate the object through 90° anticlockwise about the centre of rotation X. Label the image U.

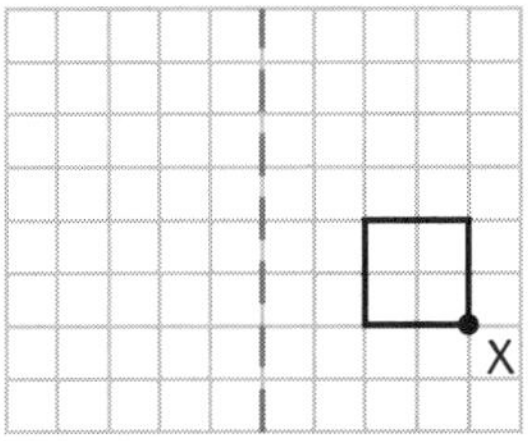

Exercise 64B

In each question start by copying the diagram onto a suitable grid.

1 (a) Reflect the object in the axis of reflection. Label the image A.
(b) Rotate the object through 180° about the centre of rotation X. Label the image B.

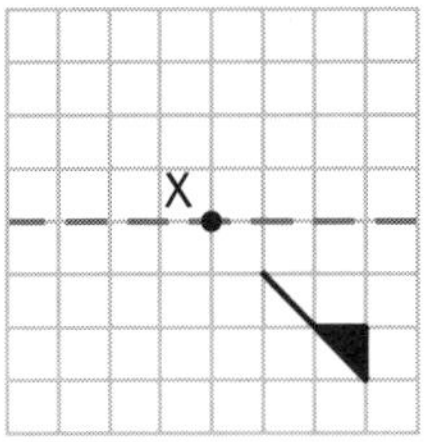

2 (a) Reflect the object in the axis of reflection. Label the image C.
(b) Rotate the object through 90° clockwise about the centre of rotation X. Label the image D.

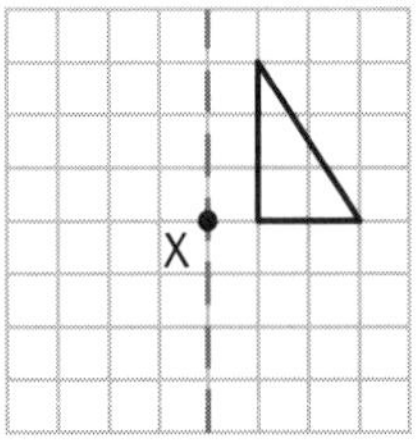

3 (a) Reflect the object in the axis of reflection. Label the image E.
(b) Rotate the object through 90° clockwise about the centre of rotation X. Label the image F.

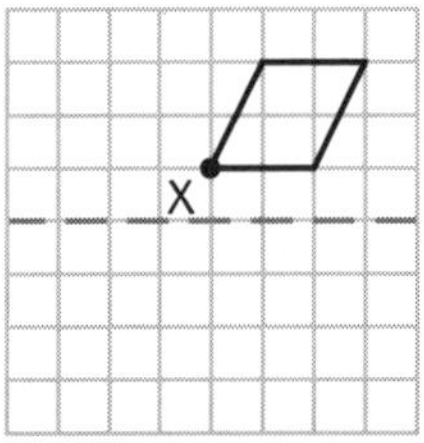

4 (a) Reflect the object in the axis of reflection. Label the image G.
(b) Rotate the object through 90° anticlockwise about the centre of rotation X. Label the image H.

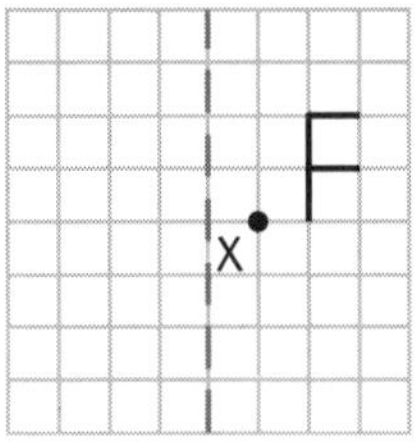

5 (a) Reflect the object in the axis of reflection. Label the image I.
(b) Rotate the object through 180° about the centre of rotation X. Label the image J.

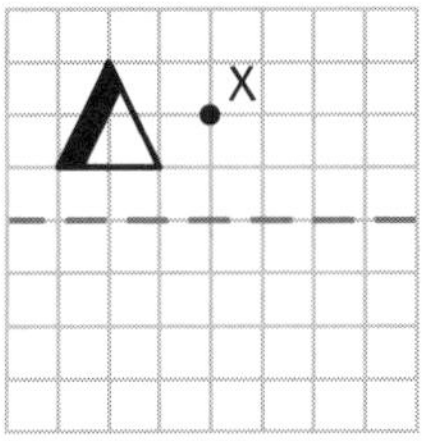

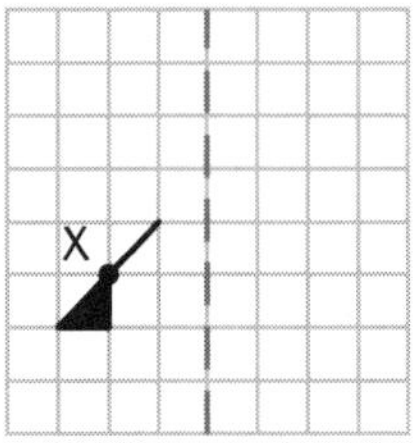

6 (a) Reflect the object in the axis of reflection. Label the image K.
(b) Rotate the object through 90° clockwise about the centre of rotation X. Label the image L.

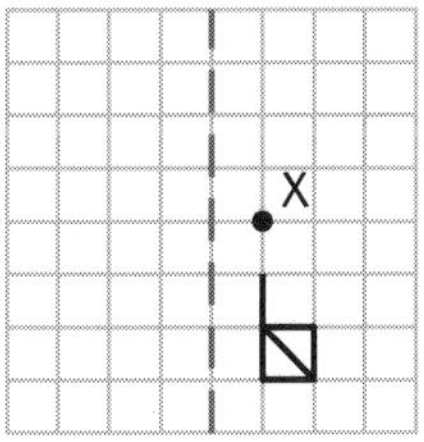

7 (a) Reflect the object in the axis of reflection.
Label the image M.
(b) Rotate the object through 270° clockwise about the centre of rotation X.
Label the image N.

8 (a) Reflect the object in the axis of reflection.
Label the image P.
(b) Rotate the object through 180° about the centre of rotation X.
Label the image Q.

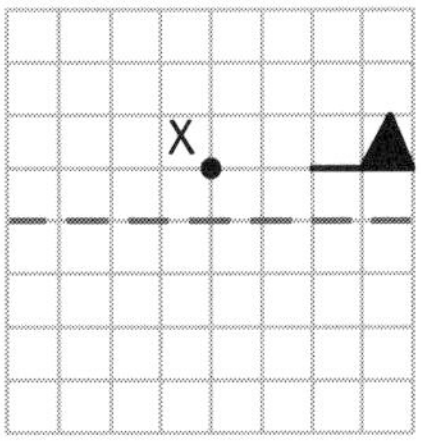

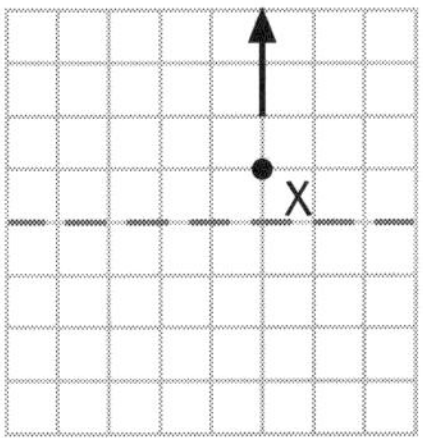

9 (a) Reflect the object in the axis of reflection.
Label the image R.
(b) Rotate the object through 90° anticlockwise about the centre of rotation X.
Label the image S.

10 (a) Reflect the object in the axis of reflection.
Label the image T.
(b) Rotate the object through 45° anticlockwise about the centre of rotation X.
Label the image U.

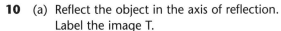

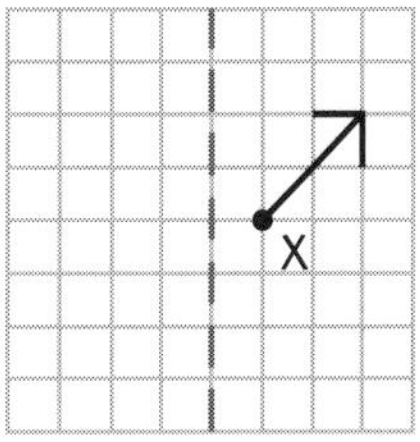

REVISION

Exercise E

1 For each example measure the angle to the nearest degree and state the type of angle.

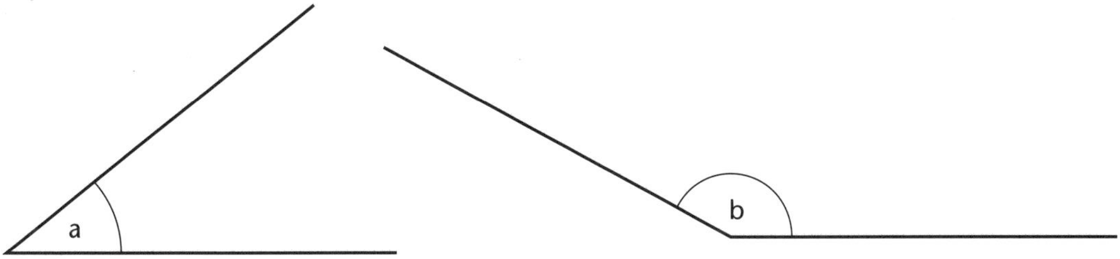

2 Draw each of these angles to the nearest degree and state the type of angle.
(a) 57° (b) 122° (c) 200° (d) 90°

3 State the size of each of the unknown angles marked with a letter.

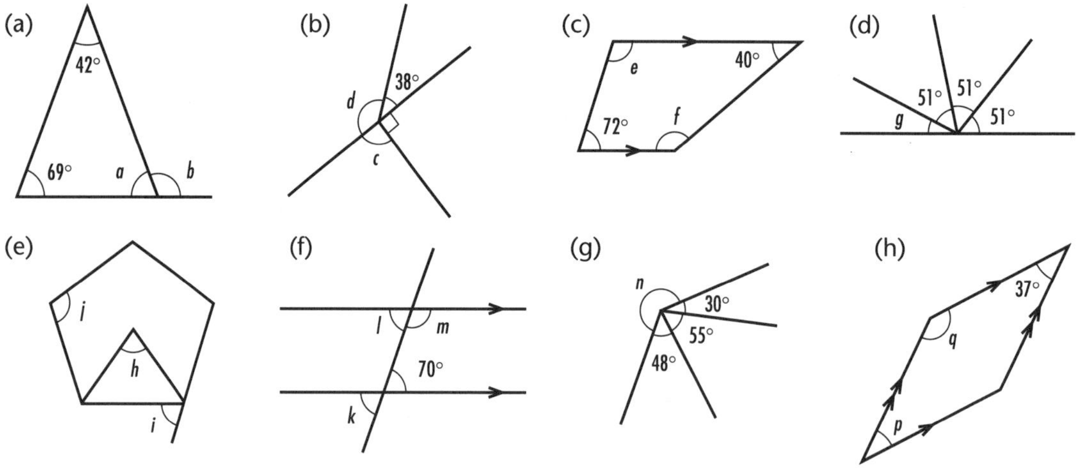

4 State the *best* name for each of the following.

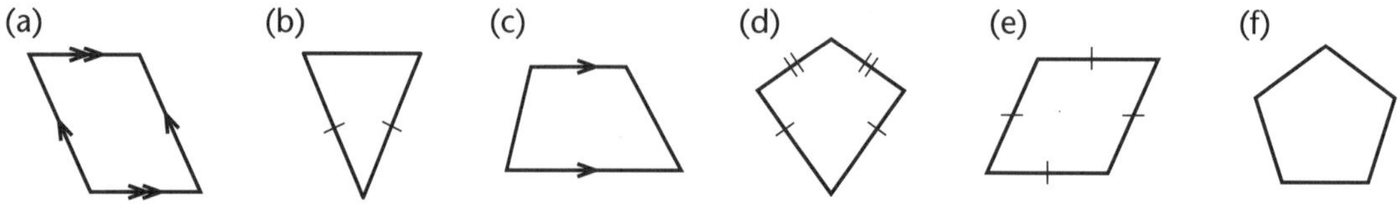

5 Copy each of the diagrams and show clearly any axes of reflection and any centre of rotation.

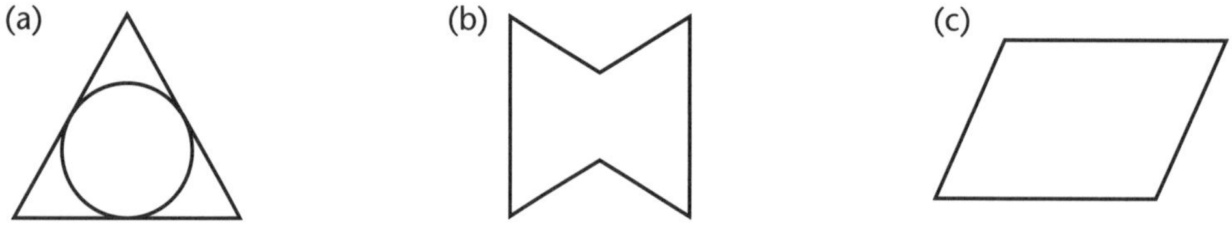

6 Copy the diagram and complete it by reflecting the shape in the axis of reflection.

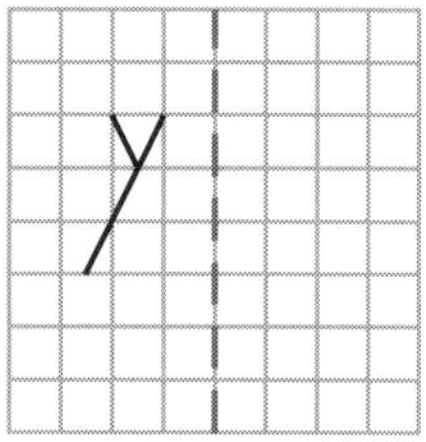

7 Copy and complete the diagram so it has rotational symmetry of order 4 about the centre of rotation X.

Exercise EE

1 Draw accurately the two triangles shown in the diagrams. Measure and record the remaining lengths and angles.

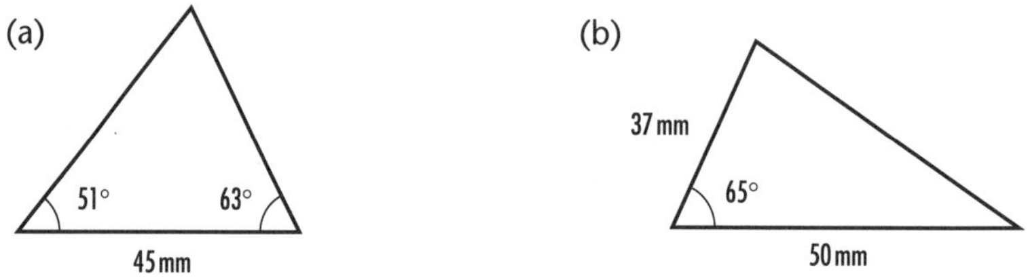

2 Nick is making a model bridge. She uses four struts of equal length to hold the two main beams in place. She starts by making one angle 70° and another 90° as shown in the diagram. Copy the diagram and fill in the missing angles.

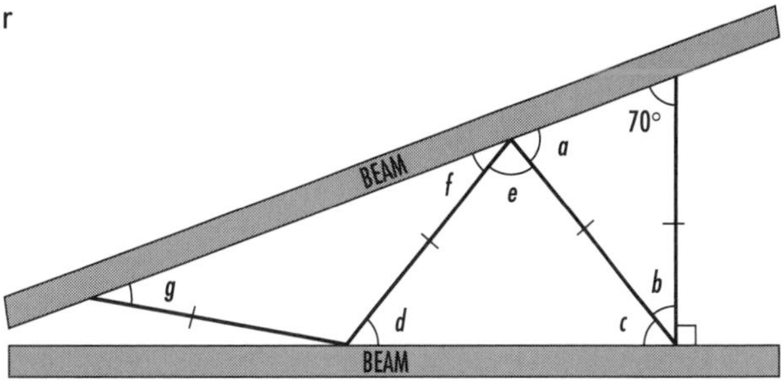

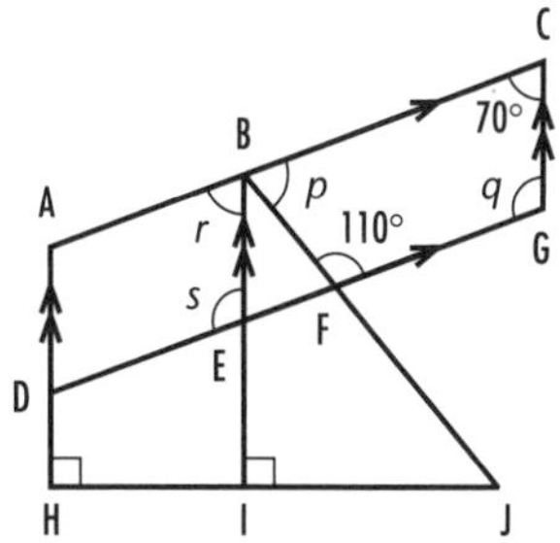

3 The diagram shows part of a clothes airer. AC and DG are parallel to each other. AH, BI and CG are vertical and HJ is horizontal.
Angle BFG = 110° and angle BCG = 70°, as shown.
(a) State the size of each of the angles p, q, r and s.
(b) Give the name which best describes each of the following shapes:
BCGF, ABED, BIJ, BEF, DEIH

4 State the size of each of the angles marked with a letter. Give reasons.

(a)

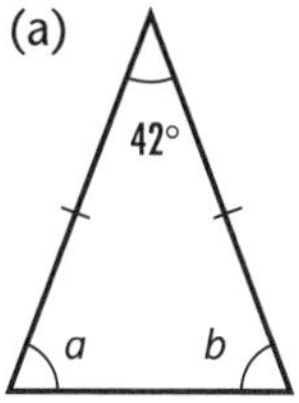

(b)

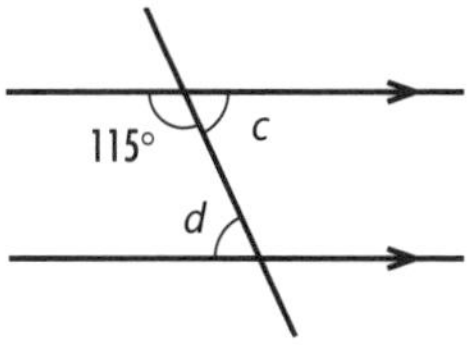

(c)

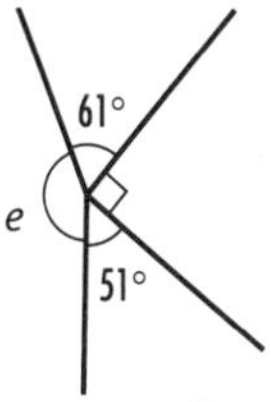

(d)

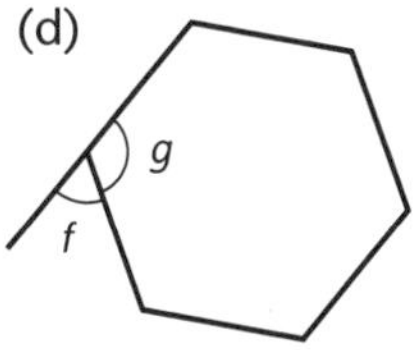

(e)

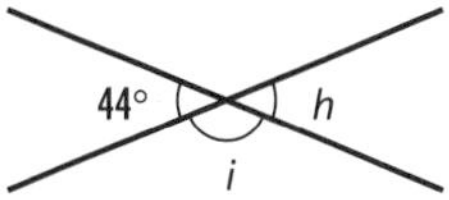

(f)

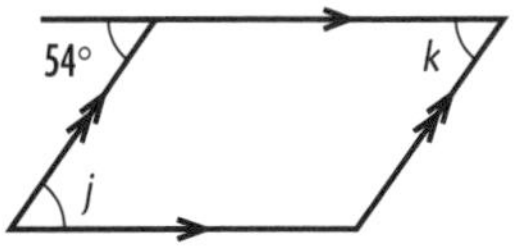

5 A regular polygon has an exterior angle of 40°. How many sides does it have?

6 State the size of the exterior and interior angles of a regular octagon.

7 Copy the letters carefully and show any axes of reflection and any centres of rotation. State the order of any rotational symmetry.

D T F H Z

8 Copy the two diagrams carefully onto squared paper and show the image in each case after reflection in the axes of reflection shown.

(a)

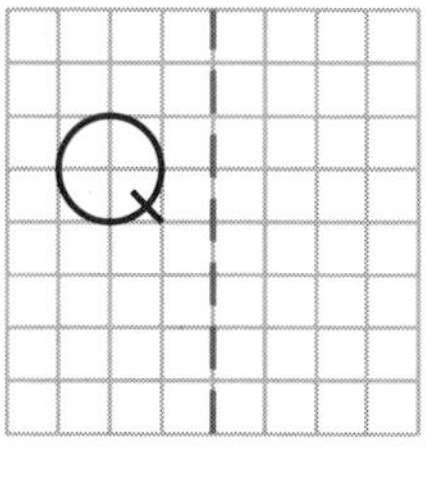

(b)

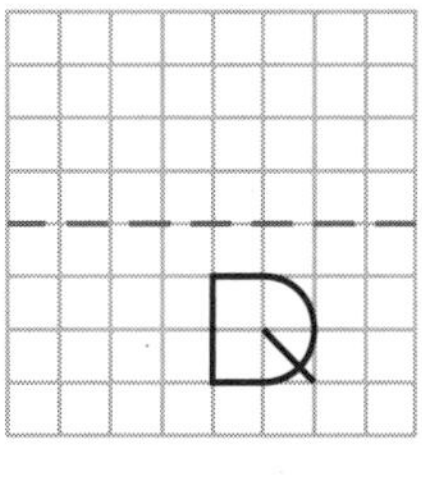

9 Copy each diagram carefully onto squared paper and show the image after rotation by 90° anticlockwise about the centre of rotation X.

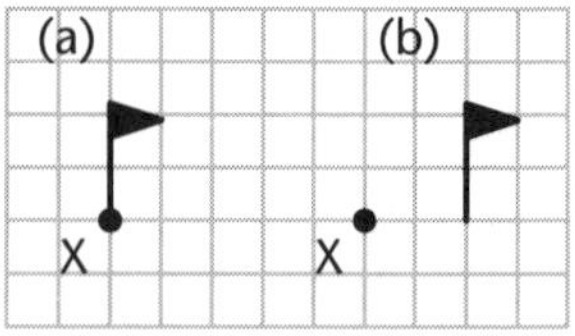

10 Copy the diagrams used in question 9 onto squared paper and show the image after rotation by 180° about the centre of rotation X.

65/ UNDERSTANDING SCALE

Here are two different ways of writing the scale of a map that uses 1 cm on the map to represent 2 km in actual length.

A 1 cm ≡ 2 km
Some people write 1 cm = 2 km but this is not a good idea as 1 cm does not *equal* 2 km, it *represents* 2 km.

B 1 : 200 000
That is, the scale is shown as a ratio: there are 200 000 cm in 2 km.

EXAMPLE

▶ What is the actual length that is represented by 5.6 cm on a map drawn to a scale of 1 cm ≡ 5 km?

1 cm ≡ 5 km
5.6 cm ≡ $5 \times 5.6 = 28$ km

EXAMPLE

▶ What length is used to represent 38.5 m on a drawing which is drawn to the scale 1 : 500?

1 : 500 means that 1 mm represents 500 mm.
So 1 mm represents 0.5 m.
$38.5 \div 0.5 = 77$
The length is 77 mm.

EXAMPLE

▶ Estimate the actual length of Crosshills on the map of Stony Stratford (bottom of map).

Length on map = 13 mm
The scale is 1 : 10 000.
Actual length = 130 000 mm = 130 m

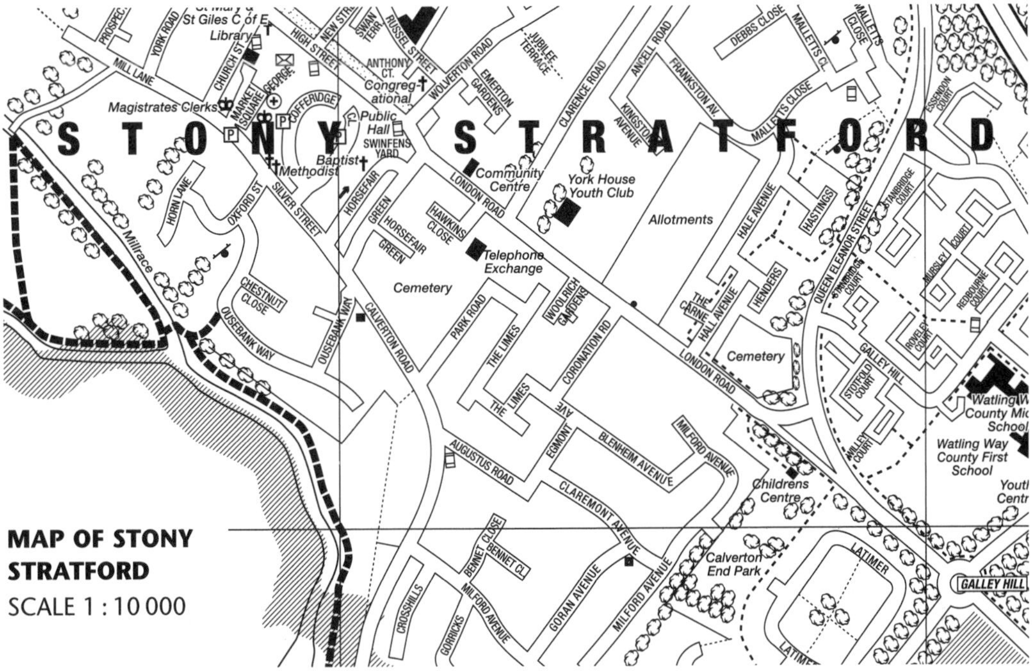

MAP OF STONY STRATFORD

SCALE 1 : 10 000

Exercise 65A

Copy the table and complete it by filling in the missing values.

Question number	Length on drawing or map	Actual length	Scale
1	3 cm	m	1 : 100
2	54 mm	km	1 cm ≡ 1 km
3	7.5 cm	km	1 cm ≡ 2 km
4	83 mm	km	1 : 1 000 000
5	65 mm	m	1 : 2000
6	10.4 cm	km	1 cm ≡ 50 km
7	mm	5 m	2 mm ≡ 1 m
8	cm	35 m	1 : 500
9	mm	12 km	1 : 2 000 000
10	cm	300 miles	1 cm ≡ 50 miles

In the following questions measure the lengths on the maps and record them. Then use these lengths to estimate the actual distances.

11 Using the map of Stony Stratford find the length and width of the allotments.

12 Using the map of Le Havre and District find the distance from Bayeux to Caen.

13 Using the map of Aldeburgh and District find the distance from Aldeburgh to Orford Ness.

14 Using the map of Milton Keynes Area find the distance on the H7 road between the V8 and V10 roads.

15 Using the map of Le Havre and District find the distance from Dives to Deauville.

16 Using the map of Aldeburgh and District find the distance from Thorpeness to Sizewell.

17 Using the map of Milton Keynes Area find the distance along the V10 road from the River Ouzel to the H7 road.

18 Using the map of Stony Stratford find the length of Chestnut Close (halfway down on the left).

19 Using the map of Le Havre and District find the distance from Port-en-Bessin (near Bayeux) to Aunay-sur-Odon through Bayeux.

20 Using the map of Aldeburgh and District find the distance from Aldeburgh to Snape.

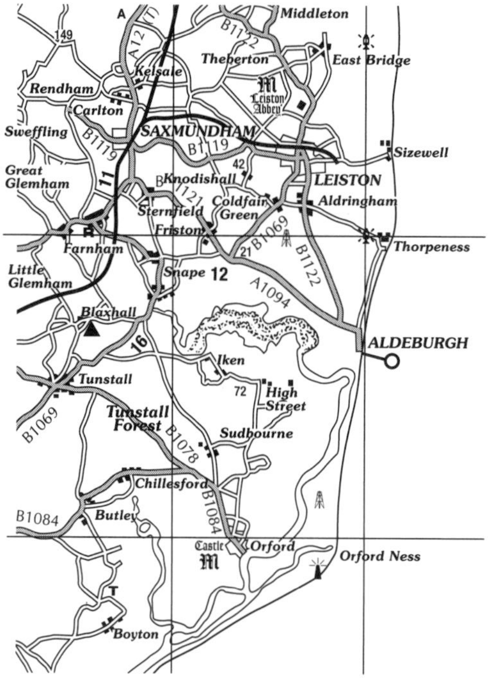

MAP OF ALDEBURGH & DISTRICT
SCALE 1 : 250 000

Exercise 65B

Copy the table and complete it by filling in the missing values.

Question number	Length on drawing or map	Actual length	Scale
1	5.8 cm	km	1 cm ≡ 1 km
2	75 mm	m	1 : 1000
3	8.2 cm	km	1 cm ≡ 5 km
4	7 cm	km	1 : 100 000
5	55 mm	m	1 : 2000
6	4.6 cm	km	1 cm ≡ 10 km
7	mm	5 m	1 : 5000
8	cm	20 m	2 mm ≡ 1 m
9	mm	75 km	1 : 5 000 000
10	inches	110 miles	1 inch ≡ 20 miles

In the following questions measure the lengths on the maps and record them. Then use these lengths to estimate the actual distances.

11 Using the map of Le Havre and District find the distance from Caen to Pont-l'Evêque.

12 Using the map of Stony Stratford find the distance from the junction of London Road and Coronation Road (opposite Allotments) to the Children's Centre.

13 Using the map of Milton Keynes Area find the distance on the A4146 (V11) road between the H6 and the H7 roads.

14 Using the map of Aldeburgh and District find the distance from Thorpeness to Aldringham.

15 Using the map of Le Havre and District find the distance from Ste. Adresse (just North of Le Havre) to Etretat.

16 Using the map of Stony Stratford find the length of Claremont Avenue (bottom middle).

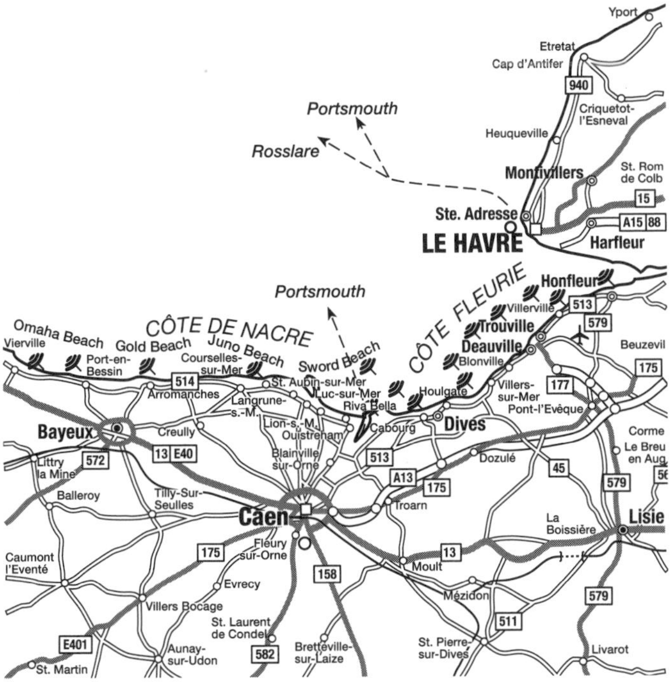

MAP OF LE HAVRE & DISTRICT

SCALE 1 cm ≡ 10 km

17 Using the map of Milton Keynes Area find the distance along the V10 road between the H3 and the H8 roads.

18 Using the map of Aldeburgh and District find the distance from Sizewell to Orford Ness.

19 Using the map of Le Havre and District find the distance from Balleroy (near Bayeux) to Tilly sur Seulles.

20 Using the map of Milton Keynes Area find the distance along the V11 road between the H4 and the A509(H5) roads.

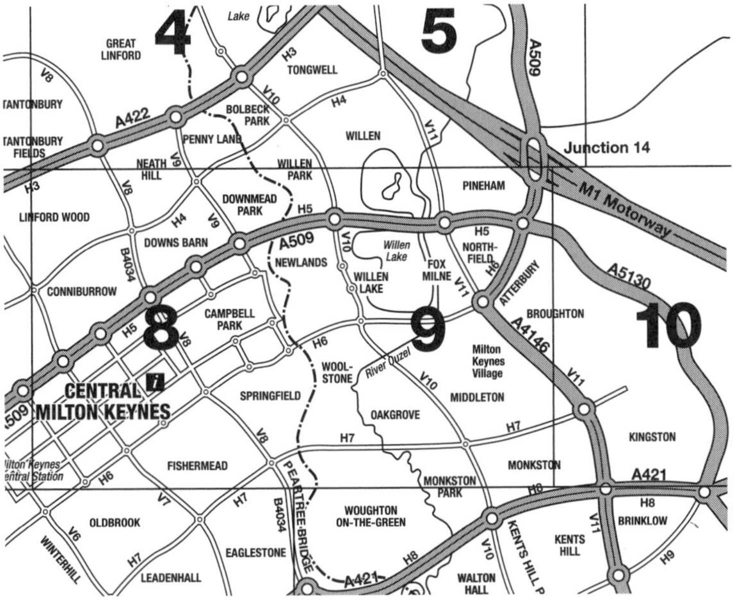

MAP OF MILTON KEYNES AREA

SCALE 2.5 cm ≡ 1 mile

EXAMPLE

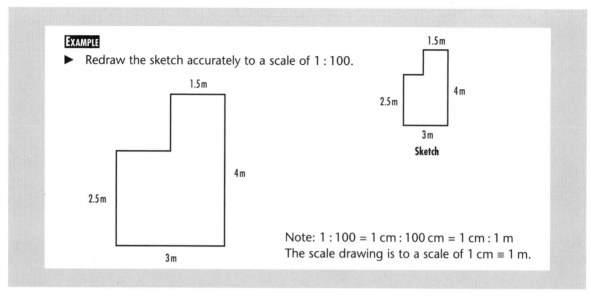

▶ Redraw the sketch accurately to a scale of 1 : 100.

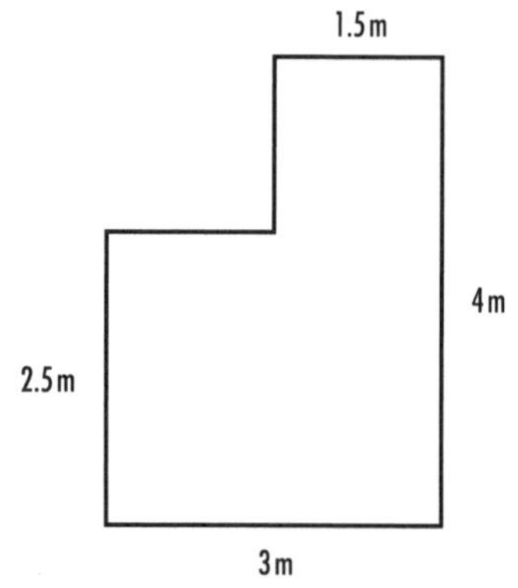

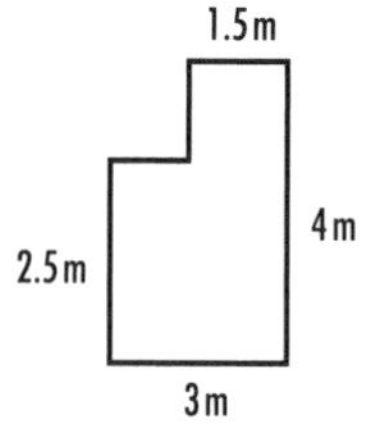

Sketch

Note: 1 : 100 = 1 cm : 100 cm = 1 cm : 1 m
The scale drawing is to a scale of 1 cm ≡ 1 m.

Exercise 66A

Redraw each shape accurately as a scale drawing to the scale stated.

1

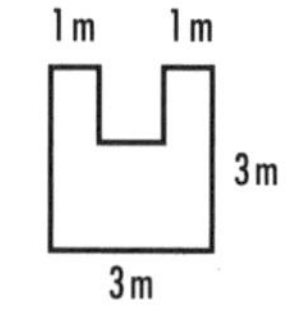

1:100

2

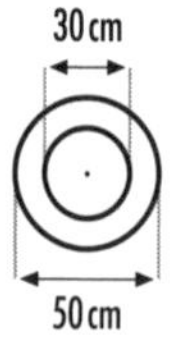

1:10

3

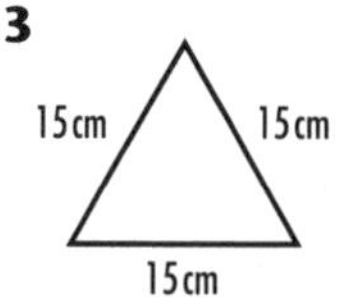

1 cm ≡ 5 cm

4

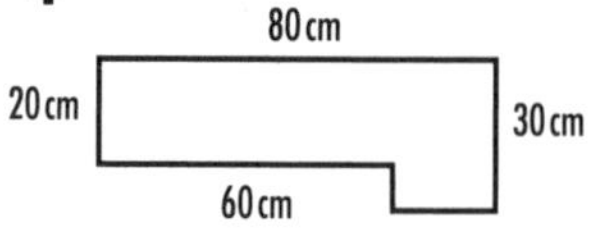

1:20

5

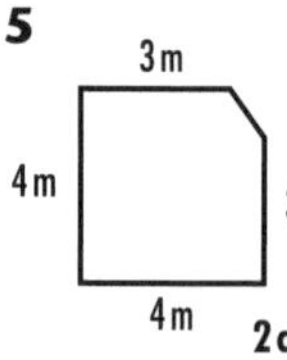

2 cm ≡ 1 m

6

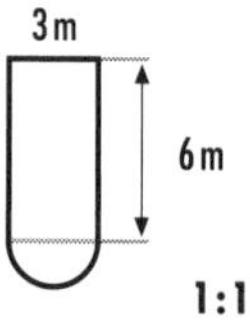

1:100

7

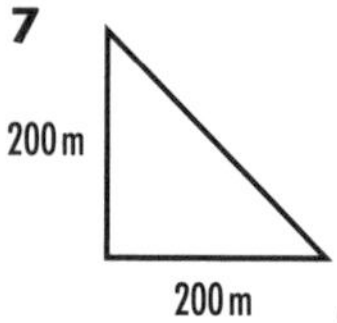

1 cm ≡ 50 m

8

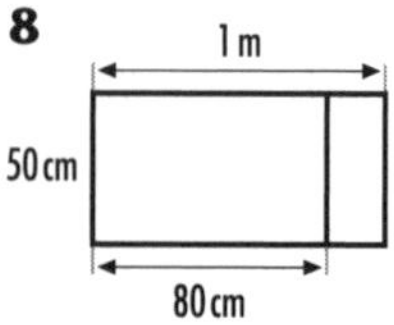

1:20

9

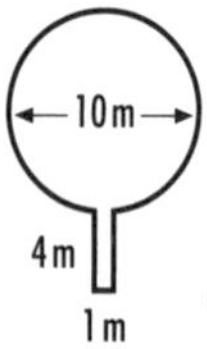

1 cm ≡ 2 m

10

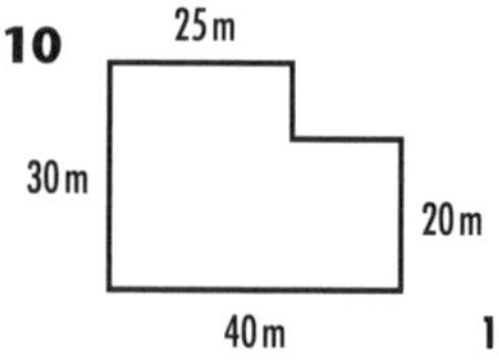

1 cm ≡ 10 m

Exercise 66B

Redraw each shape accurately as a scale drawing to the scale stated.

1

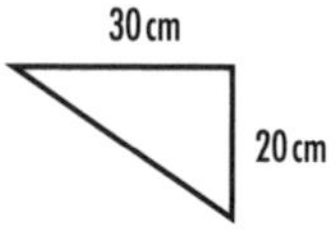

1:10

2

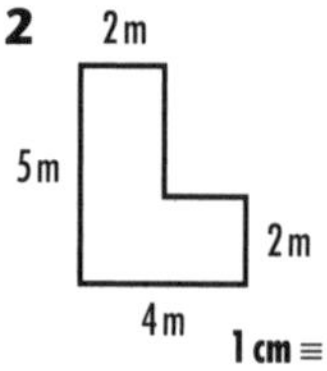

1 cm ≡ 1 m

3

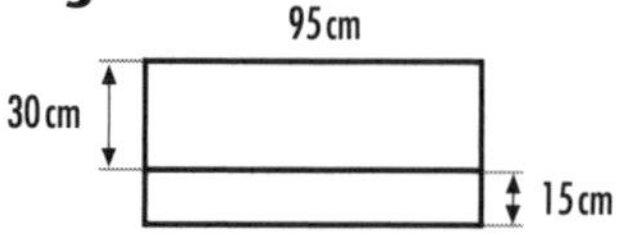

1:10

4

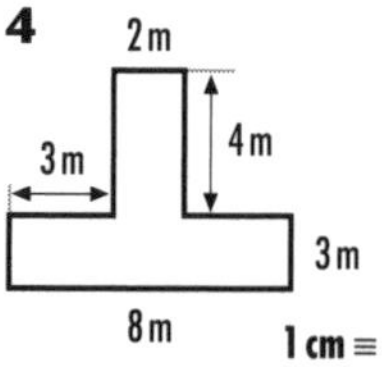

1 cm ≡ 2 m

5

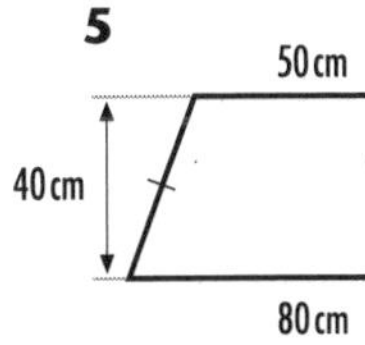

1:20

6

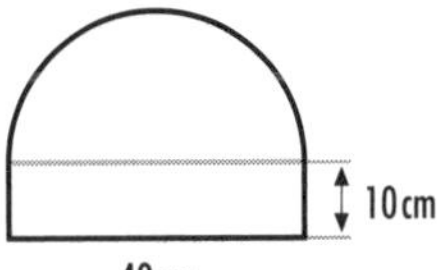

1 cm ≡ 10 cm

7

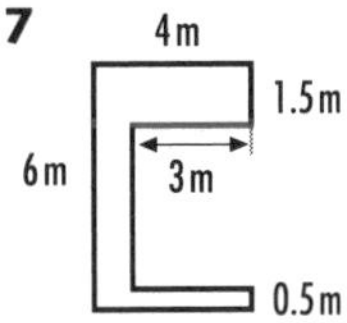

1 cm ≡ 1 m

8

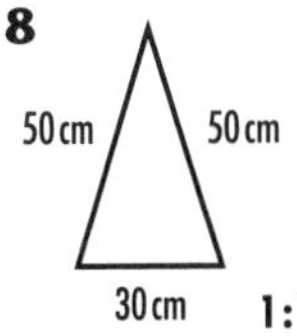

1:10

9

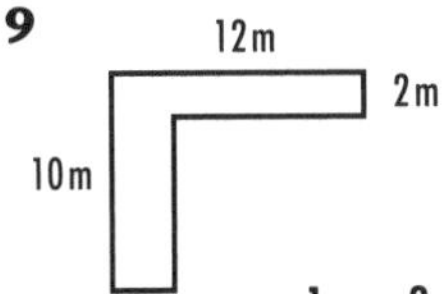

1 cm ≡ 2 m

10

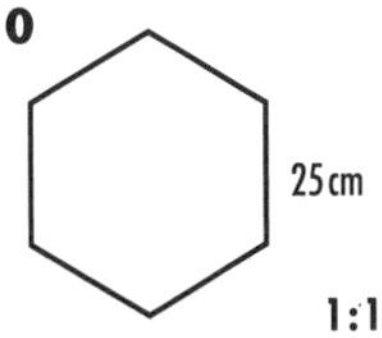

1:10

67/ FINDING THE SCALE FACTOR AND CENTRE OF ENLARGEMENT

If an **object** has been enlarged to give an **image**, then all the lengths in the image will have been multiplied by the same **scale factor**.

The enlargement will have a **centre of enlargement** from which lines can be drawn to pass through each point on the image and then on to the corresponding point on the object.

EXAMPLE

▶ Copy the diagram onto squared paper and show the centre of enlargement.
State the scale factor.

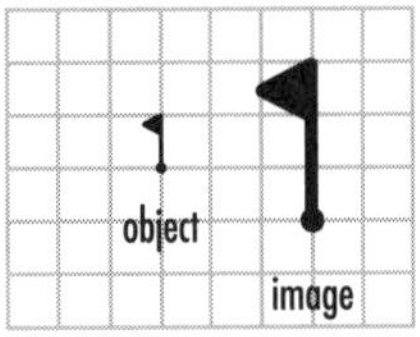

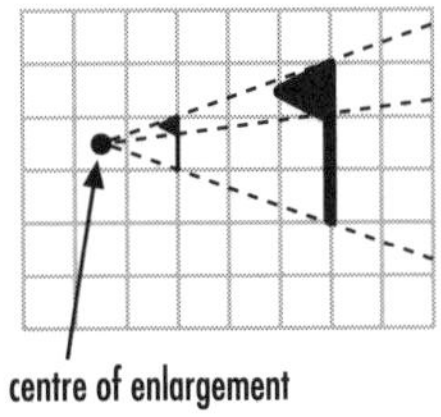

By joining corresponding points on the image and object and extending these, we find that they meet at the centre of enlargement.

All the lengths in the image are three times the lengths in the object. This means that the scale factor is 3.

Exercise 67A

For each of the following copy the diagram onto squared paper and show the centre of enlargement. State the scale factor.

1

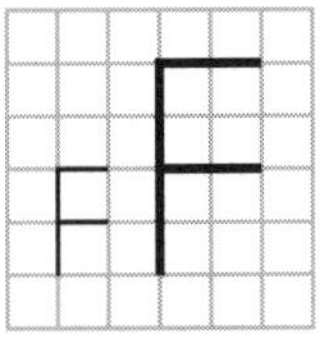

2

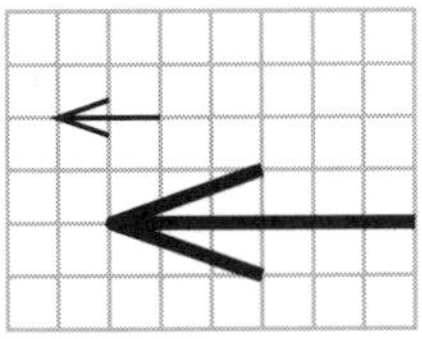

3

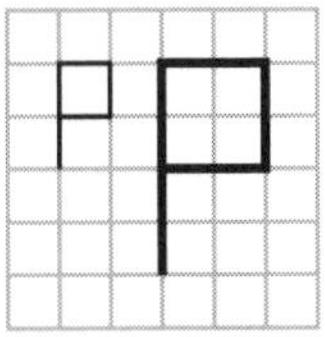

4

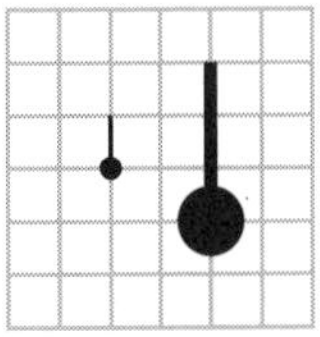

5

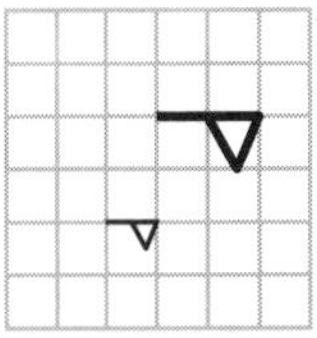

6

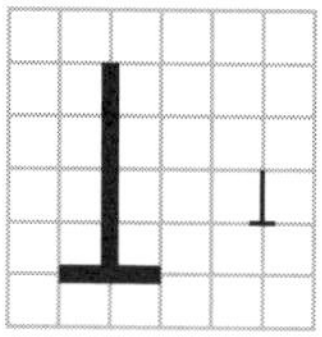

7

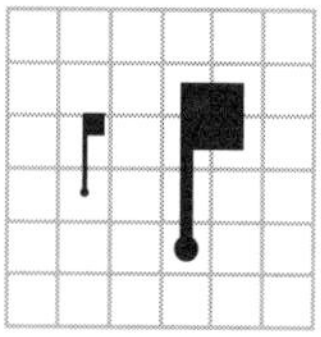

8

9

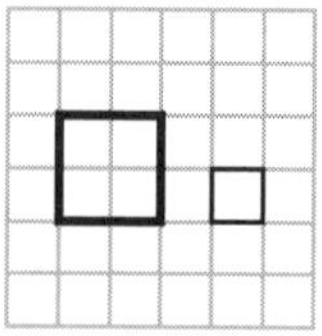

10

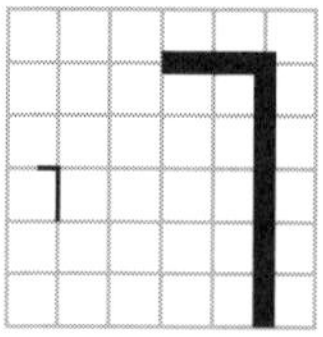

Exercise 67B

For each of the following copy the diagram onto squared paper and show the centre of enlargement. State the scale factor.

1

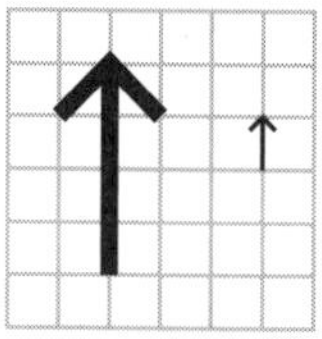

2

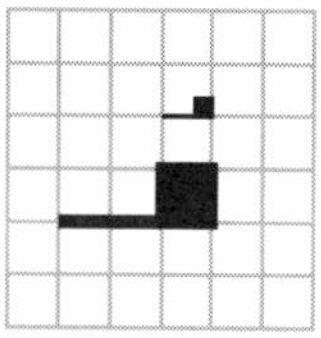

3

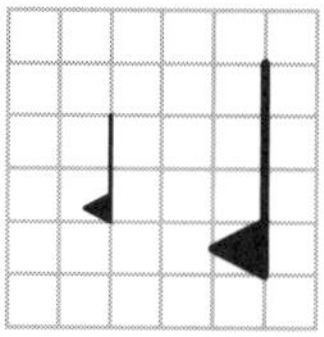

4

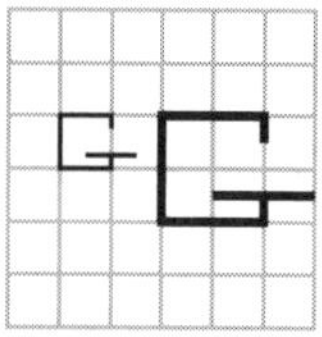

5

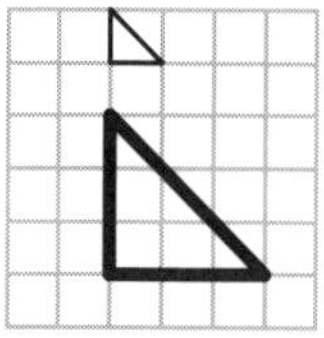

6

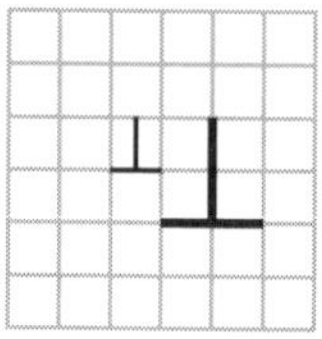

7

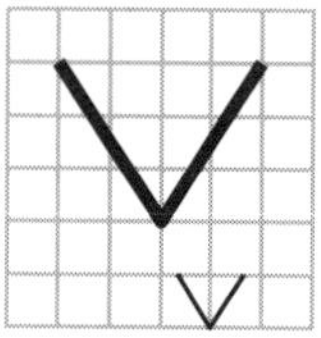

8

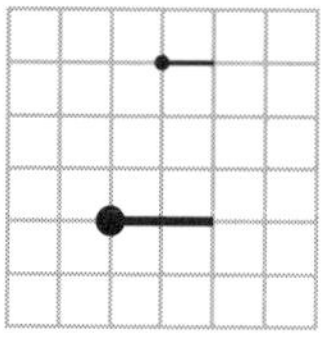

9

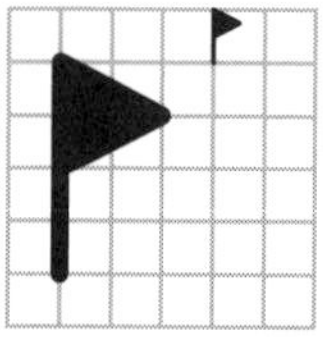

10

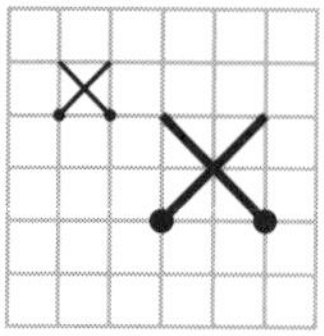

68/ DRAWING ENLARGEMENTS

To find the size and position of the image, lines are drawn outwards from the centre of enlargement through points on the object. The distance to each point on the object is measured and then multiplied by the scale factor. This distance is marked off from the centre of enlargement on the line and gives the corresponding point on the image. This is repeated for as many points as is necessary to complete the image.

EXAMPLE

► Enlarge the object by a scale factor of 3 from the centre of enlargement X.

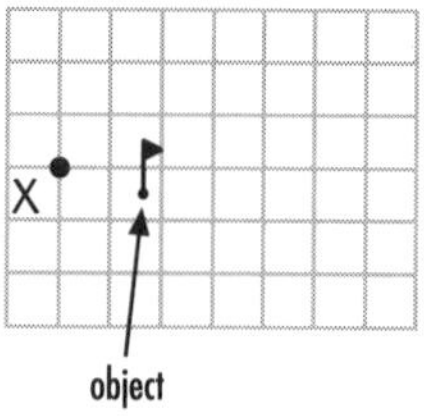

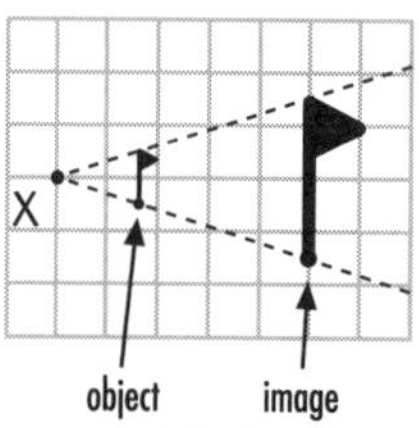

S.F. = 3

Exercise 68A

Copy and complete each diagram by drawing the image after enlargement by the stated scale factor from the centre of enlargement X.

1

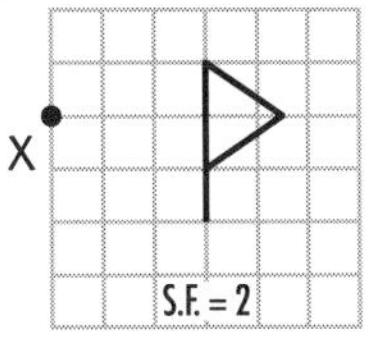

2

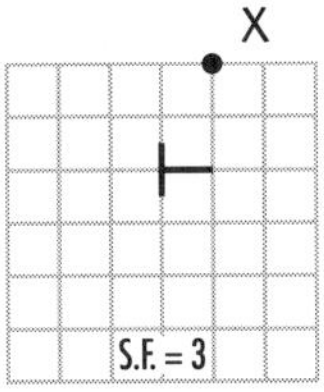

3

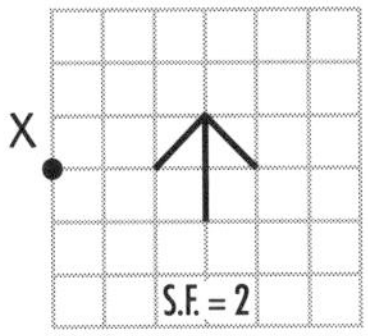

4

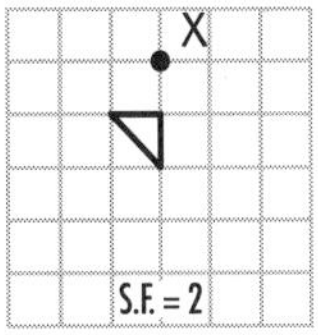

5

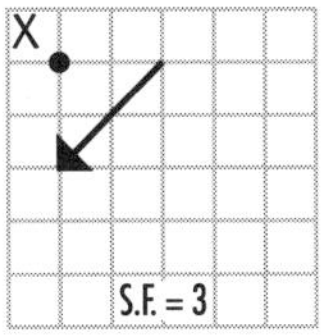

6

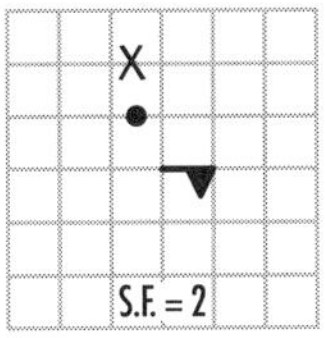

7

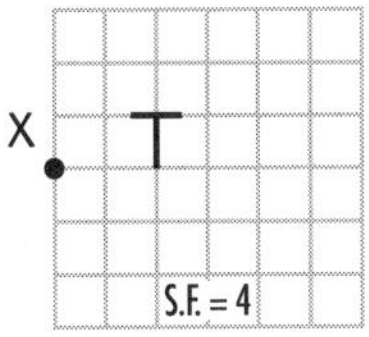

8

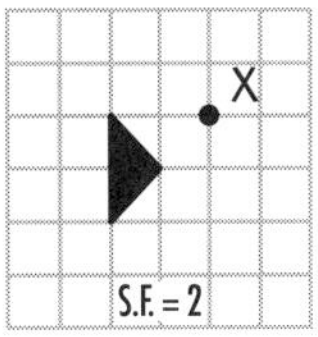

9

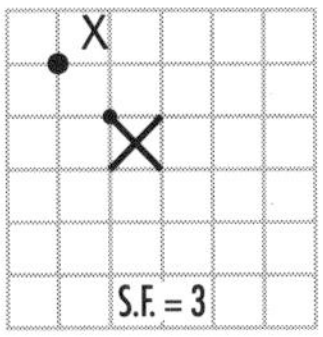

10

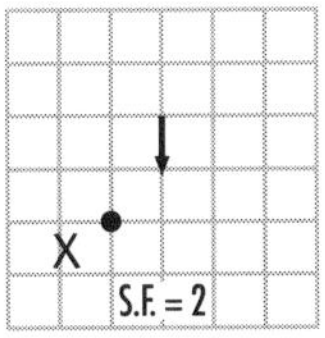

Exercise 68B

Copy and complete each diagram by drawing the image after enlargement by the stated scale factor from the centre of enlargement X.

1

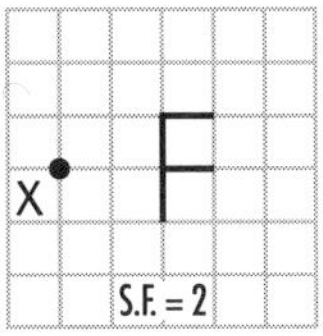

2

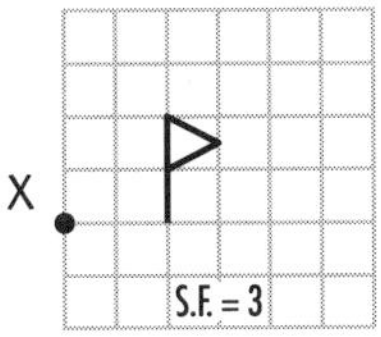

3

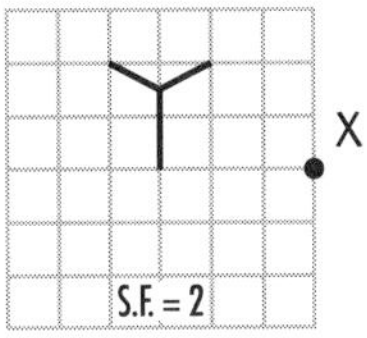

4

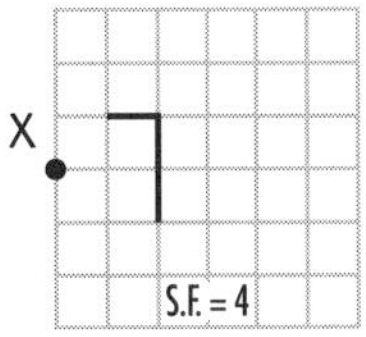

5

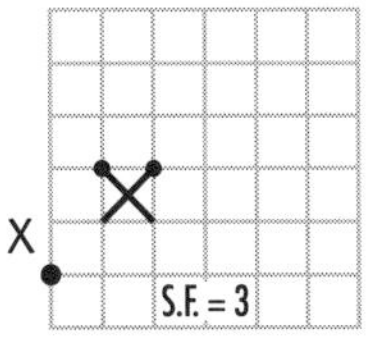

6

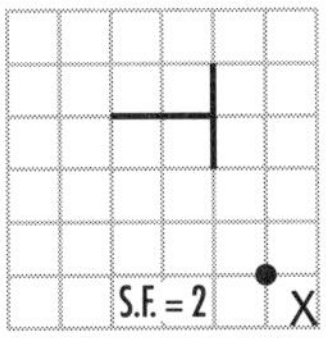

7

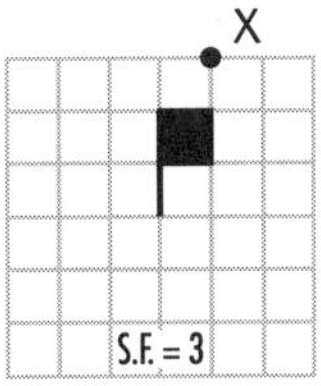

8

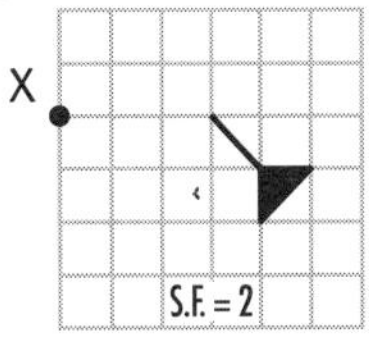

9

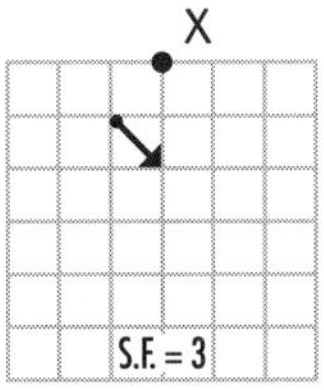

10

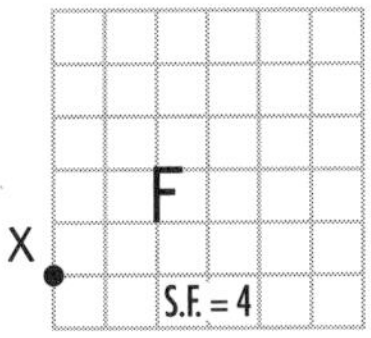

69/ METRIC UNITS

The metric system is based on 10, 100 and 1000.
The gram, the litre and the metre can be split into smaller units whose names start with **milli** or **centi**. Larger units have names with **kilo** at the front.

milli —10→ **centi** —100→ **metric unit** —1000→ **kilo**

milli —1000→ **metric unit**

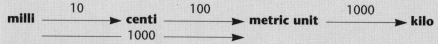

Abbreviations used:

Length	**Weight (mass)**	**Capacity**
millimetre (mm)	milligram (mg)	millilitre (ml)
centimetre (cm)		centilitre (cl)
metre (m)	gram (g)	litre (*l*)
kilometre (km)	kilogram (kg)	
	tonne (t)	
10 mm = 1 cm		10 ml = 1 cl
100 cm = 1 m		100 cl = 1 *l*
1000 mm = 1 m	1000 mg = 1 g	1000 ml = 1 *l*
1000 m = 1 km	1000 g = 1 kg	
	1000 kg = 1 t	

To move from one unit to another simply multiply or divide by 10, 100 or 1000. Multiplying can be achieved by adding noughts or moving the decimal point to the right. Dividing can be achieved by removing noughts or moving the decimal point to the left.

EXAMPLE

► Convert 124.6 cm to (a) metres (b) millimetres.

(a) 124.6 cm ÷ 100 = 1.246 m (move decimal point 2 places to the left to divide by 100)

(b) 124.6 cm × 10 = 1246 mm (move decimal point 1 place to the right to multiply by 10)

EXAMPLE

► Convert 25 kg to grams.

25 kg × 1000 = 25 000 g ('add' 3 noughts)

Exercise 69A

Convert the following:

1 4 m to mm
2 3500 g to kg
3 2.5 *l* to cl
4 550 ml to cl
5 3.5 cm to mm
6 7.450 kg to g
7 170 mm to cm
8 4500 mg to g
9 75 cl to ml
10 2.3 t to kg
11 4.75 km to m
12 35 000 g to kg
13 6 m to cm
14 75 cl to *l*
15 1.435 *l* to ml
16 17.5 kg to g
17 37.5 cm to mm
18 17 500 mg to g
19 4.665 t to kg
20 500 ml to cl
21 11.250 kg to g
22 7500 mm to m
23 45 cl to ml
24 0.007 kg to g
25 12 500 mg to g
26 130 cm to m
27 7.75 km to m
28 $\frac{1}{2}$ *l* to ml
29 1 250 000 g to kg
30 $\frac{1}{4}$ m to cm

Exercise 69B

Convert the following:

1 2500 g to kg	**2** 34 m to cm	**3** 700 cl to *l*	**4** 12 t to kg
5 340 mm to cm	**6** 3.2 *l* to ml	**7** 13.6 kg to g	**8** 175 cm to m
9 1500 ml to cl	**10** 0.065 km to m	**11** 976 ml to *l*	**12** 3 kg to g
13 45 000 mg to g	**14** 3.540 kg to g	**15** 4.675 m to cm	**16** 1.045 t to kg
17 450 cl to *l*	**18** 3.5 km to m	**19** 125 mm to m	**20** 3500 ml to cl
21 2735 g to kg	**22** 1.35 *l* to ml	**23** 35 cm to mm	**24** 0.002 g to mg
25 340 cm to m	**26** 1.265 m to cm	**27** 3 t to g	**28** 450 ml to cl
29 $\frac{1}{2}$ kg to g	**30** $\frac{1}{4}$ km to m		

Exercise 69C

1 A jar contains 240 grams of dried milk. What is the smallest number of jars needed to have more than 2 kg.

2 A can contains a litre of paint-thinner. Neil uses 640 ml. How much is left?

3 One lap of a running track is 400 m. How many laps must be run to complete a 10-km race?

4 Floyd estimates that his car weighs $\frac{3}{4}$ of a tonne. How many kilograms is this?

5 How many 30-ml doses can be poured from a 60-cl bottle of medicine?

6 Kerry measures the length of a room in two sections: 3.5 m and 85 cm. What is the total length of the room?

7 How many 75-mm lengths can be cut from 3 metres?

8 Ester weighs a small quantity of a chemical. If it weighs 0.457 g, how many milligrams more does she need to make half a gram?

9 Nathan always wanted to be 2 metres tall. At the present time he measures 1876 mm. How much more does he need to grow?

10 How many litres are contained in twenty 70-cl bottles?

Exercise 69D

1 The maximum weight that Sue can afford to send in an overseas parcel is 1 kg. She has presents weighing 320 g and 465 g. The wrapping weighs 95 g. How much more weight is Sue allowed?

2 Tarik has a device that tells him that he has walked 14 350 metres. Express this in kilometres.

3 How much more than a litre is the content of three bottles of sauce each containing 340 ml?

4 Roger needs 1 tonne of loam for a cricket pitch. He counts that he has seventeen 50-kg bags. How many more bags does he need?

5 Denzil measures the height under his work surface as 90 cm. How much space will there be if he puts a dishwasher of height 855 mm under the work surface?

6 Barry needs $\frac{3}{4}$ g of copper sulphate. How many milligrams is this?

7 Amanda needs 3.5 litres of oil in her car engine. She fills it using a jug which holds 700 ml. How many times will she need to fill the jug?

8 The width of a room is 5.5 metres. How many centimetres is this?

9 A factory produces five hundred roof-racks per day. Each roof-rack weighs 4.2 kg. What is the total weight, in tonnes, of one day's production?

10 Caenwen uses pieces of wallpaper that are 530 mm wide. How many pieces will she need to cover a wall that is 4.9 m wide?

70/ SENSIBLE ESTIMATES

Exercise 70A

For each question write down the letter of the estimate which best matches the statement. *Each letter is used once only.*

1	The weight of a bag of sugar	**A**	125 kg
2	The width of a kitchen	**B**	1320 kg
3	The capacity of a wine bottle	**C**	1.2 m
4	The total weight of two ordinary ladies	**D**	10 litres
5	The height of a mountain	**E**	60 cm
6	The capacity of a watering can	**F**	5000 m
7	The weight of a car	**G**	650 km
8	The capacity of an egg cup	**H**	50 kg
9	The distance from London to Glasgow	**I**	15 cm
10	The weight of a bag of cement	**J**	1 kg
11	The capacity of a large plastic bottle of cola	**K**	70 cl
12	The distance diagonally across a large family TV	**L**	25 km
13	A reasonable distance to cycle in 2 hours	**M**	20 cl
14	The weight of a bicycle	**N**	10 g
15	The capacity of a bath	**O**	90 litres
16	The weight of a £1 coin	**P**	40 ml
17	The length of an ironing board	**Q**	400 g
18	The weight of the contents of a tin of cat food	**R**	12 kg
19	The capacity of a cup	**S**	2.8 m
20	The width of a bathroom tile	**T**	300 cl

Exercise 70B

For each question write down the letter of the estimate which best matches the statement. *Each letter is used once only.*

1	The capacity of a garden pond	**A**	250 cl
2	The weight of ten sheets of writing paper	**B**	8500 g
3	The length of a pencil	**C**	1500 litres
4	A reasonable distance to walk in an hour	**D**	900 g
5	The weight of a pair of shoes	**E**	4.2 m
6	The height of a door	**F**	440 ml
7	The capacity of a medicine spoon	**G**	2 g
8	The height of a house	**H**	5 km
9	The weight of the contents of a can of baked beans	**I**	800 mm
10	The length of a car	**J**	20 g
11	The capacity of a large tea pot used in a café	**K**	2 m
12	The weight of a small car	**L**	0.850 t
13	The width of a computer disk	**M**	5 ml
14	The capacity of a small drinking glass	**N**	10 m
15	The weight of an exercise book	**O**	425 g
16	The width of a finger	**P**	0.1 mm
17	The capacity of a vacuum cleaner	**Q**	90 mm
18	The capacity of a can of fizzy drink	**R**	22 mm
19	The width of a single bed	**S**	145 mm
20	The thickness of a sheet of paper	**T**	150 ml

71/ IMPERIAL AND METRIC UNITS

The following are common metric and Imperial equivalents:

5 miles ≈ 8 kilometres	1 kilogram ≈ 2.2 pounds (lb)
1.1 yard (yd) ≈ 1 metre	1 stone (st) ≈ 6.5 kilograms
1 foot (ft) ≈ 30 centimetres	1 litre ≈ 1.75 pints (pt)
1 inch (in) ≈ 2.5 centimetres	1 gallon (gal) ≈ 4.5 litres

EXAMPLE

▶ Change (a) 48 km into miles (b) 14 pints into litres.

(a) 48 km ≈ (48 x 5) ÷ 8 = 30 miles
(b) 14 pints ≈ 14 ÷ 1.75 = 8 litres

Exercise 71A

Change the following into their approximate equivalents.

1 22 yd to m	**2** 9 *l* to gallons	**3** 44 lb to kg	**4** 75 cm to ft
5 5 cm to in	**6** 16 km to miles	**7** 12 *l* to pt	**8** 130 kg to st
9 10 m to yd	**10** 22 lb to kg	**11** 14 pt to litres	**12** 4 gal to litres
13 4 in to mm	**14** 3 ft to cm	**15** 100 miles to km	**16** 55 yd to m
17 1 t to lb	**18** 150 cm to in	**19** 18 in to cm	**20** 10 st to kg

21 A shirt collar measures 14 in. What is this approximately in centimetres?

22 Bronwen notices a speed limit of 130 km/h whilst on holiday. Which is the nearest equivalent speed limit: 40, 50, 60, 70, 80 or 90 miles per hour?

23 An old Imperial measure is the hundredweight which is 112 lb. Which is the nearest metric equivalent: 30, 40, 50, 60 or 70 kg?

24 How much is $\frac{1}{2}$ lb approximately in grams (to the nearest 50 g)?

25 Roger finds that his old shed measures 2 ft 6 in. How much is this approximately in centimetres?

26 A tile measures 15 mm. State the approximate equivalent in inches.

27 Mark knows that he weighs 8 st 10 lb. Is he lighter or heavier than Martin who weighs 50 kg and is the difference more than 10 kg?

28 A drum holds 18 litres. How many gallons will it hold approximately?

29 Marion has a sack weighing 50 kg. She needs to know if this is bigger or smaller than a sack weighing 112 lb. Calculate the approximate equivalent in pounds and say how much more or less than 112 lb this approximation is.

30 A recipe for a fruit drink needs 7 pints of water. How much is this approximately in litres?

Exercise 71B

Change the following into their approximate equivalents.

1 120 cm to ft	**2** 20 kg to lb	**3** 6 gal to litres	**4** 33 lb to kg
5 60 miles to km	**6** 6 st to kg	**7** 75 cm to ft	**8** 20 m to yd
9 8 *l* to pt	**10** 64 km to miles	**11** 110 yd to m	**12** 65 kg to st
13 10 *l* to pt	**14** 60 m to yd	**15** 10 kg to lb	**16** 80 km to miles
17 25 cm to in	**18** 880 yd to m	**19** 21 pt to litres	**20** 55 lb to kg

21 Jon-Paul knows that it is 40 miles to the ferry. How much is this approximately in kilometres?

22 Francis weighs 10 st. How much is this in kilograms approximately?

23 A pencil case is 20 cm in length. How many inches is this approximately?

24 A vegetable plot measures 20 metres in length. What is its approximate length in feet?

25 A small child weighs 26 kg. How many stones is this approximately?

26 Fatima knows that her petrol tank can hold up to 8 gallons of petrol. How much is this approximately in litres?

27 A jug can hold $3\frac{1}{2}$ pints. Approximately how many centilitres is this?

28 Which is bigger, $\frac{1}{2}$ litre or 1 pint?

29 The distance between two camp sites is 72 km. How many miles is this approximately?

30 The Imperial ton is 2240 lb. Using that 1 kg ≈ 2.2 lb, state which is bigger, 1 metric tonne or 1 Imperial ton.

72/ **NETS**

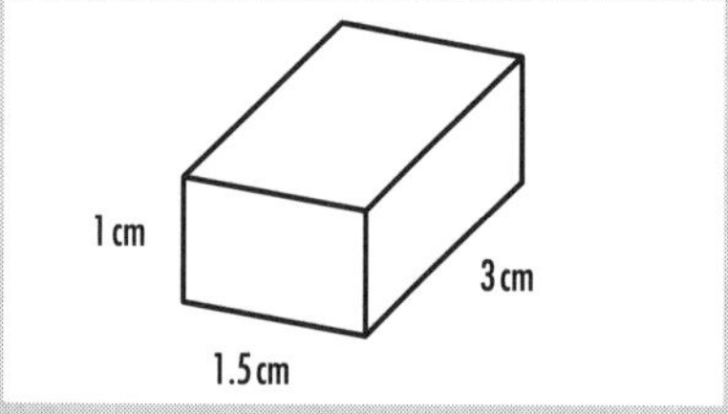

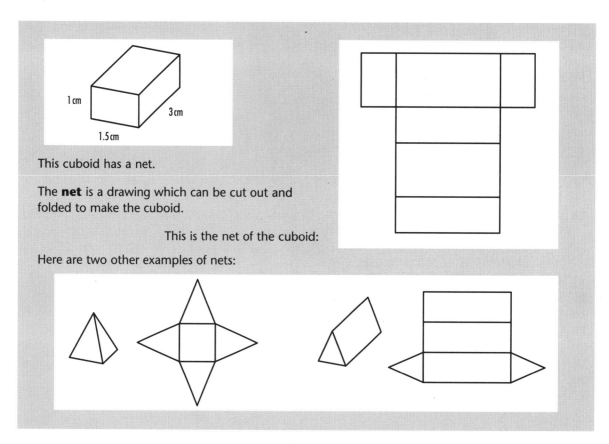

This cuboid has a net.

The **net** is a drawing which can be cut out and folded to make the cuboid.

This is the net of the cuboid:

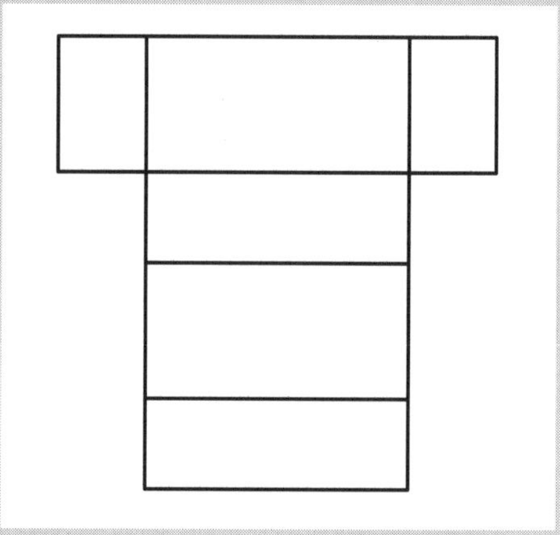

Here are two other examples of nets:

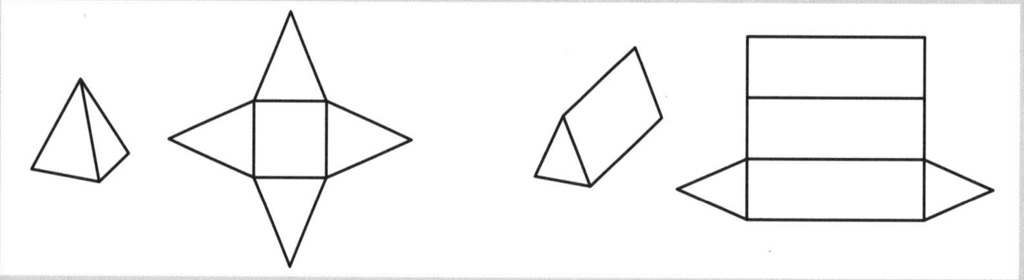

Exercise 72A

Draw a net for each of the following cuboids. If you do not draw the net to actual size, write the lengths of the sides on the diagram.

1

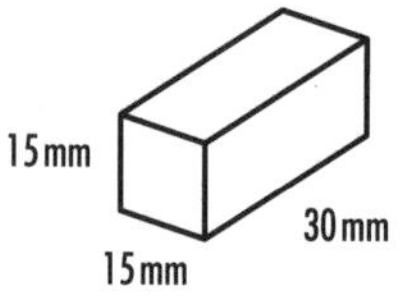

2

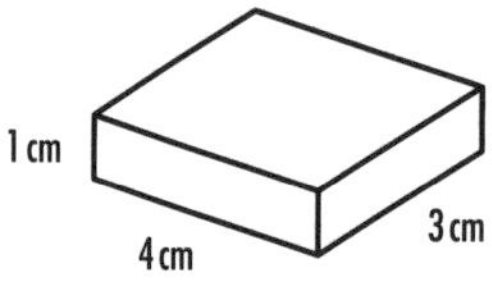

3

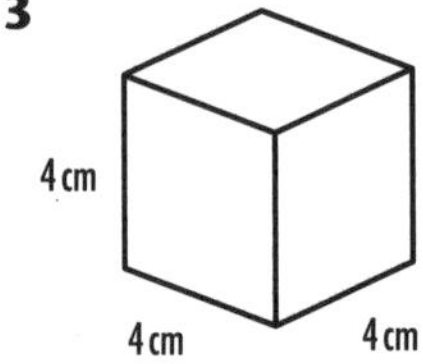

4

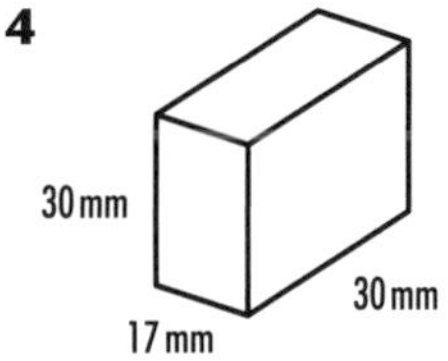

5

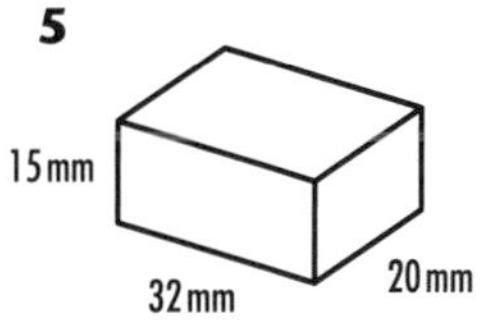

6

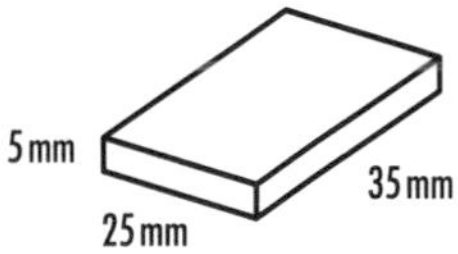

Draw a good sketch of the net of each of these 3-dimensional shapes.

7

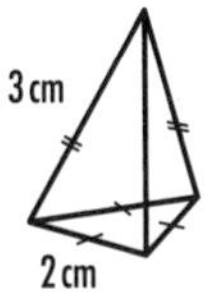

8

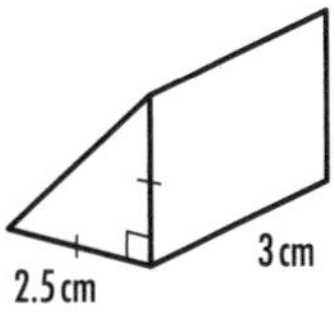

9

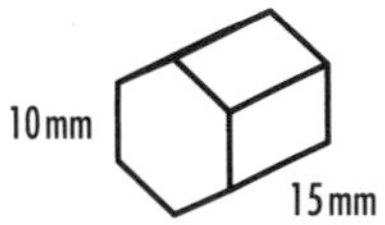

10

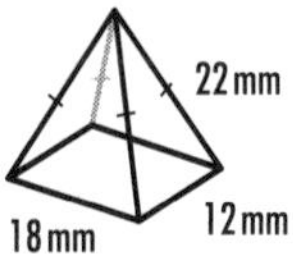

11

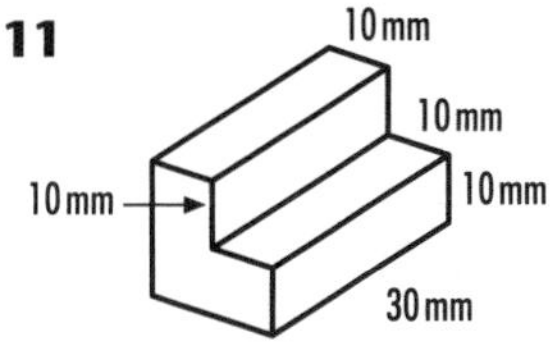

12

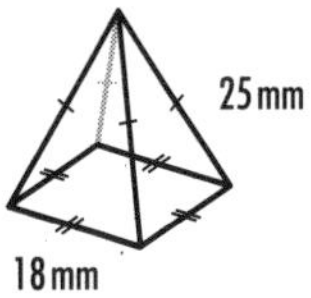

Exercise 72B

Draw a net for each of the following cuboids. If you do not draw the net to actual size, write the lengths of the sides on the diagram.

1

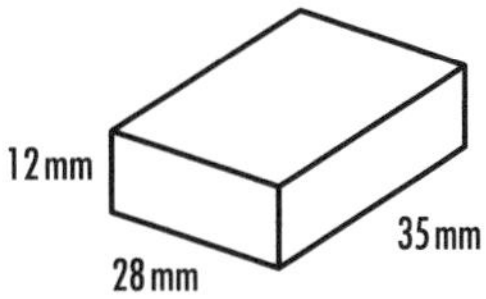

2

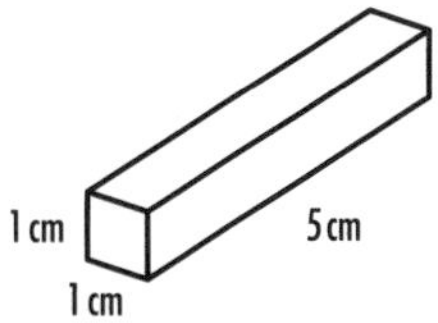

3

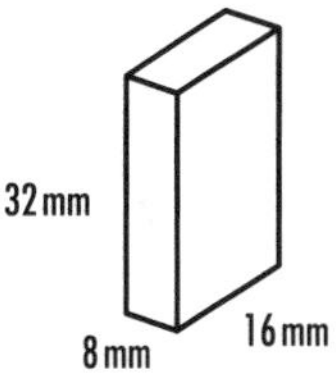

4

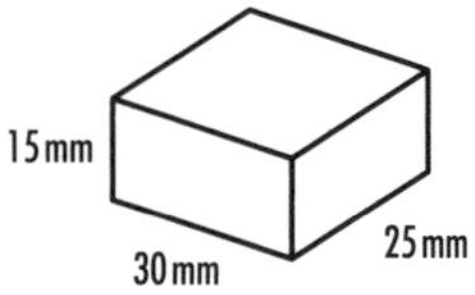

5

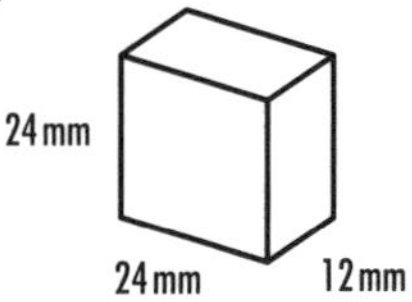

6

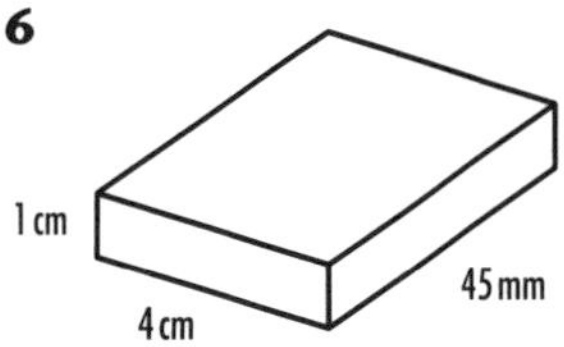

Draw a good sketch of the net of each of these 3-dimensional shapes.

7

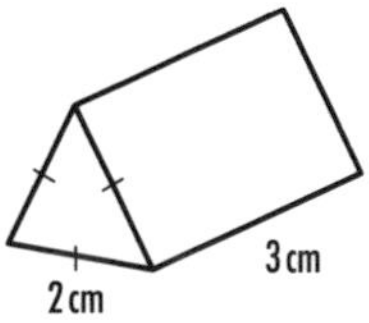

8

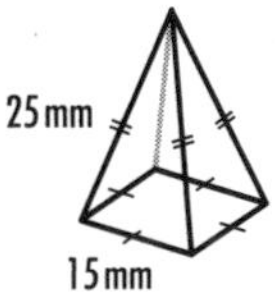

9

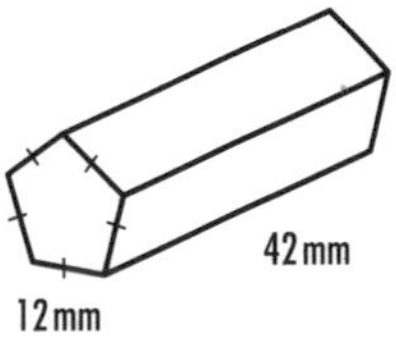

10

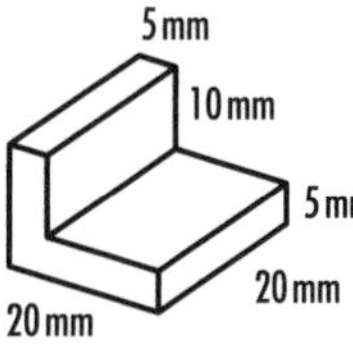

11

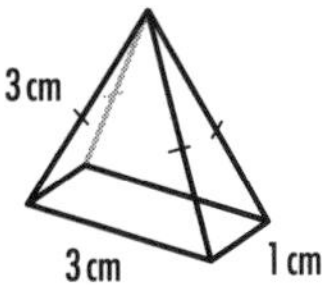

12

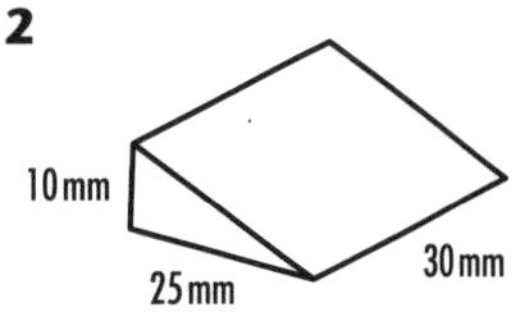

73/ AREAS OF SQUARES, RECTANGLES AND PARALLELOGRAMS

The area of squares, rectangles and parallelograms can be calculated using one formula:

$A = bh$

where b is the base length and h is the height.
The area is found by multiplying the base by the height.

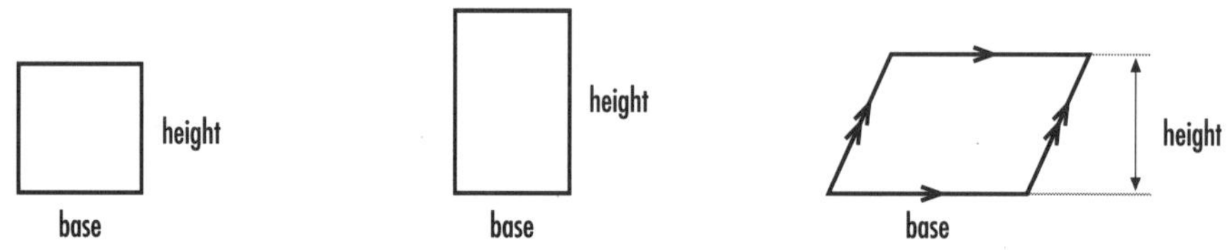

In the case of a square the base and height are the same so the formula becomes:

$A = l^2$ where l is the length of a side.

With the parallelogram make sure that the height is perpendicular to the base. *Do not* use the slant height.

Remember: Area is measured in square units such as mm^2, cm^2, m^2 etc.

EXAMPLE

► Calculate the area of the parallelogram in the diagram.

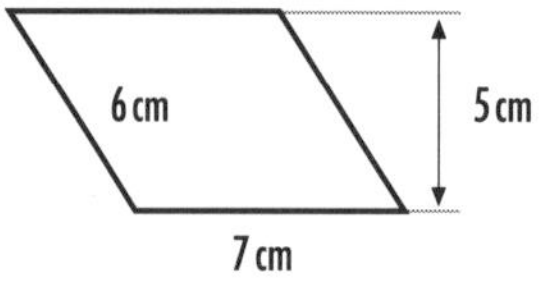

Area = base × height (Note: Ignore the *slant* height of 6 cm.)

$= 7 \times 5 = 35\ cm^2$

Exercise 73A

Sketch each of the following showing the positions of the known lengths. Calculate the area of each shape. Do not forget to write the unit of area with each answer.

1 Rectangle; base = 4 cm, height = 3 cm
2 Square; side = 6 cm
3 Parallelogram; slant height = 3 cm, base = 5 cm, height = 2.5 cm
4 Rectangle; base = 3.5 cm, height = 8 cm
5 Rectangle; base = 30 mm, height = 40 mm
6 Square; side = 2.5 m
7 Rectangle; base = 0.9 m, height = 1.2 m
8 Parallelogram; base = 40 mm, height = 25 mm, slant height = 28 mm
9 Square; side = 12 cm
10 Rectangle; base = 7.5 cm, height = 8 cm

11 Square; side = 0.8 m
12 Parallelogram; base = 12 mm, height = 10 mm, slant height = 11 mm
13 Rectangle; base = 13 cm, height = 7 cm
14 Rectangle; base = 60 mm, height = 35 mm
15 Square; side = 21 mm

Calculate the area of each of the following shapes, which are not drawn to scale.

16

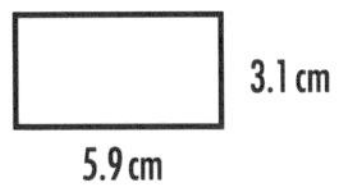

17

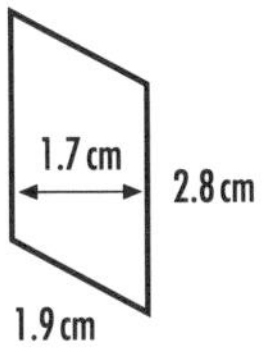

18

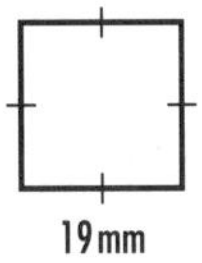

19

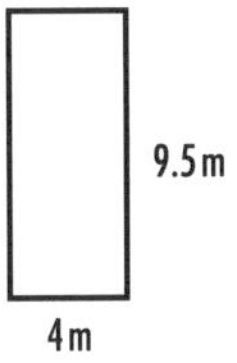

20

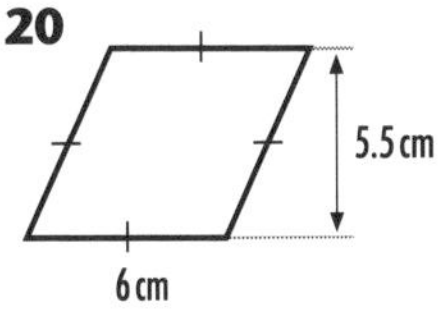

Exercise 73B

Sketch each of the following showing the positions of the known lengths. Calculate the area of each shape. Do not forget to write the unit of area with each answer.

1 Parallelogram; slant height = 5 cm, base = 6 cm, height = 4 cm
2 Rectangle; base = 3.2 m, height = 1.8 m
3 Parallelogram; base = 10 mm, height = 23 mm, slant height = 25 mm
4 Square; side = 7 m
5 Parallelogram; slant height = 7 cm, base = 5 cm, height = 6 cm
6 Square; side = 14 cm
7 Rectangle; base = 17 mm, height = 16 mm
8 Square; side = 20 cm
9 Parallelogram; base = 80 mm, height = 75 mm, slant height = 8 cm (answer in mm^2)
10 Rectangle; base = 10 cm, height = 90 mm (answer in cm^2)
11 Square; side = 0.8 m
12 Rectangle; base = 22 cm, height = 11 cm
13 Parallelogram; slant height = 4.5 cm, base = 4.2 cm, height = 4.2 cm
14 Square; side = 17 mm
15 Rectangle; base = 12 cm, height = 8.5 cm

Calculate the area of each of the following shapes, which are not drawn to scale.

16

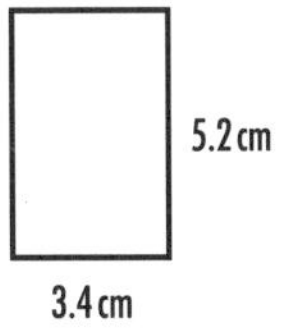

17

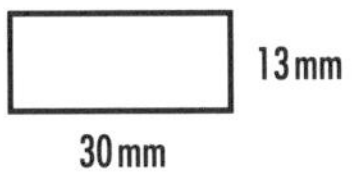

18

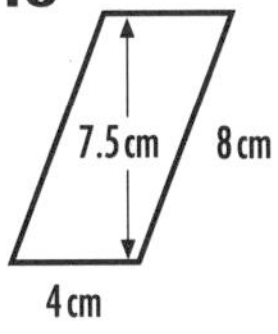

19

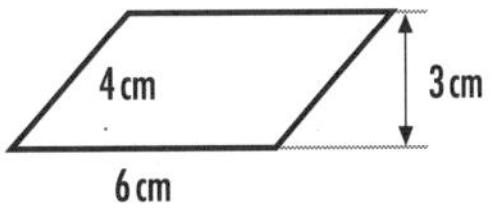

20

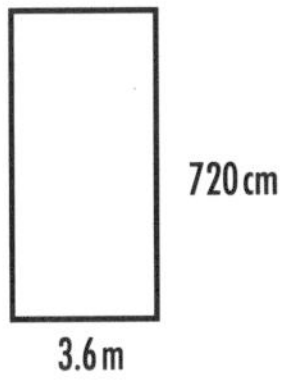

74/ AREA OF A TRIANGLE

Every triangle can be shown to be half a parallelogram (including squares and rectangles).

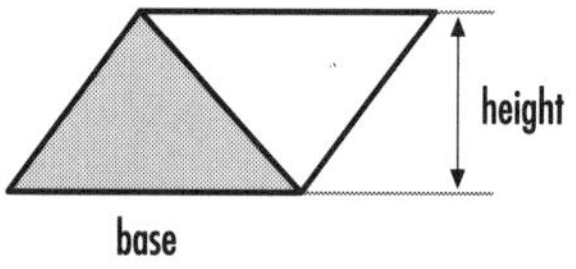

The area is therefore half that of a parallelogram and the formula is:

$$\text{area of a triangle} = \tfrac{1}{2} \times \text{base} \times \text{height} = \tfrac{1}{2}bh$$

Do not forget that each of the three sides of a triangle can be the base and there are three possible heights. You should choose the base that gives the easiest calculation.

EXAMPLE

► Calculate the area of the triangle.

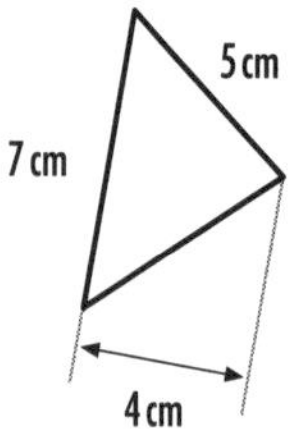

The base is 7 cm and the height to go with this base is 4 cm. Ignore the other side of 5 cm since it is not the base that goes with the height given.

$A = \tfrac{1}{2}bh$

$= \tfrac{1}{2} \times 7 \times 4 = 14\ \text{cm}^2$

Exercise 74A

Calculate the area of each of the following triangles. Do not forget to write the units for each answer.

1. Base = 3 cm, height = 4 cm
2. Base = 5 cm, height = 6 cm
3. Base = 7 cm, height = 4 cm
4. Base = 20 mm, height = 12 mm
5. Base = 10 cm, height = 8 cm
6. Base = 8 cm, height = 12 cm
7. Base = 17 mm, height = 14 mm
8. Base = 2 m, height = 1.4 m
9. Base = 25 mm, height = 2 cm (answer in mm^2)
10. Base = 21 cm, height = 20 cm
11. Base = 7 cm, height = 7 cm
12. Base = 1500 cm, height = 1.8 m (answer in m^2)
13. Base = 6.2 m, height = 3 m
14. Base = 3.2 cm, height = 1.6 cm
15. Base = 0.8 m, height = 0.6 m

Calculate the area of each of the following triangles, which are not drawn to scale. Do not forget to write the unit of area with each answer.

16

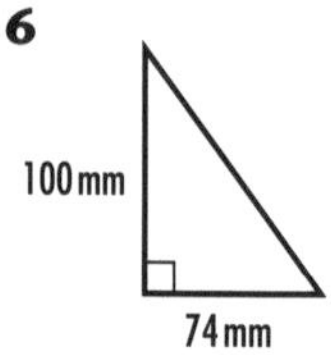

17

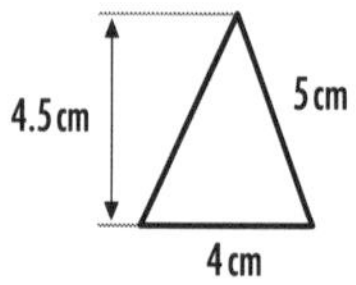

18

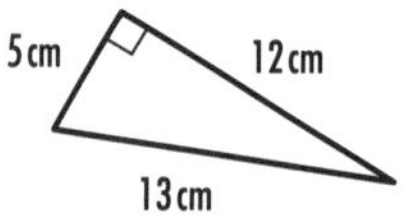

19

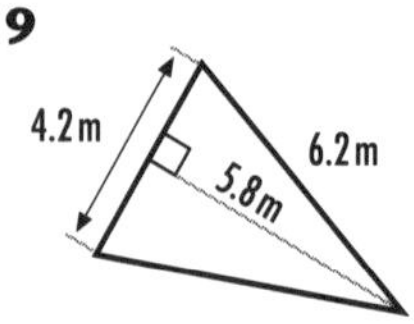

20

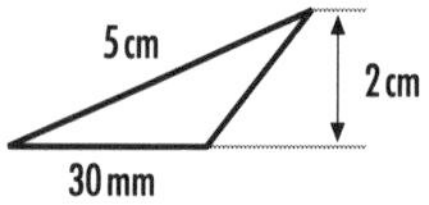

Exercise 74B

Calculate the area of each of the following triangles. Do not forget to write the units for each answer.

1. Base = 6 cm, height = 3 cm
2. Base = 9 cm, height = 4 cm
3. Base = 8 cm, height = 2.5 cm
4. Base = 10 cm, height = 7.2 cm
5. Base = 30 mm, height = 16 mm
6. Base = 0.8 m, height = 0.4 m

7 Base = 64 mm, height = 5 cm (answer in mm^2)

8 Base = 12 cm, height = 11 cm

9 Base = 4.8 cm, height = 50 mm (answer in cm^2)

10 Base = 24 mm, height = 30 mm

11 Base = 1.4 m, height = 1.2 m

12 Base = 56 mm, height = 42 mm

13 Base = 0.44 m, height = 40 cm (answer in cm^2)

14 Base = 16 cm, height = 20 cm

15 Base = 2.4 m, height = 2.4 m

Calculate the area of each of the following triangles, which are not drawn to scale. Do not forget to write the unit of area with each answer.

16

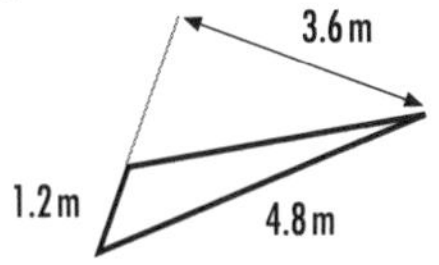

17

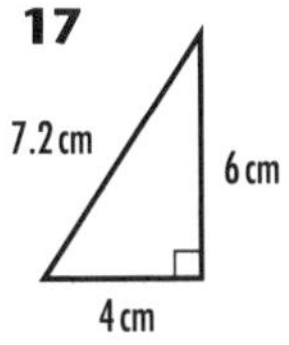

18

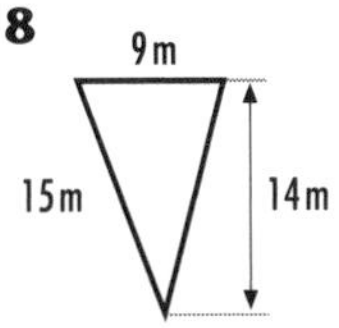

19

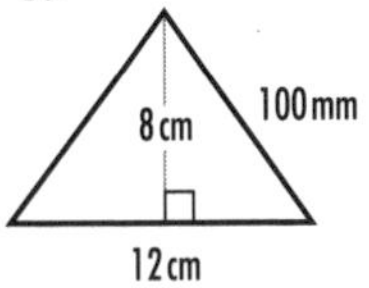

20

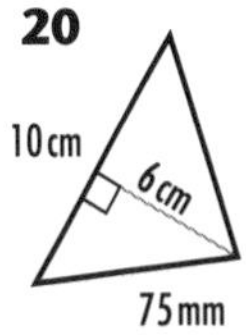

75/ AREA OF A TRAPEZIUM

There are two methods for finding the area of a trapezium.

Method 1

Divide the trapezium into two triangles and find the area of each. The area of the trapezium is found by adding these two areas together.

Method 2

Use the formula for the area of a trapezium:

$$A = \frac{1}{2}h(a + b)$$

where a and b are the lengths of the two parallel sides and h is the distance between them.

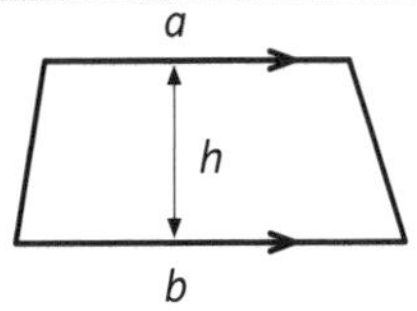

EXAMPLE

► Calculate the area of the trapezium.

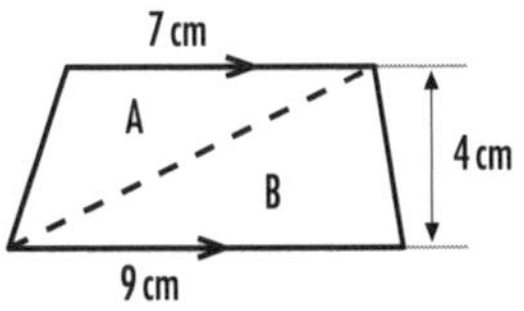

Method 1

Area of A $= \frac{1}{2} \times 7 \times 4$

$= 14\ cm^2$

Area of B $= \frac{1}{2} \times 9 \times 4$

$= 18\ cm^2$

Area of trapezium = 14 + 18

$= 32\ cm^2$

Method 2

Area $= \frac{1}{2}h(a + b)$

$= \frac{1}{2} \times 4 \times (7 + 9)$

$= \frac{1}{2} \times 4 \times 16$

$= 32\ cm^2$

Exercise 75A

Calculate the area of each of the following trapezia. Do not forget to write the units for each answer.

1 $a = 7$ cm, $b = 5$ cm, $h = 4$ cm

2 $h = 6$ cm, $a = 3$ cm, $b = 5$ cm

3 $a = 3$ cm, $b = 2$ cm, $h = 8$ cm

4 $b = 7$ cm, $a = 9$ cm, $h = 5$ cm

5 $a = 12$ mm, $h = 14$ mm, $b = 15$ mm

6 $a = 10$ cm, $b = 9$ cm, $h = 4$ cm

7 $a = 21$ cm, $h = 10$ cm, $b = 13$ cm

8 $h = 11$ cm, $a = 9$ cm, $b = 13$ cm

9 $a = 12\,\text{cm}$, $b = 8\,\text{cm}$, $h = 7\,\text{cm}$

10 $h = 3\,\text{cm}$, $a = 4\,\text{cm}$, $b = 6\,\text{cm}$

11 $b = 25\,\text{mm}$, $a = 35\,\text{mm}$, $h = 30\,\text{mm}$

12 $a = 7.5\,\text{cm}$, $b = 6.5\,\text{cm}$, $h = 3.2\,\text{cm}$

13 $a = 0.6\,\text{m}$, $h = 0.4\,\text{m}$, $b = 0.5\,\text{m}$

14 $h = 27\,\text{mm}$, $a = 23\,\text{mm}$, $b = 21\,\text{mm}$

15 $a = 1.5\,\text{m}$, $b = 1.3\,\text{m}$, $h = 120\,\text{cm}$ (answer in m^2)

Calculate the area of each of the following trapezia, which are not drawn to scale. Do not forget to write the unit of area with each answer.

16

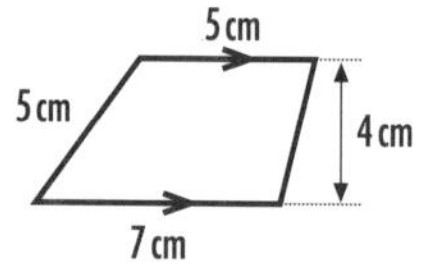

17

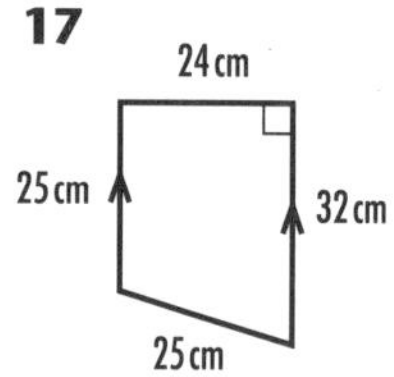

18

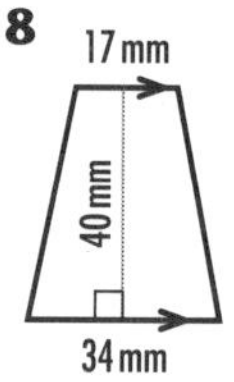

19

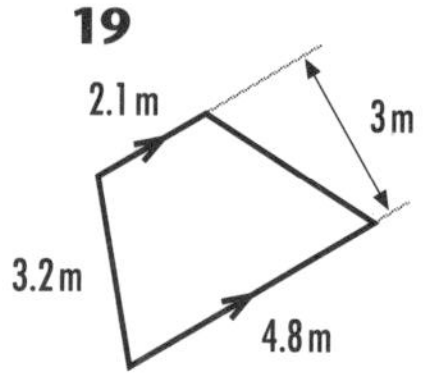

20

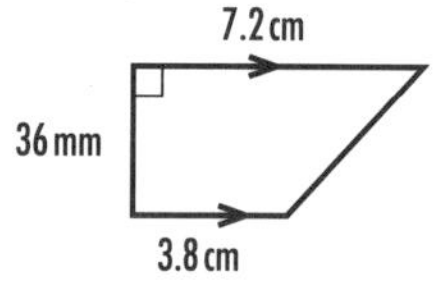

Exercise 75B

Calculate the area of each of the following trapezia. Do not forget to write the units for each answer.

1 $a = 6\,\text{cm}$, $b = 9\,\text{cm}$, $h = 8\,\text{cm}$

2 $b = 4\,\text{cm}$, $a = 5\,\text{cm}$, $h = 2\,\text{cm}$

3 $a = 9\,\text{cm}$, $b = 7\,\text{cm}$, $h = 6\,\text{cm}$

4 $h = 12\,\text{cm}$, $a = 10\,\text{cm}$, $b = 8\,\text{cm}$

5 $a = 3\,\text{cm}$, $b = 5\,\text{cm}$, $h = 5\,\text{cm}$

6 $b = 14\,\text{mm}$, $a = 18\,\text{mm}$, $h = 10\,\text{mm}$

7 $a = 11\,\text{cm}$, $h = 7\,\text{cm}$, $b = 9\,\text{cm}$

8 $b = 4\,\text{cm}$, $a = 7\,\text{cm}$, $h = 12\,\text{cm}$

9 $a = 20\,\text{mm}$, $b = 15\,\text{mm}$, $h = 12\,\text{mm}$

10 $h = 7\,\text{cm}$, $a = 9\,\text{cm}$, $b = 5\,\text{cm}$

11 $a = 0.5\,\text{m}$, $b = 0.6\,\text{m}$, $h = 0.8\,\text{m}$

12 $b = 34\,\text{mm}$, $a = 38\,\text{mm}$, $h = 25\,\text{mm}$

13 $a = 15\,\text{cm}$, $b = 16\,\text{cm}$, $h = 20\,\text{cm}$

14 $a = 3.8\,\text{cm}$, $h = 4.5\,\text{cm}$, $b = 2.2\,\text{cm}$

15 $b = 11\,\text{cm}$, $a = 12\,\text{cm}$, $h = 60\,\text{mm}$ (answer in cm^2)

Calculate the area of each of the following trapezia, which are not drawn to scale. Do not forget to write the unit of area with each answer.

16

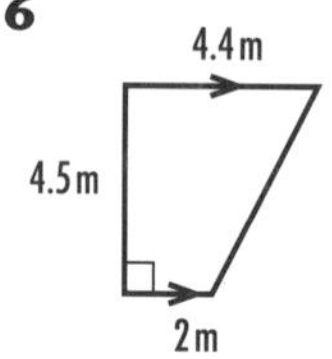

17

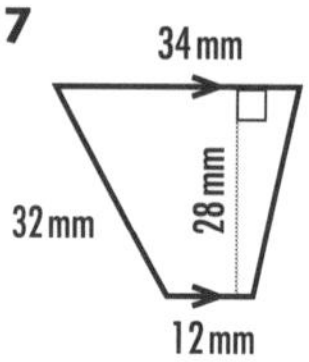

18

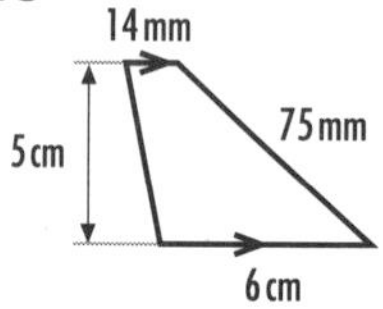

19

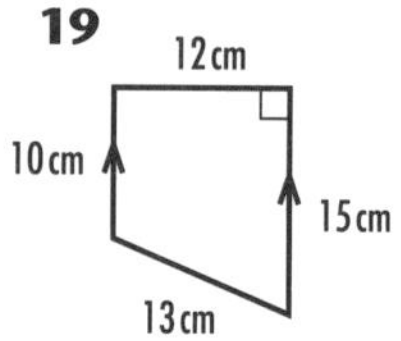

20

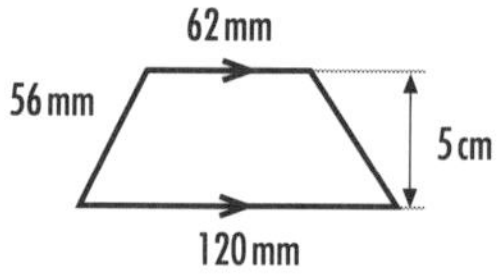

76/ VOLUMES OF CUBES AND CUBOIDS

A **cuboid** is a 3D shape with six faces, each of which is a rectangle.
Volume of a cuboid = width × length × height

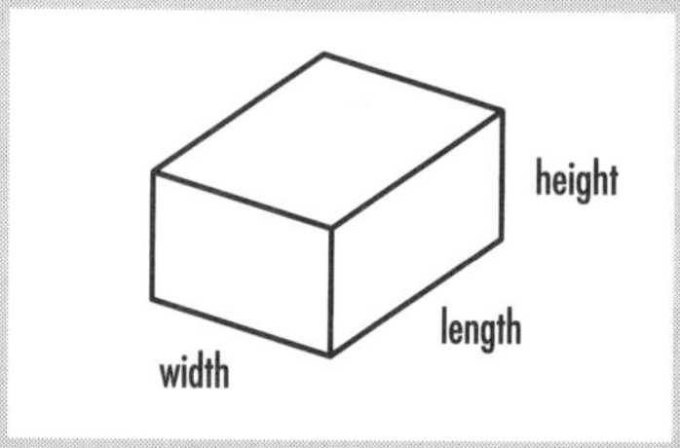

A **cube** is a type of cuboid which has all six faces the same.
Each face is a square.
The length, width and height of a cube are all the same.
Volume of a cube = l^3 where l is the length of an edge.

EXAMPLE

▶ Calculate the volume of the cuboid.

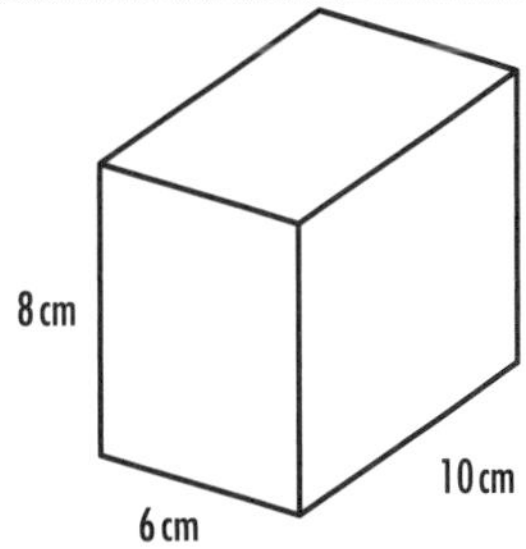

Volume $= w \times l \times h$
$= 6 \times 10 \times 8$
$= 480\ \text{cm}^3$

EXAMPLE

▶ Calculate the volume of a cube with edges of length 1.2 m.

Volume $= l^3$
$= 1.2 \times 1.2 \times 1.2$ (or use the x^3 key on your calculator)
$= 1.728\ \text{m}^3$

Exercise 76A

Calculate the volume of each of the following. Diagrams are not drawn to scale. Do not forget to write the units for each answer (cm^3, m^3 etc.).

1 A cube with edges of length 5 cm
2 A cuboid with edges of length 3 cm, 5 cm and 7 cm
3 A cuboid with edges of length 10 mm, 12 mm and 20 mm
4 A cube with edges of length 3 cm
5 A cuboid with edges of length 4 cm, 6 cm and 7 cm
6 A cuboid with edges of length 8 mm, 8 mm and 6 mm
7 A cube with edges of length 1.5 cm
8 A cuboid with edges of length 4 cm, 12 cm and 10 cm
9 A cube with edges of length 30 mm
10 A cuboid with edges of length 0.3 m, 0.5 m and 0.7 m
11 A cube with edges of length 9 cm
12 A cuboid with edges of length 2.5 cm, 2.2 cm and 1.6 cm
13 A cuboid with edges of length 36 mm, 45 mm and 28 mm
14 A cube with edges of length 0.9 m

15

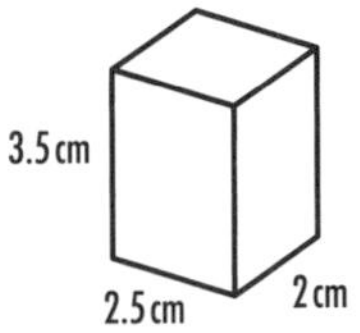

16

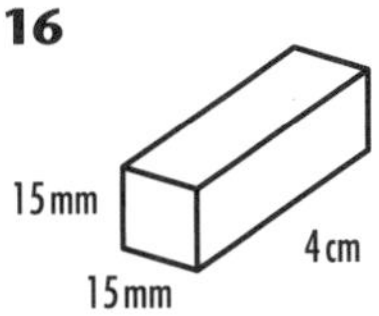

17

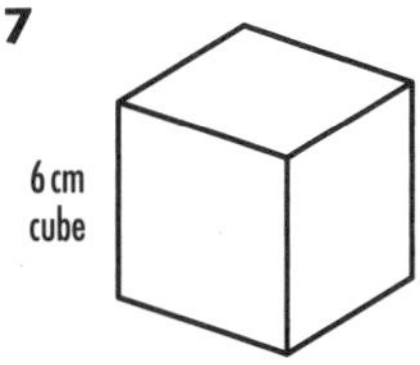

18

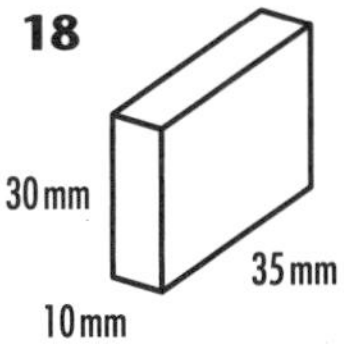

19

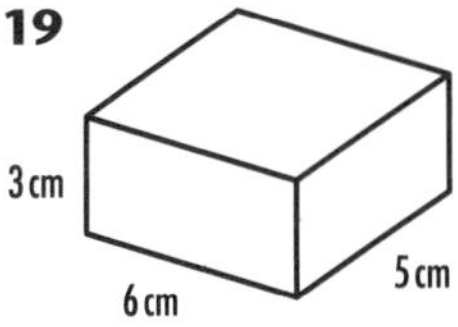

20

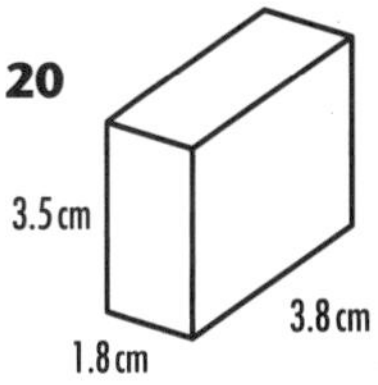

Exercise 76B

Calculate the volume of each of the following. Diagrams are not drawn to scale. Do not forget to write the units for each answer (cm^3, m^3 etc.).

1 A cuboid with edges of length 2 cm, 6 cm and 8 cm
2 A cube with edges of length 6 cm
3 A cuboid with edges of length 12 cm, 10 cm and 8 cm
4 A cuboid with edges of length 8 cm, 7 cm and 4 cm
5 A cube with edges of length 4 cm
6 A cuboid with edges of length 13 cm, 10 cm and 8 cm
7 A cuboid with edges of length 12 cm, 8 cm and 7 cm
8 A cube with edges of length 0.6 m
9 A cuboid with edges of length 56 mm, 48 mm and 3.2 cm (answer in mm^3)
10 A cube with edges of length 21 mm
11 A cuboid with edges of length 0.7 m, 0.5 m and 0.6 m
12 A cuboid with edges of length 2.5 cm, 2.1 cm and 1.5 cm
13 A cube with edges of length 11 cm
14 A cuboid with edges of length 1.1 m, 1 m and 1.2 m

15

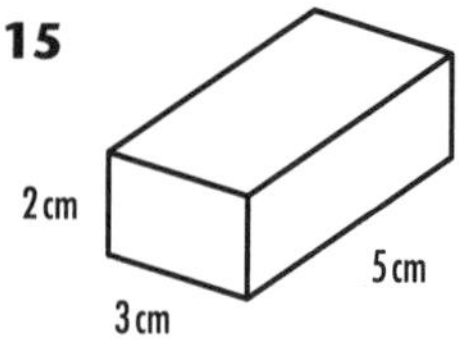

16

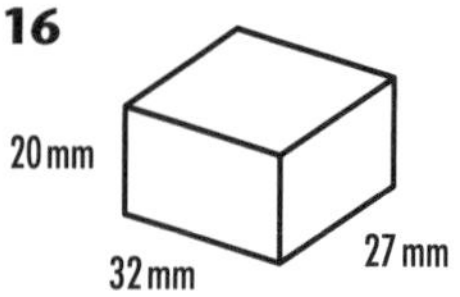

17

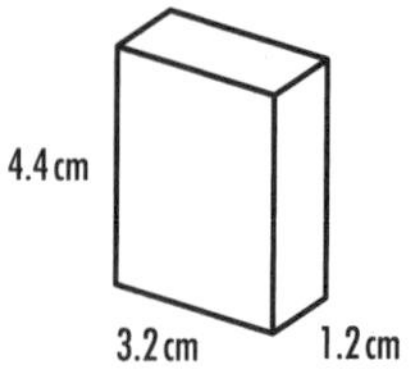

18

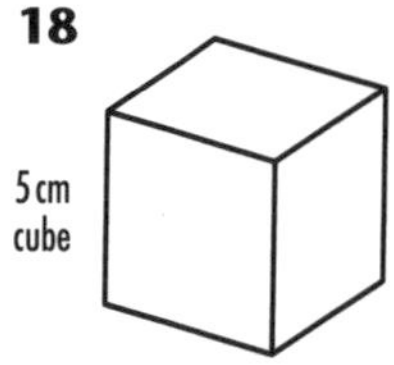

19

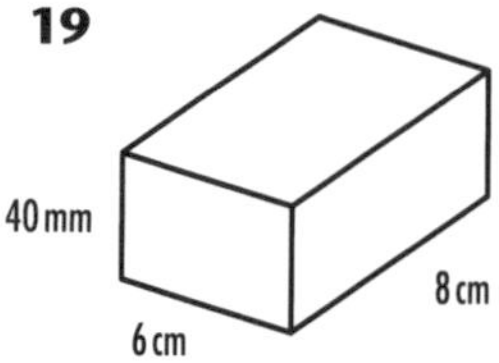

20

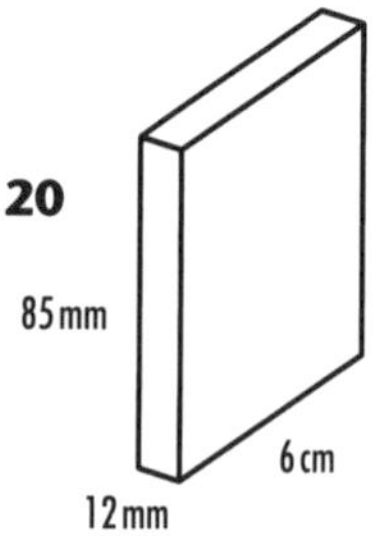

77/ CIRCUMFERENCE OF A CIRCLE

The **circumference** (the distance around the outside) of a circle is given by the formula:

$$C = \pi d$$

where d is the diameter of the circle.

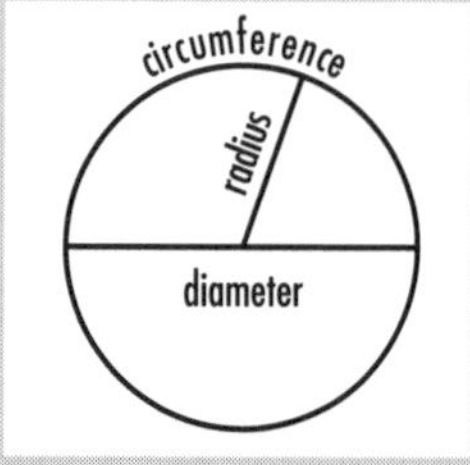

The number π is an example of an **irrational number**, which is a number that cannot be written down exactly. Use the π key on your calculator or one of these values: 3.14 or 3.142.

The diameter is twice the length of the radius. If you know the radius of a circle, double it to find the diameter and then use the length of the diameter in the formula $C = \pi d$.

Alternatively, you can use the formula $C = 2\pi r$ where r is the radius. However, the formula $C = \pi d$ is all you need to remember.

EXAMPLE

▶ Calculate the circumference of a circle of radius 4 cm.

Radius = 4 cm
Diameter = 8 cm
$C = \pi d$
$= \pi \times 8$
= 25.13 cm (to 2 decimal places)

Exercise 77A

Calculate the circumference of each of the following circles using the value of π stated. Give your answer to 3 significant figures.

Use $\pi = 3.14$.

1 Diameter = 12 cm **2** Radius = 4 cm **3** Radius = 6 m **4** Diameter = 10 cm
5 Radius = 8 mm **6** Diameter = 5 cm **7** Radius = 12 mm **8** Diameter = 2.5 m
9 Diameter = 3.2 cm **10** Radius = 15 cm

Use the π key or $\pi = 3.142$.

11 Radius = 6 cm **12** Radius = 1.2 m **13** Diameter = 3.6 cm **14** Radius = 8.5 cm
15 Diameter = 18 cm **16** Radius = 7 cm **17** Diameter = 7 cm **18** Radius = 10.5 cm
19 Radius = 3.5 m **20** Diameter = 21 mm

21 Diameter = 6.5 cm; use π key or $\pi = 3.142$.
22 Radius = 8 mm; use $\pi = 3.14$.
23 Radius = 17 cm; use $\pi = 3.14$.
24 Diameter = 6.4 cm; use π key or $\pi = 3.142$.
25 Radius = 9.2 cm; use $\pi = 3.14$.
26 Diameter = 20 cm; use π key or $\pi = 3.142$.
27 Radius = 14 cm; use $\pi = 3.14$.
28 Diameter = 17 cm; use π key or $\pi = 3.142$.
29 Diameter = 1.4 m; use $\pi = 3.14$.
30 Radius = 4.8 m; use π key or $\pi = 3.142$.

Exercise 77B

Calculate the circumference of each of the following circles using the value of π stated. Give your answer to 3 significant figures.

Use $\pi = 3.14$.

1 Radius = 10 cm **2** Diameter = 8 mm **3** Radius = 9 cm **4** Radius = 16 mm
5 Diameter = 15 cm **6** Diameter = 10.2 cm **7** Diameter = 6 cm **8** Radius = 4.5 m
9 Diameter = 11 cm **10** Radius = 7.5 cm

Use π key or $\pi = 3.142$.

11 Radius = 1.25 m **12** Diameter = 5.4 cm **13** Radius = 65 mm **14** Diameter = 23 cm
15 Radius = 0.9 m **16** Radius = 28 cm **17** Diameter = 1.8 cm **18** Radius = 3.8 m
19 Diameter = 35 mm **20** Radius = 21 mm

21 Radius = 25 cm; use $\pi = 3.14$.
22 Radius = 4.6 m; use π key or $\pi = 3.142$.
23 Radius = 40 mm; use $\pi = 3.14$.
24 Radius = 49 mm; use π key or $\pi = 3.142$.
25 Diameter = 112 mm; use π key or $\pi = 3.142$.
26 Diameter = 6.4 m; use π key or $\pi = 3.142$.
27 Diameter = 0.75 m; use $\pi = 3.14$.
28 Diameter = 120 mm; use π key or $\pi = 3.142$.
29 Diameter = 2.8 m; use $\pi = 3.14$.
30 Radius = 1.45 m; use π key or $\pi = 3.142$.

78/ AREA OF A CIRCLE

The area of a circle can be calculated using the formula:

$A = \pi r^2$

where r is the radius of the circle.

There is not a formula in general use for the area of a circle using the diameter. If the diameter of a circle is given, find the radius by dividing the diameter by 2.

The number π is an example of an **irrational number**, which is a number that cannot written down exactly. Use the π key on a calculator or one of the following values: 3.14 or 3.142.

EXAMPLE

▶ Find the area of a circle of diameter 2.65 m. Use $\pi = 3.14$.

Diameter = 2.6 m

Radius = 1.3 m

$A = \pi r^2 = 3.14 \times 1.3 \times 1.3$ (Remember: r^2 means $r \times r$ *not* $r \times 2$.)

$= 5.31\ \text{cm}^2$ (to 3 s.f.)

Remember: Area is measured in square units such as cm^2.

Exercises 78A and 78B

Find the area of each circle in Exercises 77A and 77B. Give your answers to 3 significant figures.

REVISION

Exercise F

1 The distance between two junctions on a motorway is measured as 3.5 cm on a map, which is drawn to a scale of 1 : 200 000. What is the actual distance?

2 Tony is drawing to a scale of 5 cm ≡ 1 m. He wishes to show an actual length of 40 cm; what length will he draw this?

3 Draw a line to represent a distance of 5.4 km using a scale of 1 cm ≡ 2 km.

4 Draw a line to represent a distance of 9.2 m using a scale of 1 : 400.

5 Copy the diagrams and, for each, show clearly the position of the centre of enlargement. State the scale factor.

(a)

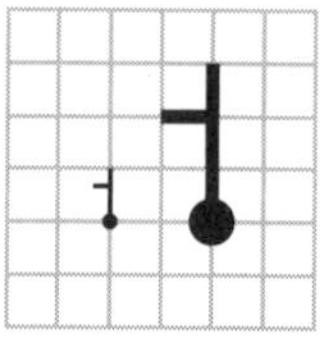

(b)

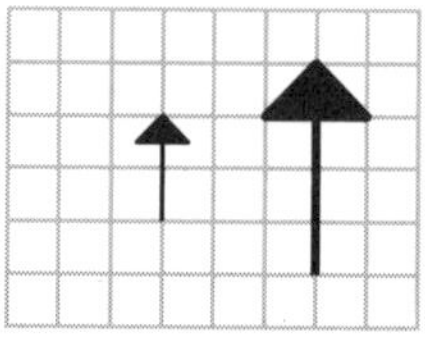

6 Convert the following.

(a) 1.2 m to mm (b) 15 400 cm to m (c) 12 500 g to kg (d) 0.975 t to kg

(e) 340 cl to *l* (f) 7.5 *l* to ml

7 Draw the net of the cuboid shown in the diagram to the actual size indicated.

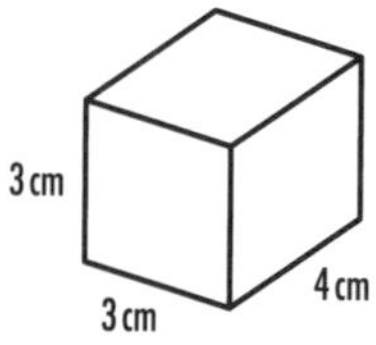

8 Calculate the area of each of these shapes.

(a) (b) (c) (d) (e)

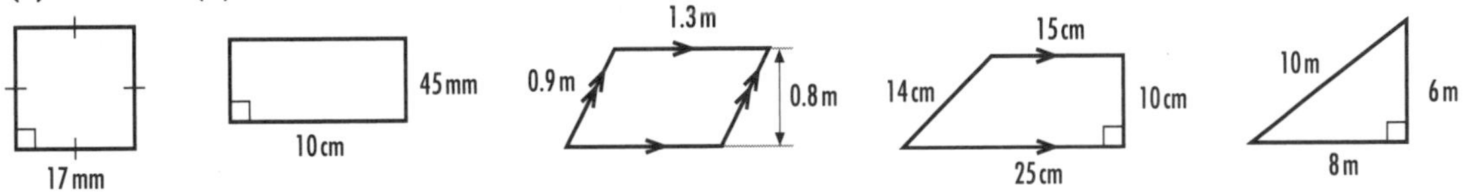

9 Which of the four solids best matches the net shown?

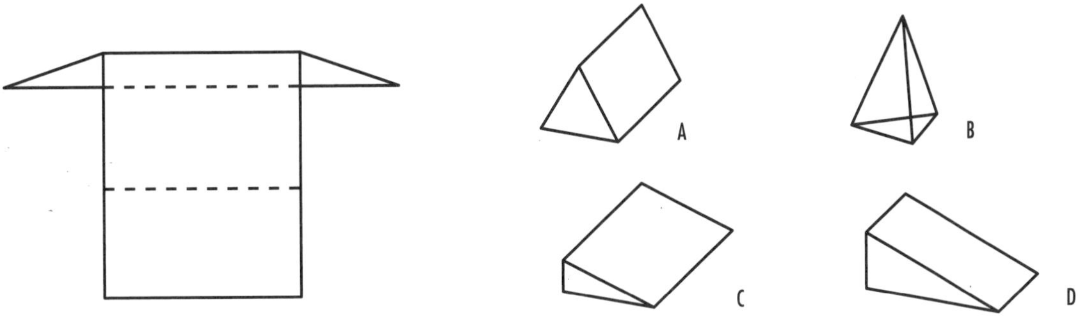

10 Calculate the volume of a cube with edges of length 4.5 cm.

11 Calculate the volume of a cuboid which measures 4.2 cm by 4.6 cm by 8 cm.

12 Calculate the circumference of a circle of radius 5.1 cm using the π key on your calculator or $\pi = 3.142$.

13 Calculate the area of a circle of diameter 10 m using $\pi = 3.14$.

Exercise FF

1 Referring to the map of Milton Keynes Area on page 101, measure the distance on the V11 road between the junctions with the H6 and the H8 roads. Use this value to estimate the actual distance.

2 Referring to the map of Le Havre and District on page 101, measure the distance from Bayeux to Pont-l'Evêque passing through Caen. Use this value to estimate the actual distance.

3 Malcolm sketches a room in his new house. Redraw Malcolm's drawing accurately to a scale of 1 : 50.

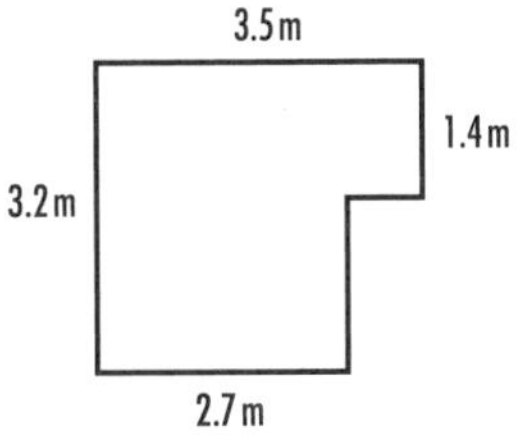

4 Copy the diagram carefully and enlarge the shape by a scale factor of 3 from the centre of enlargement X.

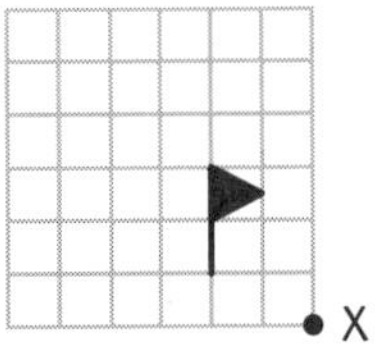

5 William is confused! A chart tells him that his healthy weight is 75 kg but he has weighed himself on some old scales as $12\frac{1}{2}$ stone. Is he overweight and, if so, by how many kilograms approximately?

6 Leigh's fish tank can hold 36 gallons. Estimate the capacity of the tank in litres.

7 Which of the following is the most sensible estimate for the weight of a small cat: 130 g, 75 kg, 0.0025 t?

8 Which of the following is the most sensible estimate for the length of a car: 1700 mm, 4.5 m, 200 cm?

9 Which is heavier, twenty bags of sugar weighing 1 kg each or a 40-lb bag of potatoes, and by how much approximately?

10 A tank has a base which measures 50 cm by 50 cm. It is filled with water to a height of 40 cm. What is the volume of the water in cm^3. Using the fact that $1\ cm^3 = 1$ ml, calculate the volume of water in litres.

11 A block of lead which measures 4 cm by 2 cm by 8 cm is melted down and reshaped into a cube. Calculate the length of the edges of this cube.

12 Sarah makes a wheel which she hopes will measure 1 metre in circumference. The radius of her wheel is 30 cm. Will Sarah's wheel have a circumference of 1 metre? If not, by how much is the circumference incorrect?

13 Talat needs to put 50 grams of fertiliser on every square metre of a circular flower bed. The radius of the flower bed is 5 m.

(a) Calculate the area of the flower bed.

(b) Calculate the amount of fertiliser required.

14 Calculate the area of each of the following.

(a)

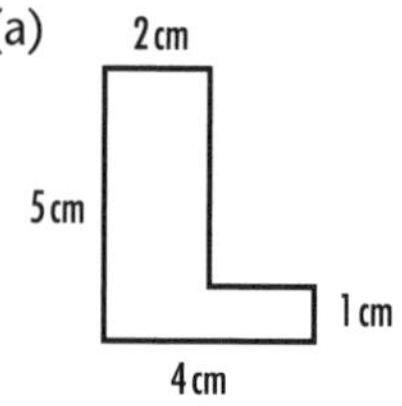

(b)

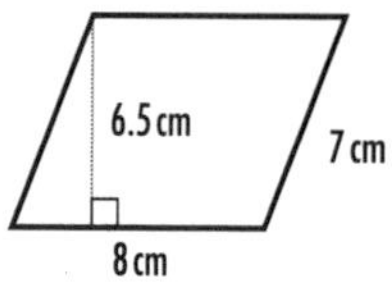

(c)

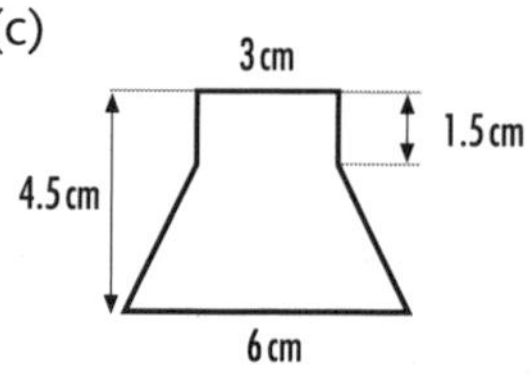

(d)

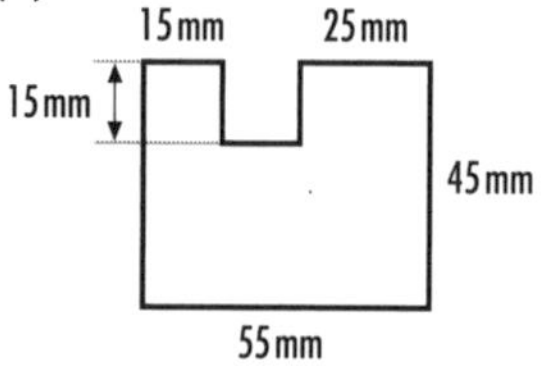

(e)

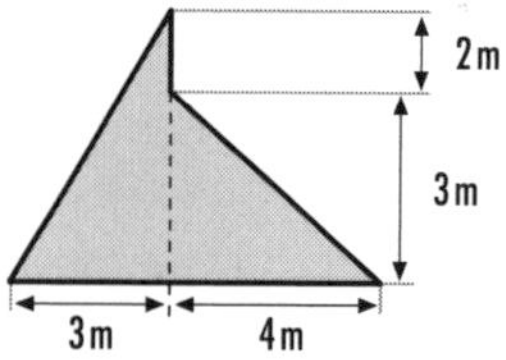

Handling data

79/ MEAN AND RANGE

The **mean** is a type of average.

$$\text{Mean of a set of values} = \frac{\text{the sum of all the values}}{\text{the number of values}}$$

The **range** tells us how widely spread the numbers are.
Range = largest number − smallest number

EXAMPLE

▶ Calculate the mean and the range of this set of numbers:
13, 19, 15, 10, 18, 17, 21, 14

Sum of all the values = 13 + 19 + 15 + 10 + 18 + 17 + 21 + 14 = 127
Number of values = 8
Mean = 127 ÷ 8 = 15.875
The largest number is 21 and the smallest is 10.
Range = 21 − 10 = 11

Exercise 79A

For each set of values find (a) the mean (b) the range.

1 5, 7, 2, 10
2 6, 1, 5, 8, 3
3 12, 16, 8, 8
4 45, 21, 63
5 5, 6, 2, 4, 3
6 1, 9, 4, 12
7 31, 25, 39, 30, 25
8 5, 1, 9, 4, 6
9 12, 8, 4, 3, 7, 2
10 18, 15, 11, 14
11 3, 1, 2, 1, 0, 5, 3, 6, 7, 2
12 11, 9, 8, 6, 3, 7, 12
13 1, 0, 3, 5, 0, 1, 9, 3, 5, 4
14 44, 41, 47, 39, 51, 0
15 2, 1, 6, 0, 8, 7, 5, 5, 4, 5, 6, 5
16 45, 61, 31, 8, 25, 31
17 0.7, 0.6, 0.2, 0.9
18 2.1, 3.2, 1.8, 1.5, 0.4
19 101, 103, 105, 104, 102, 102, 102, 104
20 41, 37, 36, 39, 45, 46, 47, 49, 47, 50

Exercise 79B

For each set of values find (a) the mean (b) the range.

1 6, 5, 2, 7
2 5, 1, 1, 3, 5
3 7, 8, 6, 1, 9, 11
4 21, 18, 17, 24
5 5, 2, 1, 6, 3, 0, 1, 6
6 15, 11, 8, 12, 4
7 7, 9, 5, 1, 8, 9
8 58, 79, 34
9 19, 11, 12, 13, 15, 20
10 42, 1, 54, 13, 75
11 3, 2, 1, 6, 4, 5, 8, 7
12 9, 11, 7, 4, 10, 11, 4
13 68, 45, 31, 96
14 10, 11, 8, 13, 15, 13, 14, 6
15 44, 41, 47, 39, 51, 42
16 103, 99, 102, 14
17 3, 5, 0, 4, 1, 6, 7, 6, 5, 7
18 20, 19, 22, 18, 14, 3, 6, 14, 18, 2, 23, 24
19 1.5, 1.3, 0.9, 1.1, 0.8, 1.6
20 223, 105, 56, 46, 17, 95, 116, 12

EXAMPLE

► The mean number of phone calls received over a period of four days is seven per day. If an extra day is included in the results, the mean drops to six. How many phone calls were there on the extra day?

Total number over 4 days = $4 \times 7 = 28$ phone calls
Total number over 5 days = $5 \times 6 = 30$ phone calls
So there were two phone calls on the extra day.

EXAMPLE

► The range of scores for six players in a 9-hole golf tournament is 17. Five of the scores, including the lowest, are: 31, 29, 34, 42 and 39. What is the sixth score?

Lowest score = 29
Highest score = $29 + 17 = 46$

EXAMPLE

► Eight students compare their scores in English language and English literature tests:

English language	23	14	25	30	32	45	11	20
English literature	42	25	48	47	15	37	1	17

Calculate the mean and range for the two sets of scores. Which test has the higher mean, and which test has the greater spread?

English language: mean = $200 \div 8 = 25$, range = $45 - 11 = 34$
English literature: mean = $232 \div 8 = 29$, range = $48 - 1 = 47$
The English literature test has the greater mean value and the results are more widely spread.

Exercise 80A

1 The mean of seven numbers is 17. Calculate the total of the numbers.
2 The total ages of a group of eight pupils is 128 years. What is the mean age?
3 The mean of five prices is £13. What is the total of the prices?
4 The total of a set of numbers is 120 and the mean is 5. How many numbers are there?
5 The total rainfall for the first six months of a year is 162 mm. What is the mean rainfall per month?
6 The range of temperatures recorded over 14 days is 15°C. If the highest recorded temperature is 32°C, what is the lowest temperature?
7 Tarik adds up his goals and finds that he has scored 27 goals at an average of three goals per game. How many games has he played?
8 The mean of eleven numbers is 13. What is the total of the numbers?
9 The range of the heights of a group of pupils is 34 cm. There are 32 pupils in the class. If the height of the tallest pupil is 178 cm, what is the height of the smallest pupil?
10 The numbers of visitors to a small zoo are noted:

Day	Mon.	Tue.	Wed.	Thu.	Fri.	Sat.	Sun.
Visitors	53	?	207	236	344	580	972

If the mean value is 351 visitors per day, how many visitors were there on Tuesday?

11 The mean of three numbers is 9 and the range is 7. If the largest number is 13, calculate the other two numbers.

12 A group of 20 students sit a test and their mean score is 6.5. Another group of 10 students achieve a mean score of 5. Calculate the mean score for all 30 students.

13 The mean number of phone calls made by the six members of a family in a week is 11. Without Bill's phone calls the mean for the other five members of the family drops to 5. How many phone calls does Bill make in the week?

14 The number of sunny days is recorded for two resorts for the first eight months of a year:

Month	J	F	M	A	M	J	J	A
Eastend	15	12	8	10	15	16	22	18
Northpoint	14	12	15	16	14	15	19	20

Calculate the mean and range for each of the resorts and comment on which has the higher mean number of sunny days and which is more reliable for sunny days.

15 The mean weight of class 8A is 47 kg with a range of 12 kg. Class 8B has the same number of pupils and a mean weight of 45 kg with a range of 21 kg. Which class has the higher total weight and which is more likely to have the heaviest and lightest pupils?

Exercise 8OB

1 The total of a set of numbers is 72 and the mean is 8. How many numbers are there?

2 A party of elderly people goes out on a day trip in coaches. The mean number of persons on each of seven buses is 39. How many people were there in total?

3 Simone cycles an average of 126 km per day over four days. What is the average distance that she cycles in a day?

4 Ray makes a note of the number of hours per day that he has worked during the month of September. His shortest working day is 5 hours and the range is 7 hours. How long does he work on his longest day?

5 Stephanie adds up her earnings and finds that she has earned £112 and that her average earnings are £28 per day. How many days did she work?

6 A class has a total of 135 absences over a week of ten sessions. What is the mean absence per session?

7 Nigel lists the number of pages he reads per day over an eight-day period. He finds that the range is 11 pages. If the least number of pages he reads is 18, what is the greatest number of pages that he reads in a day?

8 Three numbers have a range of 12 and a mean of 15. If the smallest number is 8, calculate the other two numbers.

9 The highest night-time temperature is noted for each of eight months. If the range is 13°C, what is the missing value for September?

Month	Sep.	Oct.	Nov.	Dec.	Jan.	Feb.	Mar.	Apr.
Highest temperature (°C)	?	19	17	13	9	11	14	18

10 Seven members of a running team have an average score of 16. If the last member of the team is not included, the mean score for the remainder drops to 12. How many points did the last member of the team score?

11 The mean rainfall in the first six months of the year is 52 mm per month. The rainfall in June is only 22 mm. What is the mean rainfall for the first five months of the year?

12 A group of 15 students sit a test and their mean score is 7. Another group of ten students sit the same test and their mean score is 4.5. Calculate the mean score for all 25 students.

13 Six students compare their scores in two science tests:

Test 1	67	15	35	83	20	54
Test 2	85	67	72	89	69	80

Calculate the mean and range for each of the tests. Which test has the higher mean and which test has the greater spread?

14 The mean waiting time for a bus is 7 minutes but is 5 minutes for a coach. The range of the waiting times for a bus is 2 minutes but is 20 minutes for a coach. If it is essential for Ann to catch either within 10 minutes, to which stop should she go and why?

15 The number of cups of tea and coffee drunk in a small office is noted.

Day	Mon.	Tue.	Wed.	Thu.	Fri.
Coffees	7	6	9	8	4
Teas	6	5	5	7	5

Calculate the mean number of coffees per day and the mean number of teas per day. What is the range for each? Comment on which drink is more popular and which has the more reliable numbers.

81/ CONTINUOUS DATA: CREATING FREQUENCY TABLES AND FREQUENCY DIAGRAMS

Discrete data is information which is measured in definite steps (normally whole numbers). Examples of discrete data are:

The number of people in a room – this can be counted and, for example, 3.6 people has no meaning.

The number of books in a bookcase – this can also be counted.

The size of a shoe – this increases in steps: 7, $7\frac{1}{2}$, 8 etc. but 7.6, 7.7, 7.8 have no meaning.

Continuous data includes all types of data produced by measurement (for example 11.3 cm, 4.1 km, 10 seconds) and can be all types of number, including whole and decimal numbers. Continuous data that are widely spread can be grouped together.

EXAMPLE

► Group this continuous data in a frequency table. The data represents lengths, L, in centimetres.

76.1	69.3	65.4	63.2	70.5	90.5	75.9	22.7	88.4	49.3
38.0	92.3	72.9	39.6	67.6	27.4	47.2	68.9	78.4	72.5
74.7	19.8	85.3	48.6	52.8	93.3	49.4	83.8	58.9	50.1

Length L (cm)	Tally	Frequency
$0 \le L < 10$		0
$10 \le L < 20$	I	1
$20 \le L < 30$	II	2
$30 \le L < 40$	II	2
$40 \le L < 50$	IIII	4
$50 \le L < 60$	III	3
$60 \le L < 70$	~~IIII~~	5
$70 \le L < 80$	~~IIII~~ II	7
$80 \le L < 90$	III	3
$90 \le L < 100$	III	3
	Total	30

Each of the groups, for example $0 \le L < 10$, is called a **class interval**.

The table is a **frequency table**.

Note: The interval $0 \le L < 10$ includes 0 cm and is up to but does not include 10 cm.

The frequency table can be shown as a bar chart, which is also called a **frequency diagram**.

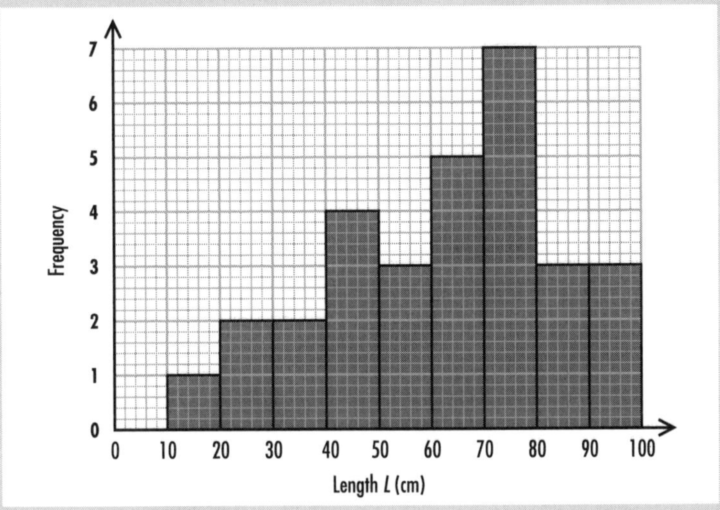

Note: The horizontal axis should show a continuous scale.

Exercise 81A

For each set of continuous data (a) draw and complete a frequency table (b) draw a frequency diagram.

1 A set of measurements of weight, in kilograms.

60	66	50	61	55	60	68	51	59	60
69	57	62	62	56	67	56	63	53	69
58	64	59	54	64					

Use class intervals $50 \le M < 55$, etc.

2 A set of measurements of length, in centimetres.

9.1	11.2	7.6	10.6	12.4	8.7	9.0	11.9	10.3	9.3
12.5	8.0	10.9	11.5	9.8	11.1	8.5	10.8	9.0	9.2
12.8	10.2	12.4	7.0	12.5	11.7	8.4	12.3	9.5	10.3

Use class intervals $7.0 \le L < 8.0$, etc.

3 Speeds of cars, recorded in miles per hour.

38	3	36	21	10	31	40	6	45	24
32	42	35	50	12	37	46	51	49	27
44	33	53	41	15	55	25	39	30	22
47	14	37	29	55	57	8	33	44	35

Use class intervals $0 \le s < 10$, etc.

4 Masses, recorded in kilograms.

2.1	3.1	0.4	3.4	1.5	3.6	2.0	2.7	3.2	1.5
2.3	1.5	2.5	3.5	3.0	1.3	1.0	3.2	2.3	0.7
3.5	1.5	4.4	2.8	3.8	1.9	4.4	2.0	3.2	3.5
3.5	2.9	1.6	4.7	3.0	3.9	2.4	2.1	4.0	1.6

Use class intervals $0 \le M < 1.0$, etc.

5 Capacities of various containers, recorded in millilitres.

413	660	575	465	610	522	641	550	475	572
502	519	671	517	641	534	434	622	535	681
580	618	635	482	548	592	543	447	540	463

Use class intervals $400 \le c < 450$, etc.

6 Daily mileage of various cars, in miles.

30	41	51	66	48	40	19	42	33	55
38	49	32	43	54	24	37	46	45	65
31	42	51	56	40	39	47	54	27	40

Use class intervals $10 \le m < 20$, etc.

7 Times, recorded in seconds.

18.5	15.1	18.8	19.3	19.7	16.5	18.2	17.6	17.0	18.9
19.9	20.4	17.0	18.4	19.5	17.6	19.6	18.0	18.2	19.1
18.8	17.0	19.6	15.5	17.4	17.7	20.3	16.8	20.2	19.3
19.1	16.7	18.3	18.5	19.5	20.0	19.7	19.9	18.5	17.3

Use class intervals $15 \le t < 16$, etc.

8 Weights of sacks, in kilograms.

51	61	38	74	45	52	54	41	50	67
32	45	53	87	66	42	59	75	46	52
49	64	48	73	60	33	45	56	48	59
57	34	65	40	47	55	43	30	54	40

Use class intervals $30 \le w < 40$, etc.

9 Distances, measured in metres.

101	14	123	50	76	107	33	78	109	61
134	69	26	112	126	93	19	52	129	96
43	83	171	66	132	29	89	118	70	104
21	53	122	136	120	48	72	155	35	58
161	64	81	170	141					

Use class intervals $0 \le d < 25$, etc.

10 Masses, recorded in kilograms.

71.1	43.8	65.7	78.1	50.9	72.1	62.2	85.3	54.7	65.7
71.1	50.1	61.1	484.	82.9	51.8	89.3	79.4	76.3	65.9
62.9	88.7	69.2	75.3	73.1	73.4	76.0	53.6	70.4	76.8
84.4	94.3	48.2	74.5	67.7	87.5	73.2	45.7	96.8	85.3
77.8	85.1	60.7	99.5	57.3	68.7	65.6	70.6	80.8	53.6

Use class intervals $40 \le M < 50$, etc.

Exercise 81B

For each set of continuous data (a) draw and complete a frequency table (b) draw a frequency diagram.

1 Times, recorded in seconds.

10.4	4.1	22.3	5.2	8.7	11.3	5.6	15.5	7.3	8.0
19.5	6.3	21.0	13.4	24.5	9.3	3.2	16.3	17.2	18.3
24.5	23.7	17.9	6.6	10.1	29.4	31.4	26.4	28.3	27.1
32.5	24.3	34.7	25.2	23.3					

Use class intervals $0 \le t < 5$, etc.

2 Masses, recorded in tonnes.

0.4	3.1	1.5	2.4	6.2	0.7	4.2	1.5	1.8	2.7
3.8	5.9	8.5	0.9	2.3	4.5	7.6	1.7	0.5	2.6
0.1	1.3	8.3	1.2	3.4	0.4	2.7	0.6	5.1	7.0

Use class intervals $0 \le m < 2.0$, etc.

3 Ages of various persons, in years.

31.1	39.5	15.7	20.4	15.5	20.3	33.4	21.2	18.4	36.7
17.2	22.1	40.7	35.1	17.8	29.6	34.4	38.8	42.1	16.2
25.9	24.2	28.3	38.3	23.6	27.9	42.0	33.0	16.3	21.2
16.6	45.7	25.3	30.3	20.5	19.6	43.7	16.5	26.8	32.8

Use class intervals $15 \leq A < 20$, etc.

4 Times, recorded in seconds.

30.3	40.1	16.1	35.8	30.8	33.2	29.4	35.3	41.3	26.3
31.2	36.4	39.9	32.7	11.3	38.3	28.4	25.6	31.8	32.3
21.4	38.3	44.9	31.6	27.4	30.7	23.5	28.5	43.5	34.5
25.0	39.1	28.5	33.2	27.6	37.1	44.7	31.9	33.6	36.1

Use class intervals $10 \leq t < 15$, etc.

5 Distances, measured in metres.

71	81	36	63	50	76	84	45	55	76
65	44	85	77	77	53	65	74	92	58
50	68	65	38	42	81	51	77	49	60
75	89	60	45	93	31	59	69	63	77

Use class intervals $30 \leq d < 40$, etc.

6 Masses, recorded in kilograms.

11.1	13.2	12.5	14.1	9.0	12.1	15.3	14.9	11.4	15.4
12.7	15.5	13.2	14.2	14.8	11.0	10.9	12.7	13.5	10.0
14.6	12.3	14.0	11.7	10.7	14.5	12.3	13.0	14.6	11.6
13.5	12.3	12.4	11.5	10.8					

Use class intervals $9.0 \leq M < 10.0$, etc.

7 Heights of a group of school-leavers, measured in centimetres.

151	142	171	165	184	140	155	175	193	150
161	197	172	199	156	175	164	176	184	165
160	188	148	198	178	173	142	162	157	175
184	150	155	169	173					

Use class intervals $140 \leq h < 150$, etc.

8 Floor areas, measured in square metres.

318	679	61	252	433	151	314	571	487	385
527	126	328	402	519	52	676	194	109	460
315	665	87	235	157	565	401	300	511	332
154	465	443	143	303	94	293	127	328	300

Use class intervals $0 \leq A < 100$, etc.

9 Crop yields of fields, measured in tonnes.

8.1	4.3	0.1	5.7	2.0	5.2	3.3	4.9	7.6	5.6
3.5	6.3	2.8	4.5	0.5	5.6	7.1	6.5	1.7	4.9
8.4	4.0	6.9	7.2	5.5	5.3	3.7	4.8	4.0	5.8
4.4	1.2	6.5	2.3	1.9	6.4	10.2	3.8	10.7	8.5
6.0	7.3	2.7	5.6	9.4	10.5	3.1	4.0	9.5	5.7

Use class intervals $0 \leq Y < 2.0$, etc.

10 Wingspans of birds, measured in centimetres.

10.1	14.1	18.9	13.9	16.7	12.5	14.3	18.0	12.1	15.6
19.5	14.3	14.2	16.2	13.2	14.5	10.0	16.4	12.5	14.9
16.5	19.7	15.9	13.2	16.0	12.1	14.2	16.3	17.6	20.9
11.6	18.6	12.8	15.9	15.7	17.9	11.5	17.8	14.4	17.7
15.2	15.0	18.5	20.8	13.4					

Use class intervals $10.0 \leq W < 12.0$, etc.

82/ CONTINUOUS DATA: INTERPRETING FREQUENCY DIAGRAMS

Continuous data is grouped together within a class interval, for example 20 cm $\leq L <$ 30 cm. This interval means that the length L is 20 cm *or more* but is *less* than 30 cm.

EXAMPLE

▶ The frequency diagram shows the weights of a group of students.

(a) How many students are there in the group?
(b) What is the size of the class interval?
(c) How many students weigh less than 45 kg?
(d) What percentage of the group weigh 50 kg or more?

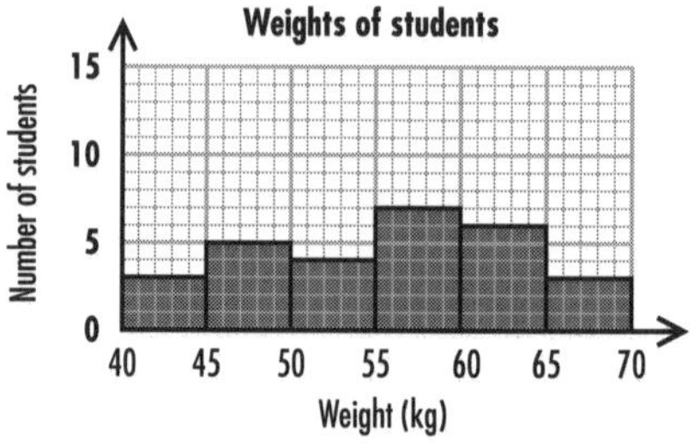

(a) Adding up the frequencies: 3 + 5 + 4 + 7 + 6 + 3 = 28
(b) 5 kg
(c) 3
(d) Students weighing 50 kg or more = 20
Percentage of students = $\frac{20}{28} \times 100 = 71.43\%$

Exercise 82A

1 The ages of people going on a day trip are shown. Use the graph to answer the following:

(a) How many people are going on the trip?
(b) Neil is 20 years old. How many people are there in his class interval?
(c) How many of the people on the trip are under 10 years old?
(d) What fraction of the people on the trip are 25 and over?

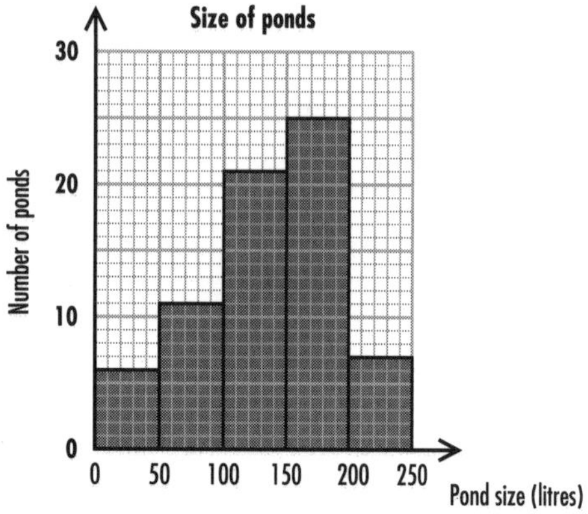

2 A garden centre carries out a survey of the size (in litres) of the small garden ponds sold. Use the graph to answer the following:

(a) What size of pond is most popular?
(b) What is the total number of ponds sold?
(c) Four of the ponds are exactly 200 litres. How many more ponds are there in the same class interval?
(d) What percentage of the ponds are less than 100 litres?

3 Dara keeps records of the weather every day. She draws a graph of the rainfall per day (in millimetres) over a period of time. Use the graph to answer the following:

(a) Over how many weeks does she record the rainfall?
(b) During this period there are 15 days in a row without any rain. How many other days are there with less than a millimetre of rainfall?
(c) On how many days is there 4 mm or more of rain?
(d) What percentage of the days have less than 3 mm of rain?

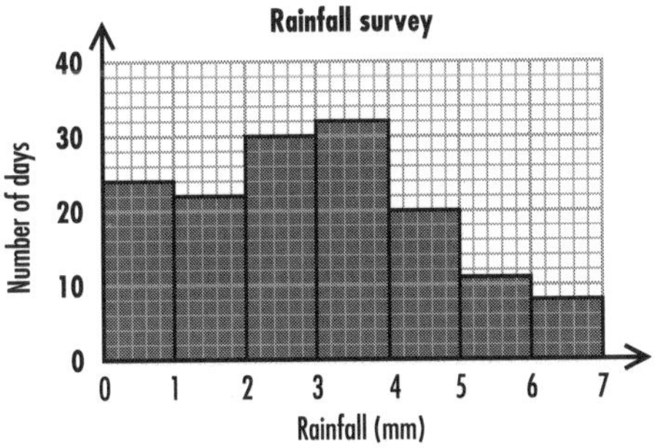

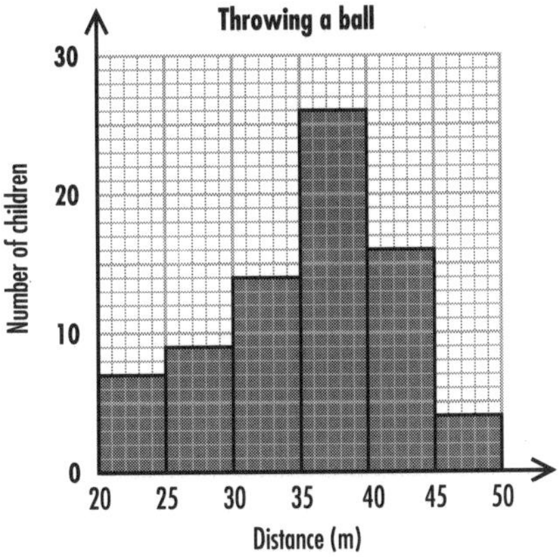

4 A junior school wants to find the best pupil at throwing a ball. Every pupil has a try at throwing the ball, the results are noted and a frequency diagram is drawn to show these results. Use the graph to answer the following:

(a) How many of the pupils failed to throw the ball 30 m?
(b) How many pupils managed to throw the ball 35 m or more?
(c) How many pupils are there in total?
(d) What fraction of the pupils throw the ball 40 m or more?

5 A firm produces sacks of peat which should weigh 50 kg. As part of a survey to check on the quality of its products, a worker weighs a sample of sacks and notes the weight of each sack. She then draws a frequency diagram to show how the weights of the sacks vary. Use the graph to answer the following:

(a) How many sacks were weighed?
(b) If 150 of the sacks appeared to weigh exactly 50 kg, how many more sacks were there in that particular class interval?
(c) How many of the sacks weighed less than 50 kg?
(d) What percentage of the sacks weighed 50 kg or more?

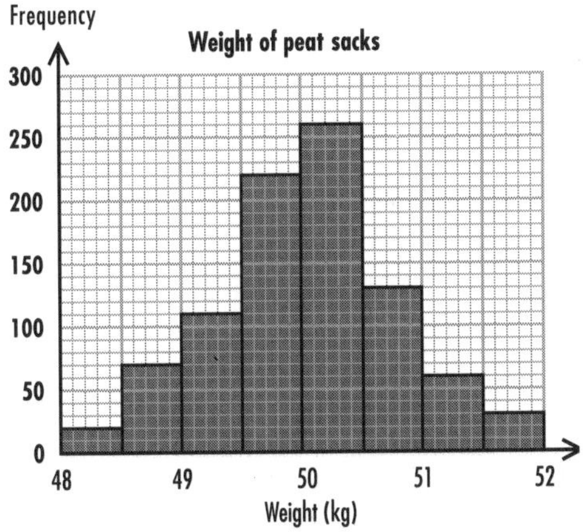

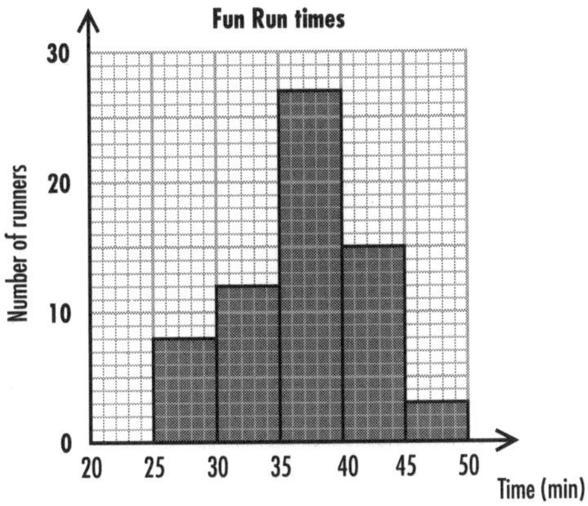

6 The times recorded by those taking part in a 'Fun Run' are noted and then shown in a frequency diagram. Use the graph to answer the following:

(a) How many runners complete the run in less than 25 minutes?
(b) Toby completes the 'Run' (he walks half of it!) in exactly 45 minutes. How many other runners are there in his class interval?
(c) How many complete the run?
(d) Runners receive a certificate if they complete the run in less than 40 minutes. What percentage of those completing the run receive a certificate?

Exercise 82B

1 The quantity (in litres) of orange drink sold at a café varies greatly according to the weather. The quantity sold is recorded over a period of days and the information used to produce a frequency diagram. Use the graph to answer the following:

(a) What is the total number of days?
(b) On how many days are less than 10 litres sold?
(c) There are no days when exactly 35 litres are sold. On how many days are more than 35 litres sold?
(d) On what percentage of the days are 20 litres or more sold?

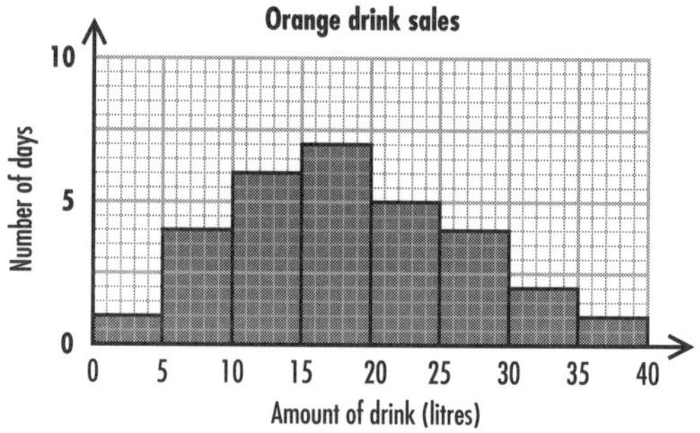

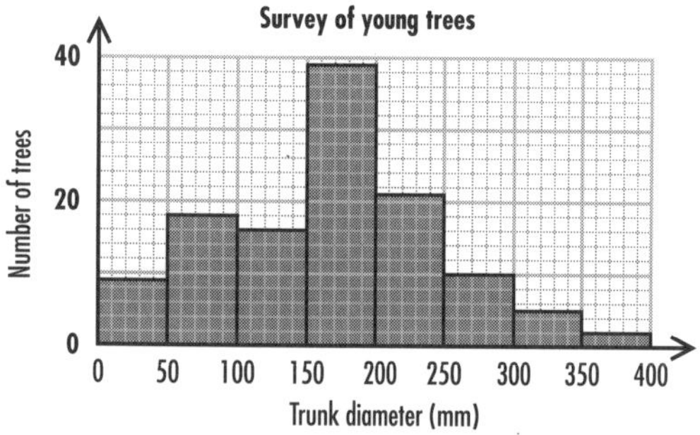

2 The diameter of the trunk of each tree in a large garden is measured and recorded to the nearest 10 millimetres. This information is used to produce a frequency diagram. Use the graph to answer the following:

(a) How many trees are there in total?
(b) Ten of the trees appear to measure exactly 150 mm. How many other trees are there in this class interval?
(c) How many of the trees measure 300 mm or more?
(d) What fraction of the trees measure less than 50 mm?

3 Sita recorded the temperature at midday every day over a period of time. She used the information to produce a frequency diagram. Use the graph to answer the following:

(a) Over how many days did Sita record the temperatures?
(b) The temperatures on 22 days appeared to be exactly 15°C. How many other days are there in the same class interval?
(c) On how many days was the temperature 20°C or more?
(d) What is the class interval that includes 20% of the days of the survey?

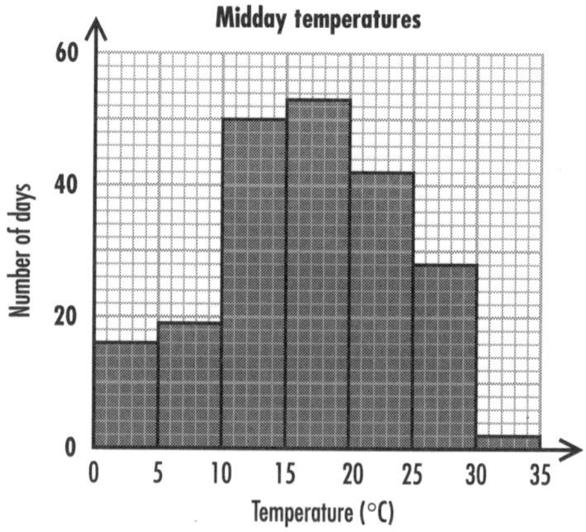

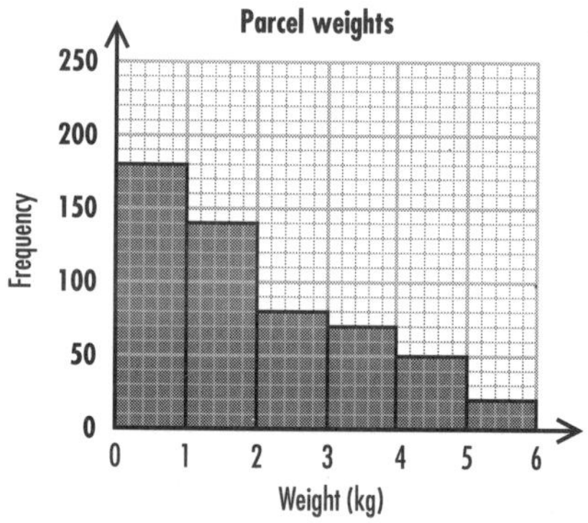

4 The weight of each parcel posted by an office was recorded on a particular day. The information is used to draw a frequency diagram where the number of parcels for each class interval is approximated to the nearest 10. Use the frequency diagram to answer the following:

(a) What was the total number of parcels posted?
(b) There were 320 parcels that weighed less than a particular weight. What is the weight?
(c) How many parcels weighed 4 kg or more?
(d) What percentage of the parcels weighed less than 1 kg?

5 The frequency diagram shows the distribution of the ages of members of a Young People's Club.
Use the graph to answer the following:

(a) How many members are less than 15 years old?
(b) Two of the members have their sixteenth birthday on the day of the survey. How many of the other members are aged 16?
(c) How many of the members are aged 17 or over?
(d) What fraction of the members are aged 18?

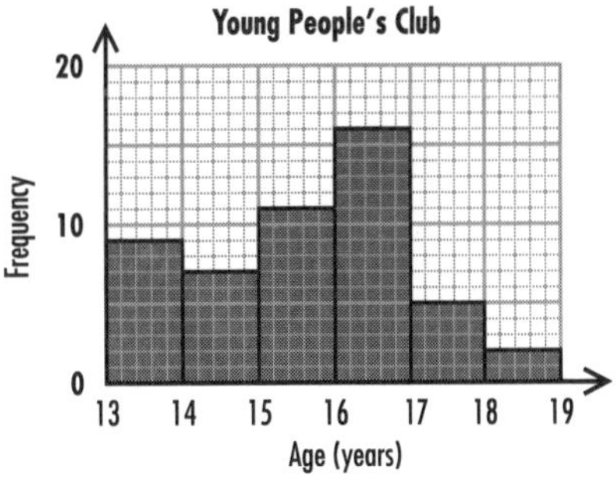

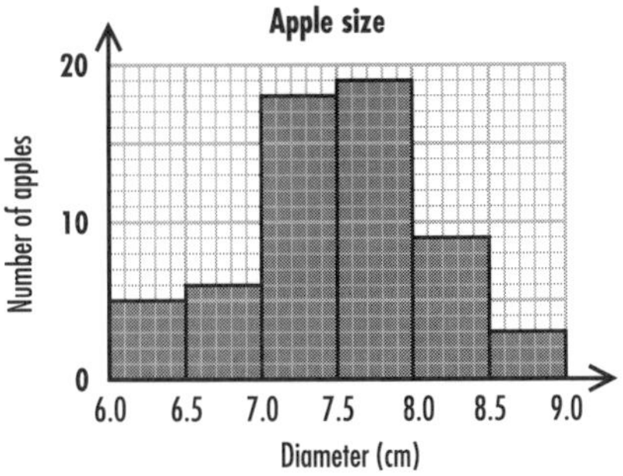

6 An apple producer measures the size (the diameter in centimetres) of a sample of apples. He produces a frequency diagram to show the results of the survey.
Use the graph to answer the following:

(a) What is the total number of apples measured in the survey?
(b) How many of the apples are less than 75 mm in diameter?
(c) Three of the apples appear to measure exactly 6.5 cm. How many other apples are there in the same class interval?
(d) What percentage of the apples measure 80 mm or more?

83/ PIE CHARTS: CALCULATION OF ANGLES AND CONSTRUCTION

The angles at the centre of a pie chart total 360°.
Each 'slice' of the pie chart is called a **sector**. The number of people, items etc. in a group is called the **population** of that group.
The angle for each sector can be calculated by dividing the population for the sector by the total population and multiplying by 360°.

EXAMPLE

▶ Calculate the angle of a sector which shows 17 out of a total population of 60.

$$\text{Angle} = \frac{17}{60} \times 360° = 102°$$

Exercise 83A

Calculate the angle required to show each of the following sectors of a pie chart. Give your answer to the nearest 0.1°, if necessary.

1 4 out of 15	**2** 7 out of 20	**3** 9 out of 10	**4** 60 out of 90
5 27 out of 60	**6** 19 out of 40	**7** 15 out of 36	**8** 25 out of 30
9 5 out of 18	**10** 55 out of 120	**11** 60 out of 72	**12** 50 out of 240
13 23 out of 100	**14** 125 out of 250	**15** 67 out of 75	**16** 7 out of 48
17 450 out of 1000	**18** 1 out of 50	**19** 9000 out of 81 000	**20** 38 out of 190

Exercise 83B

Calculate the angle required to show each of the following sectors of a pie chart. Give your answer to the nearest 0.1°, if necessary.

1 4 out of 20	**2** 7 out of 30	**3** 7 out of 15	**4** 9 out of 40
5 15 out of 36	**6** 5 out of 18	**7** 18 out of 72	**8** 42 out of 90
9 17 out of 120	**10** 42 out of 45	**11** 31 out of 60	**12** 40 out of 100
13 35 out of 150	**14** 11 out of 92	**15** 3 out of 29	**16** 1500 out of 45 000
17 95 out of 270	**18** 19 out of 300	**19** 1200 out of 5000	**20** 32 out of 125

When constructing a pie chart, first make a frequency table to show the data and put in another column to show the angle required for each sector of the pie chart.

EXAMPLE

► Construct a pie chart to show how the pupils of a class travel to school. The data is as follows: Car 3, Bus 15, Walk 10, Taxi 1

Total = 3 + 15 + 10 + 1 = 29

Method	Frequency	Angle of sector
Car	3	$\frac{3}{29} \times 360° = 37.2424° = 37.2°$
Bus	15	$\frac{15}{29} \times 360° = 186.2069° = 186.2°$
Walk	10	$\frac{10}{29} \times 360° = 124.1379° = 124.1°$
Taxi	1	$\frac{1}{29} \times 360° = 12.4138° = 12.4°$
Total	29	360° (359.9° – see note)

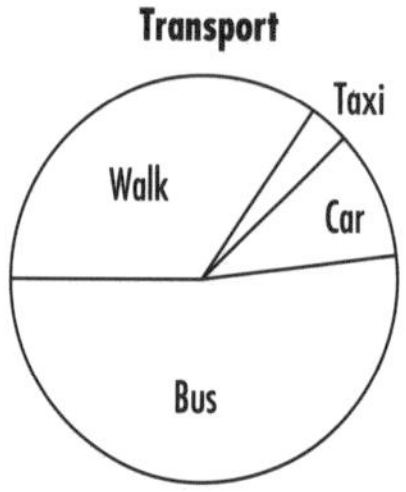

Note: If the angle is approximated to the nearest 0.1°, then the total may not be exactly 360°. This is because of rounding errors. If you use the value for each angle as displayed on the calculator, the total will be *exactly* 360°. However, it is not possible to draw this accurately so draw to the nearest degree only.

Exercise 83C

For each question (a) draw a frequency table (including the total); add an extra column to write the results of your calculations to find the angle of each sector (b) construct the pie chart.

1 The households in a street were asked which source of energy they used most. The responses were as follows:

Oil 6 Gas 12 Electricity 9 Solar 3

2 The distribution of the five most popular colours of cars in a car-park were analysed as part of a survey. The results were as follows:

White 7 Blue 5 Red 4 Green 2

3 A group of six pupils recorded the grades they had received in ten subjects as follows:

A 6 B 15 C 24 D 9 E 6

4 A travel agent asks a sample of customers where they intend to go for their holidays next year. The results are as follows:

UK 21 Europe (outside UK) 48 Africa 7 India 5 America 23 Other 16

5 A group of members of a Young Persons' Sporting Club are asked their weight, to the nearest kilogram. The results are as follows:

40–49 kg...3 50–59 kg...7 60–69 kg...16 70–79 kg...5 80–90 kg...1

6 As part of a survey, a group of people are asked to state their favourite TV sport. The results are as follows:

Football 15 Cricket 7 Tennis 11 Boxing 4 Motor sports 8
Rugby 6 Swimming 3 Athletics 2 Other 4

7 The owner of a computer shop asks a sample of her customers, 'What is the main use for your computer?' The results are as follows:

Games 112 Word processing 44 DTP 24 Spreadsheets 6
Music 12 Encyclopedia 32 Other 10

8 Tom thinks that a dice he is using has a bias towards a score of 3. He decides to throw the dice 100 times and record the results:

Score on the dice	Frequency
1	15
2	12
3	25
4	17
5	16
6	15

9 A travel firm asks a large number of its clients how they are going to travel to their UK holiday destination. The results are analysed and reported as percentages to the nearest 1%:

Car 41% Bus 18% Coach 15% Plane 2% Train 11% Others 13%

10 The imports per year of a developing country are analysed and reported as follows, to the nearest million American dollars:

Fuel $33 Transport equipment $12 Chemicals $8 Metals $24
Manufactured goods $9 Others $4

Exercise 83D

For each question (a) draw a frequency table (including the total); add an extra column to write the results of your calculations to find the angle of each sector (b) construct the pie chart.

1 A teacher asks the class how long they took to do their mathematics homework. The students all tell the truth! Their responses are as follows:

Less than 30 min...4 30–45 min...13 45–60 min...6 More than 60 min...7

2 The owner of a small shop asks a sample of his customers to tell him their favourite crisps. He records the results of his survey:

Smoky bacon 22 Ready salted 6 Salt and vinegar 15 Chicken 5 Pickled onion 3 Other 9

3 Paul is doing a survey. He asks as many students as he can to say what their favourite subject is:

Maths 3 English 15 Geography 11 Technology 21 Sport 27 Art 13
Science 15 History 7 Other 8

4 The sales of four tabloid papers are noted by the newspaper girl for a particular road:
Mail 6 Sport 5 Mirror 7 Sun 9

5 An office is checking on postage. The post on a busy day is listed as follows:
Letter 1st class 215 Letter 2nd class 312 Packages 45 Parcels 28

6 The pupils at a junior school are asked to say what pets they have. The results are as follows:
Cat 15 Dog 11 Rabbit 6 Mouse 3 Gerbil 4 Bird 7
Tortoise 2 Others 3 None 9

7 An ice-cream van is loaded with litre tubs of ice cream as follows:
Raspberry 8 Vanilla 5 Chocolate 13 Coffee 2 Other 9

8 The age of each of the members on the two coaches on a day trip is noted:
Under 20... 45 20–30... 9 30–40... 17 40–50... 9 50–60... 3
Over 60... 12

9 Morag receives £10 per week as pocket money. She reckons that she spends the following over the course of a year:
Clothes £64 Sweets £36 Drinks £46 Food £145 Entertainments £48
Presents £45 Travel £42 Other £94

10 A supermarket manager wants to know how far shoppers travel in order to shop at that store. She arranges for a large sample of customers to be asked how far they have travelled to shop at the store:
Under 1 km...2155 1–2 km...2690 2–5 km...8011 5–10 km...3750
10–20 km...2051 Over 20 km...1343

84/ PIE CHARTS: INTERPRETATION

EXAMPLE

▶ The pie chart shows the percentage of the world's total energy consumed by each region in 1987.

(a) The angle for the sector 'Rest of world' is 90°. What percentage of the world's energy was consumed by the rest of the world?
(b) What region used a little less energy than the rest of the world?
(c) How does the energy used by Japan compare with the energy used by Africa?
(d) The angle for the sector for USSR is 63°. What percentage of the world's energy was used by USSR?

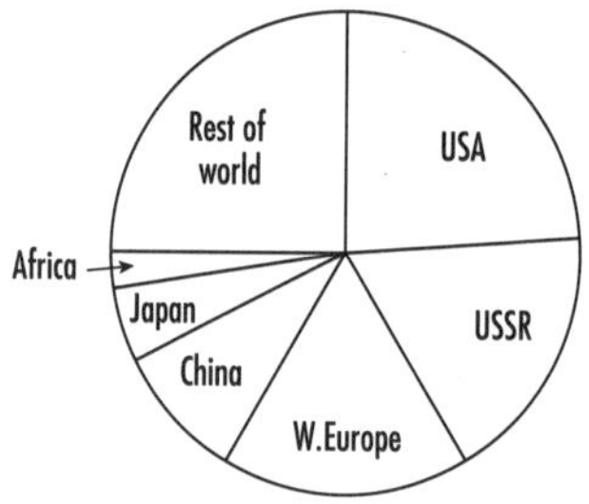

(a) As 90° is a quarter of 360°, the rest of the world used 25% of the world's energy.
(b) USA
(c) Japan used twice as much energy as Africa.
(d) 1% is represented by $\frac{360°}{100} = 3.6°$

63° represents $63 \div 3.6 = 17.5\%$

Exercise 84A

1 A survey of the heights (in centimetres) of 90 people is carried out and the results are shown as a pie chart.

(a) Estimate the number of people in the group '170–179 cm'.
(b) The angle for the sector '180 cm and over' measures 24°. Use this to calculate the number of people in that group.
(c) Which group is the same size as '180 cm and over'?
(d) Measure and record the angle for the sector '160–169 cm'. Use this to calculate the number of people in this group.

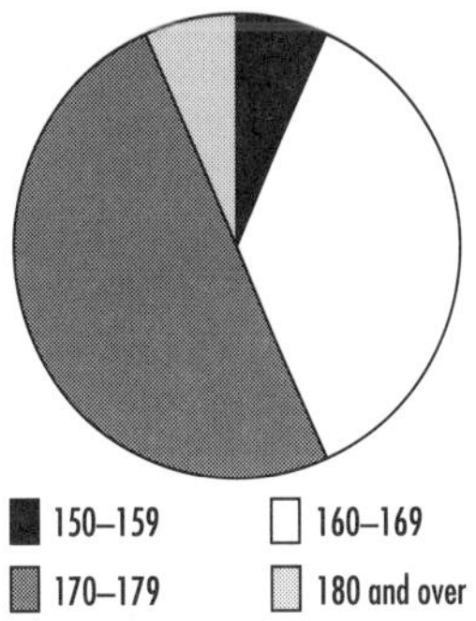

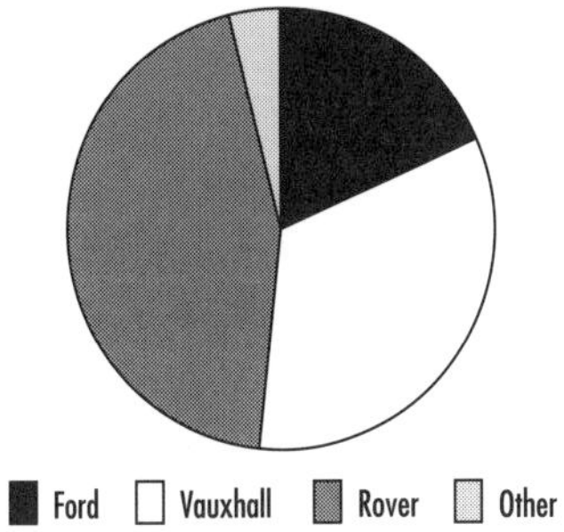

2 A car dealer lists his recent sales and draws a pie chart to show this information.

(a) Which make was the most popular with the sample of customers?
(b) Which group had the smallest number of sales?
(c) The sector for 'Vauxhall' measures 120° and there were 90 cars of this make sold. Calculate the total number of cars sold.
(d) Measure and record the angle of the 'Rover' sector and use this to calculate the number of cars in this group. *Show your working.*

3 The results of a survey of the way that 300 students travel to college is shown as a pie chart.

(a) Which is the most popular method of travel?
(b) Which group is approximately double the size of the group that cycle?
(c) If 45 students cycle to college, what size is the angle for this sector. *Show your working.*
(d) Measure and record the angle of the sector 'Bus' and use this to estimate the number of students who use this form of transport.

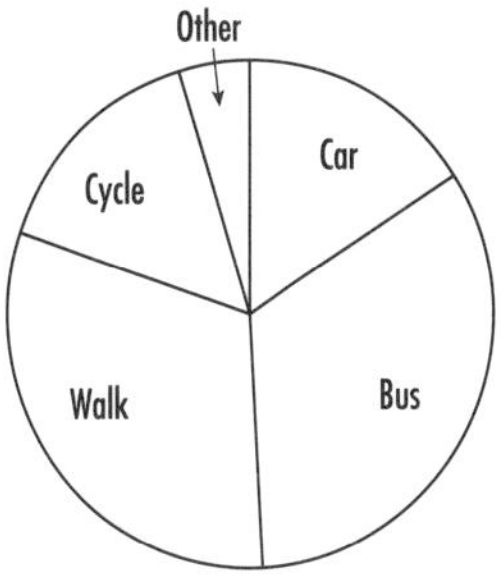

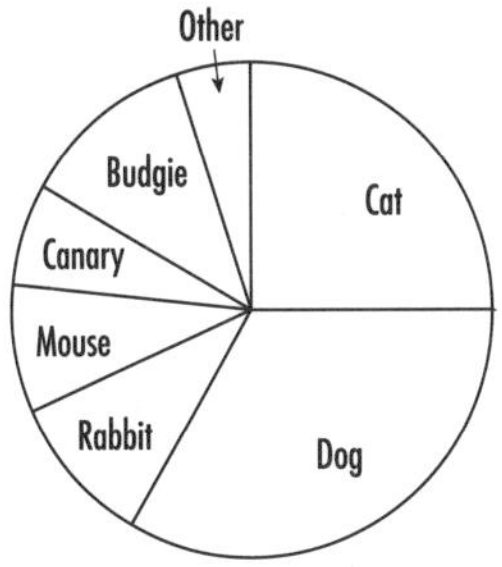

4 A survey of favourite pets is shown as a pie chart.

(a) Which pet is the most popular?
(b) Which pet is favourite with a quarter of the children?
(c) The sector for 'Mouse' measures 30° and was the favourite of five children. Use this to calculate the angle used to represent one child. Calculate the total number of children.
(d) Measure and record the angle of the sector 'Other' and use this to calculate the number of children with other favourite pets.

5 The main source of energy for each house in a road of 48 houses is listed and is shown as a pie chart.

(a) Which source of energy is least popular?
(b) What angle is used to represent one house on the pie chart?
(c) The angle for the sector 'Oil' measures 150°. Use this fact to calculate the number of houses that use oil. *Show your working.*
(d) Measure and record the angle for the sector 'Electricity; and use this to estimate the number of houses that use electricity.

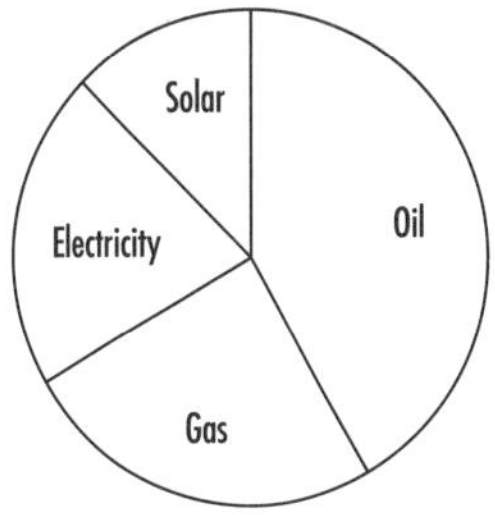

6 The results of a survey of a group of children about their favourite ice creams are shown.

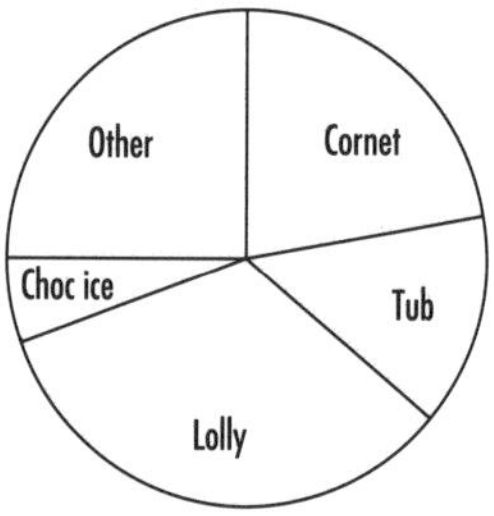

(a) Which was most popular with a third of the children?
(b) What fraction of the total is the number that liked 'Other'?
(c) The sector 'Tub' measures 50° and represents ten children. What is the size of the angle used to represent one child. How many children are there in total? *Show your working.*
(d) Measure and record the sector 'Cornet' and use this to estimate the number of children who chose this.

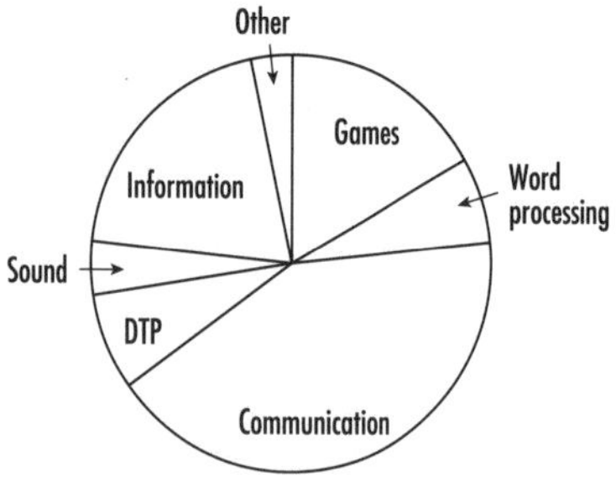

7 A survey of 300 users of personal computers (PCs) is shown as a pie chart.

(a) Which group is smallest?
(b) Which group is largest?
(c) The angle of the sector 'Games' measures 60°. Use this fact to calculate the number of users in this group. *Show your working.*
(d) Measure and record the angle of the sector 'Information' and use this to estimate the number of users in this group.

8 The people at a Young People's Disco are asked their ages and this information is used to produce the pie chart shown.

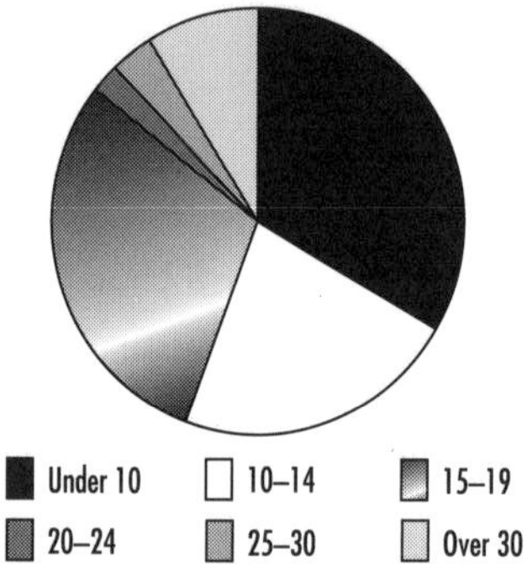

(a) Which age group has the smallest number of people?
(b) Which group has the largest number of people?
(c) The sector '10–14' measures 80° and there are 20 people in this age group. Use this information to calculate the angle that represents one person.
(d) How many people are there at the disco?

Exercise 84B

1 A survey of the number of cars of particular colours is shown as a pie chart.

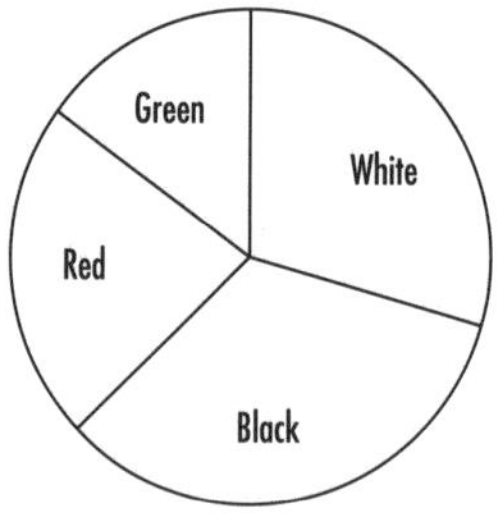

(a) Which colour is most popular?
(b) Which colour is least popular?
(c) The 'Red' sector has an angle of 80° and there are six red cars. What angle represents three cars?
(d) Measure and record the angle of the 'Black' sector. Use this measurement to estimate the number of black cars.

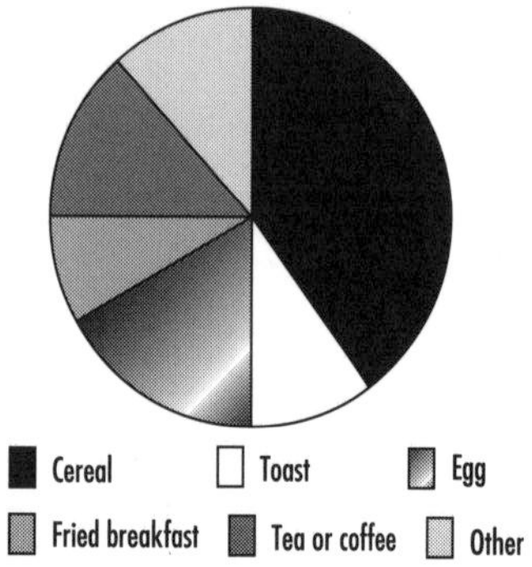

2 A group of 60 people were asked to say which one from a list they were most likely to eat for breakfast. Their responses were used to produce a pie chart.

(a) Two of the choices account for exactly half of the total. Name the two choices.
(b) Which of the choices is least popular?
(c) The 'Tea or coffee' sector has an angle of 48°. Calculate the number of people making this choice. *Show your working.*
(d) Measure and record the angle of the sector 'Egg' and use this to estimate the number of people making this choice.

3 The manager of a small office records the number and type of postage on a typical day. This information is shown as a pie chart.

(a) Which group is the largest?
(b) Which group is smallest?
(c) The 'Letter 1st' sector has an angle of 160° and there are 60 such letters. What angle is used to represent three letters?
(d) Measure and record the angle for '500 g and over'. Use this angle to estimate the number of such items.

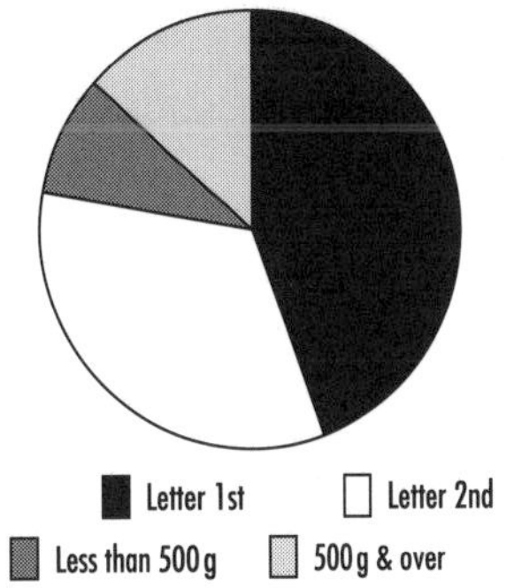

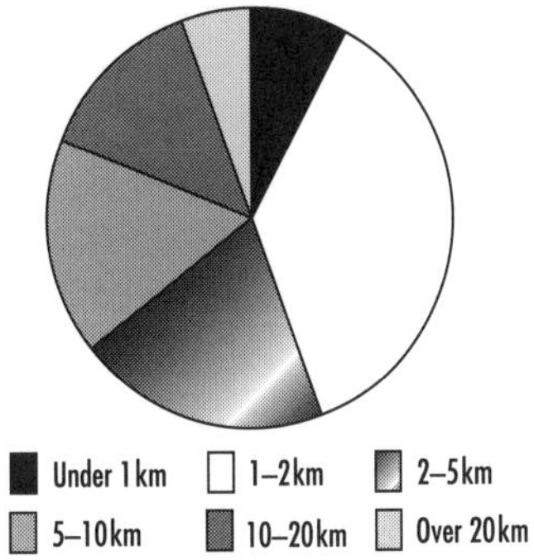

4 The management of a factory wants to know how far its 150 workers travel to work. The results of a questionnaire are used to produce a pie chart.

(a) Which distance is most common?
(b) Which two groups, together with the group '5–10 km', account for exactly half of the total?
(c) The angle for the '5–10 km' sector is 60°. Calculate the number of workers who travel this far. *Show your working.*
(d) Measure and record the angle of the sector '10–20 km' and use this to estimate the number of workers who travel this far.

5 A magazine carries out a survey of 60 fish and chip shops. They award each with a rating and the results of the survey are shown as a pie chart.

(a) Which rating was given to the smallest number of shops?
(b) Which two groups account for exactly half of the shops?
(c) The angle of the sector for the rating 'Poor' is 30°. Use this to calculate the number of shops with this rating. *Show your working.*
(d) Measure and record the angle for the sector 'Good'. Use this to estimate the number of shops with this rating.

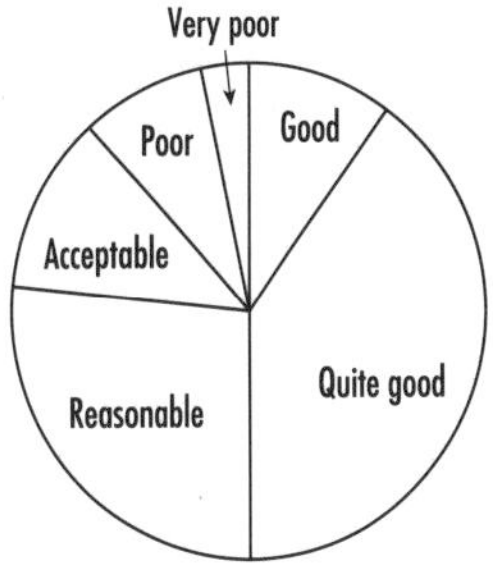

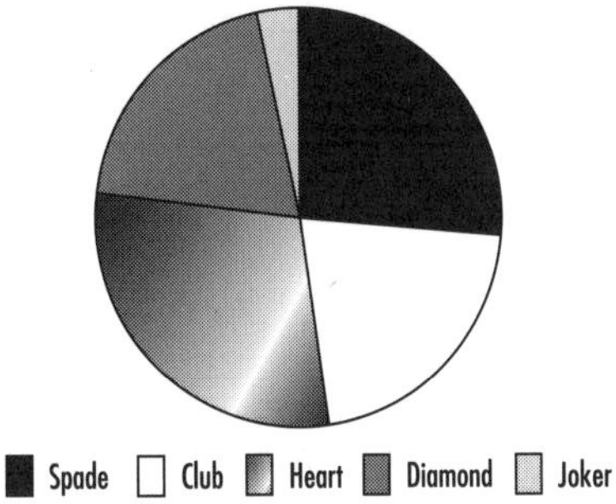

6 As part of her probability project Jessie records the results of choosing a card at random and replacing it. This was repeated a number of times. She used the results to produce a pie chart.

(a) Which sector is largest?
(b) Two of the sectors account for exactly half of the total. Name these two sectors.
(c) Which type of card accounts for exactly a quarter of the total?
(d) Measure the angle for the sector 'Joker' and use this to estimate the number of jokers chosen.

7 A group of 150 people are asked, 'What sport do you like watching best on TV?' The results are analysed and used to produce a pie chart.

(a) Estimate the number of people who choose football.
(b) Which sport is most popular after football?
(c) The angle for the 'Boxing' sector is 24°. Use this fact to calculate the number of people making this choice. *Show your working.*
(d) Measure and record the angle for the sector 'Tennis' and use this to estimate the number of people making this choice.

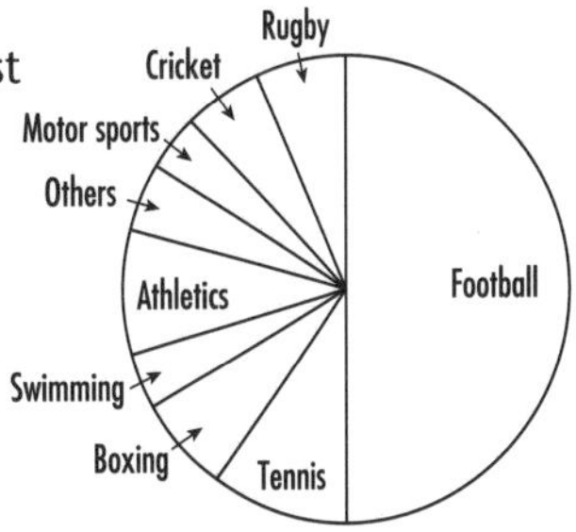

8 A group of people are asked which housework chore they hate most. The results are recorded and used to produce a pie chart.

(a) Which choice accounts for a quarter of the total?
(b) Which chore is hated most?
(c) The angle for the choice 'Meals' measures 36° and ten people made this choice. Calculate the angle used to represent one person.
(d) Calculate the total number of people in the survey. *Show your working.*

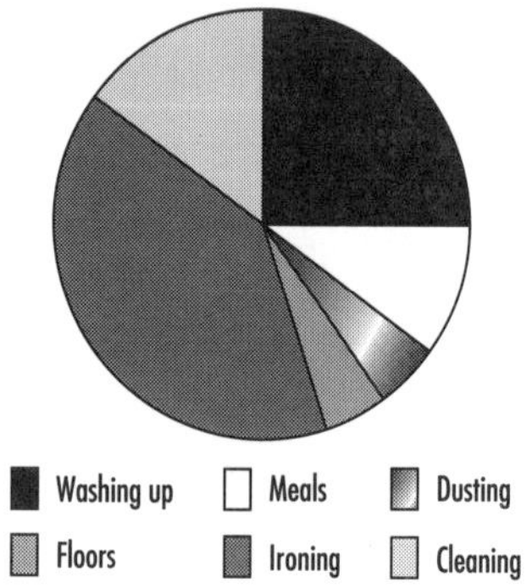

85/ DRAWING SCATTER GRAPHS

A **scatter graph** (or **scatter diagram**) is created by plotting one quantity on the horizontal axis against another quantity on the vertical axis. The result is a number of points.

EXAMPLE

► A small group of pupils record their heights and weights:

Pupil	Claire	Adam	David	Flora	Jeda	Rachel	Tom	Winston
Height (cm)	167	158	155	167	154	167	174	169
Weight (kg)	52	42	41	45	39	47	55	49

(a) Plot these results as a scatter graph. Use the horizontal axis for height from 150–180 cm and the vertical axis for weight from 30–60 kg.
(b) Label the point that shows the height and weight of Adam and also the point for Rachel.

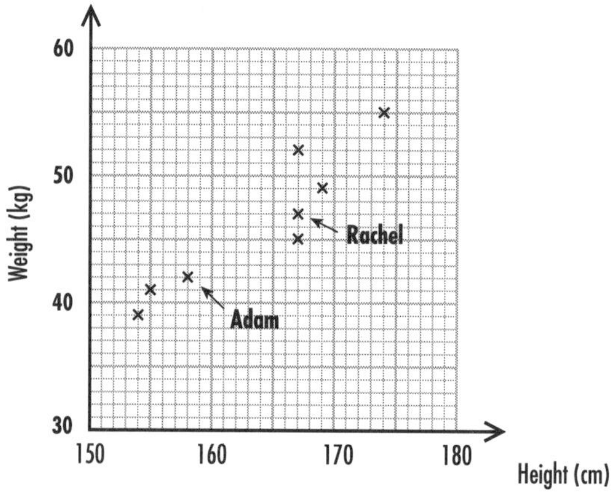

Exercise 85A

Draw a scatter diagram for each of the following sets of data and label the required points.

1 Heights and weights of six pupils.

Pupil	Fiona	Sita	Vijay	Harry	James	Karen
Height (cm)	162	178	191	169	181	173
Weight (kg)	47	58	65	54	61	57

Use the horizontal axis for height: 160–200 cm; 2 cm to represent 10 cm.
Use the vertical axis for weight: 40–70 kg; 2 cm to represent 10 kg.
Label the point that shows the height and weight of (a) Sita (b) Vijay.

2 The entries at a jam-making competition are given points for appearance and taste:

Competitor	A	B	C	D	E	F	G	H
Taste	1	7	3	3	8	4	6	5
Appearance	8	2	7	5	3	6	4	1

Use the horizontal axis for taste: 0–8; 1 cm to represent 1 point.
Use the vertical axis for appearance: 0–8; 1 cm to represent 1 point.
Label the point that shows the appearance and taste for competitor (a) C (b) G.

3 A group of six men compare their height and shoe size:

Name	John	Mark	Wes	Nick	Terry	Toby
Height (cm)	180	178	169	173	181	176
Shoe size	10	$10\frac{1}{2}$	8	$8\frac{1}{2}$	$9\frac{1}{2}$	9

Use the horizontal axis for height: 165–185 cm; 1 cm to represent 5 cm.
Use the vertical axis for shoe size: 8–11; 1 cm to represent each half size.
Label the point that shows the height and shoe size for (a) Terry (b) Wes.

4 The temperatures (in °C) in the morning (at 6 a.m.) and in the afternoon (at 3 p.m.) are noted over a period of seven days:

Day	Mon.	Tue.	Wed.	Thu.	Fri.	Sat.	Sun.
Morning (°C)	11	13	12	15	16	18	17
Afternoon (°C)	19	21	22	27	27	29	15

Use the horizontal axis for morning: 10–20°C; 1 cm to represent 2°C.
Use the vertical axis for afternoon: 14–30°C; 1 cm to represent 2°C.
Label the point that shows the temperature in the morning and afternoon for (a) Wednesday (b) Sunday.

5 The engine size in litres and the average fuel economy in m.p.g. (miles per gallon) are listed for various models of Ford Fiesta:

Car no.	1	2	3	4	5	6
Engine size (litres)	1.0	1.1	1.3	1.4	1.6	1.8
Fuel economy (m.p.g.)	41	42	40	33	32	30

Use the horizontal axis for engine size: 1.0–1.8 litres; 1 cm to represent 0.1 litres.
Use the vertical axis for fuel economy: 30–45 m.p.g.; 1 cm to represent 2 m.p.g.
Label the point that shows (a) car no. 1 (b) car no. 5.

6 The marks for eight students in two science tests are listed:

Student	Chris	Dara	Danny	Niven	Nesta	Tim	Jason	Pat
Test 1 mark	75	87	34	56	39	45	92	69
Test 2 mark	66	72	29	58	32	58	87	59

Use the horizontal axis for Test 1: 30–100 marks; 1 cm to represent 10 marks.
Use the vertical axis for Test 2: 20–90 marks; 1 cm to represent 10 marks.
Label the point that represents (a) Danny (b) Jason.

7 John lists his trial examination grades and his actual GCSE grades for eight subjects:

Subject	Science	Maths	Eng. lit.	Eng. lang.	French	History	Art	Tech.
Trial	A*	D	D	C	B	A	E	C
GCSE	C	B	C	D	A	B	E	A*

Use the horizontal axis for trial grades; A*–E; 1 cm to represent a grade.
Use the vertical axis for GCSE grades: A*–E; 1 cm to represent a grade.
Label the point that represents his grades in (a) science (b) art

8 The temperatures at midday and the sales of ice cream are noted:

Day	Mon.	Tue.	Wed.	Thu.	Fri.	Sat.	Sun.
Temperature (°C)	19	23	25	28	27	30	26
Sales (litres)	17	22	27	29	30	36	29

Use the horizontal axis for temperature: 15–30°C; 2 cm to represent 5°C.
Use the vertical axis for sales: 10–40 litres; 2 cm to represent 10 litres.
Label the point that represents the sales and temperature on (a) Saturday (b) Monday.

Exercise 85B

Draw a scatter diagram for each of the following sets of data and label the required points.

1 The weights of parcels of various lengths are noted:

Parcel	A	B	C	D	E	F
Length (cm)	14	28	22	36	30	19
Weight (g)	250	450	420	190	580	540

Use the horizontal axis for length: 10–40 cm; 2 cm to represent 10 cm.
Use the vertical axis for weight: 0–600 g; 2 cm to represent 100 g.
Label the point that represents the length and weight of (a) parcel C (b) parcel E.

2 Eight athletes run against each other in two races, the 100 m and the 1000 m. Their positions in each race are listed:

Name	Carol	Sue	Nina	Jo	Ester	Dilys	Jill	Peta
Position 1000 m	1	2	3	4	5	6	7	8
Position 100 m	7	8	6	5	3	4	1	2

Use the horizontal axis for position in 1000 m: 1–8; 1 cm to represent 1 position.
Use the vertical axis for position in 100 m: 1–8; 1 cm to represent 1 position.
Label the point that represents the position in both races for (a) Peta (b) Carol.

3 The percentage of positive breath-tests for car drivers and the percentage of accidents that involve a driver who is affected by drink are noted over the Christmas period:

Day	22 Dec.	23 Dec.	24 Dec.	25 Dec.	26 Dec.	27 Dec.
Positive breath-tests (%)	12	10	15	6	11	9
Drivers affected (%)	21	18	34	21	20	16

Use the horizontal axis for positive breath-tests: 0–20%; 1 cm to represent 2%.
Use the vertical axis for drivers affected: 10–40%; 1 cm to represent 5%.
Label the point that represents (a) 25 December (b) 27 December.

4 A teacher notes the time taken by each student to complete a test and also the mark achieved by that student:

Student	Ann	Carolyn	Sam	Denise	Fred	Sean	Zak	Sunesh
Time taken (min)	21	18	24	17	15	23	20	19
Mark	17	13	9	20	24	18	25	23

Use the horizontal axis for time: 15–25 min; 1 cm to represent 1 min.
Use the vertical axis for marks: 8–26 marks; 1 cm to represent 2 marks.
Label the point that represents the time and the mark for (a) Sam (b) Zak.

5 Six students list their grades in trial and GCSE examinations in English:

Student	Mark	Paul	Peter	Karen	Gillian	Beth
Trial grade	C	D	B	A	E	A*
GCSE grade	A	B	A	A*	C	A*

Use the horizontal axis for trial grades: A*–E; 1 cm to represent a grade.
Use the vertical axis for GCSE grades: A*–E; 1 cm to represent a grade.
Label the point that represents the grades in each examination for (a) Peter (b) Beth.

6 The number of points scored by a sample of eight basketball players in a tournament is listed against their ages:

Player	A	B	C	D	E	F	G	H
Points scored	25	18	20	5	12	42	34	17
Age (years)	21	16	17	16	17	22	21	19

Use the horizontal axis for points: 0–50; 2 cm to represent 10 points.
Use the vertical axis for age: 15–22 years; 1 cm to represent 1 year.
Label the point that represents (a) player D (b) player F.

7 The marks awarded for Paper 1 and Paper 2 of a mathematics examination are listed for six candidates:

Candidate no.	1098	1099	2001	2003	2010	2011
Paper 1	75	67	89	45	65	49
Paper 2	79	66	93	59	67	66

Use the horizontal axis for Paper 1: 40–100; 1 cm to represent 10 marks.
Use the vertical axis for Paper 2: 40–100; 1 cm to represent 10 marks.
Label the point that show the mark for each paper for candidate no. (a) 2003 (b) 1098.

8 The sales of hot drinks and the temperature at midday are noted for a period of one week by the owner of a market stall:

Day	Sat.	Sun.	Mon.	Tue.	Wed.	Thu.	Fri.
Temperature (°C)	9	13	14	11	8	6	5
Sales (£)	450	340	320	420	510	600	640

Use the horizontal axis for temperature: 5–15°C; 1 cm to represent 1°C.
Use the vertical axis for sales: £300–£650; 2 cm to represent £100.
Label the point that represents the temperature and sales for (a) Monday (b) Friday.

86/ CORRELATION

Positive correlation between two variables means that as one variable *increases* the other variable will also tend to *increase.*
Negative correlation between two variables means that as one variable *increases* the other variable will tend to *decrease.*
No correlation between two variables means that if one variable increases there is no way of knowing what will happen to the other variable.

Scatter diagrams of various correlations are shown:

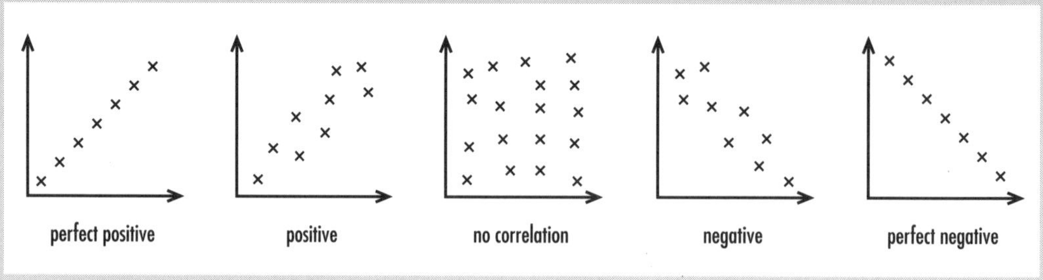

Exercise 86A

Examine each of the scatter graphs sketched below and state the type of correlation it has. Choose from the following correlations: perfect positive, positive, no correlation, negative, perfect negative

1

2
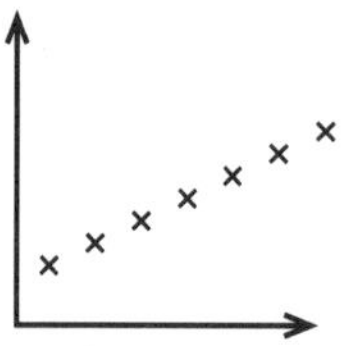

3
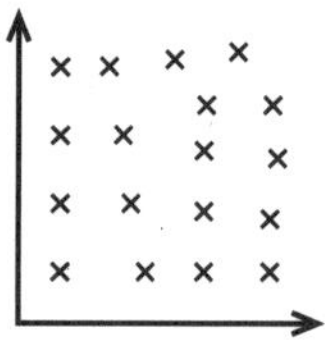

4
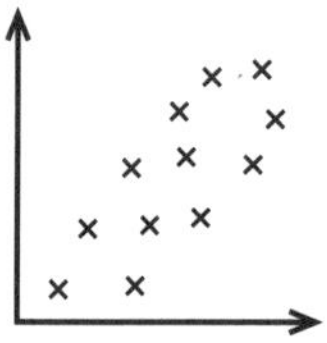

5

6
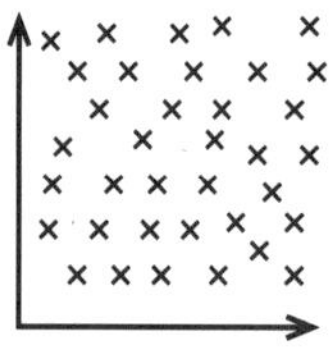

7
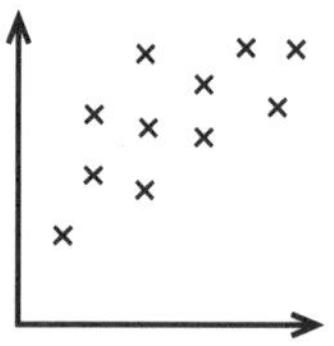

8
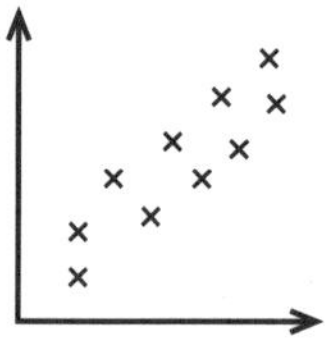

9
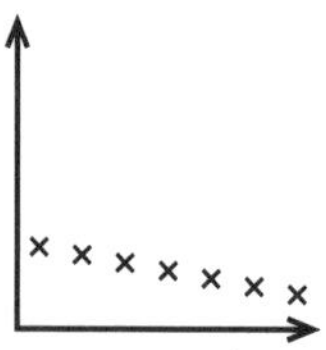

10
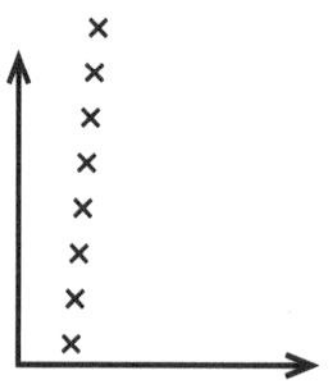

11
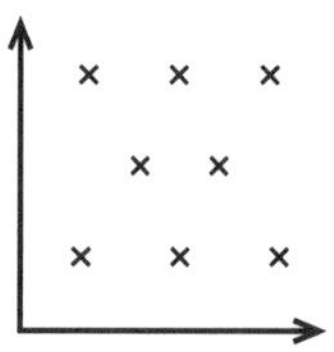

12
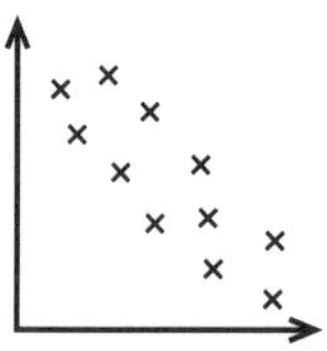

Exercise 86B

Examine each of the scatter graphs sketched below and state the type of correlation it has. Choose from the following correlations: perfect positive, positive, no correlation, negative, perfect negative.

1
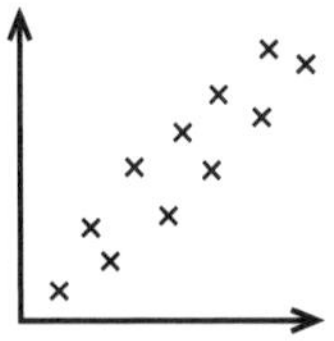

2
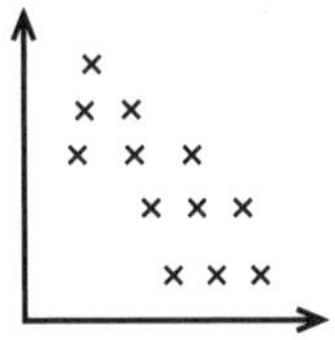

3
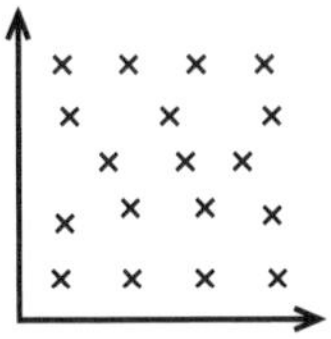

4
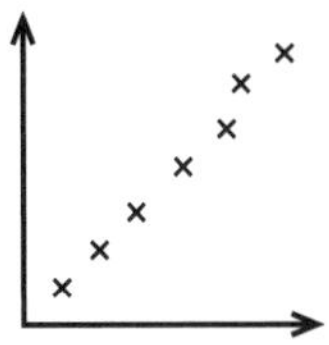

5

6
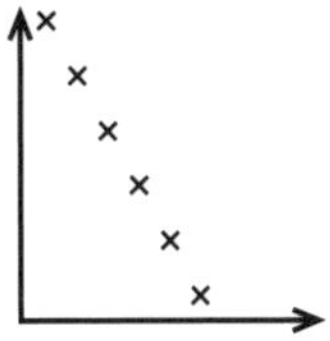

7
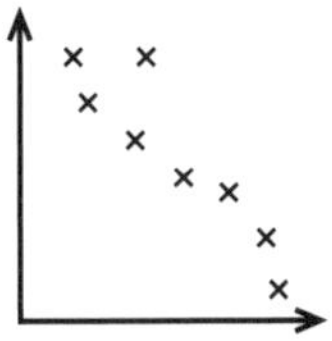

8
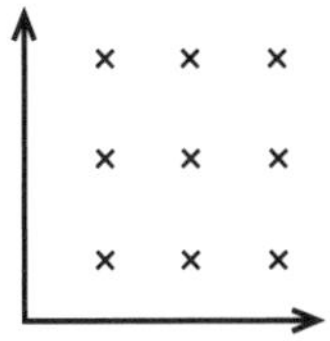

9
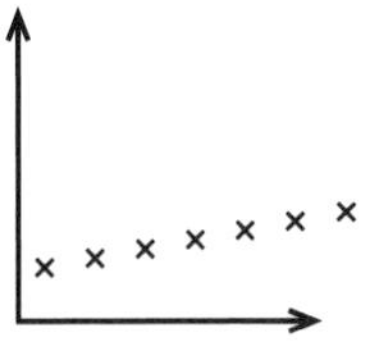

10
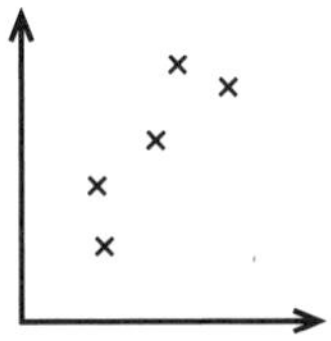

11

12
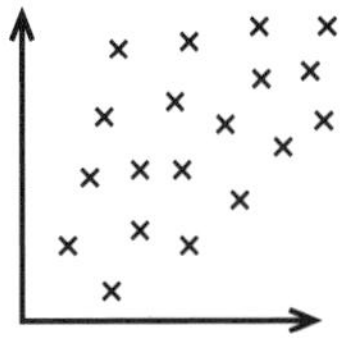

EXAMPLE

▶ The marks obtained by a group of students in two different tests are shown below:

Student	Carla	Neville	Doug	Bill	Liz	Melissa
Test 1	23	32	38	46	49	56
Test 2	31	43	47	58	48	89

Examine the marks for each of the students and comment on the correlation, if any, between the marks for the two tests.

It can be seen that as the mark for Test 1 increases so does the mark for Test 2. It is almost perfect correlation; only Liz spoils it!

EXAMPLE

▶ The owner of an hot-drinks van notes the sales on each day of a particular week. She also notes the temperature at midday.

Day	Mon.	Tue.	Wed.	Thu.	Fri.	Sat.	Sun.
Temperature (°C)	8	10	9	7	6	5	3
Sales (£)	124	100	98	146	155	220	232

Examine the data and comment on the correlation, if any, between the temperature and the sales of hot drinks.

In general, it can be seen that as the temperature *falls* so the sales of hot drinks *increase.* There is almost perfect negative correlation; the sales on Saturday and Sunday tend to be higher because it is the weekend.

Exercise 86C

Examine the data for each of the questions in Exercise 85A (page 141) and state whether there is any correlation. If there is correlation, state whether this is positive or negative, and try to comment on whether it is perfect, good, or moderate. If you have drawn the scatter graphs for Exercise 85A, use these to confirm your answers.

Exercise 86D

Examine the data for each of the questions in Exercise 85B (page 142) and state whether there is any correlation. If there is correlation, state whether this is positive or negative, and try to comment on whether it is perfect, good, or moderate. If you have drawn the scatter graphs for Exercise 85B, use these to confirm your answers.

REVISION

Exercise G

1 For each set of values find (i) the mean (ii) the range.
(a) £11, £25, £18, £15, £19 and £14
(b) 124, 132, 111, 78, 97

2 The times to complete a Fun Run are noted and a frequency table produced:

Time (min)	$30 \le T < 35$	$35 \le T < 40$	$40 \le T < 45$	$45 \le T < 50$	$50 \le T < 55$	$55 \le T < 60$
Frequency	6	8	12	11	7	3

Draw a frequency diagram to show this information.

3 Calculate the angle required to represent each of the following as a sector in a pie chart.
(a) 75 out of 300 (b) 35p out of £3.50 (c) 5 kg out of 72 kg

4 Students are choosing the colour of new carpet tiles for the common room. There are five colours available. The votes for each colour are shown below.
Green 5 Brown 7 Grey 14 Blue 23 Gold 11
Show this information as a pie chart.

5 State whether there is any correlation between the quantities represented in the scatter graphs. If there is correlation say whether it is positive or negative.

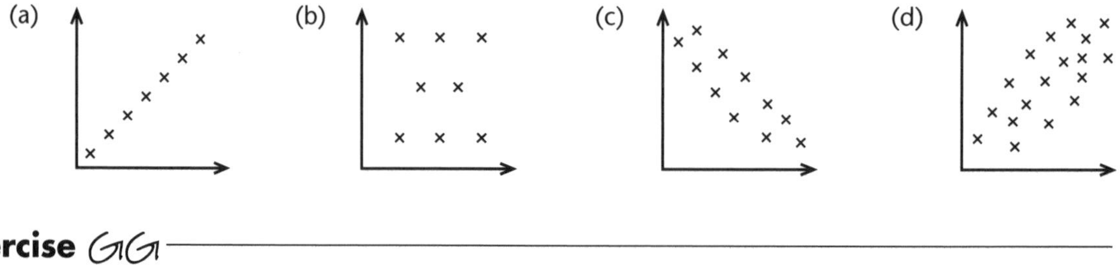

Exercise GG

1 The total ages of a family of five is 80 years. What is the mean age?

2 The mean of a set of six numbers is 23. Calculate the total of the numbers.

3 The mean of a set of numbers is 17. If the total of the numbers is 153, how many numbers are there?

4 The range of the weights of a group of people is 43 kg. There are 18 people in the group and the mean weight is 52 kg. If the weight of the lightest person is 41 kg, what is the weight of the heaviest person?

5

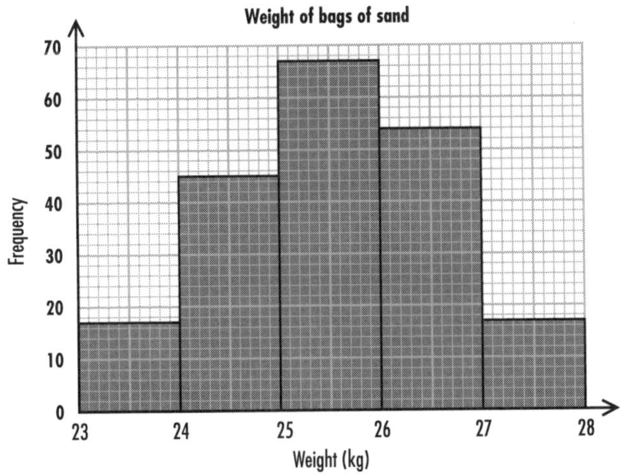

A factory packs sand in bags which are meant to weigh 25 kg. As part of a survey to check on the quality of its products, a worker weighs a sample of bags and notes the weight of each bag. He then draws a frequency diagram to show how the weights of the bags vary. Use the graph to answer the following:

(a) How many bags were weighed?

(b) There were 13 bags that appeared to weigh exactly 25 kg. How many more bags were there in that particular class interval?

(c) Bags that weigh less than 25 kg are not sold and are returned to have more sand added. How many of the sample should be returned?

(d) What percentage of the bags weighed 25 kg or more?

6 The way in which 120 pupils travel to school is shown by this pie chart. Use it to answer the questions.

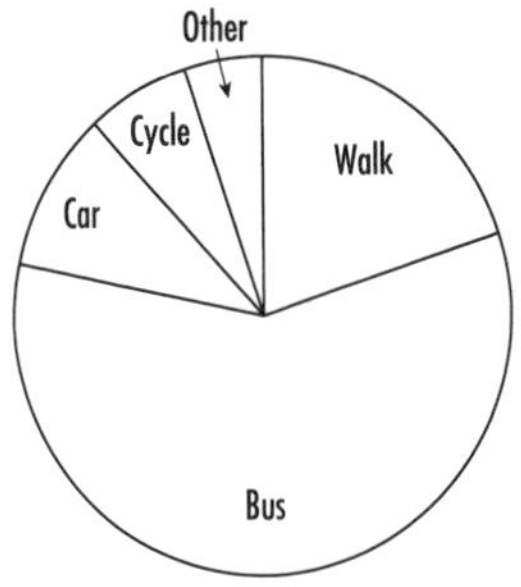

(a) How do most pupils travel to school?

(b) Calculate the angle which is used to represent one pupil in the pie chart.

(c) Two of the ways of travelling account for exactly 30 pupils. State these two groups.

(d) Measure and record the angle for the sector 'Cycle' and use this to estimate the number of pupils who travel to school by this method.

7 The time (in seconds) to accelerate from 0–60 m.p.h. and the average fuel economy (km per litre) are listed for various models of Vauxhall Astra:

Engine size (litres)	1.2	1.3	1.4	1.6	1.8	2.0
Acceleration time (s)	17.0	12.1	12.0	11.8	9.1	8.6
Fuel economy (km/litre)	12.1	11.7	11.0	11.7	9.6	10.0

(a) Plot a scatter graph of fuel economy against acceleration time.
Use the horizontal axis for time: 8–17 s; 1 cm to represent 1 s.
Use the vertical axis for fuel economy: 9–13 km/litre; 2 cm to represent 1 km/litre.

(b) Label the point that shows the model with an engine size of (i) 1.4 litres (ii) 1.6 litres.

(c) Comment on the correlation between fuel economy and the time for 0–60 m.p.h. acceleration.

87/ ESTIMATING PROBABILITIES

If an event is **impossible** it has a probability of 0.
If an event is **certain** it has a probability of 1.
An event which is **equally likely** to happen as to not (evens) has a probability of $\frac{1}{2}$ or 0.5.
These three points are shown on a probability line, along with the points at 0.1, 0.2, etc.

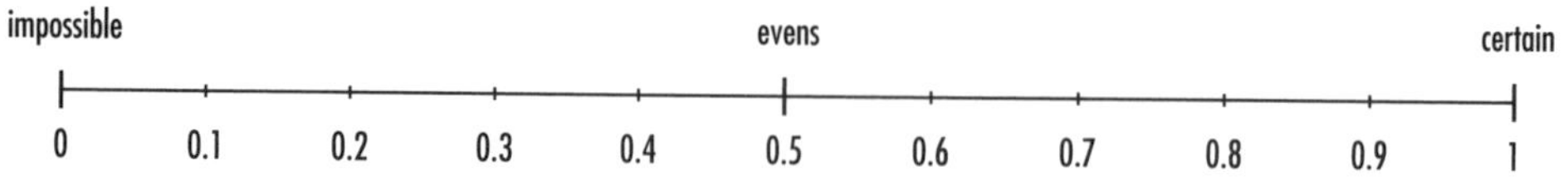

EXAMPLE

▶ Estimate (*not* calculate) where the following events would be best placed on the probability line and estimate the value of the probability at that point.
(a) There will be a shower on a day when rain has been forecast.
(b) A small ice cube will melt in the sun on a hot day.
(c) A player will be able to give 110% effort!
(d) A coin will come down 'heads' twice in row.

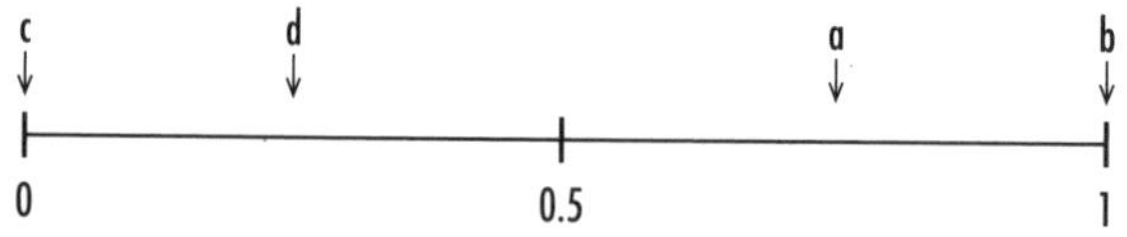

(a) This seems likely so an answer between 0.6 and 0.9 would be reasonable.
(b) This is certain and so the only answer is 1.
(c) The most effort a person can give is 100%, so 110% is impossible and the probability is 0.
(d) This has a reasonable chance but is less than evens and so estimates around 0.2 or 0.3 would be acceptable.

Exercise 87A

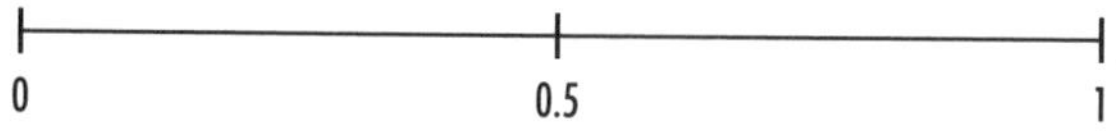

For each of the following questions you will need to draw a simple probability line as shown in the diagram.
For each question (a) put an arrow on the line to show where you estimate the probability of the particular event and (b) estimate the value of the probability.

1 The score on a dice is 5.
2 A dropped piece of toast will fall 'buttered side down'.
3 A person chosen at random is left-handed.
4 The sun will set today.

5 Two cards taken from a pack are both red.
6 A baby is born with blue hair.
7 A man aged approximately 30 years is married.
8 The total score on two dice is less than 4.
9 A window is open in the room on a very cold winter's day.
10 The score on a dice is even.
11 A five-sided, numbered spinner will score 3 twice in a row.

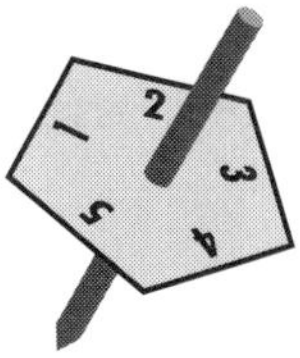

12 A clock has stopped with the hour hand between 2 and 8.
13 A person from a group of 20 people does not wear glasses, when 3 of the group do wear glasses.
14 A person winning a lottery with one ticket.
15 A square spinner has a score of less than 4.
16 A page in a newspaper has an advertisement.
17 A car can be driven from London to Glasgow in 15 minutes.
18 A word chosen at random contains the letter e.
19 A car on a motorway is driven by a woman.
20 You have answered all these questions correctly.

Exercise 87B

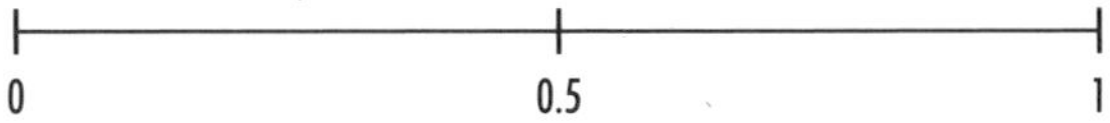

For each of the following questions you will need to draw a simple probability line as shown in the diagram.
For each question (a) put an arrow on the line to show where you estimate the probability of the particular event and (b) estimate the value of the probability.

1 A window is open in the room on a hot day.
2 A clock has stopped with the hour hand between 1 and 4.
3 The time for the 100-metre race in the next Olympics will be less than a minute.
4 A lady who is younger than 20 years old is married.
5 A good dart player will miss the dartboard.
6 The score on a dice is less than 5.
7 A page in a newspaper does not have an advertisement.
8 A word will contain the letter q.
9 The temperature in London on 1 December will be 30°C.
10 A spectator at a football match is a woman.
11 An eight-sided spinner has a score of more than 4.
12 A dog is wearing a collar.
13 The total score on two dice is less than 11.
14 A person from a group of 20 people does not wear glasses, when 12 of the group do wear glasses.
15 It will snow in London next winter.
16 The score on a dice is odd.
17 A person is right-handed.
18 A five-sided spinner will have a score of 3.
19 A baby is a girl.
20 The driver of a bus is a man.

88/ CALCULATING SIMPLE PROBABILITIES

A probability has a value which can be 0 (impossible) or 1 (definite) or any value in-between.
If all the outcomes are *equally likely* then:

Probability of a particular event happening = $\dfrac{\text{number of outcomes which make the event happen}}{\text{number of possible outcomes}}$

EXAMPLE

► State the probability of each of the following.
(a) A score of 2 or less on a dice.
(b) Picking a red pencil from a bag containing five red and three blue pencils.
(c) Picking an even number from the list: 13, 14, 15, 17, 20.
(d) Winning a raffle after buying 10 of the 200 tickets.

(a) The suitable scores are 1 and 2 from six possible scores.
$P = \frac{2}{6} = \frac{1}{3}$ (or 0.333 in decimal form to 3 s.f.)

(b) There are 5 suitable outcomes from 8 possible outcomes.
$P = \frac{5}{8}$ (or 0.625)

(c) Suitable outcomes are 14 and 20 but there are five possible outcomes.
$P = \frac{2}{5}$ (or 0.4)

(d) There are 10 suitable outcomes out of a total of 200 possible outcomes.
$P = \frac{10}{200} = \frac{1}{20}$ (or 0.05)

Exercise 88A

In each case all outcomes can be assumed to be equally likely. Write down the probability of each of the following events happening. Give your answers as fractions except for questions marked * where you should give your answer in decimal form.

1 Selecting the letter S from the word SKILL.
2 Picking a red pencil from a pencil bag containing four red pencils and five blue pencils.
3* Picking a red card from a standard pack of playing cards.
4 Throwing a score of 6 with a dice.
5* Picking an odd number from 12, 13, 14, 15, 16, 18, 19, 20.
6 The spinner in the diagram coming down on an R.
7* Winning a raffle having bought 12 tickets out of a total of 240 tickets sold.
8 Picking a heart from a standard pack of playing cards.
9 The spinner in the diagram coming down on an N.
10* Throwing an odd number with a dice.
11 Picking an even number from 5, 7, 9, 11, 13, 15.
12* Selecting the letter G from the word GIGANTIC.
13 Choosing a 5p coin from £2 in change, of which £1 is in 5p coins and £1 in 2p coins.
14* Picking a blue pencil from a pencil bag containing one black, four red and five blue pencils.
15 Picking a month that starts with the letter J from a list of months of the year.

16* Picking a square number from 1, 4, 9, 15, 16, 20, 25.
17 Picking an ace from a standard pack of playing cards.
18* Winning a raffle having bought ten tickets out of a total of 250 tickets sold.
19 Throwing a score of less than 3 with a dice.
20* Picking a red pencil from a pencil bag containing one black, four red and five blue pencils.

Exercise 88B

In each case all outcomes can be assumed to be equally likely. Write down the probability of each of the following events happening. Give your answers as fractions except for questions marked * where you should give your answer in decimal form.

1 Throwing a score of 2 with a dice.
2* Picking a spade from a standard pack of playing cards.
3* Selecting the letter S from the word SAUSAGES.
4 Winning a raffle having bought five tickets out of a total of 200 tickets sold.
5 Picking a day that starts with the letter T from a list of days of the week.
6* Picking an even number from 12, 13, 14, 15, 16, 18, 19, 20.
7 The spinner in the diagram coming down on an E.
8* Picking a green pencil from a pencil bag containing two red pencils and four green pencils.

9 Selecting the letter A from the word AMAZING.
10 The spinner in the diagram coming down on an L.
11 Throwing an odd number with a dice.
12* Picking a blue pencil from a pencil bag containing three black, five red and two blue pencils.
13 Picking a queen from a standard pack of playing cards.
14 Picking a number containing a 7 from 1, 3, 5, 7, 17, 27.
15* Winning a raffle having bought two tickets out of a total of 1000 tickets sold.
16 Choosing a 2p coin from £1 in change, of which 50p is in 5p coins and 50p in 2p coins.
17 Picking a multiple of 5 from 5, 10, 15, 20, 25, 30.
18* Throwing a score of 5 or more with a dice.
19 Picking a red seven from a standard pack of playing cards.
20* Picking a black pencil from a pencil bag containing three black, seven red and five blue pencils.

89/ PROBABILITY: COMPLEMENTARY EVENTS

Each outcome either 'happens' or 'does not happen'. An event happening and an event not happening are called **complementary** events.
Probability (event happened) + Probability (event did not happen) = 1 (certain)
This means that:

Probability (event did not happen) = 1 – Probability (event happened)

or

$P(E') = 1 - P(E)$

where E is the event happening and E' is the event not happening.
E' is the complementary event to E.

EXAMPLE

▶ State the complementary event (avoid the word 'not' if possible), and the probability of this complementary event happening in the following.
(a) A score of 2 or less on a dice.
(b) Picking a red pencil from a bag containing five red and three blue pencils.
(c) Picking the letter T from TROUBLE.
(d) Winning a raffle after buying ten of the 200 tickets.

(a) The complementary event E' is *3 or more.*
$P(E) = \frac{1}{3}$ so $P(E') = 1 - \frac{1}{3} = \frac{2}{3}$

(b) E' is *picking a blue pencil.*
$P(E) = \frac{5}{8}$ so $P(E') = 1 - \frac{5}{8} = \frac{3}{8}$

(c) E' is *NOT picking the letter T.*
$P(E) = \frac{1}{7}$ so $P(E') = 1 - \frac{1}{7} = \frac{6}{7}$

(d) E' is *losing.*
$P(E) = \frac{1}{20}$ so $P(E') = 1 - \frac{1}{20} = \frac{19}{20}$

Exercise 89A

State (a) the complementary event (b) the probability of this complementary event for each of the questions in Exercise 88A (page 150). Give your answer as either a fractional or decimal value as indicated.

Exercise 89B

State (a) the complementary event (b) the probability of this complementary event for each of the questions in Exercise 88B (page 151). Give your answer as either a fractional or decimal value as indicated.

90/ PROBABILITY: TWO COMBINED INDEPENDENT EVENTS

When one event can take place without having any effect on what happens in another event then the two events are said to be **independent**. For example, when two dice are thrown, the score on one of the dice does not affect the score on the other dice.
One way of analysing the outcomes of two independent events is to create a **possibility space**. This is a methodical way of listing all the outcomes of two independent events.

EXAMPLE

► A playing card is taken from a pack and a dice is thrown. Create a possibility space to show the possible combinations of the score on the dice and the suit of the card. Use this to calculate the probability of each of the following events:

(a) A red card and a 6 on the dice
(b) A club and a score of more than 3
(c) Any outcome except 'a red card and a 6'

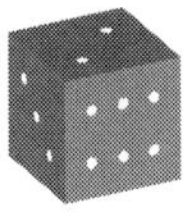

Note: A pack of playing cards contains four suits: hearts (H), diamonds (D), clubs (C) and spades (S). Each suit contains 13 cards. Hearts and diamonds are red; clubs and spades are black.

The possibility space showing all 24 possible outcomes is:

				Dice			
		1	**2**	**3**	**4**	**5**	**6**
	H	H1	H2	H3	H4	H5	H6
Suit	**D**	D1	D2	D3	D4	D5	D6
	C	C1	C2	C3	C4	C5	C6
	S	S1	S2	S3	S4	S5	S6

where, for example, H1 means 'a heart + a score of 1'.

(a) In the possibility space there are two favourable outcomes: H6 and D6.
So, P(red card + 6 on the dice) = $\frac{2}{24} = \frac{1}{12}$

(b) The favourable outcomes on the dice are 4, 5 and 6, so there are only three favourable outcomes for the two events: C4, C5 and C6.
So, P(club + score of more than 3) = $\frac{3}{24} = \frac{1}{8}$

(c) In (a), P(red card + 6 on the dice) = $\frac{2}{24} = \frac{1}{12}$
The complement of this is required, so
P(not 'red card + 6') = $1 - \frac{1}{12} = \frac{11}{12}$

Exercise 90A

For each of the following questions create a suitable possibility space to show all the possible outcomes, and then use this to calculate the probability of each of the events stated. Give your answers as fractions except for questions marked * where you should give your answer in decimal form.

1 The score on a dice and the suit of a card.
(a) A club and a score of 4
(b) A black card and a score of 1
(c) A red card and an even score
(d) Any card and an odd score

2* The colour of a card and tossing a coin.
(a) A red card and a tail
(b) A black card and a head
(c) Any card and a head
(d) Any outcome except 'red card + head'

3 Tossing a coin and the score on a dice.
(a) A head and a score of 6
(b) A tail and a score of more than 2
(c) A head and an even score
(d) Any outcome other than 'head + even score'

4* The suit of a card and a letter picked from the word *chance*.
(a) A spade and the letter *a*
(b) A red card and the letter *e*
(c) A club and the letter *c*
(d) A black card and a letter that is not *n*

5 Tossing a coin and spinning a spinner numbered 1, 2, 3, 4 and 5.
(a) A tail and a 3
(b) A head and a score of less than 4
(c) A head and an even score
(d) Any outcome that is not 'head + odd score'

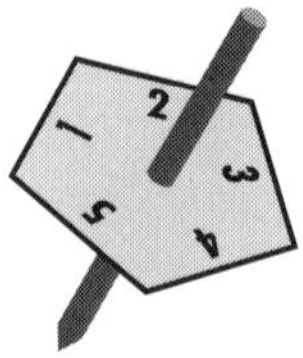

6 Picking a letter from the word *ALL* and picking a letter from the word *any*.
(a) The letter *A* and the letter *n*
(b) The letter *L* and the letter *y*
(c) One of the letters is an *a* (that is *A* or *a*)
(d) Neither letter is an *a*

7* Two coins.
(a) Both coins are heads
(b) Only one of the coins is a head
(c) One or both coins are tails
(d) Neither coin is a tail

8 The score on a dice and the colour of a disc taken from a bag containing one red disc and two black discs.
(a) A black disc and a score of 2
(b) A red disc and a score of more than 4
(c) A red disc and an even score
(d) A black disc and an odd score

9* The scores on two pentagonal spinners (five-sided spinners numbered 1, 2, 3, 4 and 5).
(a) The total score is 2
(b) The total score is more than 8
(c) The total score is 7
(d) The total score is not 6

10* The scores on two dice.
(a) Both scores are the same
(b) The total score is 7
(c) The total score is more than 8
(d) The total score is 8 or less

Exercise 90B

For each of the following create a suitable possibility space to show all the possible outcomes, and then use this to calculate the probability of each of the outcomes stated. Give your answers as fractions except for questions marked * where you should give your answer in decimal form.

1* A coin and the suit of a card.
(a) A head and a red card
(b) A tail and a club
(c) A tail and a black card
(d) Any outcome other than 'tail + black card'

2 Tossing a coin and picking a letter from the word *selected*.
(a) A head and the letter *s*
(b) A head and the letter *e*
(c) A tail and the letter *e*
(d) Any outcome other than 'head + *c*'

3* The suits of two cards. The first card is replaced before the second card is picked.
(a) Both cards are clubs
(b) Both cards are red
(c) At least one of the cards is red
(d) Neither card is red

4* The score on a dice and the colour of a card.
(a) The card is red
(b) The score is 5
(c) The card is black and the score is less than 4
(d) The card is red and the score is 4 or more

5 Tossing a coin and the score on a octagonal spinner (eight-sided spinner numbered 1, 2, 3, 4, 5, 6, 7 and 8).
(a) A tail and a score of 7
(b) A tail and a score of less than 5
(c) An even score
(d) Any outcome other than 'tail + score less than 5'

6 The score on a dice and the colour of a disc picked from a bag containing two red and four blue discs.
(a) A score of 4 and a blue disc
(b) A score of less than 3 and a red disc
(c) An odd score and a blue disc
(d) A score of 1 and a black disc

7* The scores on two square spinners (numbered 1, 2, 3 and 4).
(a) Both spinners have a score of 3
(b) Both spinners have the same score
(c) The total of the scores is 6
(d) The total of the scores is not 5

8 The suit of a card and picking a letter from the word *skills*.
(a) The card is a spade and the letter is *s*
(b) The card is red and the letter is *l*
(c) The card is black and the letter is not *s*
(d) Any outcome other than 'heart + *k*'

9 Tossing a coin and the colour of a disc picked from a bag containing three green and two yellow discs.
(a) A head and a green disc
(b) A head and a disc of any colour
(c) A tail and a yellow disc
(d) Any outcome other than 'tail + yellow'

10* Picking two letters independently from the word EXTENT.
(a) Both letters are N
(b) Both letters are E
(c) The letters are the same
(d) The letters are different

REVISION

Exercise H

1 Estimate where the following events would be best placed on the simple probability line and read off the value of the probability at that point.

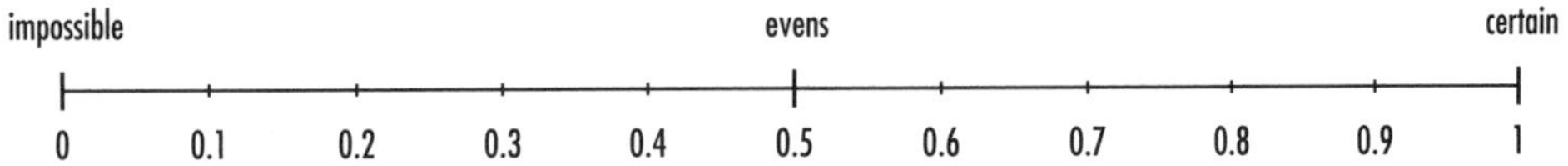

(a) The results of tossing a coin five times all being heads.
(b) There will be at least one week of warm weather next summer.
(c) Two cards taken from a pack will both be black.
(d) A person is right-handed.

2 In each case all outcomes can be assumed to be equally likely. Write down the probability of each of the following events happening.
(a) Selecting the letter S from the word SAUSAGES.
(b) Picking a blue disc from a bag containing three red discs and two blue discs.
(c) Picking an odd number from 7, 14, 21, 28, 35, 42 and 49.
(d) Throwing an even score on a dice.

3 State (i) the complementary event (ii) the probability of this complementary event:
(a) Picking a black card from a standard pack of playing cards.
(b) Winning a raffle having bought 12 tickets out of a total of 500 tickets sold.
(c) Choosing a 10p coin from £1 in change of which 50p is in 5p coins and 50p in 10p coins.
(d) Throwing a score of 4 or more with a dice.

4 A coin is tossed and a spinner with the numbers 1, 2, 3, 4 and 5 is spun.
Create a suitable possibility space for all the possible outcomes of these two events. Use this possibility space to calculate the probability of the following events.
(a) A head and a score of 2
(b) A tail and a score of 3 or more
(c) The score is a 3
(d) A tail and a score of 6

Exercise HH

1 (a) There has been no rain in the last 100 days in the Sahara Desert. Estimate the probability that the next day will be dry.
(b) A normal coin has been tossed 15 times and has come down heads every time. Estimate the probability that it will come down heads next time.

2 A letter is chosen from the word DATA and a letter is chosen from the word STATISTICS. Create a suitable possibility space to show all the possible outcomes and then use this to calculate the probability of each of the following events.
(a) One of the letters is a D.
(b) One or more of the letters is an A.
(c) The letters are the same.
(d) The letters are different.

3 Senga draws a frequency diagram to show the possible outcomes of tossing five coins. Use this to answer these questions.
(a) How many possible outcomes are there?
(b) What is the probability of getting only one head? Give your answer as a fraction.
(c) What is the probability of getting three or more heads? Give your answer as a decimal.
(d) What is the probability of getting one tail? Give your answer as a fraction.

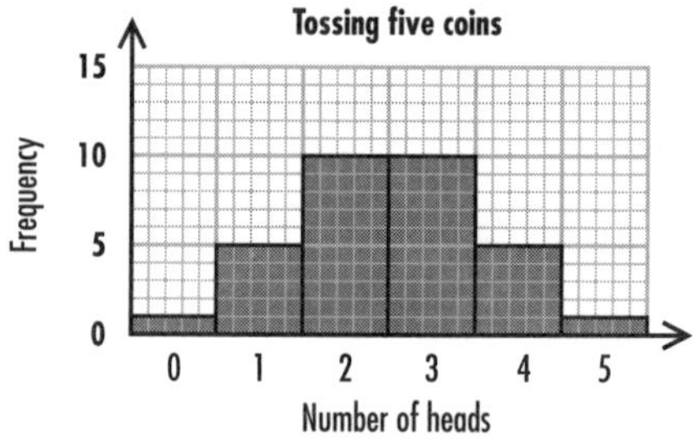

4 Ray draws a pie chart to show the number of possible outcomes of spinning two spinners both of which have sections coloured red (R), blue (B) and yellow (Y). 'BY' means that one of the spinners came down blue and the other spinner came down yellow. The total number of possible outcomes is 18.
Use the pie chart to answer the following questions.
(a) What is the probability of both spinners being red? Give your answer as a fraction.
(b) What is the probability that at least one of the spinners is yellow? Give your answer as a fraction.
(c) What is the probability that both spinners are the same colour? Give your answer as a decimal.
(d) The probability of two particular combinations of colours occurring is 0.5. State the two combinations of colours.

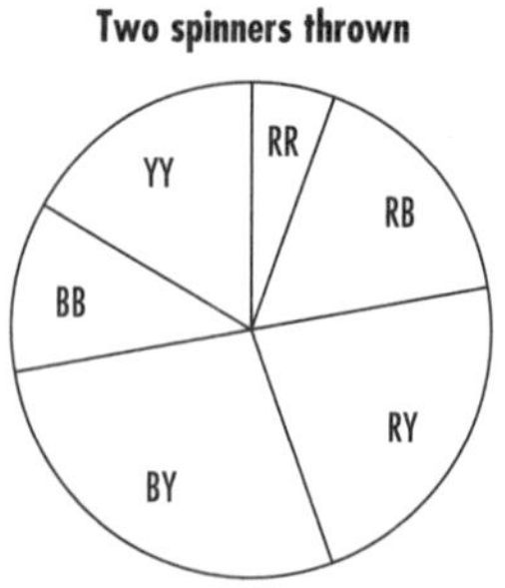